RETAIL
Before, During & After COVID-19

Bruce Winder

Bruce Winder

Copyright © 2020 Bruce Edward Winder Consulting Limited

All rights reserved

ISBN- 9798651503636

Bruce Winder

DEDICATION

This book is dedicated to my wife Karen, my daughters Claudia and Alyssa and my mom Dolores. Also to Lorne Milks, who passed away during the writing of this book.

TABLE OF CONTENTS

INTRODUCTION 3

BEFORE COVID-19.. 7
   Ryders in The Storm.. 9
   Eighty Retail Trends 81

DURING COVID-19.. 249

AFTER COVID-19 321

APOCALYPSE NEVER.. 379

ACKNOWLEDGMENTS

I would like to acknowledge all of the men and women who chose retail as a career. This industry is not for the faint of heart and I am fortunate to have learned so much from you about retail and life. I would also like to thank my students. Your curiosity and sense of community inspires me.
Finally, I wish to thank all of the front-line workers, including retail staff, who helped keep the world safe and fed during COVID-19.

INTRODUCTION

Since I was a child, I have always admired how retail works. Like a symphony, hundreds or even thousands of components work in harmony to create something beautiful. Storefronts, signage, inventory and assortments, fixtures, staff, digital experiences, sight and sound and even smell. There is something about retail that has always drawn me to it. A magical place. Colour, lights, the sound of the cash register. But like most beautiful things it can sometimes come with pain and sorrow.

Today, the retail industry is going through excruciating change brought on by significant disruption before, during and after COVID-19. Few, if any, industries have witnessed so much change in such a short period of time. Before the pandemic began to impact retail, a perfect storm of changes in customer behaviour, technology, financial markets, business models, supplier relationships, employee relationships, retail formats and more were in play. Now, with COVID-19 laying siege to the industry, the future of retail is unknown. Will retail survive? If so, what form will it take? I used to think the term retail apocalypse was highly exaggerated. Today, I'm not so sure. For some, these challenges represent a once-in-a-lifetime opportunity. For many others, they represent the end of their dream.

I originally completed this book in March of 2020 and had sent it for editing. When the virus spread across the planet, I quickly realized that my work was incomplete. The book did its job of discussing retail up to that point in time, but the world turned upside down overnight and my writing began again. I took the months of April and May to add sections that talked about how COVID-19 was impacting retail now and how I thought it would impact retail in the future. How would the trends I cited in the first part of the book translate into this new abnormal?

Many retailers will go bankrupt as a result of the virus. Coresight Research has speculated that the United States could see 15,000-plus stores close in 2020 as a result of this new normal[1]. I think this estimate is low. Many of the retailers that fall are undercapitalized and had weak value propositions to start with. The drop off in revenue and cash flow will make them insolvent within a few weeks or months. Strong, well-capitalized retailers and suppliers will weather the storm. They are too big to fail and will receive government bail-outs to keep them afloat if needed. The

---

[1] Thomas, Lauren. "Retail store closures in the U.S. could explode because of the coronavirus." March 16, 2020. Retrieved from:
https://www.cnbc.com/2020/03/16/retail-store-closures-in-the-us-could-explode-because-of-coronavirus.html

longer the crisis lasts, the more pronounced this dynamic will be. The industry will further consolidate. It's just a question of how much.

Many consumers will lose their jobs, both within the retail industry and outside of it. This will exacerbate the problem. As unemployment rises, consumer spending will drop off further. A vicious circle.

Governments will offer financial aid packages. This will help to some degree. But depending on how long the pandemic lasts, it might not be enough for retailers and consumers. Those firms that do survive the crisis will have taken on more debt or will soon face significant expenses that were deferred by governments, landlords or business partners. There is no easy fix.

Some retailers and brands will benefit from this catastrophe. Those that sell food and other essential products will continue to do well as restaurants slowly open to fewer patrons. Online retailers like Amazon will prosper as customers avoid brick and mortar stores.

Those that sell discretionary goods aren't as fortunate. Fashion, apparel and footwear will be hard-hit along with department stores — some have already begun to enter bankruptcy protection.

Although one could argue this is a one-time black swan event, it shows the fragility of the industry and the consumer it serves. Too many retailers and too many consumers are living hand to mouth. For retailers, this means having high debt levels and low cash reserves. They may have been breaking even or losing money before the pandemic started. For consumers, this means they had too much personal debt and low or non-existent savings. They may have been working on contract or through the gig economy. Those operating or living at the margin will be impacted first.

In an ironic twist of fate, as the world shuts down, the environment is healing. Pollution has plummeted and water is clear again. This pandemic has led society to revisit a number of paradigms including how we treat the vulnerable and the role of government.

The purpose of this book is to do three things. First, share my thoughts on where the industry was up to and including February 2020 — to establish a baseline from which to discuss parts two and three. Second, summarize the key impact that COVID-19 has had on retail as it opens up again. Third, offer my opinion on how retail will emerge from the pandemic and how industry dynamics as well as individual store operations will change.

Retail Before, During & After COVID-19

Retail Before COVID-19

<u>Ryders in the Storm</u>

Before COVID-19 spread, I wrote a section that discussed how a variety of retailers, suppliers and service providers were faring against so many changes in the industry up to the beginning of the 2020s. This gets you caught up on retail before the pandemic and creates a baseline that I use to show how the pandemic has and will continue to impact retail.

<u>Eighty Retail Trends</u>

The second part of this section summarizes my take on the top 80 retail trends as we entered 2020. It was originally going to be called Retail 2020, but that isn't valid anymore. I examine these trends as they relate to customers, employees, suppliers, managers, investors and retailers. I also review key technologies that enable retail and what is on the horizon.

Retail During COVID-19

In this section, I discuss the state of retail during the pandemic. With research from leading news agencies, I summarize some of the examples of how retail stakeholders are being impacted and are reacting to COVID-19. This section lays the groundwork, in part, to how I see the industry taking shape as society recovers and retail begins to open again.

Retail After COVID-19

As the world begins to move from flattening the curve to reopening economies, this section outlines a three-phase approach to retail post-pandemic. From slowly opening essential retail to living in a world where consumers coexist with the virus, stakeholders learn to survive. Finally, I examine retail once a vaccine has been discovered and the world gets inoculated. Taking the 80 retail trends from earlier in the book, I forecast whether each will accelerate, decelerate, pause, change or stay the course. I also discuss how the virus has brought forward numerous retail trends that were to take effect decades from now — and made them relevant in the near future.

Thank You For Your Support

Given the state of the world, I have decided to donate five percent of the proceeds I receive from this book to mental health care. Specifically, the Centre For Addiction and Mental Health (CAMH) in Canada and the National Institute of Mental Health (NIMH) in the United States. The COVID-19 pandemic has and will continue to negatively affect the mental health of retail industry workers and their families and this is my way of helping them. Thank you for your support of this great cause.

BEFORE COVID-19

RYDERS IN THE STORM

EIGHTY RETAIL TRENDS

Bruce Winder

RYDERS IN THE STORM

"You may be high
You may be low
You may be rich, child
You may be poor
But when the Lord get ready
You gotta move[3]"

(You Gotta Move, The Rolling Stones. Originally written by Gary Davis and Fred McDowell)

Even in good times, the retail industry can be challenging. Every day can be a battle to keep up-to-date with changing consumer needs, competitors and technology. In tough times, winners and losers are identified quickly and decisively. Those who have the resources and the intestinal fortitude to make meaningful change thrive while those who stand still find themselves in trouble. Some brands take a short-term view and fail to reinvest in the business. Some find themselves trying to sell products that no one wants anymore. Some wait too long to invest in omni-channel retail or ignore new entrants that eventually become a threat. Take big food as an example. Big food got caught flat-footed. Health-conscious consumers had no need for processed brands. Big food was left scrambling to sell unproductive divisions and buy new brands that better aligned with consumer purchase patterns.

Many retailers had too many stores. Many still do. Online shopping hurt brick and mortar productivity. Retailers at the fringe, those with weak balance sheets or weak value propositions, were the first to be hit, followed by the next layer of competitors and so forth. Not everyone suffered, though. Many national champions got busy and built new capabilities such as home delivery, click-and-collect and the use of technology to improve the shopping experience. Some built new formats that offered experiential retailing and shape-shifted in size and business model to cater to city dwellers. As the consumption sweet spot moved from baby boomer and Gen X to millennial and Gen Z, some firms quickly lost relevance and have struggled to adapt to these new customers and their strict demands.

---

[3] The Rolling Stones, "You Gotta Move." *Sticky Fingers*. 1971. *Spotify.*
https://open.spotify.com/album/29m6DinzdaD0OPqWKGyMdz

<u>Calamity Categorization</u>

I have taken a sample of retailers, suppliers and service providers that came up during my research and classified them. The classification is based on where I see them on the continuum of success and failure. The list below is far from exhaustive but hopefully gives you a sense of the disparity within the trade. I added the most recent sales trend for each going concern company as well to give you a sense of its trajectory. I focus less on profitability as too many companies use voodoo accounting and manage earnings to make themselves look better than they really are.

SWEET AISLE OF MINE

The first category, Sweet Aisle of Mine, consists of some of the best and brightest at this time. They are delivering what customers want and are positioned well for today's retail environment.

IKEA

I have a lot of respect and admiration for IKEA. I worked with a gentleman named Robert D., who was employed by the Swedish giant for years. Based on his stories and everything I have read, the company has a unique culture and was decades ahead of its time in many ways. The retailer was a pioneer in vertical integration, customer focus, value and environmental stewardship.

IKEA is adapting as it knows it has to. In a recent article in The Wall Street Journal, Saabira Chaudhuri writes about an interview with IKEA CEO Jesper Brodin and how IKEA is adapting to changing consumer shopping habits[4]. One of the first points Brodin makes is the acknowledgement that IKEA staying the course and playing it safe was the riskiest path.

<u>Store-ship Trooper</u>

IKEA is testing the redesign of its stores to eliminate the tried-and-true racetrack and make them more open-concept. The company recognizes that customers might not want to walk the entire store or have time to browse all categories. Better to let the customer decide how much he or she wants to spend in each location.

---

[4] Chaudhuri, Saabira. "Inside Ikea's strategy to stay relevant as consumers change." *The Wall Street Journal*. February 25, 2019.

IKEA plans on opening about 50 smaller city stores. The company is transforming its network to urban convenience that allows customers to shop and receive products every day, any time of the day through pick-up or delivery. Like the models tested in London and Madrid, new city stores will be showrooms that allow customers to interact with the brand in a convenient fashion where customers live.

It involves a two-pronged approach by major market — full assortments at suburban stores and convenient assortments at city stores. Managing fulfillment for this set-up has required some reengineering. It involved taking space from large suburban stores and using it for regional product storage and delivery. These mini distribution centres serve small city stores that don't have the space for large inventories. The firm will also add regional warehouses as needed to complement existing assets. IKEA recognizes the economics of city stores will be very different, but hopes to improve profitability by buying locations versus renting or leasing them.

Kitchen Bunny

The firm recently bought TaskRabbit, a platform that enables crowd-sourced delivery and assembly services. It also bought a large stake in Traemand, a North American installer of kitchens. IKEA has always been vertically integrated and owns factories and raw materials providers and designs its own products.

Love Connection

IKEA, like many big companies, is partnering with startups for new product and service ideas[5]. It knows it needs to do a better job connecting with younger millennials and future generation Z customers. The retailer recently invited 18 young companies to Sweden for its "startup boot camp," where it meets and discusses potential partnerships.

An example of the type of products it's reviewing includes a $6,000 US space-saving system. This system allows the user to raise furniture to the roof when not in use. It is made by BumbleBee Spaces and targets consumers in tight spaces such as bachelor apartments. The system uses AI and robots to help customers manage space in a fluid way. Users can touch or use voice to command the system to find items using sensors.

---

[5] Molin, Anna & Matlack, Carol. "Ikea teams up with startups to look at next-gen furniture." *Bloomberg.* May 4, 2019.

IKEA reported full-year 2019 sales growth of 6.5 percent to EUR 41.3 billion[6].

Amazon

Amazon created modern-day retail. It destroys competitors on assortment, value and convenience. It has both anticipated and directed the industry to a spot where it has no real competitors, at least in North America. In the U.S., Amazon is dominating the $600 billion US online shopping market. This market has been growing from 15 to 20 percent per annum versus traditional retail, which has been up in the low single digits[7]. Amazon recently told EMarketer, an e-commerce research firm, that it has 37.7 percent of the U.S. online market[8]. The true power and dominance of Amazon has only really started to show itself in the last five years. But with dominance comes attention and turbulence.

Optionaire

One needs to remember that Amazon is not just a seller of products. Unlike Walmart, Amazon has additional high-margin businesses to help smooth out earnings. Amazon makes more margin from its growing cloud-computing services, third-party merchant services area and digital advertising than from direct product sales[9]. Amazon's blended gross margin from all businesses was 43 percent for the quarter ending March 31, 2019. That is a large number considering the firm trades in the discount segment of retail.

Amazon's digital advertising business has grown into the third largest in the United States, only behind Google and Facebook. In the second quarter of 2019, Amazon reported sales growth of 23 percent from seller services while advertising and other revenue grew 37 percent.

---

[6] *Inter IKEA Group FY19 financial results*. Retrieved from: https://about.ikea.com/en/organisation/ikea-facts-and-figures/inter-ikea-group-fy19-financial-results

[7] Soper, Spencer. "Bezos disputes Amazon's market power as sellers feel pinch." *Bloomberg*. April 20, 2019.

[8] Day, Matt & Soper, Spencer. "Amazon U.S. downplays dominance in market." *Bloomberg*. June 14, 2019.

[9] Day, Matt. "Amazon profit up on cloud computing, ad gains." *The Financial Post*. April 26, 2019.

For the same period, half of Amazon's operating income came from Amazon Web Services (AWS). Amazon Web Services grew 37 percent while overall revenue including all businesses grew 20 percent.

Amazon has been open about moving more growth toward its third-party marketplace business, where it earns a commission on products sold and charges third-party suppliers for advertising, fulfillment services and more. Amazon recently confirmed for the first time that 58 percent of its gross sales comes from third-party marketplace vendors.

Prime Day Power Play

Amazon has made Prime Day a North American version of China's Singles Day. Sort of. The numbers don't compare, but the marketing style is similar. During Prime Day 2019, the fifth such year the promotion ran, celebrities such as Taylor Swift, Will Smith, Mark Wahlberg, Youtuber JoJo Siwa and the late Kobe Bryant were hired by Amazon to push offers and drive excitement[10].

Prime Day isn't just about Amazon anymore. RetailMeNot, a research company, claims that in 2019, about 250 other retailers offered sales during the event, up from 194 in 2018. Walmart boasted about how consumers don't need a membership to get its deals. Ebay offered an amusing "Crash Sale," making fun of Amazon's 2018 Prime Day website crash.

Some say that Amazon is now focusing more on increasing the average basket of existing Prime members versus driving new members like previous promotions. At 150 million members, it may be getting harder to gain new subscribers.

List Pay Love

As Amazon has grown, some merchants have formed a love/hate relationship with it. They love Amazon because of the customer reach and supply chain capabilities that the company provides, but hate Amazon because they see it as a competitor. Amazon can be a competitor because it harvests data in order to efficiently copy existing products and sells them under its own private label.

In fairness to Amazon, this activity has been going on for decades. We used to do it ourselves all the time when I worked at big retail. I think the difference this time is the amount of data that Amazon gleans and the amount of control it has over one

---

[10] Soper, Spencer. "Kobe and other celebs pitching deals for Amazon." *Bloomberg*. July 16, 2019.

channel. Some retailers have tried to position themselves as an alternative to Amazon, such as Walmart and Ebay. But e-commerce market share for everyone else is miniscule compared to Amazon. For some vendors, Amazon represents 80 to 90 percent of their business even though they list their products on competitors' platforms. There are plenty of entrepreneurs who have made a lot of money off Amazon, so the argument is based on one's perspective.

You Shipped Me All Night Long

Amazon is flexing its enormous channel power to make manufacturers change packaging[11]. The online giant is pursuing this initiative for at least two reasons. One is to lower its environmental footprint, the other is to streamline shipping and transportation.

Amazon has communicated with vendors, directing them to use more environmental packaging or less packaging where possible. It has also asked suppliers to make packaging more compact to accommodate Amazon supply-chain equipment.

Amazon has so much clout now that CPG companies such as P&G and Lever have created separate Amazon packaging configurations and formulas to enable lower-cost shipping and reduce leakage during home delivery[12]. Laundry brands Tide and Seventh Generation have also made major changes to their products to accommodate Amazon, a costly feat. Tide has reduced the weight of its product by four pounds and uses cardboard versus plastic. Seventh Generation opted for a mini plastic bottle that's less than nine inches tall and saves five pounds.

Let's Go

In February 2020, Amazon opened its first full-size, cashier-less grocery store in Seattle called Go Grocery. At 10,400 square feet, the unit has an expanded assortment and is five times larger than Amazon Go convenience stores. The firm clearly has its mind set on disrupting the $800 billion US grocery industry[13]. In March 2020, Amazon announced it would be selling this technology to other retailers. It has

---

[11] Gasparro. Annie. "Amazon pushes brands to be less boxy." *The Wall Street Journal*. July 31, 2019.

[12] Pisani, Joseph. "Laundry-detergent makers create lighter products for online retailers". *The Associated Press*. December 28, 2018.

[13] Pisani, Joseph. "Amazon expands no-cashier stores." *The Associated Press*. February 26, 2020.

branded the offering "Just Walk Out technology by Amazon" and reportedly has a number of chains that have signed up[14].

<u>Beautiful Monster</u>

Amazon blew away holiday 2019 expectations as total net sales increased 21 percent to $87.44 billion US for the quarter. Prime members grew by 50 percent to 150 million, and one-day shipping grew fourth-quarter deliveries by four times from 2018. Revenue from subscription fees grew 23 percent. AWS revenue grew by 34 percent and is now a $9.95 billion US division[15].

Amazon is discussed significantly throughout this book and is the benchmark that all retailers need to contemplate, at least from an e-commerce and technology perspective. The firm receives a lot of flack, but is really no different from Walmart in its competitive spirit and tactics.

Alibaba

Anyone vaguely familiar with Asia knows the power and reach of Alibaba. Some say Alibaba is the eBay of China. However, there are several similarities to Amazon from a diversification standpoint. The giant has a portfolio of businesses including the consumer products division, its largest, in addition to cloud computing, banking and entertainment.

Considering China's 1.3 billion consumers and the growth of that economy to second in the world, Alibaba is poised to become the world's largest retailer in the future. In 2019, Jack Ma, Alibaba's billionaire founder, retired on his 55th birthday as the Chinese champion he founded approached sales of $60 billion[16] US. Perhaps it's a good time for Mr. Ma to leave, as the consumer market in China has slowed. This is a result of trade wars with the U.S. and a maturing economy. Alibaba has not been immune to this cycle and has seen growth slow. The company's online sales grew by

---

[14] Porter, Jon. "Amazon will start selling cashierless Go system to other retailers." March 9, 2020. Retrieved from: https://www.theverge.com/2020/3/9/21171230/amazon-just-walk-out-technology-cashierless-go-stores-third-party-retailers

[15] Dastin, Jeffrey. "Holiday sales at Amazon jump on 1-day shipping." *Reuters with files from Bloomberg.* January 31, 2020.

[16] McDonald, Joe. "Alibaba's Ma steps down amid uncertainty." *The Associated Press.* September 11, 2019.

almost 18 percent in the first two quarters of 2019 versus about 24 percent in all of 2018. In addition, second quarter, 2019 revenue increased 42 percent but dropped from a growth rate of 51 percent in 2018. Stunning numbers nonetheless.

For the fourth quarter, 2019, Alibaba grew revenue 38 percent year over year to $23.2 billion[17] US.

Walmart

Walmart is the retailer with the biggest bullseye on its back over the last few years. The emergence and dominance of Amazon has put enormous pressure on Walmart, but it has responded by creating a new innovative organization that is surprisingly agile and effective. The Bentonville firm announced third quarter, 2019 results that were mixed. Sales were up 3.2 percent, but operating income dropped 5.4 percent[18]. Why? The firm is spending to lower prices and build out infrastructure to fight Amazon. Walmart's international business has been mixed as the UK suffers due to Brexit concerns, while growth has been strong in China and Mexico.

Pocket Pal Payday

Outside of Amazon, it would be hard to find another large retailer that has embraced technology to the same scale as Walmart. Since 2011, the big Arkansas chain has revamped its e-commerce platform, increasing its speed and offering a better user experience (UX)[19]. It integrated its massive store systems with e-commerce that enabled click and collect for not only general merchandise, but groceries as well. It made returns easier and opened Walmart Labs, which has acquired 10 startups (and counting) and moved all data on the cloud. Not an easy task considering it has well over 4,500 stores.

Grocery Battlefield

Walmart is beginning to offer a fee-based Delivery Unlimited program at 1,400 U.S. stores whereby customers pay a monthly fee for unlimited grocery delivery. A

---

[17] "Alibaba group announces December quarter 2019 Results." Retrieved from: https://www.alibabagroup.com/en/news/article?news=p200213

[18] Nassauer, Sarah. "Walmart extends sales growth streak." *The Wall Street Journal*. November 15, 2019.

[19] Bose, Nandita. "Walmart chief tech officer steps away as e-commerce competition intensifies." *Reuters*. March 21, 2019.

step-up service piloted in three cities includes food delivered into a customer's fridge for $19.95 US per month. Grocery represents 56 percent of Walmart's business and the firm has had a hard time making money on food delivery. E-commerce sales were up 41 percent in Q3, 2019 driven by grocery. The firm has 3,000 U.S. click-and-collect locations and 1,400 stores where home delivery is offered.

Blue Light Special

It looks like Walmart is starting to turn a corner. Sales are good but profitability remains a concern. I think the retailer will need to transform further to be able to compete with Amazon and others long term while still making money. Until then, look for a bumpy ride from this giant over the next few years.

In the fourth quarter of 2019, Walmart grew U.S. same-store sales by two percent[20]. For all of 2019 fiscal, Walmart grew U.S. comparable-store sales by 2.6 percent.

Target

Much like Walmart, Target was one of the U.S. giants that could stand to lose the most from Amazon and changing consumer shopping habits. But much like Walmart, it got busy upgrading itself. After an embarrassing failed expansion into Canada in the early 2010s, Target struggled for a few years before getting traction recently.

Target is on track to spend $7 billion US on store renovations and will have bettered some 1,000 stores by the end of 2020. The chain has turned its stores into pick-up depots to enable e-commerce. About 1,000 units offer curbside pickup through its click-and-collect service. It also acquired delivery startup Shipt for $500 million US and offers same-day delivery across 200 stores.

2018 Turnaround

As Target approached the fourth quarter, 2018, third-quarter results were lacklustre[21]. Higher labour costs, investments in e-commerce and price reductions

---

[20] Redman, Russell. "Walmart turns in lower-than-expected earnings for Q4, full year." February 18, 2020. Retrieved from: https://www.supermarketnews.com/retail-financial/walmart-turns-lower-expected-earnings-q4-full-year

[21] Bose, Nandita. "Target shares slump as results disappoint and inventories rise." *Reuters*. November 21, 2018.

hammered margins from an estimated 29.6 percent to an actual of 28.7 percent. Inventory jumped 18 percent while sales grew a more modest 5 percent. Investors were caught off guard and the share price dropped 11 percent on the news. It was not the best of times for the Minneapolis giant.

Things changed in a good way during holiday 2018. During Q4, 2018, online sales increased 30 percent and helped contribute to 5.3 percent comparable store sales growth, a gain not seen since 2004[22]. Store traffic picked up 4.5 percent.

Target invested in infrastructure and capabilities and saw results. With more city stores and about 75 percent of holiday 2018 online orders being filled through its stores, it has started to use its network as a competitive weapon. The retailer announced it was renovating 300 stores in 2019 on top of the 300 renovated in 2018 and is adding additional private labels to differentiate itself[23].

Merchandise by the Dashboard Light

The big discount differentiator is pointed in the right direction and has positioned itself well for future quarters. Like Walmart, though, profitability will be a challenge as it continues to spend on price and make capital investments to transform.

Holiday 2019 was a bit of a disappointment. Target's fourth quarter 2019 comp store sales grew a modest 1.5 percent year over year. Comp digital growth was up 20 percent. For 2019, full-year comp store sales growth was 3.9 percent year over year[24].

Lululemon

Lululemon is a retail success story. The mother of athleisure and yoga wear, the brand's premium prices and innovative technical garments help make it a stock market darling. Lululemon is on fire and is one of the best retailers on the planet. In the fourth quarter of 2018, sales increased an incredible 26 percent as e-commerce

---

[22] D'Innocenzio, Anne & Chapman, Michelle. "Target hits on all cylinders." *The Associated Press.* March 6, 2019.

[23] Safdar, Khadeeja & Kapner, Suzanne. "Target and Kohl's gain as rivals shrink." *The Wall Street Journal.* March 6, 2019.

[24] *Target Reports Fourth Quarter and Full-Year 2019 Earnings.* Retrieved from: https://investors.target.com/news-releases/news-release-details/target-reports-fourth-quarter-and-full-year-2019-earnings

represented 26 percent of revenue[25].

Lululemon has numerous initiatives in the works to keep the love strong. It plans on opening 25 to 30 stores outside of North America. It is adding e-commerce capabilities in various cities in Germany, France and Japan and will have click-and-collect capabilities across the U.S. by fall of 2019. The chain is also adding high-margin experiential services such as wellness retreats and other events to reinforce the company as a lifestyle brand.

It's Sweating Men

Lululemon is busy planning the next wave of growth and is aiming big. It is looking to replicate Nike, Under Armour, Adidas and other large global firms as a full assortment brand. Its target market? Those who subscribe to the "sweatlife" as Lululemon calls it[26]. The firm is looking to potentially double its sales to $6.3 billion US by 2023.

In a 2019 interview with CEO Calvin MacDonald, retail reporter Marina Strauss outlined MacDonald's vision to add categories such as cosmetics, casual wear, socks, headbands, footwear, hats, bags, swimsuits, tennis wear, hiking wear and more. One of the retailer's goals is to make menswear half its business. This may be tough, as men don't necessarily recognize Lululemon from an awareness standpoint in these categories. The Vancouver-based retailer announced quietly that it closed two men's-only stores called "The Local" in Toronto and New York[27]. The firm said the brand works better in a "dual-gender" environment. Comparable store sales for men's products were up 26 percent in 2019 through June.

Risky Business

These are all big bets and with big bets comes big risk. Lululemon risks alienating or confusing existing female customers and losing focus from what got it here in the first place. Also, some categories like footwear offer less profit margin than apparel and could tow down operating margins, making investors cringe. Also, one can assume the likes of Nike, Under Armour and Adidas will not sit idly watching. These

---

[25] Edmiston, Jake. "Lululemon Q4 profit beats expectations." *The Financial Post.* March 28, 2019.

[26] Strauss, Marina. "Lululemon looks beyond yoga." *The Globe and Mail.* May 11, 2019.

[27] Rockeman, Olivia & Rastello, Sandrine. "Lululemon to close men's-only stores." *Bloomberg.* June 20, 2019.

brands have already encroached on Lulu's home territory by offering yoga wear themselves. One of the challenges MacDonald faces is to keep Lululemon's innovative culture intact as it grows.

Stretch Plan

Either way, this powerhouse is on a roll and seemingly immune to the flight to value we are seeing in many other businesses. I hope the good times last for it.

For the fourth quarter of 2019, Lululemon's latest guidance was that its comp store sales would be up mid to high teens in percentage terms year over year[28].

Costco

Like an early version of Amazon, Costco was made for today's retail environment. Like Amazon, it offers tremendous value. Costco sells at a gross margin of only 11 to 12 percent[29]. Like Amazon too, it builds in switching costs with its membership fee, which generates a significant portion of its net income. Although stock keeping unit (sku) count is modest, Costco offers variety through changing in and out assortments, a treasure hunt for the bargain hunter. Costco has shown extraordinary results since The Great Recession as consumers look for better value for their money.

Like everyone else though, the mighty Costco has had to work harder to keep its position as one of the top retailers[30]. It expanded same-day grocery delivery to cover more U.S. cities, opened a store in China for the first time and has added Apple computers to its lineup. The U.S. club store market is competitive, with Sam's Club recently posting its 12th straight quarter of comparable store gains and smaller BJ's Wholesale recently gaining members. Although Costco is in a great segment of retail, it has fierce competitors chomping at the bit. Costco faces competition from Amazon from a convenience standpoint and will need to continue to work hard for its gains in the years ahead.

---

[28] *Lululemon Athletica Inc. Updates Guidance For The Fourth Quarter Of Fiscal 2019 Ahead Of The ICR Conference.* Retrieved from: http://investor.lululemon.com/news-releases/news-release-details/lululemon-athletica-inc-updates-guidance-fourth-quarter-fiscal-6

[29] *FY 2019 Annual Report.* December 12, 2019. Retrieved from: https://investor.costco.com/financial-information/annual-reports

[30] "Costco tops estimates, shares get 3% bump." *Reuters & Bloomberg.* March 8, 2019.

Costco reported same-store sales results for the 18 weeks ending January 5, 2020 of + 6.3 percent year over year. E-commerce comp sales for the same period grew 17.1 percent[31].

The Home Depot

The Home Depot just keeps rolling. Better than Lowe's, this Atlanta-based juggernaut quietly does almost everything right. Not too fancy but consistent and smooth in execution, Home Depot is one the best retailers on the planet. With a lock on the tradesperson, Home Depot offers great value and convenient reach.

Same-store sales increased 5.2 percent in the fourth quarter of 2019[32]. Sure, the U.S. housing market helped, but there is more to it than that. In Canada, it dominates Lowe's even more than it does in the United States.

Aldi

German discount grocer Aldi has taken America by storm with its simple yet stunning low cost and private label food offering, and Save-a-Lot has been collateral damage. According to Euromonitor, Aldi has about 60 percent of the U.S. discount grocery market, up from 56 percent in 2016. This contrasts with Save-a-Lot, which has dropped from 28 percent to 23 percent during the same time frame. Like a Costco that has only food (but without the membership fee), this chain fits in perfectly with frugal consumers.

Aldi is privately owned and does not publish sales numbers.

Nike

In September of 2019, Nike announced third-quarter financial results that beat expectations, due in part to its robust direct-to-consumer (DTC) business[33]. Nike is

---

[31] *Costco Wholesale Corporation Reports December Sales Results.* January 8, 2020. Retrieved from: https://investor.costco.com/news-releases/news-release-details/costco-wholesale-corporation-reports-december-sales-results-19

[32] "Housing market strength powers Home Depot's holiday quarter." Reuters. February 26, 2020.

[33] "Nike profit, revenue up as direct selling gains momentum." *Reuters.* September 25, 2019.

one of the most visible brands to sell direct-to-consumer and investors have applauded these efforts. Nike calls the direct initiative the "Consumer Direct Offense"[34]. The American brand has relied less on wholesale and more on its own stores, online offering and pop-up stores in select malls. This strategy allows the firm to connect directly with customers, glean insights and make more money.

I toured Nike's flagship store in New York. This location exemplifies the innovation that the retail and supplier industry needs. It is the best store I have ever toured and positions the brand as a continued leader in consumer products. Look for a brief write-up on the tour later in the book.

Nike grew total revenue by 10 percent for Q2, 2020, its most recent reported-on quarter[35].

Ulta Beauty

Ulta Beauty is known for its unique assortment of discount and premium cosmetics under one roof. It also offers a range of services including spa, hair salon and facials. I visited one of Ulta's New York City stores in late 2018 and was impressed with its assortment breadth and depth.

Since December 31, 2009, Ulta Beauty's stock rose 1,271 percent as of December 26, 2019. This was the highest 10-year performance of any stock in the S&P 500 Retailing Index[36]. After Mary Dillon became CEO in 2013, the retailer began a winning streak. Dillon relaunched the firm's loyalty program and updated stores to feel more upscale. High-end brands soon followed. E-commerce has also been a stand-out as more make-up business is marketed through online influencers. The firm recently announced it is expanding to Canada. Ulta was chosen as a key distribution partner for Kylie Cosmetics.

Ulta Beauty posted comp store sales gains of 3.2 percent in Q3, 2019, its latest reported financial performance.

---

[34] Sampath, Uday. "Nike sales fall short in North America". *Reuters*. March 22, 2019.

[35] *Nike, Inc. Reports Fiscal 2020 Second Quarter Results.* December 19, 2019. Retrieved from: https://investors.nike.com/investors/news-events-and-reports/?toggle=earnings

[36] Freund, Janet. "Ulta decade's best retail performer." *Bloomberg*. December 26, 2019.

Aritzia

Aritzia is one of retail's best-kept secrets. The 35-year-old Vancouver retailer has been slowly but surely taking women's fashion by storm in an ever-so-quiet, Canadian way. Aritzia calls itself a luxury brand but focuses on accessibility[37]. Positioned as "affordable luxury," the retailer sells proprietary brands and designs through well-informed store staff that connect with each customer and help create welcoming stores.

Putting on the Ritz

Aritzia is a retail stock market darling, delivering stellar results since its 2016 IPO. In the third quarter of 2018, it drove almost 13 percent comparable store sales growth. Profit was up 16 percent.

Prime Locations

In a recent article by Natalie Obiko Pearson from Bloomberg, she highlights how Aritzia is lighting it up in the cut-throat U.S.clothing market[38]. While other stores are closing in record numbers, Aritzia is expanding. The chain has had success setting up shop in prime real estate areas such as New York's Hudson Yards. Brian Hill, Aritzia's CEO and co-founder, was quoted as saying, "I was told a long time ago by my father: Make sure you get the best real estate. Because then if it doesn't work, you know it's you." The chain has 96 stores in all, of which 27 are in the United Sates.

Clicks and Bricks

The firm has seen a wonderful symbiotic relationship with its brick and mortar stores and its online sales. When Aritzia opens a new store in a particular market, it enjoys a significant uplift in online sales nearby.

Opportunities

One weak point, if you had to pick one, would be awareness. Those who do know the brand see it favourably, though. In January 2020, the firm signaled it is

---

[37] Strauss, Marina. "Can Aritzia cater to both luxury and mainstream clients?" *The Globe and Mail*. February 19, 2019.

[38] Obiko, Pearson, Natalie. "Boutique chain Aritzia making inroads in U.S." *Bloomberg*. July 27, 2019.

expanding into men's outerwear and offering a greater variety of sizes in women's wear, up to size 18 from 12[39]. Aritzia sees continued growth in the U.S. market and will also look to expand to China when the time is right.

In January of 2020, the firm reported comp stores sales gains of 5.1 percent for the third quarter of 2020 (period ending December 1, 2019)[40].

Canada Goose

Canada Goose has that moxy that only successful companies have. The firm has grown by an annual compound rate of 42 percent from 2016 to 2018[41]. Unlike some of the recent IPO disasters at Uber and Lyft, Canada Goose shares rose 25 percent on their first day of trading. This is even more impressive when you think that Canada Goose offers no discounts on its products. Dani Reiss, Canada Goose's CEO, is happy to let his jackets sell out each year to create market scarcity[42].

Quality Control

The firm recently announced a new factory in Quebec, which will be its ninth in Canada as the brand expands yet controls product quality[43]. The firm also has contract facilities in Italy and Romania for knitwear.

Growing Pains

With the success of lower-cost products such as down and knitwear came lower

---

[39] "Aritzia fuelled by new stores, expanded product lines." *The Canadian Press*. January 10, 2020.

[40] *Aritzia Reports Third Quarter Fiscal 2020 Financial Results.* January 9, 2020. Retrieved from: https://investors.aritzia.com/investor-news/press-release-details/2020/Aritzia-Reports-Third-Quarter-Fiscal-2020-Financial-Results/default.aspx

[41] Lewis, Michael. "Canada Goose isn't worried about a chilly market."

[42] Edmiston, Jake. "Canada Goose scarcity creates 'little bit of magic.'" *The Financial Post*. February 15, 2019.

[43] Deschamps, Tara. "Canada Goose to open new factory in Quebec." *The Associated Press*. February 15, 2019.

gross margins as compared to its core parka business[44]. Still, ringing in at a lofty 57.5 percent versus 64 percent last year, the business is extremely healthy.

Opportunity Eh?

Some of the recent growth for Canada Goose has come from Chinese retailer Alibaba's Tmall marketplace. It was one of the top 10 brands in sales on the platform on Singles Day 2018. The retailer also sees expansion in Europe as well as through select line extensions. The firm also bought Baffin Inc., maker of quality outdoor and industrial footwear, in 2018 for about $32.5 million Cdn. I recently toured Canada Goose's new brand experience store in West Toronto and was impressed. More to follow on that later.

Canada Goose reported growth in total revenue of 13.2 percent for fiscal Q3, 2020 (ending December 29, 2019)[45].

Hermès

There are few luxury brands that command the premium price of both its handbags and its stock[46]. With a forward price-to-earnings ratio of 41 (as of April, 2019), Hermès stock, like its $10,000 US handbags, is for the wealthiest of buyers. Some Hermès handbags cost more in the resale market than they do brand new! That's brand power!

Hermès grew total revenue by 15 percent for all of 2019[47].

---

[44] "Canada Goose shares down despite higher sales as loss, margins widen." *The Canadian Press*. August 15, 2019.

[45] *Canada Goose Reports Results for Third Quarter Fiscal 2020*. February 7, 2020. Retrieved from: https://investor.canadagoose.com/English/news-results-and-presentations/press-release/press-release-details/2020/Canada-Goose-Reports-Results-for-Third-Quarter-Fiscal-2020/default.aspx

[46] Ryan, Carol. "Hermès can only show its worth in a luxury downturn." *The Wall Street Journal*. April 24, 2019.

[47] *Hermès International: 2019 Results*. February 26, 2020. Retrieved from: https://www.globenewswire.com/news-release/2020/02/26/1990644/0/en/Herm%C3%A8s-International-2019-Results.html

Shopify

During the summer of 2019, Canada's Shopify eclipsed eBay from a valuation perspective[48]. In August 2019, the Ottawa-based tech giant had a market capitalization of $56 billion Cdn. The firm has become the anti-Amazon. It enables retail while Amazon, some argue, competes with retail. Never one to stand still, Shopify is adding fulfillment and an integrated payment processor along with other merchant services. With sales over $1 billion Cdn, the company almost never reports a profit but is getting a lot of attention from investors. For the fourth quarter of 2019, Shopify reported a 47 percent growth in revenue[49].

In 2018, Shopify had about 800,000 customers who sold about $41 billion US worth of product across 175 countries[50]. In October 2019, the firm announced it surpassed the millionth customer mark — a number CEO Tobi Lutke said was unexpected when he launched the business in 2004[51].

In an interesting and contrarian move, Shopify announced in February 2020 that it was signing on to Facebook's cryptocurrency Libra. Experts feel Shopify might see Libra as a way of lowering merchant fees by circumventing credit card firms such as Visa and Mastercard, who have balked at the program[52].

Shopify grew revenue by 47 percent for both the fourth quarter and full year 2019[53].

---

[48] Shufelt, Tim. "Shopify surpasses BCE market cap as shares continue to surge." *The Globe and Mail*. August 21, 2019.

[49] Deschamps, Tara. "Shopify sees profit boost from software changes, new merchants." February 13, 2020.

[50] McLeod, James. "Shopify takes on the Amazon 'gorilla.'" *The Financial Post*. April 13, 2019.

[51] "Shopify reports loss as revenue jumps." *The Canadian Press*. October 30, 2019.

[52] Shecter, Barbara. "Shopify signs on to join Facebook's cryptocurrency." *The Financial Post*. February 22, 2020.

[53] *Shopify Announces Fourth-Quarter and Full-Year 2019 Financial Results*. February 12, 2020. Retrieved from: https://investors.shopify.com/Investor-News-Details/2020/Shopify-Announces-Fourth-Quarter-and-Full-Year-2019-Financial-

Urban Warehouses

The rise of online shopping has had many winners. One of those winners has been vacant warehouses and factories near large urban centres. According to Ben Sykes from Avison Young, a real estate firm, these properties in Toronto have historically had a vacancy rate of about five to seven percent. With the growth of online shopping, Sykes says the vacancy rate is now around 2 percent. This has also increased rents 40 percent from 2014 to 2018[54].

Toronto

I may appear self-serving by mentioning my hometown. According to CBRE Group, Toronto has become the number-one city in North America for international retailer expansion.

The city and Canada overall have been a hotspot for Asian chains. These brands are looking to capitalize on diversity and Canada's high Asian population. Retailers like Muji, Miniso, Uniqlo and Oomono have set up shop in The Great White North and have, in some cases, fairly aggressive expansion plans. Miniso announced a plan for 500 Canadian stores by 2020. Muji is looking to grow to 30 stores in Canada by 2030. Canadians love value, so I think there is room for these companies. Time will tell, though, how many stores will be appropriate for the market. Look for Toronto to continue to be a North American test lab for international retailers and brands.

STREET EMOTION

The second category, Street Emotion, consists of retailers and brands that are working hard to re-gain momentum or at least hold their own. Although well established, they have a sense of urgency that is refreshing.

Apple

Apple has redefined retail with its simple yet effective stores and record-breaking sales-per-square-foot numbers. Many retailers have copied its approach with some success. In retail, though, your store is the sizzle but the steak is your product.

Results/default.aspx

[54] Wickens, Stephen. "Obsolete factories in the inner suburbs find new life." *The Globe and Mail*. November 27, 2018.

And Apple was starting to have a problem on both fronts.

Busy Signal?

Apple signalled in the fall of 2018 that it would stop reporting device unit sales for 2019. This was a big red flag in terms of loss of hardware sales momentum[55].

In the fall of 2018, Apple announced it would start selling its full range of products on Amazon for the first time[56]. Up to that point, Amazon sold only older model iPhones. The new offering included products such as the Apple Watch, Apple TV, Apple iPhone (XS and XS Max), iPad, Mac computer and Apple Beats branded headphones and accessories. Is this a sign of desperation or a clever way to expand its user ecosystem?

Counter Productive

In a recent article by Mark Gurman and Matthew Townsend from Bloomberg, the duo discusses how the Apple store has fallen from grace[57]. Once the pride of retail, the Apple store has become a headache for some customers. These are the stores that so famously generated $5,500 US in sales per square foot (2017). Fast forward to today and wait times are long and convenience is lacking. Employees have been directed to push sales and warranty service. What about actually helping customers? Quality of staff suffered as the behemoth expanded rapidly. Customer engagement suffered.

Service Side Hustle

Apple responded with new services in streaming and finance and looks to increase these new businesses to offset pressure on hardware sales. Apple will also benefit from the launch of new 5G technology in the fall of 2020.

An amazing company, Apple is dealing with another period of adversity. It has the wind at its back, though, with a user ecosystem of 1.3 billion users and a track record of incredible innovation and brand power. Investors believe in the firm. As of

---

[55] Gurman, Mark. "Apple's silence on iPhone unit sales sparks concern." *Bloomberg.* November 2, 2018.

[56] "Amazon to start selling most recent Apple products." *Bloomberg.* November 10, 2018.

[57] Gurman, Mark and Townsend, Matthew. "How the Apple store lost its lustre." *Bloomberg.* May 7, 2019.

the end of January 2020, its share price doubled from the previous 12 months as a new life on iPhones emerged[58].

Come Sales Away

In January 2020, Apple announced solid holiday 2019 sales and profit performance driven by iPhone sales, wireless headphones and AirPods. Apple posted fourth quarter 2019 revenue of $91.8 billion US versus analyst estimates of $88.5 billion US[59].

In February 2020, an article was published in Bloomberg that warned Apple's TV subscription was softer than expected with only 10 million Apple customers opting in to the free 12-month trial for the service[60].

McDonald's

McDonald's has made a tremendous comeback. Written off not so long ago as a fast-food machine that offers brutally unhealthy food, it has come back swinging and is winning.

Fast food is a tough business. According to NPD, quick-serve burger chain visits were down one percent in the U.S. in Q1, 2019. Customers have been checking out rivals. It has never been a better time to be in the burger biz if your offering is on point. Millennials and Gen Z customers are looking for premium customized burgers — things that McDonald's simply wasn't built for. McDonald's tried it and pulled back[61].

---

[58] Mickle, Tripp. "Apple had one of the highest rallies ever." *The Wall Street Journal*. January 28, 2020.

[59] Nellis, Stephen. "Apple iPhone sales return to growth, bolstering profit." *Reuters*. January 29, 2020.

[60] Vlastelica, Ryan. "Apple's push into television 'failing to resonate,' analyst says." *Bloomberg*. February 4, 2020.

[61] Haddon, Heather. "McDonald's says U.S. promotions paid off in latest quarter." *The Wall Street Journal*. May 1, 2019.

Grimace Can Dance

McDonald's hasn't sat around waiting to be a victim. Former CEO Steve Easterbrook made numerous positive changes during his tenure, including simplifying management structures, selling corporate stores to franchisees, rolling out automated order kiosks, launching all-day breakfast, switching to buy eggs from cage-free hens, using fresh beef patties in the U.S. and partnering with Uber Eats to deliver food to customers.

Quarter Pounder

McDonald's has shown that consumers are receptive to its numerous change initiatives. During the summer of 2019, the burger giant reported a whopping 6.5 percent global comparable restaurant sales growth for the quarter, above analyst expectations[62]. Some of the major updates and changes to its business include: technology-enhanced stores, delivery, new menu additions, mobile app upgrades, pay and pickup and more. The firm has also used aggressive pricing and promotions to drive traffic, such as offering $1, $2 and $3 (US) value items and the two for $5 US mix-and-match promotion. McDonald's also added donut sticks.

The food giant reported a solid third quarter in October of 2019, but missed street expectations. U.S. comparable store sales were up almost five percent and international comparable store sales were up almost six percent[63]. Outstanding results, but below lofty analyst expectations. In the U.S., foot traffic suffered as McDonald's was out-assorted by rivals Burger King, with its plant-based burger, and Wendy's, with its chicken sandwich. But McDonald's is investing for the future. Some 14,000 U.S. restaurants are being renovated to incorporate new technology and the firm is expanding delivery. Worldwide, McDonald's now offers food delivery in 80 countries from 23,000 locations.

Stop Clowning Around

While it was contemplating testing plant-based burgers, McDonald's made some changes to its existing beef patties to try to stay relevant[64]. The chain claims these

---

[62] Balu, Nivedita and Venugopal, Aishwarya. "McDonald's beats sales forecast." *Reuters*. July 27, 2019.

[63] Venugopal, Aishwarya and Russ, Hilary. "McDonald's misses on profit as competition takes bite." *Reuters*. October 23, 2019.

[64] Edmiston, Jake. "McDonald's stays on 'beef journey.'" *The Financial Post*. August 6, 2019.

changes make burgers juicier and hotter, which of course makes them taste better. The specifics of the changes from an operations perspective included thinner bottom buns, fewer patties on the grill at any given time and more sauce for Big Macs. The chain would later test plant-based burgers at several London, Ontario outlets and begin expanding the test by 2019.

Easter Island

The industry was in shock when McDonald's fired its CEO in 2019 for code of conduct breaches. The head of human resources left shortly after. It shows that in this environment, even stellar results don't make up for poor ethical judgement.

The show must go on, though, for McDonald's, which has shown it can innovate. Time will tell if the firm can keep pace with changing consumer tastes.

In January 2020, McDonald's announced that global 2019 full-year, same-restaurant sales increased a healthy 5.9 percent. One alarming issue, though, is U.S. restaurant traffic fell 1.9 percent during the same time. In the United States, more consumers are eating at home and competition is fierce. The food giant plans to spend $2.4 billion US on capital in 2020. About $1.3 billion US of this amount will go toward the U.S. division[65].

Lowe's

Lowe's is a work in progress. The U.S. home improvement giant has had a hard time keeping pace with larger rival Home Depot as supply chain issues hamper growth[66]. To get things on back on track, Lowe's hired former Home Depot senior executive Marvin Ellison as its CEO.

Handyman

Things have changed since Ellison's arrival. Lowe's has started focusing more on its core U.S. business. It exited Mexico and closed two side businesses[67]. Ellison

---

[65] Haddon, Heather and Maidenberg, Micah. "McDonald's gains sales, but U.S. guest count falls." *The Wall Street Journal*. January 30, 2020.

[66] Nassauer, Sarah. "Lowe's lays off thousands of store workers." *The Wall Street Journal*. August 2, 2019.

[67] Chin, Kimberly. "Lowe's to exit its Mexico business, shed two operations." *The Wall*

also closed 47 poor-performing stores as well as Orchard Supply and brought in leaders from his former life. He also outsourced store assembly and maintenance, resulting in thousands of layoffs.

Leaky Faucet

Lowe's appears to be making progress. In the quarter ending June 2019, the retailer grew sales faster than Home Depot for the first time since 2016. But margins remain a problem. Lowe's also has its hands full with its acquisition of Rona in Canada, which we will discuss later.

Lowe's reported a fourth quarter 2019 (ending January 31, 2020) same-store sales gain of 2.5 percent over 2018[68].

Best Buy

Many thought Best Buy was going to take a sh*t kicking from Amazon and I guess it did for a while. Then, in 2012, new CEO Hubert Joly rode in on his horse and turned the town around.

Unlike other category killers that have bitten the dust such as Circuit City, Toys "R" Us and The Sports Authority, Best Buy dusted itself off and decided to fight back[69].

Joly added services to differentiate from online retailers and price matched any would-be showroomers. He and his team also reconfigured stores to be pick-up friendly so that Best Buy online orders could be gotten quickly and efficiently, one of the first retailers to do so. He added payment plans and made acquisitions such as senior devices maker GreatCall and senior services provider Critical Signal. The firm also took advantage of Sears' problems by growing the major appliance business.

Best Buy reported enterprise comparable sales that grew 3.2 percent for the

---

Street Journal. November 21, 2018.

[68] Repko, Melissa. "Lowe's fourth-quarter sales, outlook for fiscal 2020 fall short of estimates." February 26, 2020. Retrieved from: https://www.cnbc.com/2020/02/26/lowes-low-earnings-q4-2019.html

[69] Safdar, Khadeeja and Al-Muslim, Aisha. "Best Buy performs better than expected." *The Wall Street Journal.* May 24, 2019.

fourth quarter of 2019 (13 weeks ending February 1, 2020)[70].

Starbucks

Starbucks has seen a renaissance of late. After decades of tremendous growth, sales flattened out after new CEO Kevin Johnson took the helm in 2017[71].

Mermaid Management

Times have changed, though, for the coffee giant, as a better, more convenient ordering app and a well-received loyalty program helped drive sales and share price. At over 17 million members, the loyalty program helps improve average sale and brand engagement, as well as keep customers out of the competition. In addition, China, which is Starbucks' second-largest market outside of the U.S., has continued to see strong growth and store expansion. New drinks such as Cloud Macchiato and Nitro Cold Brew have driven sales. Starbucks also partnered with Nestlé to sell Starbucks packaged coffee products.

Starbucks released an updated environmental assessment of its operations in January 2020. The company said its findings showed the use of dairy was the biggest source of carbon emissions in its system. Starbucks is targeting a 50 percent reduction in carbon emissions by 2030. In 2018, the coffee giant was responsible for throwing 868 metric kilotons of coffee cups and other garbage in landfills. It also used one billion cubic metres of water and emitted 16 million metric tons of greenhouse gases[72].

The Great Wall

Some challenges remain, though. Starbucks is making significant changes to fight off slowing traffic at its U.S. and China stores[73]. The firm recently lowered its

---

[70] "Best Buy reports better-than-expected fourth quarter results." February 27, 2020. Retrieved from: http://investors.bestbuy.com/investor-relations/news-and-events/financial-releases/news-details/2020/Best-Buy-Reports-Better-Than-Expected-Fourth-Quarter-Results/default.aspx

[71] Peltz, James F. "How a once-stalled Starbucks has picked up steam again." *Los Angeles Times*. July 30, 2019.

[72] Pfanner, Eric. "Starbucks suggests going back to green." *Bloomberg*. January 22, 2020.

[73] Jargon, Julie. "Starbucks to offer delivery across U.S. in bid to expand reach." *The Wall*

outlook for annual EPS growth from the 15 to 20 percent range down to 12 percent. It's also laying off about five percent of its global staff and has closed Teavana stores. Starbucks is also trying to improve customer service; it recently advised baristas to clean up after closing hours in order to tend to customers more.

Starbucks reported Q1 fiscal 2020 (13 weeks ending December 29, 2019) comp store sales up 5 percent globally[74].

Chipotle

Chipotle, hammered with a food quality and safety issue in 2016, has regained ground[75]. In the second quarter of 2019, the restaurant grew same-store sales 10 percent. In the third quarter of 2019, results were again solid as comparable store sales increased 11 percent, easily beating analyst estimates[76]. Why? Digital sales and delivery. Digital sales increased 88 percent. The firm has been investing in pick-up shelves to make it easier for customers and delivery drivers.

Chipotle announced a fourth quarter 2019 comp restaurant sales growth of 13.4 percent[77].

American Eagle

U.S. clothing chain American Eagle has showed some solid performance recently, as both its namesake banner and Aerie banner have been at the upper end

---

Street Journal. December 17, 2018.

[74] "Starbucks Reports Q1 Fiscal 2020 Results." January 28, 2020. Retrieved from: https://investor.starbucks.com/press-releases/financial-releases/press-release-details/2020/Starbucks-Reports-Q1-Fiscal-2020-Results/default.aspx

[75] Sampath, Uday. "Chipotle's online focus delivers same-store sales beat." *Reuters*. July 24, 2019.

[76] Russ, Hilary. "Chipotle beats Street on new items, digital." *Reuters with a file from Bloomberg*. October 23, 2019.

[77] "Chipotle announces fourth quarter and full year 2019 results." February 4, 2020. Retrieved from: https://ir.chipotle.com/2020-02-04-Chipotle-Announces-Fourth-Quarter-And-Full-Year-2019-Results

of fashion retailers' comparative store sales growth[78]. Part of the reason for its success has been its jeans. Jeans that stretch and jeans that look warn. In fact, jeans overall are making a comeback, as brands are making them more comfortable. Let's not forget jeans are also more acceptable to wear to work now versus a few decades ago.

American Eagle announced fourth quarter 2019 (ending February 1, 2020) comp store sales up two percent[79].

Levi's

As a child growing up in the 1970s (my favourite decade), I remember when Levi's was a power brand. Anyone and everyone who was cool wore Levi's. There was GWG and Wrangler or no-name jeans, but they were all sh*t compared to the San Francisco giant.

Jean Machine

I still remember the day I got my first pair of Levi's jeans. I was about 10 and I went with my mom and sisters to a mall called Square One in a city called Mississauga, which is a suburb of Toronto. It was November. I was old enough to ask my mom for specific presents for Christmas and I asked for Levi's. We walked into a Thrifty's store and I tried a pair on. My whole demeanour instantly changed. I felt like a new man or I guess a new boy. I was suddenly Peter Frampton. I was suddenly Fonzie. I was suddenly a rock star! Time passed and Levi's got its pockets kicked when it missed the designer jeans trend. It also faced new competition from private label and teen retailers and lost a lot of its stardom. Levi's was taken private in 1985 and began to take on too much debt. Sales peaked in the 1990s at $7 billion US, but dropped off to just under $5 billion US in 2011.

Denim Diva

Fast forward to 2019, and it made a comeback through an IPO. Levi Strauss & Co. (its formal name) has been working hard over the last 10 or so years to become

---

[78] Sampath, Uday. "Jeans revival lifts American Eagle." *Reuters*. June 6, 2019.

[79] "American Eagle Outfitters reports record fourth quarter and annual revenue." March 4, 2020. Retrieved from: http://investors.ae.com/news-releases/news-releases-details/2020/American-Eagle-Outfitters-Reports-Record-Fourth-Quarter-and-Annual-Revenue/default.aspx

relevant again[80]. The company improved its image, its operations and its product. The brand has such a rich heritage to play to, having made jeans in 1873 for the U.S. West Coast gold rush. Key changes made under CEO Charles Bergh consisted of increasing marketing spend, reducing staff, repaying debt and creating an innovation lab. The brand also started a direct-to-consumer channel through its own stores and website. Results have been encouraging, with direct making up about 35 percent of revenue.

Ripped

The company admits it has benefited from the denim trend, but is challenged by the yoga and athleisure movement. In the summer of 2019, Levi's stock fell as it reported a lacklustre quarter and was downgraded by a Goldman Sachs analyst[81]. Time will tell if it can get back to the glory days.

Levi Strauss and Co. announced a fourth quarter 2019 net revenue decrease of two percent. Full-year 2019 net revenue grew three percent[82].

H&M

H&M is in tough as it relates to inventory. In October 2019, the Swedish giant announced third quarter results that were mostly positive, with a 19 percent growth in U.S. sales[83].

No Clearance No Cry

For the first time in seven years, sales grew faster than inventory — a scary scenario for a retailer in the fast-fashion game, where yesterday's fad is today's markdown.

---

[80] Maheshwari, Sapna. "New and improved Levi's prepares to go public". *New York Times News Service*. March 20, 2019.

[81] "Levi Strauss hits new low after first sell rating." *Bloomberg*. July 18, 2019.

[82] "Levi Strauss & Co. reports fourth-quarter and full year 2019 earnings." January 30, 2020. Retrieved from: https://investors.levistrauss.com/news/financial-news/news-details/2020/Levi-Strauss--Co-Reports-Fourth-Quarter-and-Full-Year-2019-Earnings/default.aspx

[83] Mulier, Thomas. "H&M earnings return to growth." *Bloomberg*. October 4, 2019.

Promotional Rescue

The firm backed off on discounts, which boosted profit, and had a great summer lineup that drove top line. Sales grew for the sixth consecutive quarter, while inventories dropped slightly. H&M, like other fast-fashion players, faces headwinds as consumers grasp the environmental impact of semi-disposable garments.

The H&M group reported growth in full year 2019 net sales of 11 percent, six percent in local currencies[84].

Burberry

Burberry, like many luxury brands, depends more and more on China for sales and profits. About 20 percent of Burberry's business is from there. Demonstrations in Hong Kong during the summer of 2019 and the escalating trade war between the U.S. and China have created much uncertainty, not just for Burberry, but for many firms[85].

Department Store Detox

The company has hired a new designer and is focusing more on handbags to boost margins. Like other luxury brands, Burberry is reducing distribution through department stores to maintain its premium image and premium pricing in the market.

Burberry reported a third quarter fiscal 2019 (13 weeks ending December 28, 2019) comp store sales growth of three percent[86].

Ralph Lauren

Ralph Lauren, like other once-premium brands, is repositioning itself as less of a

---

[84] "Full-year report 2019." January 30, 2020. Retrieved from: https://hmgroup.com/content/dam/hmgroup/groupsite/documents/masterlanguage/Presentations/2019/Press%20conference%20presentation%20Handout%202019.pdf

[85] Ryan, Carol. "Burberry is down at heel without China." *The Wall Street Journal*. August 19, 2019.

[86] "Burberry Group PLC third quarter trading update." January 22, 2020. Retrieved from: file:///C:/Users/14167/Downloads/Burberry%20Third%20Quarter%20Trading%20Update%20Announcement.pdf

discounted department store brand and more of a full-priced marque[87]. With this change comes financial pain as channels are realigned and sales and profits fall. At least in the short run. The company also recognizes it must work hard to focus on younger customers.

Ralph Lauren reported its second quarter fiscal 2020 net revenue increased by one percent[88].

Cole Haan

Not all footwear retailers are hurting. Privately-held Cole Haan has decided to go public based on recent success[89]. Formerly owned by powerhouse Nike, the brand was sold off to private equity firm Apax Partners in 2013. Since changing hands, Cole Haan has reinvented itself to focus on a mix of new product development and international expansion.

Business on Top, Party on the Bottom

One of its homeruns is a new line called ZeroGrand that mixes dress shoes with comfort. The line offers flexibility and comfort on the bottom but looks dressy on the top. The firm relied on its R and D team for this modern approach to formal footwear. Cole Haan sells about 30 percent of its products online, where it enjoys greater margins.

Cashing Out

In mid-February 2020, Cole Haan made its U.S. listing application public as it plans its IPO. Cole Haan joins retailers Casper, MyTheresa and Madewell, which plan to go public in 2020. The IPO will be used to allow existing investors to cash out[90].

---

[87] Kapner, Suzanne and Chin, Kimberly. "Ralph Lauren's profit shrinks as North American sales dip." *The Wall Street Journal*. May 15, 2019.

[88] "Ralph Lauren reports second quarter fiscal 2020 results." November 7, 2019. Retrieved from: https://www.businesswire.com/news/home/20191107005224/en/Ralph-Lauren-Reports-Quarter-Fiscal-2020-Results

[89] Townsend, Matt. "Top shoemaker Cole Haan preps IPO." *Bloomberg*. August 27, 2019.

[90] "Shoemaker Cole Haan makes U.S. IPO filing public." *Reuters*. February 15, 2020.

Cole Haan's fiscal 2019 revenue increased 14 percent over 2018[91].

DSW (Now Designer Brands)

In Canada, U.S.-based shoe retailer DSW (now Designer Brands) announced it was adding up to 50 stores over the next few years[92]. After closing a mid-priced chain called Town Shoes, it realized that consumers want bargains and has focused on the growing value segment of the market.

It's a surprising move considering Payless ShoeSource closed 248 stores, including Nine West and Rockport. Designer Brands is looking to significantly grow online sales and consolidate vendors to get better costing. Capitalizing on the service business, the firm will be testing nail bars and shoe repair services at select locations.

Designer Brands reported a third quarter 2019 (three months ending November 2, 2019) comp store sales growth of .3 percent[93].

L.L. Bean

American brand L.L. Bean is taking its time and doing it right. The storied outdoor products retailer opened its first store in Canada in August, 2019[94]. The privately-held New England retailer used its years of catalogue and online sales data to pick the Canadian location and its initial assortment. Located in affluent Oakville, Ontario, about a 30-minute drive from Toronto, the town represented the geographic epicenter of previous sales.

---

[91] Garcia, Tonya. "Cole Haan is going public: 5 things to know about the shoes and accessories company." March 2, 2020. Retrieved from: https://www.marketwatch.com/story/cole-haan-is-going-public-5-things-to-know-about-the-shoes-and-accessories-company-2020-02-28

[92] Strauss, Marina. "Shoe retailer DSW aims to boost Canadian footprint." *The Globe and Mail*. March 19, 2019.

[93] "Designer Brands Inc. reports third quarter 2019 financial results." December 10, 2019. Retrieved from: https://investors.designerbrands.com/2019-12-10-Designer-Brands-Inc-Reports-Third-Quarter-2019-Financial-Results

[94] Edmiston, Jake. "Why L.L. Bean is being cautious about its foray into Canada." *The Financial Post*. August 29, 2019.

On Target

Unlike Target, L.L. Bean learned the easy way by opening one store to test and learn before considering expansion. The firm also inked a deal with HBC to offer its brand in select Hudson's Bay stores. A great way to get a feel for the brick and mortar potential of the brand without the massive investment.

The firm partnered with local Jaytex Group, which brings Canadian expertise. Another step that Target did not take. Jaytex feels that the brand could have as many as 20 stores over the next 10 years. Without a store, L.L Bean sold $32 million US in Canada in 2018, which represented about two percent of the firm's $1.6 billion US in global sales. The brand feels Canada could one day grow to about four percent of global sales.

Tesco

The U.K. grocery market is changing rapidly and Tesco, the largest player, is trying to manoeuvre to remain at the top spot. Caught in the cross hairs of online shopping growth and a lacklustre economy, Tesco, with a commanding 27 percent of the market, has been holding its own and then some compared to competitors such as Asda, Morrisons and Sainsbury's.

New Sensations

The chain has been launching new formats, too. Tesco opened Jacks, a discount format, to fight German Lidl and Aldi. It also created Metro, a daily shop destination. And it runs Express convenience stores and its namesake banners. Tesco reported it was cutting back its workforce at its Metro chain by about 4,500 as it adjusts the concept[95]. Tesco is the largest private employer in the U.K., with a workforce of about 320,000 people.

Coronation

The firm will have a new boss come 2020 when Ken Murphy takes the reins from Dave Lewis[96]. Tesco has enjoyed a rebirth during Lewis's tenure, as the grocer focused on a multi-prong strategy to win in Britain's cut-throat food business. Lewis

---

[95] Holton, Kate. "U.K. grocery giant Tesco to cut about 4,500 jobs." *Reuters*. August 6, 2019.

[96] Davey, James. "In turbulent times, Tesco's new boss can build on firmer foundation." *Reuters*. October 4, 2019.

used a number of block and tackle moves, such as differentiating Tesco from other grocers, monetizing real estate, striking a sourcing relationship with Carrefour, boosting margins, lowering costs and improving cash flow. Lewis also bought a wholesaler called Booker.

Tesco reported Christmas sales (six weeks to January 4, 2020) down 1.8 percent. The firm also reported Q3, 2019 sales (13 weeks to November 23, 2019) down 1.4 percent[97].

Marks & Spencer

Marks & Spencer was once a rock star of the British retail scene. Founded in 1884, the seller of food and clothes was the first U.K. retailer to hit one billion pounds in profit in one year[98] — that was 1998. Times have changed, though. The firm recently got kicked out of the FTSE 100 index and saw its stock plummet 36 percent at one point. It recently made a big bet in grocery e-commerce, investing 1.5 billion pounds in a new online delivery warehouse with fellow U.K. company Ocado.

Marks & Spencer reported its third quarter 2019/20 (ending December 28, 2019) trading statement, which showed revenue declined .7 percent on a constant currency basis[99].

Loblaw

For those of you who have never been to Canada, you may not have heard of Loblaw, one of our national champions. Loblaw is Canada's largest grocer and also owns our largest drug store, Shoppers Drug Mart. The firm has done a great job innovating and using technology to cater to customers' changing needs.

---

[97] "3Q and Christmas trading statement 19/20." January 20, 2020. Retrieved from: https://www.tescoplc.com/news/2020/3q-and-christmas-trading-statement-1920/

[98] Davey, James. "Troubling times for Marks & Spencer." *Reuters*. September 5, 2019.

[99] "Marks And Spencer Group PLC Quarter 3 2019/20 Trading Statement 13 Weeks to 28 December 2019." January 9, 2020. Retrieved from: https://corporate.marksandspencer.com/documents/rns-q3-2019-20-trading-statement-website.pdf

Grocery Game

Josh Rubin, a reporter with The Toronto Star, sat down with Greg Ramier, president of Loblaw's market division, to ask about the future of the 100-year-old Canadian grocer[100]. Like most executive interviews, it was well-scripted and cautious, but is still worth the read. Here are a few points I gleaned from the piece: Local will become even more important as consumers want it. Nutrition is more important to shoppers. Fresh vegetables, sustainable seafood and meatless protein are key. Environmental programs have become important and will grow. Online grocery shopping is small but will grow. Service and experience matters. Not surprisingly, the retailer has several initiatives underway to capitalize on these trends.

Amazon Light

Loblaw announced in November, 2019 that it was launching an e-commerce marketplace that offered numerous categories such as toys, furniture, household products, housewares and more. The firm is said to be capitalizing on busy shoppers to offer a convenient, one-stop shop beyond food[101]. Loblaw faces stiff competition up here. Walmart and Costco have taken share from traditional grocers, while Amazon slowly but surely builds grocery infrastructure. In February of 2020, Loblaw reported that 2019 online sales topped $1 billion Cdn for the first time — almost twice the value in 2018. Still a small percentage of the grocer's $48 billion Cdn in annual sales, it generates lower margins from this channel versus in-store[102].

Loblaw reported a fourth quarter 2019 food (Loblaw) comp store sales growth of 1.9 percent and drug (Shoppers Drug Mart) comp store sales growth of 3.9 percent[103].

---

[100] Rubin, Josh. "The shiny new future of the supermarket." *The Toronto Star.* July 22, 2019.

[101] Krashinsky Robertson, Susan. "Loblaw announces launch of new e-commerce marketplace." *The Globe and Mail.* November 21, 2019.

[102] Krashinsky Robertson, Susan. "Loblaw's e-commerce sales reached $1-billion in 2019." *The Globe and Mail.* February 21, 2020.

[103] "Loblaw Reports 2019 Fourth Quarter Results and Fiscal Year Ended December 28, 2019 Results." February 20, 2020. Retrieved from: https://media.loblaw.ca/English/media-centre/press-releases/press-release-details/2020/Loblaw-Reports-2019-Fourth-Quarter-Results-and-Fiscal-Year-Ended-December-28-2019-Results1/default.aspx

Couche-Tard

You may never have heard of Couche-Tard unless you are from Canada, but chances are you know its brand Circle K when you pump gas or buy cigarettes. Montreal-based Alimentation Couche-Tard has quietly become one of the largest convenience store outfits in the world.

Achieved mostly through smart acquisitions over a period of several years, this retailer is the biggest in Canada with revenue just under $60 billion Cdn. The firm announced in July, 2019 that it plans to double its profit in five years.[104] Look for more acquisitions over the next few years and best-in-class integration.

Alimentation Couche-Tard reported second quarter fiscal 2020 total revenue down seven percent for the 12-week period ending October 13, 2019[105].

Canadian Tire

With many strengths, including power private labels such as Mastercraft and Motomaster, Canadian Tire is starting to find it harder to compete with Amazon and a changing customer. The chain is threatened by millennials moving away from homes and cars and needs to redefine itself or face irrelevance. Canadian Tire was extremely late launching home delivery and is a laggard from a technology perspective. The firm has time but must accelerate its pace of change, in my opinion.

Clean out the Trunk

Until it can find its "A" game again, cost-cutting is in store. The firm announced in 2019 that it would cut $200 million Cdn in cost to drive profits. Canadian Tire has numerous independent divisions such as SportChek, Marks and its namesake banner, all with separate marketing and sourcing functions. In addition, the firm sees the retirement of legacy systems and processes as well as the elimination of redundant headcount as cost synergy opportunities. It is often difficult to cut your way to glory as the firm appears to be poised to do.

The firm realizes it needs to ramp up its omni channel capabilities. In February

---

[104] "Convenience store aims to double its net profit." *The Canadian Press.* July 11, 2019.

[105] "Alimentation Couche-Tard announces its results for its second quarter of fiscal year 2020." November 26, 2019. Retrieved from: https://corpo.couche-tard.com/wp-content/uploads/2019/11/2020-Q2-Press-Release-En.pdf

2020, The Tire announced it was rolling out more pick-up towers[106]. Like other retailers, Canadian Tire realizes that the economics of e-commerce home delivery are challenging. Greg Hicks, then Canadian Tire retail president, was quoted as saying:

"We collectively believe…that in-store pick up continues to be the best way for customers to have orders filled. It's always the fastest and the cheapest option."

The problem for The Tire is that customers may value the convenience of home delivery more than Canadian Tire realizes. This could drag down future earnings as home delivery increases as a percentage of Tire's sales mix.

The firm had a solid fourth quarter in 2019, with comp store sales increasing 4.8 percent.

Foot Locker

Foot Locker shares dropped nearly 20 percent in May of 2019 after posting results that missed analyst expectations[107]. Store traffic slowed and was down by low single digits. While up, online sales could not offset brick and mortar declines. Foot Locker faces many challenges, including growing duties on imported product from China and the growth of DTC athletic brands.

The chain reported fourth quarter 2019 (ending February 1, 2020) comp store sales down 1.6 percent. Full year 2019 comp store sales increased 2.2 percent[108].

Holt Renfrew

Canada's luxury segment got crowded quickly. Privately-held Holt Renfrew, the perennial luxury department store in Canada, is consolidating its stores to focus on Canada's largest luxury markets: Toronto and Vancouver[109]. The chain closed its

---

[106] Krashinsky Robertson, Susan. "Canadian Tire to build upon e-commerce strategy." *The Globe and Mail*. February 14, 2020.

[107] Novy-Williams, Eben and Edwards III, John J. "Foot Locker plunges most since 2017 as sales miss estimates." *Bloomberg*. May 25, 2019.

[108] "Foot Locker, Inc. reports 2019 fourth quarter and full year results." February 8, 2020. Retrieved from: https://www.footlocker-inc.com/content/flinc-aem-site/en/home/investor-relations.html#press-releases

[109] Strauss, Marina. "Holt Renfrew to close store in Edmonton amid tight market." *The*

Edmonton store in January of 2020 as part of a downscale from nine stores in seven cities to six stores in four cities (Toronto, Vancouver, Montreal and Calgary). Like society, luxury is polarizing and sales have grown online.

Haute Competition

Holt Renfrew faces a significant increase in competition as new players such as Saks 5th Avenue and Nordstrom, as well as a slew of new international luxury brands, have added stores in Canada. The chain is growing, though. As a private firm it does not disclose financial results but indicated it was seeing growth in the "high single digits to low double digits" range. The retailer has been spending significantly on remaining store upgrades including its Montreal store, which will be rebranded Ogilvy.

Campbell Soup

150-year-old Campbell Soup has seen its share of turbulence. Former CEO Denise Morrison left the company in May 2018 after numerous big ticket acquisitions failed to drive earnings. The only significant increase was in debt levels, which have further burdened the company.

Activist Broth

Daniel Loeb's hedge fund Third Point has taken the fight to Campbell to stir things up and drive performance[110]. With earnings down 50 percent in Q3, 2018, the firm was limping. The ancestors of the founder, who control about 40 percent of the company, are not thrilled with Third Point's aggressive approach. Third Point wanted five seats on the board.

Contrarian Taste

New CEO Mark Clouse is refocusing the brand on its namesake products to drive the soup and snack business in the U.S. market. Campbell recently announced it was selling its Australian snack division, Arnott's, to investment firm KKR for $2.2

Globe and Mail. May 15, 2019.

[110] Schwartz, Nelson D. "The battle for Campbell Soup is reaching a boiling point." *The New York Times.* November 19, 2018.

billion[111] US. Clouse is also exiting fresh foods. It's a marked difference from other CPG firms that are looking for growth from this segment. He sees differentiation from private label as a key to win the U.S. soup and snack market and rely less on discounts. Unlike other foodservice companies, Campbell is not looking to expand internationally. Clouse has reversed the downward trend and reported a sales increase of 12 percent year over year for the quarter that ended April 28, 2019[112].

Campbell Soup reported second quarter fiscal 2020 net sales flat to the same time last year. Organic sales rose one percent[113].

Nestlé

Nestlé is following the playbook of other big food companies. It recently announced it was putting its Herta brand of lunch meats for sale as it refocuses its portfolio away from processed food and into healthy plant-based products[114]. Recent acquisitions, including Sweet Earth and Blue Bottle Coffee, have reinforced this new direction. The firm is not alone in its quest for healthy brands. Unilever recently bought Vegetarian Butcher. Another growth area for the firm is the soy and wheat protein-based Incredible Burger.

Nestlé reported a full year 2019 organic revenue growth of 3.5 percent. Accounting for price increases, real internal growth came in at 2.9 percent[115].

Kellogg

It's tough to drive returns in the boxed and canned food business these days as consumers don't want processed crap anymore. Kellogg understands this as well as

---

[111] Duran, Paula and Kaye, Byron. "KKR buys biscuit maker for $ 2.2-billion from Campbell." *Reuters.* July 25, 2019.

[112] Maidenberg, Micah. "Sales rise at Campbell on snack strength". *The Wall Street Journal.* June 6, 2019.

[113] "Q2 2020 earnings press release." March 4, 2020. Retrieved from: https://investor.campbellsoupcompany.com/financial-information/quarterly-results/

[114] Gretler, Corinne. "Nestle cuts the meat in bid to build healthier food giant." *Bloomberg.* February 15, 2019.

[115] "Nestlé reports full-year results for 2019." February 13, 2020. Retrieved from: https://www.nestle.com/media/pressreleases/allpressreleases/full-year-results-2019

anyone.

Food Court

Kellogg has been holding a garage sale of unwanted brands of late, selling off its cookie and ice cream business to Ferrero for $1.3 billion US. These include the Famous Amos and Keebler marques. Kellogg is looking to offload its fruit snack business as well[116].

The list of other big food companies playing musical chairs with brands is long. Nestlé sold its U.S. candy business, Campbell Soup is dumping its international brands and J.M. Smucker kicked out the Pillsbury Dough Boy and his baking mixes. Other food firms, such as Conagra and General Mills, are looking for buyers for parts of their portfolio as well.

Cereal Entrepreneur

Another big ugly problem for Kellogg is the cereal business. It's too big to cut loose. Kellogg must find a way to reinvent the category based on today's changing consumer preferences. Not an easy task.

On a Diet

The American cereal icon announced in the summer of 2019 that it was laying off about 150 employees from its North American business[117]. The firm is retooling its organization structure to enable faster decision making. It also requires less support staff as it sells off large parts of its North American division. The cost to eliminate these workers and right size the business: $35 million US before taxes. The company is also reorganizing Europe, which will result in a one-time hit of $57 million US.

Kellogg reported a fourth quarter 2019 net sales decrease of 2.8 percent and a full year 2019 sales increase of .2 percent. Fourth quarter 2019 organic sales increased by 2.7 percent and organic full year 2019 sales increased by 1.9 percent[118].

---

[116] Gasparro, Annie and Maidenberg, Micah. "Kellogg considers selling its fruit-snacks, cookies businesses." *The Wall Street Journal.* November 14, 2018.

[117] Maidenberg, Micah and Kellaher, Colin. "Kellogg plans job cuts amid North American reorganization." *The Wall Street Journal.* June 19, 2019.

[118] "Kellogg Company reports solid finish to 2019 and issues 2020 financial guidance."

Reckitt Benckiser

Reckitt Benckiser, the maker of Lysol cleaner and Durex condoms, has a new boss and some operational issues to deal with[119]. Known for its high margins, the British CPG firm has underperformed within its health division. This is problematic, as health makes up over 60 percent of its revenue. The company has also been challenged by store brands and lower birthrates in China. It is contemplating selling off its home division in the near future.

The brand reported full year 2019 revenue increased by two percent[120].

Mattel

Mattel has fallen on hard times over the last few years. One of its largest customers, Toys "R" Us, went bankrupt. It lost the Frozen licence to its arch enemy, Hasbro. Its cash cow, Barbie, hasn't been performing well. The company went through four CEOs in four years.

Mollywood

Things could be looking up, though, for the California firm. Its latest CEO, Ynon Kreiz, is an entertainment man and sees the value Mattel's brands have beyond the toy aisle[121]. He opened a Mattel film studio and inked movie deals for Barbie, Hot Wheels and other key Mattel brands. Kreiz is also developing TV shows and will be looking to license key brands more widely on categories such as live-action events and games.

The toy giant continues to work on positioning its Barbie line as more diverse and inclusive. In late January 2020, the firm launched several new Barbie dolls, including a doll with vitiligo, a doll with a prosthetic limb and a bald Barbie. Mattel

---

February 6, 2020. Retrieved from: https://investor.kelloggs.com/QuarterlyResults

[119] Ryan, Carol. "Lysol's new boss has messy decisions to make." *The Wall Street Journal*. July 31, 2019.

[120] Castia, Mettia. February 27, 2020. "Reckitt Benckiser swings to net loss for 2019." Retrieved from: https://www.marketwatch.com/story/reckitt-benckiser-swings-to-net-loss-for-2019-2020-02-27

[121] Ziobro, Paul. "Barbie, Hot Wheels go Hollywood in Mattel CEO's plan." *The Wall Street Journal*. April 18, 2019.

claims that the 2020 line has "more skin tones, hair types and body shapes than ever before.[122]"

Workshop Wind Down

Mattel announced in February 2020 that it was closing three factories — two in China and one in Canada. The firm also closed facilities in China and Indonesia in 2019 and planned to sell its Mexican plant. At one time Mattel owned 13 factories. Unlike rival Hasbro, the El Segundo toy giant made its products in-house[123].

Mattel reported 2019 fourth quarter net sales down three percent. 2019 full year net sales were flat to 2018[124].

Coca-Cola

The soft drink market is changing rapidly and giants like Coca-Cola have had to change with it. Soda, or pop as we call it in Canada, has been in decline for the last 10 years as consumers have flocked toward bottled water and flavoured seltzer[125]. Coke has seen strong growth in tea, water and coffee. It also launched Orange Vanilla Coke and Orange Vanilla Coke Zero Sugar in an effort to draw interest to the brand. The firm also relaunched Diet Coke with new flavours and a cool skinny can shape. Flavours include Zesty Blood Orange and Ginger Lime. These are bold moves for a giant that is so synonymous with its original cola. The company has also been busy improving its environmental impact as we shall discuss later.

Coke reported a net sales increase of 16 percent in Q4, 2019. Global organic revenue grew seven percent for the same period[126].

---

[122] Cramer, Maria. "Barbie, now 61, is still reinventing herself." *The New York Times*. January 31, 2020.

[123] Ziobro, Paul. "Mattel closes factories amid toy slump." *The Wall Street Journal*. February 11, 2020.

[124] "Mattel reports full year and fourth quarter 2019 financial results." Retrieved from: https://news.mattel.com/news/mattel-reports-full-year-and-fourth-quarter-2019-financial-results

[125] Maloney, Jennifer and Al-Muslim, Aisha. "Coca-Cola expects sales growth to slow in 2019." *The Wall Street Journal*. February 15, 2019.

[126] "Coca-Cola stock rises as earnings meet estimates and Coke brand boosts sales."

Monster

The energy drink market has become complicated. Monster, the U.S. market leader, has decided to get bold and branch out into non-energy and even alcoholic drinks. It's a big departure for the firm, which has 42 percent of the market, according to Neilson[127]. Big brother Coca-Cola, with its 18.5 percent stake in Monster, has launched its own energy drink in Europe called Coca-Cola Energy and Monster has fought to prevent Coke from releasing it in the U.S. market. In March of 2020, Coke rival PepsiCo bought energy drink brand Rockstar for $3.8 billion[128] US.

Musical Chairs

It appears beverage is the new battleground as firms are jumping into each other's verticals for growth. Coke launched an alcoholic lemon-flavoured drink in Japan. Anheuser-Busch launched an energy drink as well as cold coffee and iced tea.

Sweet Leaf

Monster has also talked about entering the weed business. If Uncle Sam makes it legal federally, Monster could launch a cannabis-infused drink.

Monster Beverage reported a fourth quarter 2019 net sales increase of 10.1 percent[129].

January 30, 2020. Retrieved from: https://www.cnbc.com/2020/01/30/coca-cola-ko-earnings-q4-2019.html

[127] Maloney, Jennifer. "Monster looks beyond energy drinks to alcohol." *The Wall Street Journal*. June 10, 2019.

[128] Manskar, Noah. "PepsiCo to buy Rockstar Energy for $3.8 billion." March 11, 2020. Retrieved from: https://nypost.com/2020/03/11/pepsico-to-buy-rockstar-energy-for-3-8-billion/

[129] "Monster Beverage reports 2019 fourth quarter and full year financial results." February 27, 2020. Retrieved from: https://www.globenewswire.com/news-release/2020/02/27/1992239/0/en/Monster-Beverage-Reports-2019-Fourth-Quarter-and-Full-Year-Financial-Results.html

Conagra Foods

Investors are looking for growth and that growth must come from spending on new products and marketing. One company that has excelled in this space while others have struggled has been Conagra Foods. Conagra has realized it can't slash its way to glory and has been successfully spending to kickstart dusty brands such as Marie Callenders and Healthy Choice.

Conagra announced a second quarter fiscal 2020 (ending November 24, 2019) net sales increase of 18.3 percent. Organic net sales grew 1.6 percent for the quarter[130].

FUMBLING DICE

The third category, Fumbling Dice, represents gambles — retailers or brands that have fallen down and are trying to make another go of it. Time will tell if they are successful or retire to the history books. I wish them well.

Tru Kids

What happened to Toys "R" Us (TRU)? It has been reincarnated by former executives who launched privately-held Tru Kids Inc[131]. The new entity will explore a variety of go-to-market strategies including e-commerce, brick and mortar stores and stores within a store[132]. After TRU's 2017 death, Tru Kids announced it was getting back in the market by opening up its online operations and two small 6,500-square-foot stores in the fall of 2019. The two stores, in Houston and New Jersey, will be experiential with room for birthday parties and special events — more interactive product showcases and play and less stack-it-high and watch-it-fly. The new store concept is the child of b8ta, an electronics retailer, and Tru Kids.

---

[130] "Conagra Brands reports solid second quarter results." December 19, 2019. Retrieved from: https://www.conagrabrands.com/news-room/news-conagra-brands-reports-solid-second-quarter-results-prn-122715

[131] D'Innocenzio, Anne. "Toys R Us plans second act in U.S. under new name." *The Associated Press.* February 12, 2019.

[132] "Spin Master slides on Toys 'R' Us fallout." *The Canadian Press.* March 8, 2019.

IOU

Not everyone is keen to make peace with this once-iconic retailer[133]. In an article by Tiffany Hsu, written during the annual 2019 New York Toy Fair, she discusses the storied toy retailer "rising from the ashes." Not everyone is giddy with excitement, though. Hsu quotes former TRU vendor Mark Carson as saying he still has a "bitter taste" in his mouth from the $100,000 US Toys "R" Us owed him before it went under. This is chump change compared to what TRU owed big kids Mattel and Hasbro.

Barnes & Noble

Reuters recently reported that hedge fund Elliot Management is buying distressed U.S. book retailer Barnes & Noble[134]. Bruised and battered from too many dust-ups with Amazon, sales at Barnes & Noble have been declining for three years. Elliot Management paid a 40 percent-plus premium to the pre-sale stock price or about $476 million US. The hedge fund has a thing for book stores, as it bought U.K. book retailer Waterstone in 2018.

Barnes & Noble reported second quarter fiscal 2020 (ending October 26, 2019) comp store sales down 5.9 percent[135].

FAO Schwarz

The toy business has changed. Take the rebirth of FAO Schwarz in 2018. Owned by private equity firm ThreeSixty Group, the business model for the brand has been updated radically[136]. Beyond its flagship in New York City, many units are "stores within other stores." Others are located in airports, where the firm receives franchising fees.

---

[133] Hsu, Tiffany. "Toys "R" Us tries to rise from the ashes in U.S., while wary partners try not to get burned." *The New York Times News Service.* February 18, 2019.

[134] "U.S. hedge fund to buy Barnes & Noble." *Reuters.* June 8, 2019.

[135] "Barnes & Noble education reports second quarter fiscal year 2020 financial results." December 4, 2019. Retrieved from: https://www.businesswire.com/news/home/20191204005163/en/Barnes-Noble-Education-Reports-Quarter-Fiscal-Year

[136] Corkery, Michael. "FAO Schwarz to start playing a different tune." *The New York Times.* November 23, 2018.

Some toy suppliers have become disenchanted with the new business model, as they take all the risk on inventory. The company sees big growth in international markets such as China.

Sunrise Records/HMV

Privately-held Canadian Sunrise Records bought the assets of defunct U.K. record store HMV[137]. Sunrise picked up 100 stores in the U.K. and saved about 1,500 jobs. As vinyl is making a comeback, Sunrise offers a niche for music and entertainment lovers. This move is not without significant risk as Spotify and Apples iTunes have turned the business upside down. The challenge for Sunrise will be to create a valuable music experience that cannot be replicated online. This may include expert music advice, live entertainment, community, artist interaction and other services.

In January 2020, Sunrise announced it was buying For Your Entertainment (FYE), a U.S. chain of 200 stores, for $13 million Cdn. The stores focus on entertainment, pop culture and music[138].

GLAZED AND CONFUSED

The fourth category, Glazed and Confused, represents retailers and brands that are lost in the woods and can't find their way. They may be lacking a solid strategy, find themselves without strong leadership, have a weak balance sheet or be having brand trouble. Some have been caught on the wrong side of consumer changes or have pressure from investors. For whatever reason, they had better get their act together quick.

Tim Hortons

Tim Hortons is a Canadian tragedy. Bought by 3G Capital in 2014 and tucked into parent Restaurant Brands Inc. (RBI), the cherished brand has fallen from grace. RBI, known for its radical cost-cutting programs, generated about 20 percent compound average share appreciation over three years, but things went off the rails at Tims[139].

---

[137] "Canada's Sunrise Records to buy failing HMV." *The Canadian Press*. February 6, 2019.

[138] Friend, David. "Sunrise Records shining in U.S." *The Canadian Press*. January 25, 2020.

[139] Haddon, Heather and Monga, Vipal. "Tim Hortons parent defends strategy as growth

Global Brand?

Tim Hortons has had a hard time expanding in the U.S. outside of border towns. It's having problems finding the right master franchisors with fast-food experience and capital[140]. It has turned to China and is investing there as we shall discuss later.

Third Wheel

Tim Hortons lost momentum in the quarter ending September 30, 2019. The donut and coffee slinger posted same store sales of minus 1.4 percent[141]. This was down from the same period last year when comparable store sales increased .6 percent. Management blamed the results on sandwich and cold drink sales[142]. Tims has become the runt in the Restaurant Brands litter as siblings Burger King increased sales 4.8 percent and Popeyes increased sales 9.7 percent during the same timeframe.

Marketing Miss

Tims launched an institutional advertising campaign focusing on hockey, but it didn't move the needle. Experts feel the company has an outdated positioning and should focus more on Gen Z and millennials. Tim Hortons has launched a plethora of new products, but may be missing the boat by not designing specific offerings for these groups. The company also launched a "Winning Together" plan to re-engage franchisees after a fallout a couple of years ago that made its way into the Canadian media. The firm lost significant brand perception but gained some of it back last year as it cracked the top 10 again of most trusted brands.

The firm recently partnered with Post Foods to offer a breakfast cereal branded Timbits (with the Tim Hortons logo on the box top). The cereal is available in two flavours: birthday cake and chocolate glazed. Many marketing experts fear Tims is diluting its brand by spreading itself too thin over too many menu items and novelty products such as the cereal[143].

---

cools." *The Wall Street Journal*. May 16, 2019.

[140] Olive, David. "Tim Hortons' expansion in the U.S. has been a dismal flop." *The Toronto Star*. May 21, 2019.

[141] Desai, Devika. "A cup half empty." *The Financial Post*. October 30, 2019.

[142] Lewis, Michael. "Tim's sales miss expectations." *The Toronto Star*. October 29, 2019.

[143] Sagan, Aleksandra. "Timbits cereal is a novelty but may dilute brand, experts say." *The

Double Dipping

In late February 2020, Tim Hortons received a lawsuit from its U.S. franchisees regarding alleged overcharging of supplies. The Great White North Franchise Association U.S. (GWFA U.S.A.) claims that the parent company charges franchisees as much as 50 percent more than competitors for basic supplies such as paper, coffee, meat and baking goods[144]. The association alleges TDL (affiliate of Tims) sells supplies to Tim Hortons, which then sells supplies to a distributor, which then sells supplies to the store owners. Sounds like a lot of cooks in the kitchen.

Plain Donut

In February 2020, Tim Hortons announced a back-to-basics strategy to simplify its menu and get the business back on track. Tims wants to improve drive-thru efficiency and improve the quality of its core offering including coffee, baked goods and breakfast[145].

The firm reported fourth quarter 2019 comp store sales were down over four percent and full-year comp store sales were down 1.5 percent.

HBC

HBC is starting to feel like the HBC from the Netflix series *Frontier*. The oldest company in North America, HBC is a bit of a gong show and has been so for some time.

Smooth Sailing?

Things were looking solid for the retailer in the early- to mid-2010s as it sold off Zellers leases to Target for a cool $1.8 billion US, bought Saks Fifth Avenue and went public. It looked like it was going to become a powerhouse in global department store retail. Then all hell broke loose. The department store sector tanked, the firm realized it had spread itself too thin across too many banners and was drowning in debt. HBC hired a new CEO and she started taking out the trash,

---

Canadian Press. January 13, 2020.

[144] Deschamps, Tara. "Lawsuit accuses Tim Hortons of 'fraudulent business scheme.'" *The Canadian Press.* February 29, 2020.

[145] Krashinsky Roberston, Susan. "Tims to streamline offerings in push for profit." *The Globe and Mail.* February 11, 2020.

selling its European division, closing banners and simplifying the business. In June of 2019, the firm was the subject of a takeover bid as discussed later in the book.

Taking on Water

In September 2019, HBC reported a staggering quarterly loss from continuing operations of $462 million US for the quarter ended August 3[146]. Revenue was stagnant at $1.85 billion US for the same period. Gross margins plummeted by a stunning 530 basis points to 34 percent. The retailer's net loss from all operations (continuing and discontinued) rang up to a blistering $984 million US! Comparable store sales at The Bay and Saks Off 5th were both down 3.4 percent while sales at Saks Fifth Avenue were up a meager .6 percent.

Bay Watch

At The Bay, the company said it went too low-end to try to pick up Sears Canada's business. The move backfired and negatively impacted sales and margins. The company is dumping about 300 brands and adding another 100 to freshen its offering. The banner is also promoting more exclusive products to differentiate itself and build margins.

Thrown Overboard

The company reported that it was selling off its 193-year-old Lord & Taylor banner to Le Tote Inc. for $132.7 million US. HBC keeps the real estate but Tote gets the brands and the inventory to use for its sales and rental business. A segment that has been growing.

Her Majesty

In my opinion, the firm's crown jewel is the Saks Fifth Avenue brand. The Hudson's Bay brand has brand recognition in Canada, but poor prospects as department stores become less relevant. The monetization of real estate is the company's biggest opportunity for improved cash flow generation.

HBC reported a third quarter 2019 comp store sales decrease of 1.7 percent[147].

---

[146] Krashinsky Robertson, Susan. "HBC losses grow as brand transition dents Bay sales." *The Globe and Mail*. September 13, 2019.

[147] "HBC reports third quarter 2019 financial results." December 10, 2019. Retrieved from: http://investor.hbc.com/news-releases/news-release-details/hbc-reports-third-quarter-2019-financial-results

L Brands

L Brands and its famous Victoria's Secret chain has been under fire from a number of fronts. Already at odds with women over the positioning of females as a plaything for men, the firm also wandered into a public relations nightmare with the disclosure of the relationship between its long serving CEO Leslie Wexner and the late disgraced financier and sexual predator Jeff Epstein[148].

Modern Love

The brand, once embraced as the ultimate sexy garment with its lingerie collection, capitalized on celebrity models through its prime-time televised fashion shows and its "angel" designation. But then society changed. Beauty was redefined to include all shapes and sizes, all sexual orientations and a sense of loving oneself as oneself is. The idea of needing to look like a Victoria's Secret model in order to be sexy faded away — or at least was reduced significantly.

Fallen Angel

Women's movements such as #metoo and #timesup also took flight, which reinforced this new sentiment. Euromonitor, a market research firm, estimates that the firm dropped from 34 percent to 26 percent market share from 2016 to 2018 in the U.S. women's bra, underwear and lingerie space. In January 2020, the firm reported that quarter-to-date comp store sales at Victoria's Secret had fallen 12 percent. Traffic was down even more[149].

Cover Up

In February 2020, L Brands announced it had sold 55 percent ownership of Victoria Secret & PINK to private equity firm Sycamore Partners for $525 million US. With Victoria Secret now private, L Brands was left with Bath & Body Works[150].

---

[148] Maheshwari, Sapna. "Victoria's Secret had increasing troubles even before Epstein scandal." *New York Times News Service*. September 9, 2019.

[149] Freund, Janet. "Victoria's Secret is fading into obscurity: analyst." *Bloomberg*. January 10, 2020.

[150] Chapman, Michelle and D'Innocenzio, Anne. "Struggling Victoria's Secret sold." *The Associated Press*. February 21, 2020.

L Brands reported a full year 2019 (ending February 1, 2020) comp store sales increase of 10 percent for Bath & Body Works and a decrease of seven percent for Victoria's Secret[151].

Gap

Gap has had a hard time over the last decade. It was the worst performing stock on the S & P 500 Retailing Index for the decade as of December 26, 2019 with a 15 percent decline[152]. Once a powerhouse, it has been heavily criticized for using stronger Old Navy results to mask the Gap's and Banana Republic's poor performance. Pundits and customers complain the company lost its fashion sense and connection to young consumers.

<u>Nasty Breakup</u>

The company recognized the disparity and decided to break itself into two parts[153] — Old Navy on one side and Gap, Banana Republic and some other niche brands on the other. Investors liked the idea, at least initially, as the share price jumped 16 percent on the day the announcement was made.

The fun was short-lived, though. In August of 2019, Gap announced a quarterly same store sales drop of four percent[154]. Old Navy, the more productive of the banners historically, fell five percent. Quarterly net income dropped from $297 million US in 2018 to $168 million US.

Gap reported a third quarter 2019 comp store sales decrease of four percent across all banners. Comp store sales at the Gap were down seven percent, while Banana Republic and Old Navy dropped three percent and four percent respectively for the same timeframe[155].

---

[151] "L Brands reports fourth quarter and full-Year 2019 earnings." February 26, 2020. Retrieved from: http://investors.lb.com/news-releases/news-release-details/l-brands-reports-fourth-quarter-and-full-year-2019-earnings

[152] Freund, Janet. "Ulta decade's best retail performer." *Bloomberg*. December 26, 2019.

[153] Townsend, Matt and Boyle, Matthew and Holman, Jordyn. "Gap Inc. surges on plan to spin off Old Navy." *Bloomberg*. March 2, 2019.

[154] "Gap same-store sales disappoint as Old Navy struggles." *Reuters*. August 23, 2019.

[155] Thomas, Lauren. "Gap shares rise on earnings, sales beat; retailer says making 'progress' on split." November 21, 2019. Retrieved from:

Abercrombie & Fitch

The clothing business can be tough. Abercrombie and Fitch reduced its 2019 full year sales forecast amid trade war fears with China. Its share price slid about 14 percent after the firm announced Q2, 2019 results and lowered its full-year forecast from a range of plus two percent to four percent down to a range of flat to plus two percent[156]. The retailer also projected gross margins would drop between 50 and 90 basis points. The brand lost its cache and has had a hard time selling itself at a premium. Time for an overhaul.

The firm reported a fourth quarter comp store sales increase of one percent[157].

Bed Bath & Beyond

Activist investors have a ton of control these days and aren't afraid to flex their muscles in the boardroom. Bed Bath & Beyond was recently in the news as its CEO left following pressure from an activist investor[158]. With its share price down some 80 percent over the last five years, long-time CEO Steven Temares was under significant pressure to resign. With comp store sales up about one percent in 2018, Legion Partners Asset Management LLC, Macellum Advisors GP LLC and Ancora Advisors LLC turned up the heat until the change was made. Later in 2019, the firm announced it was chopping about seven percent of its corporate staff, including the COO[159].

In January 2020, the retailer announced it would be closing 60 stores. This was in addition to the 14 units it had closed at the end of 2019. Of the 60 stores to be

---

https://www.cnbc.com/2019/11/21/gap-inc-gps-reports-q3-2019-earnings-beat-shares-rise.html

[156] "Abercrombie cuts full-year sales forecast." *Reuters*. August 30, 2019.

[157] "Investor Presentation: 4th quarter 2019." March 4, 2020. Retrieved from: https://abercrombieandfitchcompany.gcs-web.com/system/files-encrypted/nasdaq_kms/assets/2020/03/04/7-21-26/Q4%202019%20Investor%20Presentation.pdf

[158] "Bed Bath & Beyond CEO steps down following pressure." *Reuters*. May 14, 2019.

[159] "Bed Bath & Beyond cuts 7% of corporate employees, including COO." *Reuters*. July 24, 2019.

shuttered, 20 will close later, once inventories have been drawn down[160].

Bed Bath & Beyond reported a drop in comp store sales for the third quarter 2019 of 8.3 percent[161].

Chick-fil-A

Chick-fil-A has grown significantly since 2012. Revenue has doubled to $9 billion US and restaurant count has more than tripled from 700 to 2,300. The firm claims its franchise model is one of its secret weapons, as each owner is vigorously screened and interviewed for the right fit. It only costs about $15,000 to obtain a franchise, but operators can have only one store and must work there full time.

Out of Touch

The chain is very successful, but out of touch with modern society. The billionaire Cathy family, which owns the chain, are devout evangelical Southern Baptists who have at times been vocal opponents of gay marriage. This led to protests by the LGBTQ community. The Atlanta-based chain launched its first location in Toronto in the summer of 2019 to significant public protest[162]. The restaurant plans 15 stores in Canada.

Making Amends

Chick-fil-A has since tempered its stance and appears to want to rebuild relations with LGBTQ members of society. In November 2019, Reuters reported that Chick-fil-A announced it stopped funding two Christian organizations. These include The Salvation Army and the Fellowship of Christian Athletes (FCA). Both oppose same-sex marriage[163].

---

[160] Jones, Charisse. "Bed Bath & Beyond still plans to close 60 stores." *USA Today*. January 10, 2020.

[161] Lucas, Amelia and Thomas, Lauren. "Bed Bath & Beyond shares plunge after earnings miss, company withdraws fiscal 2019 outlook." January 8, 2020. Retrieved from: https://www.cnbc.com/2020/01/08/bed-bath-beyond-bbby-earnings-q3-2019.html

[162] Ebner, David. "U.S. fast-food chain Chick-fil-A expanding in Canada." *The Globe and Mail*. July 25, 2018.

[163] "Chick-fil-A cuts off donations to pair of Christian groups." *Reuters*. November 19, 2019.

Subway

Privately-held Subway sandwich shops accelerated store closings in 2018 as consumers' tastes changed and sales decreased. The chain increased the pace of closings from 800 in 2017 to 1,100 in 2018[164]. It's the third straight year of shrinking U.S. store numbers. What was healthy or perceived to be healthy 10 years ago has changed from a consumer perspective. Bread is now a nasty carb. Who wants a Subway sandwich when you can stroll into Chipotle?

Harley-Davidson

Even legendary motorcycle brand Harley-Davidson needs to keep up with changes in consumer purchase patterns. Sales at the Milwaukee firm have been in decline since 2015[165]. Its share price dropped by over 40 percent since 2014.

Electric Avenue

In the fall of 2019, the brand unveiled a new e-bike called LiveWire. Priced at $30,000 US, many dealers thought it was too expensive. The bike also had quality problems, which led to a delay and shut down of the assembly line shortly after launch. LiveWire is targeted at millennials with an annual salary of $100,000 US or more. Harley has competition in this space as Zero Motorcycles offers models ranging from $8,500 US to $21,000 US.

In January 2020, Harley-Davidson announced it had experienced its fifth straight annual decline in U.S. sales. Asia Pacific was the only area to show increased revenue[166]. The brand announced a fourth quarter 2019 global retail sales decline of 1.4 percent and a full year 2019 global sales decline of 4.3 percent[167].

---

[164] Patton, Leslie. "Sandwich shop Subway closings accelerate in 2018." *Bloomberg*. March 29, 2019.

[165] Singh, Rajesh Kumar. "Harley-Davidson struggles to fire up new generations of riders." *Reuters*. October 8, 2019.

[166] Coppola, Gabrielle. "Harley-Davidson misses estimates, looks overseas for opportunities." *Bloomberg*. January 29, 2020.

[167] "Harley-Davidson announces fourth quarter, full-year 2019 results." January 28, 2020. Retrieved from: https://investor.harley-davidson.com/news-releases/news-release-details/harley-davidson-announces-fourth-quarter-full-year-2019-results

Under Armour

Under Armour needs to train harder if it wants to compete against Adidas and Nike. In July 2019, the firm reduced its balance of year forecast for North America as sales in that market were down three percent. During the same time, powerhouse Nike grew North American sales seven percent[168].

DTC Fumble

Under Armour's DTC strategy has not been firing on all cylinders. Its direct-to-consumer growth was a meager two percent, while Adidas grew its DTC unit 40 percent during Q2, 2019.

I Fought the Law

In November 2019, Under Armour chopped its financial forecast for that year for the second time and is now facing an inquiry from U.S. federal regulators over its accounting methodologies[169]. Its executives also face alleged code of conduct breaches.

On the DL

In February 2020, Under Armour announced its fourth quarter 2019 results and gave guidance on Q1, 2020. Citing a number of headwinds, including issues with its new flagship in New York, softening demand in North America and a bloated costs structure, the firm is going to take it on the chin in 2020. It forecasted full-year revenue to be down low single digits and charges to profit of between $325 million and $425 million US[170]. Nike and Lululemon have out-manoeuvred the brand with assortment and marketing.

Indigo

Canada's Indigo is a story of ups and downs. The firm received accolades for surviving and even thriving as a book retailer. Many argue that this is a no-win

---

[168] Venugopal, Aishwarya. "Under Armour stock plummets." *Reuters*. July 31, 2019.

[169] "Under Armour cuts revenue forecast for 2nd time in 2019." *Reuters*. November 5, 2019.

[170] Chapman, Michelle and D'Innocenzio, Anne. "Under Armour looking for tighter fit amid weak sales." *The Associated Press*. February 12, 2020.

category, as the main competition is Amazon and that books are directly comparable from a price standpoint. Also, the book business can be assortment-driven, especially if you claim to be a category-killer like Indigo. So how do you compete with an online retailer the size of Amazon and its legendary endless aisle?

Chapter 1

Indigo's CEO, Heather Reisman, came up with a novel idea (pardon the pun). Make Indigo a lifestyle brand[171]. She turned her stores into a fun hangout for book lovers. Sort of a Disneyland for the reader. She added complementary items such as candles, wall art, throw pillows, champagne flutes and more. She built an educational toy shop within stores. She partnered with Starbucks to drive traffic. Indigo price-matched Amazon on high-profile books. From a business standpoint, it was smart. The complementary items were unique to Indigo and commanded strong gross margins. The new strategy enabled Indigo to grow sales and improve profits.

Quick Read

The glory would not last, though. In 2018, the firm broke stride as general merchandise sales slowed. Indigo reported a loss that neared $40 million Cdn on comparable store sales that were down 1.1 percent[172]. In response, Indigo hired a new creative expert to rebuild general merchandise, which it feels is a key pillar to its growth.

Unfortunately, 2019 was not kind to it. Both Q1 and Q2, 2019 revenue dropped $13 million Cdn each quarter. Q2 comparable store sales dropped by eight percent[173].

Chapter 2

Indigo subsequently announced several initiatives to turn things around. It launched a subscription loyalty program called Plum Plus. It costs $39 per annum and includes free shipping and 10 percent off purchases. It cut $20 million Cdn in

---

[171] Alter, Alexandra. "How Indigo is reinventing the book store." *The New York Times.* May 3, 2019.

[172] Sagan, Aleksandra. "Indigo Books has 'hit a wall', chases new creative direction." *The Canadian Press.* May 30, 2019.

[173] Wells, Jennifer. "Indigo isn't working. But what's the fix?" *The Toronto Star.* November 9, 2019.

costs. It committed to manage cash flow better. It said it would sell more high-margin, on-trend items while lowering reliance on low-margin promotional products. It also paused its U.S. expansion.

Indigo reported a third quarter fiscal 2020 (13 weeks ending December 28, 2019) comp store sales decrease of 10.5 percent[174].

Peloton

Peloton is pricey. First, customers have to buy an exercise bike for $2,000 US. Then they have to pay $40 US per month to use it with its interactive, internet-based features. Who can afford to be healthy anymore?

The firm reported that second quarter 2020 revenue grew 77 percent, while the company lost $55.4 US for the quarter[175].

American Greetings

In January 2020, privately-held American Greetings announced it was closing 254 Carlton Cards and Papyrus stores in North America, impacting 1,400 workers. The company will focus on its wholesale division. Carlton started in 1950 as an importer of European paper products[176].

Kraft Heinz

One could argue that the acquisition of Kraft and Heinz by 3G Capital and Berkshire Hathaway has been a legendary cluster f*ck. In March of 2019, the firm wrote down $15 billion US of goodwill as a result of lacklustre sales and an outdated valuation of the merged brands[177]. In August of 2019, the firm reported an

---

[174] "Indigo Books & Music Inc. third quarter fiscal 2020 financial results." February 7, 2020. Retrieved from: https://static.indigoimages.ca/2020/corporate/indigo_q3-fiscal-2020_feb-7-2020_transcript.pdf

[175] "Peloton Q2 2020 shareholder letter." Retrieved from: https://investor.onepeloton.com/static-files/ca5b1b77-4dcc-4e45-a191-8e4242b87662

[176] "Carlton Cards closing all stores." *The Canadian Press*. January 24, 2020.

[177] Wells, Jennifer. "The link between profit and purpose." *The Toronto Star*. March 13, 2019.

impairment charge of $1.2 billion US[178].

Chop House

3G is notorious for ruthlessly cutting back expenses through its zero-based budgeting approach. On paper, this approach sounds good. Start with a zero budget each year and make each expense earn itself time and again. The problem is that you can starve growth by axing advertising and marketing and lose sales. That's exactly what happened. Now under new leadership, Kraft Heinz looks to reinvest in its stable of brands to reinvigorate sales.

Channel Mismanagement

Another problem Kraft Heinz has created for itself involves its deteriorating relationship with key retailers[179]. It tried to pull a fast one by lowering trade spend while significantly increasing prices. It probably thought the power of its brands would see it through this, but it backfired. It lost business. Private label has grown and consumers have changed. Processed food just doesn't have the draw it once did, as customers prefer healthier dishes. It also fired about five percent of its workforce and lost some of the people who had the experience and relationships to keep grocers happy.

Kraft Heinz is attempting to reverse the damage by investing back in promotions and discounts. It has also increased in-store sales teams by about 80 percent year over year. Lesson learned?

Head In The Sand?

It looks like Kraft Heinz is sleeping through the recent protein alternative trend. At least that's what shareholders might be thinking based on its annual meeting in Pittsburgh in September 2019[180]. Shareholders made a proposal to get an update from the food giant on how it was looking to take advantage of the recent food

---

[178] Haddon, Heather and Maidenberg, Micah. "Kraft Heinz books $ 1.22 billion in impairment charges." *The Wall Street Journal*. August 9, 2019.

[179] Haddon, Heather. "Kraft Heinz's approach on cost hurt grocery relationships." *The Wall Street Journal*. February 27, 2019.

[180] Naidu, Richa and Cavale, Siddharth. "Where's the fake beef? Not at Kraft Heinz, investors worry." *Reuters*. September 13, 2019.

trend. No plan materialized, at least as communicated at the meeting. The company has also been the subject of an SEC investigation of its accounting practices relating to its procurement division.

The firm reported a decrease in fourth quarter 2019 revenue of 5.1 percent. Organic revenue decreased by 2.2 percent for the same period[181].

FedEx

FedEx recently announced it would stop serving Amazon with its air delivery service[182]. The change doesn't impact ground and international, but represents the coming of age of Amazon as a competitor.

Castaway

FedEx continues to struggle. The global delivery behemoth spooked investors with a 25 percent reduction in forecasted profit for 2019[183]. FedEx blamed the results on the slowing world economy caused in part by President Trump's trade war with China.

The street was skeptical and cited recent internal problems with the company. These include a problematic European acquisition, the recent walk away from Amazon, slow capital cuts in the air delivery business and extra cost as the firm tries to position itself successfully for growth in e-commerce.

FedEx reported second quarter fiscal 2020 revenue down 2.8 percent[184].

---

[181] "Kraft Heinz reports fourth quarter and full year 2019 results." February 13, 2020. Retrieved from: http://ir.kraftheinzcompany.com/index.php/news-releases/news-release-details/kraft-heinz-reports-fourth-quarter-and-full-year-2019-results

[182] "FedEx won't renew air delivery deal with Amazon." *Bloomberg*. June 8, 2019.

[183] Black, Thomas and Unsted, Sam and Remondini, Chiara. "FedEx plunges most since 2008 as outlook cut." *Bloomberg*. September 19, 2019.

[184] "FedEx Corp. reports second quarter results." December 17, 2019. Retrieved from: http://investors.fedex.com/news-and-events/investor-news/news-release-details/2019/FedEx-Corp-Reports-Second-Quarter-Results/default.aspx

Roots

Canadian brand Roots has had a hard time getting back to its glory days. Founded in 1973 by two Americans, the brand was very cool back in the 1980s, but went to sleep for a few decades.

Maple Mishap

Most recently, the brand attempted a comeback with new funding from private equity and new management. It hasn't worked so far[185]. Traffic has been soft. It has problems in its Asian business. Its new warehouse system caused shipping delays.

Moose Droppings

In the second quarter of 2019, the firm announced it would not hit previous yearly targets and that the loss for the quarter would double from 2018. Comparable store sales fell almost three percent. EBITDA dropped to a loss of $4.4 million US versus a gain of $32,000 US in 2018.

In January 2020, the retailer announced it was parting ways with its CEO, Jim Gabel. Roots share price has fallen 85 percent since its high in May, 2018[186].

Roots reported third quarter fiscal 2019 sales down one percent. Comp store sales for this period were up three percent[187].

Private Equity and Hedge Funds

Private equity, or PE as it is sometimes known, along with hedge funds, have a reputation of being scavengers that buy something cheap, strip it, rebuild it from the ground up and sell it for a hefty profit.

---

[185] McClelland, Colin. "Roots stock plunges after retailer lowers profit targets." *The Financial Post*. September 12, 2019.

[186] Krashinsky Robertson, Susan. "Tangled Roots: Iconic Canadian retailer struggles with global expansion, operational woes at home." *The Globe and Mail*. January 7, 2020.

[187] "Roots reports fiscal 2019 third quarter results." December 6, 2019. Retrieved from: https://investors.roots.com/news-and-events/press-releases/press-release-details/2019/Roots-Reports-Fiscal-2019-Third-Quarter-Results/default.aspx

Waste Of Time

Sometimes their antics backfire, though. According to Kenneth Goldman, an analyst at JPMorgan, the Kraft Heinz merger has created no value for shareholders. The combined entity's 2019 adjusted EBITDA guidance was no more than the combined value of the two separate companies in 2014, before the merger[188].

Squeeze Them Dry

Kraft Heinz is not the only large consumer goods giant to try to take cost out of its business. Unilever set an $8 billion US cost reduction target. Even Nestlé, with significant pressure from activist investor Third Point, set an operating margin target for the first time. In fact, consumer companies were the third most targeted sector for acquisitions for 2018.

Botox

Not everyone sees PE as vultures. Take, as an example, big consumer products firms looking to dump assets. As per Carol Ryan's 2019 article in The Wall Street Journal, PE firms can help create healthy competition, sidestep competitive issues and avoid brand cherry-picking, which other CPG firms sometimes like to do[189]. This is important, as many big consumer companies are in transition, dumping legacy brands that can't keep up with millennials or that have been disrupted by start-ups doing it better and cheaper.

Silver and Gold

Also, private equity can make a lot of money, if done correctly. Take the case of Onex and its purchase and subsequent sale of southern U.S. chain Jack's.[190] Onex bought the chain in 2015 and sold it the summer of 2019 for a significant profit for itself and its investors. Onex itself invested about $79 million US in the company and received back $255 million US, an annual average return of 38 percent. Onex brought the storied chain to "new communities" in the south to assumingly drive sales and

---

[188] Back, Aaron and Ryan, Carol. "The failure of Kraft Heinz." *The Wall Street Journal.* February 22, 2019.

[189] Ryan, Carol. "Private equity is more friend than foe to consumer giants." *The Wall Street Journal.* March 13, 2019.

[190] Milstead, David. "Onex cashes out on U.S. chain Jack's." *The Globe and Mail.* July 19, 2019.

margins. Much about the deal is confidential, though, including the sale price, the buyer and exactly what was done to make this much cash!!

Retail Witcher

I still think more often than not that private equity destroys retail. Sometimes short-term results can be magnificent. But when I look medium to long term, I see starved brands and a failure to invest in must-do initiatives. Bare bones infrastructure that reduces customer service and shatters local employment. Rant complete.

KNOCKING ON HEAVEN'S STORE

The fifth category, Knocking on Heaven's Store, includes retailers and brands that are close to death. They may be a year, two or three away from bankruptcy and may be bought on the cheap. Many are department stores that have found themselves in the wrong format at the wrong time. Others have outdated business models and will pass away as part of a natural purge in the industry.

Sears Holdings

Sears has been on a downward spiral for years. Following hedge fund ESL Investments Inc.'s purchase of the chain in the mid-2000s, the brand has been in freefall. I worked for Sears Canada back in the early 2010s and although I feel sad for the company's remaining workers and suppliers, I can personally attest to it being the poster child for what not to do in modern-day retail.

Sky Diving

When ESL took ownership of the combined Sears and Kmart chains, they had retail sales of $55 billion US. Since then, the retailer has been milked like a goat for assets and brands while investing little in new formats and the like. Its 2018 revenue was approximately $13.5 billion US.

Reincarnated

In its previous legal entity, Sears Holdings Corp. entered bankruptcy protection in the U.S. in October 2018. In 2019, Edward Lampert (owner of ESL Investments) rescued Sears by buying it again for $5.2 billion US under the name Transformco. The new entity had a smaller footprint of 425 stores. With this new announcement, the brand will have just 182 stores nationwide. Interestingly, Sears bought 414 Sears Hometown stores as well.

A Little Late

The retailer announced in April 2019 that it was opening smaller U.S. stores[191]. Fresh from bankruptcy protection, Sears announced it will focus on appliances, mattresses and home services. No more clothing. These "Sears Home & Life" units will be approximately 10,000 to 15,000 square feet, a wide departure from the average Sears store of about 150,000 square feet.

Alimony

It was announced in April 2019 that the company that was Sears Holdings Corp. (before being sold to Transformco) is suing Edward Lampert and other board members[192]. The suit claims that Lampert squeezed about $2 billion US from the former entity for use at his own companies, such as ESL Investments. Mark Cohen, director of retail studies at Columbia Business School and former CEO of Sears Canada, was quoted as saying, "Lampert ran the company like it was a private company owned by him."

Life Support

The company announced in early November of 2019 that it had secured $250 million US in financing to remain a going concern ahead of the holiday season but with 96 fewer stores[193]. The chain would also close 45 Kmart stores during the fall of 2019. In February 2020, Sears announced it had secured $100 million US in financing from Brigade Capital Management LP, a hedge fund to help with continuing operations[194].

Macy's

Macy's finds itself in a death spiral not unlike Sears. Macy's, like Sears and other department stores, finds itself over-stored. That is, it has too much brick and mortar

---

[191] D'innocenzio, Anne. "Sears to open smaller stores in the U.S." *The Associated Press*. April 5, 2019.

[192] Bhattarai, Abha. "U.S. treasury secretary in crosshairs of Sears lawsuit." *The Washington Post*. April 20, 2019.

[193] Dinapoli, Jessica and Spector, Mike. "Sears secures lifeline, but will close 96 stores." *Reuters*. November 8, 2019.

[194] "Sears snags new financial lifeline as losses continue." *Reuters*. February 21, 2020.

square footage to justify sales. Macy's, like Sears, did not invest in store renovations and upkeep over the years and is now paying the price as its stores look old and dusty.

Year of the Dog

The year 2018 was not a great one for the firm. Although sales were down 2.5 percent in the fourth quarter, its profit shrunk to $740 million US from $1.35 billion US a year earlier[195]! As a result, the retailer planned to cut 100 senior management positions as part of a larger plan to save $100 million US per annum.

Chainsaw Management

This sounds prudent, but investors have heard this story before. It is the sixth year in a row that Macy's has announced year-end cost cuts. The firm has already cycled through several rounds of asset sales over the past few years, including selling its San Francisco Union Square property. Attention has now turned to selling its New York Herald Square location.

Overstored

The retailer operates about 680 department stores under banners such as Bloomingdale's and its namesake in addition to another 190 stores under specialty banners such as Story, Macy's Backstage, Bluemercury and Bloomingdale's The Outlet.

2 Tier Health Care

One of the ways that CEO Jeff Gennette is managing through this freefall is by putting up walls to shrink select stores[196]. The retailer has segmented its vast store network into two basic classifications. Magnets, the first category, are top performing stores and offer the best productivity. Neighbourhood stores, the second category, have poor productivity and are too big.

The magnets are receiving significant capital to give them a facelift with new lights, added assortments, new carpets, additional staff and even a Starbucks to drive

---

[195] Kapner, Suzanne and Al-Muslim, Aisha. "Macy's looks to thin upper management as sales fall." *The Wall Street Journal.* February 27, 2019.

[196] Kapner, Suzanne. "Macy's radical plan to save itself? Shrink." *The Wall Street Journal.* November 14, 2018.

traffic. In 2018, Macy's renovated 50 of these magnets at a cost of $50 million US. It has another 100 magnets planned for renovations in 2019. Some of the magnets include new technology such as virtual mirrors where customers can simulate trying on cosmetics. Results at the magnet stores have been encouraging.

Ziggy Floor-Dust

In the neighbourhood stores, retail space is cut by as much as 20 percent, assortments are pruned and payroll is chopped. The neighbourhood stores have become quasi self-serve stores in categories like footwear, as product is displayed in boxes on the retail floor. Macy's has had some success renting out stores within its stores to complementary retailers such as LensCrafters and Sunglass Hut. But in some locations the economics don't work.

Macy's had another tough year in 2019 but exceeded expectations. Comp store sales dropped .6 percent in November and December, while analysts expected a drop of 1.75 percent[197]. Still, in February 2020, Macy's announced it was closing an additional 125 stores and firing 2,000 workers over the next three years[198].

Neiman Marcus

U.S. department store Neiman Marcus joined other department stores in posting poor financial performance. In the quarter ending June 2019, its last public financial report, revenue was down nine percent. Comparable store sales were down 1.5 percent. Losses for the quarter grew from $19.9 million US in 2018 to $31.2 million US in 2019.

Like other department stores, the firm is owned by private equity and is riddled with debt. Ares Management LLC and The Canadian Pension Plan are the primary investors. Neiman Marcus runs its namesake stores along with other banners that include Mytheresa, Last Call, Cusp, Horchow and Bergdorf Goodman.

---

[197] Thomas, Lauren. "Macy's holiday same-store sales fall 0.6%. Smaller-than-expected decline boosts shares." January 8, 2020. Retrieved from: https://www.cnbc.com/2020/01/08/macys-0point6percent-holiday-sales-decline-wasnt-as-bad-as-expected-shares-jump.html

[198] "Macy's to close 125 stores, cut more than 2,000 jobs over three years." *Reuters*. February 5, 2020.

J.C. Penney

J.C. Penney has struggled as well. The retailer posted same-store sales declines of 5.5 percent for Q1, 2019 and lost $148 million US for the quarter, about double what it lost in Q1, 2018[199]. Like Sears and Macy's, it is in slow decline and has limited prospects. A symbol of America's middle class, it is fading away.

The firm announced fourth quarter 2019 comp store sales down seven percent. Full-year 2019 comp store sales were down 7.7 percent[200].

GameStop

GameStop, the parent company that owns EB Games, is facing significant headwinds. In a recent article in Bloomberg, it was reported that the retailer lost 22 percent of its value when it signalled that comparable store sales for 2019 would come in at negative teens percent[201]. Gamers are buying more games online these days and the used cartridge business has dried up.

Gamestop announced that 2019 holiday sales from continuing operations were down 27.5 percent[202].

Blue Apron

The meal kit industry is not for the faint of heart. Perhaps the most popular brand in the space is Blue Apron. In 2015, Blue Apron had a U.S. market share of about 67 percent of meal kit customers. Since then, its customer count has fallen by two-thirds.

---

[199] "J.C. Penney sales fall short of expectations, net loss nearly doubles." *Reuters*. May 22, 2019.

[200] "J. C. Penney Company, Inc. reports fourth quarter and full year 2019 financial results." February 7, 2020. Retrieved from: https://ir.jcpenney.com/news-events/press-releases/detail/608/j-c-penney-company-inc-reports-fourth-quarter-and-full

[201] Palmeri, Christopher. "GameStop forecast falls short of predictions." *Bloomberg*. September 12, 2019.

[202] "GameStop reports 2019 holiday sales results." January 13, 2020. Retrieved from: https://www.globenewswire.com/news-release/2020/01/13/1969887/0/en/GameStop-Reports-2019-Holiday-Sales-Results.html

It appears investors and consumers are still not sold on this business — at least from Blue Apron's track record. Investor confidence remains low as the share price dropped to below $1 US in March 2019[203].

Blue Apron reported that net revenue decreased 33 percent in the fourth quarter of 2019 and decreased 32 percent for full year 2019[204].

Save-a-lot

Save-a-l-a-lot is an example of a private equity deal in the wrong place at the wrong time. Canada's Onex bought the chain in 2016 for $1.4 billion US with plans to presumably work its typical turnaround magic[205]. Fast forward to 2019, and the 1,300 store grocer has become an albatross. German food discounters Aldi and Lidl have eaten their lunch.

According to Supermarket News, the chain posted a sales decrease of 9.2 percent for the 2018/2019 fiscal year[206].

NOVEMBER PAIN

The sixth and final category is November Pain. It includes retailers and brands that have entered bankruptcy or liquidated in some or all markets. These retailers may be reincarnated as smaller entities or bought as a trademark for another going concern. Some will go away permanently.

---

[203] "Blue Apron sinks back below US $1 as shares fall 10%." *Bloomberg*. March 5, 2019.

[204] "Blue Apron Holdings, Inc. reports fourth quarter and full year 2019 results and provides corporate update." February 18, 2020. Retrieved from: https://investors.blueapron.com/press-releases/2020/02-18-2020-212423334

[205] Doherty, Katherine and Coleman-Lochner, Lauren. "Save-a-Lot debt goes for half off as grocery rivals squeezing sales." *Bloomberg*. August 24, 2019.

[206] Redman, Russell. "Save A Lot eyes rebound with capital infusion." January 3, 2020. Retrieved from: https://www.supermarketnews.com/retail-financial/save-lot-eyes-rebound-capital-infusion

Toys "R" Us U.S.

One needs to look no further than the plight of Toys "R" Us (TRU) in the United States. Bought by a private equity company for $6.5 billion US in 2005, TRU was mostly purchased with debt. This is known in the industry as a leveraged buy-out or LBO.

<u>Fairy Tale Finance</u>

LBOs involve the new owner borrowing a large portion of the purchase price of the acquired company from banks or other lenders. Then they use the cash from operations of the company being bought to pay back the large interest and principle borrowed. The assumption is that the target company will provide a steady and predictable stream of cash flow to make sure the debt is paid. It's sort of like buying a mansion for $10 million and borrowing $9 million from the bank. You really, really hope that you keep that $250,000-a-year job or you lose the house. Well, the same thinking goes for LBOs and specifically TRU.

<u>Toy Story</u>

After the privatization of TRU, the economy fell and the toy industry changed. Mass merchant retailers such as Walmart and Target decided they wanted to invest heavily in toys to drive traffic. Amazon started to get serious about the category too. But TRU could react, right? No. Too much of its cash flow went to service debt. There was no money left over for renovations, omni-channel development, strategic acquisitions or reinvention.

<u>Island of Misfits</u>

Sadly, over time, TRU's market share was eaten by competitors until, one day, its operation could not make enough money to pay creditors. In 2017, the storied retailer entered Chapter 11 bankruptcy protection. In 2018, it closed its U.S. operation but still operates in a few other markets like Canada and parts of Europe. There are many other retailers and suppliers that have suffered a similar fate at the hands of financiers who know more about money management than they do about retail.

Pier 1 Imports

With more than 965 stores in the U.S. and Canada, Pier 1 Imports accelerated its planned number of closings in 2019 from 45 to 57[207]. It signalled that up to 15

---

[207] Tyko, Kelly. "Pier 1 Imports warns of more stores closing." *USA Today*. June 28, 2019.

percent of its stores could close depending on how negotiations went with landlords.

In January 2020, the retailer announced it was closing almost half its stores (450) and select distribution centres. It has also added two board members with expertise in restructuring[208].

In February 2020, the retailer entered Chapter 11 bankruptcy protection in the U.S. and announced it was closing all of its stores in Canada. The firm has debtor in possession financing and is looking for a buyer. Some pundits have cited Pier 1's late e-commerce push as well as a bloated real-estate portfolio.

Gymboree

Children clothing store Gymboree filed for bankruptcy for a second and final time in January 2019[209]. San Francisco-based Gymboree started in 1976 and employed about 11,000 workers across Crazy 8 and its namesake stores.

What happened? Sadly, it's a common story and a combination of factors. First, the firm was bought by private equity firm Bain Capital in 2010, which increased its debt to $1 billion US. Investment was starved to service debt and costs were cut. Sales faltered and the retailer slid into bankruptcy in 2017.

It got through the bankruptcy with fewer stores and lower debt. It wasn't enough to save the chain, though, as the market shifted. Internet retailers and big box stores doubled down on prices and folks like Gap and Children's Place did a better job. At the same time, mall traffic plummeted and margins tanked as revenue slid 27 percent for the first nine months of 2018.

Fred's

In September of 2019, southeast discounter Fred's filed for Chapter 11 bankruptcy protection with plans to close all stores within 60 days. Despite efforts to merge with Rite Aid and Walgreens in 2017, the retailer fell short. The chain had 556 stores, including 169 pharmacies, in 15 states as of May 2019[210].

---

[208] "Pier 1 Imports closing nearly half of stores as sales falter." *The Associated Press*. January 8, 2020.

[209] "Gymboree begins winding down operations." *The Associated Press*. January 18, 2019.

[210] Wu, Jasmine. "Retail discounter Fred's files for Chapter 11 bankruptcy, to close all its stores." September 9, 2019. Retrieved from: https://www.cnbc.com/2019/09/09/retail-discounter-freds-files-for-bankruptcy-to-close-all-its-stores.html

Shopko

In January 2019, Shopko announced it was entering Chapter 11 bankruptcy. The regional retailer had been closing stores in waves and was involved in a nasty lawsuit with supplier McKesson over $67 million US in unpaid bills. As of filing, the chain had 360 stores in more than 24 states[211].

Forever 21 Canada

The dismantling of Forever 21 during the fall of 2019 created a fairly sizable debate by pundits about the role of fast fashion in modern society. The bankruptcy and subsequent closing of numerous stores for the California-based retailer included the outright shuttering of all Canadian locations. The main reason for the downfall was the over-aggressive expansion of the brand into retail footprints that were too big. In addition, the company expanded too quickly into too many markets and lost control.

Private Dancer

In a recent article by Sapna Maheshwari from The New York Times, the inner workings of Forever 21 are examined as a potential reason for the once dominant chain's downfall[212]. Maheshwari talks to the firm's insulated management team, which was too inward looking. Being a private company, the retailer did not have the critical eye of outside stock analysts and independent board members to challenge direction. Most, if not all, key decisions were made by family members with limited input or consultation from other executives or team members.

Land Lord

The remaining Forever 21 entity was sold in February 2020 to Simon Property Group, Brookfield Property Partners and Authentic Brands for $81 million US[213].

---

[211] Bollier, Jeff. "Shopko files for Chapter 11 bankruptcy protection, will close 38 more stores across country." January 16, 2019. Retrieved from: https://www.usatoday.com/story/money/business/2019/01/16/shopko-files-bankruptcy-close-38-more-stores/2591759002/

[212] Maheshwari, Sapna. "Forever 21's family ties played role in retailer's ultimate demise." *The New York Times*. October 25, 2019.

[213] Thomas, Lauren. "Forever 21 reaches $81 million deal to sell its retail business to US mall owners and Authentic Brands." February 3, 2020. Retrieved from:

Barneys NY

Barneys NY, a fixture on Madison Avenue that once personified hip department-store fashion, has fallen[214]. The retailer, controlled by Perry Capital, entered Chapter 11 protection and plans to close 15 of its 22 stores.

Manhattan Skyline

Once a great way for small designers to gain traction, the retailer lost ground due to a combination of online shopping, direct-to-consumer brands and increasing real-estate costs. At one time, the Madison Avenue store represented about one-third of the chain's sales. Unfortunately, this location had its rent raised by almost 100 percent in 2019. This dynamic, coupled with a decline in traffic, left the company cash-strapped.

Up In Smoke

Management tried to reinvent the brand by adding a high-end weed shop in its Beverly Hills unit.

Second Life

This is the firm's second brush with bankruptcy protection. Barneys NY entered Chapter 11 in 1996 when the Pressman family owned the firm, but things were easier then and they were able to merge intact.

In late 2019, the Barneys NY brand was purchased by Authentic Brands Group for $271.4 million US and will be licensed to Saks Fifth Avenue.

FTD

The flower retailer FTD recently filed for bankruptcy and is selling itself in parts[215]. Once a flower broker in the early 20th century, the U.S. company is one of

---

https://www.cnbc.com/2020/02/03/forever-21-reaches-deal-to-sell-its-retail-business-for-81-million.html

[214] Friedman, Vanessa and De La Merced, Michael J. "Luxury retailer Barneys NY files for protection." *Reuters*. August 7, 2019.

[215] Hill, Jeremy. "FTD files for bankruptcy protection, will sell assets." *Bloomberg*. June 4, 2019.

many legacy retailers disrupted by e-commerce. FTD tried to fight back by buying ProFlowers in 2014, but couldn't make a go of it.

David's Bridal

If you f*ck up omni-channel basics, customers will punish you. That's what I gained from reading about troubled retailer David's Bridal[216].

Blushing Bride

The company launched an online website that had higher prices versus in store. A major no-no. Customers stopped shopping and the retailer entered Chapter 11. This compounded the problem as brides got scared off and went elsewhere. In November 2019, the retailer announced it had secured new financing, mostly from previous creditors. With 300 stores across the United States, U.K. and Canada, it would be a shame for this gem to shut down.

David's Footwear

It was a bad year for David's in the retail business. Canadian luxury retailer David's Footwear fell victim to a common problem in luxury retail. Its suppliers started opening up their own stores.

DTC Destruction

Brands such as Louboutin used to be a big draw to the store, says Lisa Hutcheson, managing partner at consultancy J.C. Williams Group, but the brand opened up its own store just around the corner in Toronto's famous Yorkville. With its recent drop in sales, rent at its flagship Toronto location represented a staggering 30 percent of revenue, twice what it should be, says Larry Rosen, part owner of the small chain and CEO of famed Canadian fashion retailer Harry Rosen.

The men's shoe retailer had graced Toronto since 1951 and had locations in other major Canadian centres, including Ottawa[217]. It is now closing down and liquidating inventory.

---

[216] Doherty, Katherine. "David's Bridal debt deal will keep chain running." *Bloomberg*. November 5, 2019.

[217] Rubin, Josh. "The other shoe has dropped at Toronto's David's Footwear." *The Toronto Star*. September 21, 2019.

Dean Foods

One casualty of the move consumers have made to plant-based milk alternatives is Dean Foods, the largest milk company in the United States. Dean, which has been around since 1925, filed for U.S. bankruptcy protection in mid-November, 2019[218]. The firm had a lot of debt and did not change fast enough to meet consumer preferences.

Bench Canada

In January 2020, Bench announced it was closing all of its 24 Canadian stores. The company said it will focus on e-commerce and wholesale. Experts cite the strength of competitors such as Lululemon as well as a lack of innovation at the brand's brick and mortar stores[219].

Modell's

In March 2020, eastern U.S. sporting goods retailer Modell's announced it was entering Chapter 11 protection. The family-owned chain of 153 locations was founded in 1889. Online shopping and strong competition were cited as reasons for the store's demise[220].

---

[218] Yaffe-Bellany, David. "As a beverage, milk losing ground." *The New York Times*. November 16, 2019.

[219] Rubin, Josh. "Bench closing all Canadian locations." *The Toronto Star*. January 24, 2020.

[220] Meyersohn, Nathaniel. "Modell's Sporting Goods files for bankruptcy and will close all stores." March 11, 2020. Retrieved from: https://www.cnn.com/2020/03/11/business/modells-sporting-goods-bankruptcy/index.html

EIGHTY RETAIL TRENDS

"Blood stains the ivorys
Of my daddy's baby grand
I ain't seen no daylight
Since we started this band
No more, no more
No more, no more[221]"

(No More No More, Aerosmith)

In this chapter, I summarize my top 80 retail trends as of here and now. I have separated each by key stakeholder.

CUSTOMERS

1) Demographic Change-Up — OK Millennial

It's not a news flash that global demographics are in flux. Seniors are moving into care homes or passing away. Baby boomers are retiring and living it up as best they can while actively aging. Generation X-ers are hitting mid-life crisis and millennials are settling down with condominiums, townhomes and maybe even the odd child. Generation Z are in high school or post-secondary school and thinking about their future.

<u>Photograph</u>

These combined groups represent today's snapshot of consumer markets. It's a snapshot, as the mix of these segments is ever changing. In 2040, today's Generation X will be seniors, today's millennials will be tomorrow's boomers and Generation Z will be the key spending generation that millennials currently occupy.

---

[221] Aerosmith. "No More No More." Toys In The Attic. 1975. *Spotify.* https://open.spotify.com/album/36IxIOGEBAXVozDSiVs09B

Moving Target

As each group passes through its respective spending lifecycles, how can companies position themselves to be relevant and attractive to each? It sounds simple but it is far from it. You can't be everything to everyone (or you end up being nothing to everybody), so you need to pick a customer segment and go hard to be the best for it. But which one and when?

Retailers and suppliers need to understand the current positioning of their brand. Based on research, what will customers give them permission to do or represent? What assets and capabilities do firms currently have? How and where do they currently distribute products and services? Should they buy a start-up that targets a new demographic? Can they reposition their current brand or add a new brand themselves? Will they alienate their current customer base? Or do firms stick with current customers and follow them through their aging and spending lifecycle?

Retailers and suppliers need not get too comfortable with a particular segment either, as needs change within segments as different age and lifestyle stages take hold. I have noticed countless brands flick a switch and awkwardly target millennials when just a year or two ago they were chasing Gen X and Boomers. Millennials aren't stupid. They see through this and brands look shallow and opportunistic. Companies must be careful and approach this new group in a different fashion.

Dog Days

An example of how changes in demographics have changed consumer purchasing habits can be found in the pet category. According to research from PricewaterhouseCoopers, affluent millennials were to spend $183 US per person during holiday 2018 on their furry friends[222]. This is above the $67 US that the average U.S. consumer was to spend on pets during this same time. This generation sees pets as children and is willing to spoil them the same way. Pet retailers like Petco are capitalizing on this trend with large assortments of Christmas and Hanukkah-themed pet gifts. Walmart recently announced it would increase the number of stores with on-site vet clinics from 21 to 100 and will open an online pet pharmacy[223]. U.S.

---

[222] Porter Jr., Gerald. "Millennials to spend big this holiday season – on their pets." *Bloomberg*. November 19, 2018.

[223] Thomas, Lauren. "Walmart is opening dozens of veterinary clinics in its stores and launching an online pet pharmacy." May 7, 2019. Retrieved from: https://www.cnbc.com/2019/05/06/walmart-to-open-dozens-of-vet-clinics-launch-online-pet-pharmacy.html

consumers were expected to spend $75.3 billion US on this category in 2019.

Party Rock Tantrum

Another example can be found in the party category. Millennials have become parents and are having parties for their kids. Canadian general merchandiser Canadian Tire bought dusty category killer Party City Canada and its 65 stores to try to connect with millennials[224]. It isn't alone. I noticed expanded party stores within the prototypical Walmart in Toronto and in a large Loblaw Superstore in Georgetown, Ontario.

Sister Sledgehammer

Retailers and brands need to be aware of who in a household is influencing purchases. Although one can argue that millennials are the sweet spot for many categories, one can't forget the silent minority. According to Adweek, Gen Z's influence on spending rings in at $1.2 trillion US[225]. How can marketers ensure they appeal to not only the person who makes the actual purchase but key influencers as well? The death is in the data. Speaking of Generation Z, teenagers are spending about $2,600 US per annum on clothes and food, according to Lauren Thomas from CNBC[226]. Teens' favourite stores include Chipotle, Amazon, Lululemon and UltaBeauty.

2) Customization: Me, Myself and I

Beyond the high-level demographic stereotypes above, retail must also embrace

---

[224] "Canadian Tire buying Party City business for $174.4M cash." *The Canadian Press.* August 9, 2019.

[225] Fleming, Jameson and McCoy, Kimeko. "Gen Z's influence on purchases." September 26, 2019. Retrieved from: https://www.adweek.com/digital/gen-zs-influence-on-purchases-the-good-places-final-hurrah-thursdays-first-things-first/

[226] Thomas, Lauren. "Teens are spending $2,600 a year on food and clothes. Here's where they like to shop." April 8, 2019. Retrieved from: https://www.cnbc.com/2019/04/08/teens-spend-2600-a-year-on-food-clothes-heres-where-they-shop.html

the notion of infinite segmentation. That is, everyone on the earth is their own market segment.

Technology and data have enabled this granular level of marketing to not only be possible but demanded by consumers. There is zero tolerance for anything but personal one-on-one offers. This creates obvious challenges from a production, inventory and supply chain perspective.

Retailers and suppliers must deliver exactly what consumers want in near real-time the way they want it with the exact specification they want it with.

Some retailers have used customization as a major theme in their recent flagship stores, too.

Shoemaker

At Nike's House of Innovation 000 in New York, it offers a best-in-class example of customer-driven product customization. Customers work with experts and each other in sessions to build a running shoe from scratch. Like a product manager or product developer, they build their own shoe within this small-scale footwear factory.

Elf

The FAO Schwarz flagship store in New York is full of customization. Customers can build their own toy race car from scratch — picking body, wheels, accessories and more. Watching the faces of children (and adults) creating their very own vehicles confirms how cool this is for customers.

3) Community: Serenity Squad

Although somewhat over-used in retail, creating a sense of community for customers can be important. It creates a sense of loyalty and allows shoppers to learn and share with others who often feel the same as they do about their love for the brand. Numerous loyalty programs play on this sense of community. Brands are starting to create community in-store as well.

Foot Fetish

Community is alive and kicking at Nike's New York flagship. Workshops facilitate a connection with other Nike enthusiasts and you can't help but bond with other customers as your mouth drops in awe at the concept.

4) Customer Convenience: Time Wastes For No One

The value of time has increased for most consumers. Why? People are working more and have less disposable time. Less time to shop. Less time to sleep. Less time for leisure.

Purchasing Power Outage

Numerous millennials and Generation Z consumers work several low-to-medium-wage jobs to pay the bills and fuel their modern lifestyle of frequent travel, dining out and experiences. Generation X and baby boomers work several precarious jobs to makes ends meet. Seniors try to stay in the work force longer with lower-paying service jobs to help with expenses and keep health care.

All in all, consumers have less time available for basic shopping needs such as grocery, drug and other staple products and for the preparation of meals.

Impact to Grocery

According to Dr. Sylvain Charlebois, the Canadian grocery business is in tremendous flux[227]. Canadians are migrating toward more convenient channels to buy food. Corner stores, specialty stores, online food delivery companies and even vending machines have seen sales grow while big box grocers have struggled.

Ready–to-eat solutions such as meal kits and pre-cooked foods are growing. In addition, non-traditional grocers such as Walmart and Costco have gained market share in Canada and have put pressure on the big three players: Loblaw, Empire (Sobeys) and Metro. This has fragmented the way customers shop and has created inefficiencies with legacy stores and distribution models. Grocers must innovate quickly to keep pace with changing customer purchasing habits or face serious financial consequences.

I have outlined a few examples below of how companies are responding to the need for convenience.

Meal Kits

Consider Canadian meal kit company Fresh Prep, one of many start-ups that

---

[227] Charlebois, Sylvain. "Canadians want convenience and grocers are paying the price." *The Globe and Mail.* July 25, 2018.

has jumped into the fairly new but hotly contested meal kit delivery business[228]. This small firm is taking it slow and it appears to be working. It is estimated that one in 10 American households have tried meal kits and although it has garnered attention, companies like Blue Apron have struggled. It is hard not to see this category growing and eventually being done right by someone; behemoths such as Amazon, Walmart and large grocery stores have experimented with it.

Snacks

You might think snacks are dead. The unhealthy kind might be, but big food loves snacks due to their sales and profitability potential.

In a recent article by Micah Maidenberg in The Wall Street Journal, she writes about the high profile snack business and how it still fits into modern society[229]. Research firm Mintel claims the U.S. snack category is worth $150 billion US per annum and is expected to rocket to $180 billion US by 2022.

Some experts feel the business is going to slow down due to health concerns, but the food giants are full steam ahead. J.M. Smucker is building a new Colorado snack factory. Mondelez started an in-house venture capital division that finds and invests in snack start-ups. In 2016, 93 percent of Americans reported snacking at least once per day.

Food Delivery

Food delivery has become incredibly popular, especially with Gen Z and millennials. Even seniors are getting into it. Competition between providers is heating up too.

DoorDash said that by the end of 2019, it will be able to cover 90 percent of the U.S. market from a population perspective. Instacart can cover about 80 percent. Shipt, the delivery company bought by Target in 2017, can reach 250 markets.

One of the challenges for participating restaurants is the 25 percent commission

---

[228] Ebner, David. "Fulfilling an increasing appetite for meal kits." *The Globe and Mail*. November 19, 2018.

[229] Maidenberg, Micah. "Food makers crowd snack aisle despite uneven growth." *The Wall Street Journal*. July 3, 2019.

taken by meal delivery companies. Some restaurant owners aren't making much profit and are not seeing the benefit. Others say it's the best thing to happen to the industry in a long time. It depends on the average ring per delivery, the food category being ordered and overhead costs at the individual restaurant.

A recent survey by Cowen and Co. indicates that cities with less than 200,000 residents use restaurant delivery about half as much as cities above this population. A survey by UBS indicated that seven percent of suburban customers use meal delivery versus 14 percent of urban customers. One of the many challenges that food delivery companies face is the ability to economically service smaller communities[230]. Being able to locate and sign on qualified drivers and the need to travel further with food have been tough barriers to overcome. In addition, rural customers have gotten used to picking up their own food, so delivery takes time to get used to.

Walmart is offering a new service called Walmart InHome. It allows customers to ask the retailer to not only deliver groceries, but to put them in their fridge[231]. Launched in the fall of 2019, the service is available in Pittsburgh, Vero Beach (Florida) and Kansas City and reaches about one million people. Walmart delivery staff wear cameras and drive Walmart-owned vehicles. The service was tested with a third-party provider in 2017 in California. Walmart charges customers $9.95 US for delivery services across about 100 cities with another 200 cities on the way.

Drive Thrus

McDonald's made drive-thrus commonplace in the 1970s. Some fast-food chains sell between 50 and 65 percent of their food through this method. Now, fast-casual chains such as Chipotle, Panera Bread and Noodles & Co. are launching drive-thru service in more stores as customer convenience becomes more important[232]. Even Starbucks, known for its in-store ambience, is growing this business.

Other Examples

If you like that certain sauce or an entrée at your favourite fast-food spot, you may soon be able to enjoy it at your grocery store. Grocers have partnered with

---

[230] Haddon, Heather and Jargon, Julie. "Food-delivery companies acquire a taste for smaller markets." *The Wall Street Journal*. March 13, 2019.

[231] Boyle, Matthew. "Walmart will stock your fridge." *Bloomberg*. June 12, 2019.

[232] Patton, Leslie. "Chipotle turns to drive-thrus as fast-food stigma fades." *Bloomberg*. May 28, 2019.

restaurant chains to carry their products in consumer packaged goods form[233]. Both sides need the sales and profits due to heightened competition and slimming margins. In Canada, you can enjoy Tim Hortons or McDonald's coffee as well as a St-Hubert chicken pot pie at your local supermarket.

Rogers, a Canadian telecommunications giant, recently announced it was piloting a new service that would involve no-charge personal delivery and set-up of cellular phones[234]. The new service, called "Pro-on-the-Go," was to launch in Toronto in the fall of 2019. It uses technology to confirm a two-hour delivery window to the location of the customer's choice. The service is being provided by third party Enjoy, founded by former Apple head of retail Ron Johnson. Johnson was quoted as saying, "This isn't just a delivery service. It's kind of like Uber combined with the Apple store."

5) City Living - Uptown Flunk

Consumers are migrating back to cities. Urbanization is a parallel trend to income disparity as well as a product of demographic and generational preferences. Millennials and soon-to-be-independent Generation Z are flocking to downtown condominiums to both save on commuting time and live close to where work is. These folks want to live, work and play in a downtown setting. Getting married later (if at all), they are opting for one (if any) child and have abandoned the suburban lifestyle that their parents coveted. Transportation has changed from cars to ride sharing, public transit, bicycles or electric scooters.

This trend plays heavily into retail as merchants cater to this new urban lifestyle. Everything from store size, assortment and product mix, delivery services, promotion and more are being modified to cater to this important consumer segment. Living more of a Manhattan lifestyle, consumers shop for fresh food more often and dine out significantly more. Millennials are asset-light and would rather spend their disposable income on travel and experiences. Numerous retailers and brands have started to adapt to this trend with downtown formats and services as described below.

---

[233] Sagan, Aleksandra. "Fast-food chains make menu items available in grocery stores." *The Canadian Press*. October 10, 2019.

[234] Rubin, Josh. "Rogers to offer in-person cell delivery and setup option." *The Toronto Star*. October 10, 2019.

City Stores

Grocers have begun to change-up how they are serving this new breed of city dweller. More downtown grocers have had to adjust to smaller store footprints, some as small as 13,000 square feet as in the case of Toronto's Organic Garage[235]. This store in Liberty Village boasts aisles of no more than 20 feet long. Big brands such as Walmart, Loblaw and Sobeys have followed suit. Second-floor spaces are also becoming popular. Cheaper per square foot versus main floor venues, the lower rent helps make the economics work better. New builds have planned second floors with grocers in mind as millennials love the convenience of having a food store where they work or where they live. This new approach puts pressure on assortments and transportation considerations, but where there's a will there's a way!

IKEA

Downtown formats are not unique to the grocery space. As mentioned previously, IKEA recently announced it will be opening 30 smaller urban stores in cities around the world[236]. Like grocers, IKEA realizes that millennials and other urban customers don't want to spend half a day driving outside the city to look at furniture. IKEA's new stores are about 25 percent of their traditional size. An example of this is the new second-floor Warsaw location that recently opened. Other units with the same approach are currently open in London and Madrid.

IKEA opened a downtown Paris store in May 2019. This 5,400-square-foot, two-level store acts as a lab to test products and services and glean insights[237]. The store will eventually test furniture rental and will offer unique services including workshops on home renovation, Feng Shui, cooking and furniture repair. Items too big to be taken home can be ordered online. They can then be delivered at home or picked up at one of 350 locations.

Each of IKEA's downtown stores has its own special focal point. The London store features personalized renovation planning. The Sweden store features a dedicated showroom for kitchens. The Madrid location offers a special living room furniture section. The company is also looking at the United States and Japan as well.

---

[235] Attfield, Paul. "Urban grocery stores squeeze into tight spaces." *The Globe and Mail*. November 27, 2018.

[236] Gera, Vanessa. "Ikea moving into city centres to adapt to consumer changes." *The Associated Press*. December 1, 2018.

[237] Vidalon, Dominique. "Ikea opens store in central Paris." *Reuters*. May 7, 2019.

The biggest urban store will be about 50,000 square feet — a fraction of IKEA's suburban footprint of about 300,000 square feet.

IKEA announced in November of 2019 that Toronto will be getting a city store too[238]. There will be one location downtown that shows one of each IKEA item. This will complement other smaller stores around the city that showcase kitchens, living rooms and other slice-of-life showrooms.

IKEA Canada president Michael Ward was quoted as saying, "There are many more people coming into the city. Fewer people own cars. People want to live, work and shop in a closer area, especially when you're living in the middle of a dense city with smaller spaces and expensive rents."

Target has also recognized this trend and has adapted to changing consumers with downtown formats.

6) Healthy Eating: Food Fight

Consumers have made healthy living a priority. The days of large fries, a hotdog and a Coke for breakfast, lunch and dinner are gone. Retailers and brands realized this and are waged in a war to win this customer. They know that more people have become foodies and that what is eaten has become more fashionable. Just look at social media. They also know that consumers want to eat healthy and will pay a premium for it. They know that grocery and food shopping has a high purchase frequency and can help with declining traffic to brick and mortar stores. They also know that healthy foods command greater margins. These factors have driven numerous retailers to invest heavily in the food category.

Burger King recently launched a controversial ad campaign that features a Whopper turning mouldy using time-lapse photography. The ad was meant to show that the company has removed many artificial flavours, colours and additives[239].

Entrepreneur Shelby Taylor has taken advantage of changing consumer eating

---

[238] Rubin, Josh. "Ikea to launch smaller urban stores in downtown Toronto." *The Toronto Star*. November 7, 2019.

[239] "Burger King trims artificial additives-with big exception." *Bloomberg*. February 26, 2020.

habits. She founded Chickpea, which sells gluten-free pasta made from chickpeas[240]. Her chickpea lentil pasta is now sold in 3,500 to 4,000 North American stores.

Taylor says of changing consumer eating habits, "I definitely think it's part of a larger movement, both towards plant-based eating and plant-based proteins, and towards convenient health foods."

7) Meat & Protein Alternatives – Synthetic Sizzle

Plant-based food is on the rise and is now mainstream. In the U.S., plant-based food sales grew 20 percent to $3.3 billion US from 2016 to 2017[241]. The market for plant-based protein and lab-generated proteins could be as much as $85 billion US per annum by 2030. Many consumers have become vegetarians, vegan or flexitarians due to health benefits such as lower cholesterol and lower saturated fats.

In a recent op-ed in The Globe and Mail, well-respected food expert Sylvain Charlebois cites the new "protein war" in Canada[242]. He goes on to say, "Plant-based product providers are trying to democratize the notion of proteins. As a result, we are seeing more innovation coming from the food industry than we have in the past 20 years."

He talks about how burger chains are picking camps between Beyond Meat and Impossible Foods, the two major faux meat suppliers.

First Mover Advantage

With companies such as Beyond Meat and Impossible Foods tearing up the market, this trend may have turned into a movement[243]. Taste will be a major factor

---

[240] Dixon, Guy. "Gluten-free pasta maker counts on simplicity." *The Globe and Mail*. June 10, 2019.

[241] Shanker, Deena. "Plant-based food sales jump $3.3B in past year." *Bloomberg*. July 31, 2018.

[242] Charlebois, Sylvain. "Major restaurant chains choosing sides as 'protein war' heats up." *The Globe and Mail*. August 17, 2019.

[243] Wells, Jennifer. "Beyond Meat reveals our changing tastes." *The Toronto Star*. April 3, 2019.

and so far Beyond Meat tastes the best, according to some. Plant-based meats offer enormous benefits not only to customers but also to the environment by lowering energy consumption and carbon monoxide through production.

Beyond Meat is asking grocers to merchandise its product in the meat section[244]. Many grocers still aren't sure whether to stock meat alternatives in the vegan section, the meat section or both! These new products are taking aim at the $1.4 trillion US meat industry.

Big Food Takes a Bite

Plant-based foods have enticed companies new and old to enter the market[245]. Since the launch and success of Beyond Meat and Impossible Foods, plant-based applications have spread to sausages, chicken and fish. Big-name food companies are jumping in. These include: Nestlé, Tyson, Perdue, Hormel, Smithfield, Conagra, Kellogg, Campbell Soup and McCain, just to name a few[246]. Some food companies have offered blended or hybrid products that combine original animal protein with plant-based protein. They see huge growth in this segment and like the higher average price point protein alternatives yield. With billions of dollars in marketing behind them, look for a war of the meatless world to erupt.

Campbell Soup Co. is launching Bolthouse Farms Plant Protein Milk, which is made with peas. Nestlé plans to launch its own Incredible Burger in Europe and Awesome Burger in America.

Kellogg announced its own version of a plant-based hamburger[247]. Its Morningstar Farms division will launch the "Incogmeato" burger in early 2020. The firm is also relaunching vegetarian chicken nuggets and chicken tenders.

Meat giant Tyson Foods is launching a hybrid product that includes a burger

---

[244] Bellon, Tina. " Vegan section or the meat aisle?" *Reuters*. June 7, 2019.

[245] Yaffe-Bellany, David. "Jumping on the plant-based bandwagon." *The New York Times*. October 19, 2019.

[246] Back, Aaron. "The food giants are coming for Beyond Meat." *The Wall Street Journal*. June 3, 2019.

[247] Shanker, Deena. "Plant-based burger will 'sear wonderfully.'" *Bloomberg*. September 5, 2019.

made of pea protein and beef[248]. The patty will be branded Raised and Rooted, a new brand that will focus on the growing faux meat category. Tyson currently has about a 20 percent market share of the U.S. pork, chicken and beef market.

Fast Food Frenzy

Fast food entered the meat alternative market in Canada during the summer of 2018 when A&W restaurants started carrying the Beyond Meat burger. They couldn't keep them in stock.

Since then, fast-food restaurants such as Burger King, White Castle, Little Caesars Pizza, TGI Fridays, Del Taco, Red Robin, Carl's Jr., American Wildburger and many others have scrambled to add meatless hamburgers and other meatless products. Beyond Meat and Impossible Foods were the main suppliers and had a hard time keeping up[249]. As of June 2019, about 20,000 restaurants in the U.S. alone were offering the two firms' products. Burger King reported a 17 percent increase in visits from locations that carried the Impossible Whopper. Even Taco Bell finally succumbed to the trend and announced the addition of plant-based proteins to its menu in 2021[250].

McDonald's has also jumped into the meatless burger arena — albeit very late compared to competitors. The giant tested a Beyond Meat fake hamburger at 28 locations in southwestern Ontario (Canada) starting late September 2019 and running for 12 weeks[251]. The item is called the P.L.T., standing for plant, lettuce and tomato, and will inform further global decisions as to if and when to expand the product into other markets. Since the test began, the firm has expanded the product to more Ontario restaurants.

Dunkin' Donuts tested a Beyond Meat sandwich for three months in the summer and fall of 2019 at its 1,603 Manhattan locations. In October 2019, it

---

[248] Mulvany, Lydia and Patton, Leslie. "Meat giant moves into veggie protein." *Bloomberg*. June 14, 2019.

[249] Bunge, Jacob and Haddon, Heather. "Fast food embraces meatless burgers, but there's not enough." *The Wall Street Journal*. June 5, 2019.

[250] "Taco Bell changes tack on plant-based fare." *Bloomberg*. February 25, 2020.

[251] Krashinsky-Robertson, Susan. "Ontario serves up test market for McDonald's." *The Globe and Mail*. September 27, 2019.

announced it was rolling it out to all 9,000 U.S. stores[252].

Burger King announced in November 2019 that it was launching a faux-meat burger to 2,400 restaurants in Europe[253]. The new Whopper won't be made by Impossible Foods due to regulatory hurdles not met at launch. Instead, it will use Vegetarian Burger, a Dutch company. The new burger will be called the Rebel Whopper.

Tim Hortons added a slew of Beyond Meat products during the summer of 2019, including breakfast sandwiches and even a burger. It didn't work. Tim Hortons announced in September 2019 it was delisting the Beyond Meat burger across Canada after just a few weeks of sales[254]. It went on to keep Beyond Meat breakfast sandwiches in select stores in Ontario and British Columbia, but exited these items within a few months due to poor sales. This could be a good lesson — for retailers to use caution when expanding assortments and menu items outside their core brand positioning.

After sitting on the meatless bench for a long time, Starbucks announced it was launching breakfast sandwiches from Beyond Meat in Canadian locations[255].

You know meat alternatives are here to stay when IKEA starts selling its famed Swedish meatball in vegan form. In the fall of 2019, IKEA started testing the new offering, with a worldwide rollout at its 400 stores in 2020[256].

In January 2020, Impossible Foods announced it was testing a plant-based

---

[252] Shanker, Deena and Darie, Tatiana. "Beyond Meat gets big boost." *Bloomberg*. October 22, 2019.

[253] Durbin, Dee-Ann. "Burger King brings a plant-based Whopper to 2,400 restaurants across Europe." *Associated Press*. November 13, 2019.

[254] Healing, Dan. "Tim Hortons to stop selling Beyond Meat burgers." *The Canadian Press*. September 19, 2019.

[255] Rubin, Josh. "It didn't work at Tims. But will Beyond Meat be a Starbucks hit?" *The Toronto Star*. February 27, 2020.

[256] "IKEA to roll out new vegan Swedish 'meatballs' starting this fall." *Bloomberg*. May 24, 2019.

sausage patty in 139 Burger King restaurants[257].

The race is on for faux-meat sellers in Asia, too. Beyond Meat recently announced it plans to be producing product in Asia by the end of 2020[258]. Beyond Meat products are currently available in Hong Kong, Singapore and Taiwan, but the firm sees enormous potential in China.

Other Protein Alternatives

Seafood is getting a lot of play in the protein alternative market. There are a number of firms jockeying for first mover advantage in this space. In a recent article by David Yaffe-Bellany from The New York Times, he talks about how Impossible Foods is hot on the trail of fishless fish[259]. AquaBounty Technologies is offering genetically-modified salmon that grows twice as fast as in the wild[260]. Gathered Foods Corp. recently received $32 million US from General Mills to develop its Good Catch brand of plant-based seafood. In June of 2020, the firm plans on launching plant-based fish burgers and crabcakes[261]. Others exploring this category include Wild Type and Good Catch. Several science and regulatory barriers are still to be solved, but one can see this arena gaining momentum in the years to come.

Hong Kong start-up Green Monday wants to do for pork what Beyond Meat has done for beef. It has developed a faux pork offering made from soy, mushroom, rice and peas that has the same texture and taste as pork. The firm is targeting China, where over 50 percent of the world's almost 80 million tons of pork is consumed each year[262]. Green Monday was a successful distributor for Beyond Meat in Asia.

---

[257] "Impossible Foods to trial plant-based sausage patty." *Reuters*. January 8, 2020.

[258] "Beyond meat eyes production in Asia before end of 2020." *Reuters*. November 8, 2019.

[259] Yaffe-Bellany, David. "The biochemistry and science behind the flavour of fish." *The New York Times*. July 13, 2019.

[260] Mulvany, Lydia and Petri, Josh. "The race to become the Beyond Meat of fish." *Bloomberg*. June 15, 2019.

[261] Leigh Painter, Kristen. "Plant-based seafood next on the plate." *The Star Tribune (Minneapolis)*. January 18, 2020.

[262] Wei, David. "Beyond Meat's Asia ally taking alt-pork to China." *Bloomberg*. June 28, 2019.

The lab-grown meat movement has also spawned another Frankenstein of sorts. Synthetic whey[263]. Start-ups such as San Francisco-based Perfect Day are capitalizing on society's trend toward more responsibly-made and consumed protein.

Dairy, too, is on the radar, as Perfect Day and other firms have been testing animal-free ice cream[264].

Finally, there is talk of finding a plant-based alternative to eggs[265]. Think animal welfare, cholesterol, risk of salmonella and tainted eggs. About 80,000 Americans get sick from bad eggs every year, according to the Food and Drug Administration. It's a natural extension to the meat alternative movement.

8) Subscriptions: Rent Is The New Own

Numerous consumers are renting things instead of owning them. Why? Renting offers more flexibility and does not require big upfront payments. As the cost of living increases, while for many, wages stagnate, renting is a preferred option. Millennials and Generation Z would prefer to spend the little disposable income they have on experiences and travel.

More retailers and brands recognize the opportunity for rental and subscriptions. Whether it's teeth-straightening kits or online beauty boxes, retailers and marketers sneak a little disposable income out of customers' wallets monthly instead of all at once.

Big brands have jumped on the rental band wagon, as it can be quite lucrative and allows them to tap into new markets. Ann Taylor, American Eagle and others have started partnering with rental start-ups such as Caastle. The CEO of Caastle, Christine Hunsicker, says brands can generate about a 25 percent operating profit through rental, which is significantly higher than the low single digit operating margin when running a retail store.

---

[263] Zimberoff, Larissa. "Forget synthetic meat, lab grown dairy is here." *Bloomberg*. July 12, 2019.

[264] Hui, Ann. "Lab-made milk – the next food frontier." *The Globe and Mail*. February 15, 2020.

[265] Zimberoff, Larissa. "There's a growing, multibillion-dollar race to replace eggs." *Bloomberg*. May 25, 2019.

Let's take a look at some examples across different categories.

Clothing

Urban Outfitters recently announced its rental program[266]. For $88 US per month, members can rent six outfits at a time. The new venture, called Nuuly, allows members to rent from Urban Outfitters brands such as Free People and Anthropologie, as well as select outside brands such as Reebok and Gal Meets Glam.

Children's Footwear

Nike announced the launch of "Adventure Club," which targets parents with children aged two to 10[267]. The program is available in three price tiers, $20 US, $30 US and $50 US per month. Depending on the package, the child receives a new pair of Nike shoes once a month, once every two months or once every three months. Nike's app SNKRS lets users know when a new shoe is available. Parents use a fridge magnet foot sizing guide to help with the purchase. The program was piloted with 10,000 households before launch. It allows Nike to connect with kids at a young age and takes away the pain point of frequent shopping trips by parents as their children grow. It doesn't hurt Nike's margins either, as it cuts out the retailer. In the United States, the kids' shoe market is worth about $10 billion US per annum.

Furniture

IKEA is testing furniture rental[268]. IKEA is one of those retailers that takes environmental stewardship seriously. It has aggressive targets in place to make all products from renewable and recyclable materials by 2030. It also sees a change in consumer sentiment. Consumers, especially IKEA consumers, want to act responsibly toward the earth when they buy (or rent) things. Why sell them cheap, disposable furniture when you can rent them furniture that can change as consumers progress through life's various stages? IKEA has been testing this concept close to home in the Netherlands, Sweden (of course), Poland and Switzerland and plans to

---

[266] Safdar, Khadeeja. "Urban Outfitters to start renting clothes." The Wall Street Journal. May 22, 2019.

[267] Balu, Nivedita. "Nike aims sneaker subscriber scheme at kids." *Reuters*. August 13, 2019.

[268] Thomasson, Emma. "IKEA to test furniture rental in 30 markets." *Reuters*. April 4, 2019.

roll out the test to all of its 30 markets. This will require a fundamental change in IKEA's business model and will be gradual in uptake. It is one of a number of key initiatives that puts the firm on a bold new path.

Automobiles

The auto subscription business took an interesting turn when Porsche announced it was adding four North American cities to its Atlanta "Porsche Passport" program[269]. The cities added to the list include San Diego, Las Vegas, Toronto and Phoenix.

There are a few different packages available. At $3,100 US per month, users can "borrow" up to 20 different vehicles and don't pay for insurance or maintenance — just gas. Cars are delivered to users who pay a one-time activation fee of $595 US. A less-expensive, four-hour rental version, called Porsche Drive, is also available at $269 US per occasion. The monthly fees are up to 20 percent more expensive than fixed lease rates. The company is trying to stimulate trial and ultimately increase purchases. This approach allows Porsche to target a new generation of drivers who are accustomed to subscription payment plans that offer variety and flexibility.

Volvo recently announced it will be utilizing a Netflix-like subscription model to sell its Polestar electric vehicles[270]. Customers will pay a monthly subscription that includes the car, insurance and maintenance. No money is required initially. In addition, the company will be opening "guide shops" in prime malls. These stores will be commission-free and will enable the touch-and-feel required to buy an automobile — a key part of the purchase process. Consumers can also buy the car online.

9) Used Products: Cheapish and Cheerful

As consumers feel the pinch, many are turning to used products to save money and save the planet. Used products are nothing new. Think vehicles, homes and condominiums, musical instruments and more. What *is* new is the categories now part of the market. These include fashion, shoes, accessories and more.

---

[269] Coppola, Gabrielle. " Want to drive a Porsche for a few hours?" *Bloomberg*. September 3, 2019.

[270] Elliott, Hannah. "Volvo to sell by Netflix-style subscription." *Bloomberg*. September 22, 2018.

Global Data PLC, a research company, says that the overall U.S. market for resale footwear, accessories and clothing was $24 billion US and is expected to hit a stunning $51 billion US by 2023. Bain & Company, a consulting firm, estimates that the U.S. market for used luxury products was worth about $6 billion US in 2018.

There are several consumer sub-segments within the used products market. There are the luxury wannabes who want to look rich but are not. There are environmentally-conscious people who want to minimize their impact on the planet. There are people who are squeezed by stagnant wages and rising costs and need to stretch each dollar or euro further. Consumers can fall in one or many of the segments above.

Luxury

RealReal has an interesting business model. The firm runs a used luxury goods website where everything is sold on consignment[271]. Sellers earn between 55 and 70 percent of the resale price and RealReal keeps the rest. There are a few players in this space such as Poshmark and Fashionphile, now owned by department store Neiman Marcus. One of the tricks of winning in the used luxury market is authentication. RealReal and others dedicate a lot of time and money making sure products are real and not fake. One of the benefits RealReal has is its reputation that products being sold on the site are not counterfeit.

According to the Organization for Economic Cooperation and Development (OECD), the fake goods market rang in at $509 billion US as of 2016, the latest year statistics were available. That is up from $461 billion US in 2013.

In 2018, RealReal had 29 percent of its sales volume returned or cancelled. This is a big number and eventually must be lowered if the firm is to make money. RealReal went public during the summer of 2019 and like many IPOs that year, has struggled out of the gate.

Handbags and Watches

Handbags and watches are two of the most popular used luxury product categories. Through online platforms such as Watchfinder & Co., RealReal and Vestiaire Collective, it is easy to match buyers and sellers[272].

---

[271] Kapner, Suzanne. "RealReal's biggest hurdle will be keeping it real after IPO." *The Wall Street Journal*. June 26, 2019.

[272] Ryan, Carol. "Some luxury brands look frayed second-hand." *The Wall Street Journal*.

This growing market has impacted full-line retail in at least two ways. Firstly, the resale market for some brands is negatively impacting sales at full price. Secondly, some brands have had a harder time increasing prices if their resale products aren't holding their value. Watch companies have therefore started to take more control of the resale market through acquisition. An example of this is Richemont's purchase of Watchfinder in 2018.

Non-Luxury

IKEA, a leader in environmental stewardship, has already started offering customers an opportunity to trade in their used furniture. Other retailers will consider following as they learn to make money at this new and growing market. Existing sites such as Kijiji and used-clothing stores such as Plato's Closet are examples of this trend.

Patagonia announced in 2019 that it would open up its first Worn Wear clothing store in Boulder, Colorado[273]. The store allows customers to trade in, repair and buy used clothing and includes consignment. Some of the clothing is remade by Patagonia from other used clothing that customers have provided.

StockX, a web platform that facilitates the purchase and sale of used running shoes, has been a good college hobby-turned-big business for founder Nic Wilkins[274]. The firm has been valued at $1 billion US, with sales over $1 million US and a healthy 25-percent profit margin. StockX is not alone as others including Bump, Stadium Goods and Goat Group take advantage of the exploding used-products market, geared toward millennials and Gen Z.

10) Authenticity, Inclusivity, Equality and Transparency (AIET)

The trend of consumers looking for authenticity, inclusivity, equality and transparency (AIET) in brands is growing significantly. Society has had enough of

---

May 29,

[273] Murphy, Mary. "Patagonia opens first 'Worn Wear' clothing store." November 14, 2019. Retrieved from: https://gearjunkie.com/patagonia-worn-wear-shop-upcycled-recycled

[274] Griffith, Erin. "The new investment mantra: Buy low (top), sell high (top)." *The New York Times*. June 29, 2019.

corporate spin and can see through this type of retail and marketing. We are tired of listening to company PR people covering up, blaming others or just plain lying to us. Also, not many people look like models or are anywhere near perfect, whatever that is. Society has demanded equality for all people, regardless of gender, ethnicity, sexual orientation, disability and more. Recent women's movements underscore this. Customers want to buy from brands that give them the straight goods, celebrate diversity, empower them and offer inclusion of all kinds.

Beautiful Mind

Let's take the $470 billion US (2017) global beauty and personal care industry as an example[275]. Consumers are looking for more authentic brands to help them stay beautiful and healthy. Big beauty brands such as CoverGirl, Estée Lauder, L'Oreal and Shiseido have all been under threat from start-up brands such as Glocier and others. Beauty customers want brands that connect to them. They don't see pricier as better. They buy online and not just in store. They share brands they like with friends on social media. They don't want some big brand telling them what they should look like. The beauty industry is now defined as one of entrepreneurship, inclusivity, empowerment and shopping the way the customer wants, not the way big brands want them to.

Doing it Right

Banana Republic has woken up to the fact that not everyone is thin and has the "perfect" shape. The firm announced it will be expanding sizing and colours to reach a wider customer base[276]. Not everyone is white and garments need to better match different skin tones. Just ask Fenty, Rihanna's beauty brand, which caters to a variety of users' skin colours. Banana Republic currently offers up to size 16 in store and up to 20 online. It will now look to increase that range up to size 26. This makes sense, as 70 percent of U.S. women buy a pant size 14 and above.

Ingredient transparency has become a hot topic as well. Michelle Pfeiffer recently launched a line of cosmetics that had 100 percent ingredient transparency, a first for the cosmetics industry[277]. Chemical transparency has gained traction with

---

[275] Lachapelle, Tara. "Beauty industry thriving in makeover." *Bloomberg*. December 26, 2018.

[276] Holman, Jordyn. "Banana Republic diversifies offerings in turnaround effort." *Bloomberg*. September 21, 2019.

[277] Kary, Tiffancy and Roeder, Jonathan. "Pfeiffer pushes for transparency in perfumes."

numerous groups and consumers due to the link between chemical ingredients and cancer and other health issues. Giant consumer goods firms such as Procter and Gamble, Unilever and Johnson & Johnson started publishing ingredients for shampoo and makeup. Big perfume has resisted so far.

The clothing industry has been forced to become transparent about which suppliers retailers source from. Sadly, much of this reform came to pass after the Rana Plaza incident, in which 1,100 workers lost their lives in Bangladesh at a garment factory. Since then, many brands have led this initiative, including Patagonia, Nike and many others. Consumers are demanding retailers disclose factory names to labour and human rights groups for approval[278].

Swing and a Miss

Hasbro is one of the many brands that is looking to capitalize on the women's movement. Spawned by the popular #timesup and #metoo hashtags, there is a renewed discussion on women's rights and representation in business. Many brands are looking to take advantage of this movement and connect with women. Hasbro dropped the ball recently when it launched Ms. Monopoly in September 2019[279]. The game includes an advocate for investing in women start-ups and for compensating women more than men. But the firm does not give enough credit to the actual woman, Elizabeth "Lizzie" Magie, who helped invent an original version of the game. Brands need to use extreme caution when marketing themselves through deep-rooted causes unless they get their facts straight.

During the summer of 2019, numerous retailers aggressively marketed Pride merchandise to commemorate Pride month across the U.S. and Canada[280]. The reaction has been fairly positive for the most part, although some gay leaders see this effort as nothing more than opportunistic and labelled the efforts "rainbow capitalism". Some firms have donated part of all profits from the sale of the merchandise to LGBTQ causes to recognize the tremendous challenges gay people

---

Bloomberg. April 9, 2019.

[278] Wells, Jennifer. "Retailers revealing more on suppliers." *The Toronto Star.* December 18, 2019.

[279] Chokshi, Niraj. "New Monopoly celebrates all women, except game's creator." *The New York Times.* September 14, 2019.

[280] Dobnik, Verna. "U.S. retailers promote LGBTQ apparel during Pride." *Associated Press.* June 24, 2019.

face even in today's society. Retailers that participated in the event and gave donations included Target, Macy's, H&M and others. Gay leaders have noticed the transition of Pride marketing from the U.S. coasts into small town America. Several years ago some brands resisted marketing the event for fear of straight consumers' backlash. This backlash failed to materialize for the most part. Gay leaders have also criticized some brands for marketing to gays but manufacturing Pride products in countries where being gay is illegal.

Cold drink maker Pepsi took significant heat when it used Kendall Jenner in a commercial that many thought played on the complicated "Black Lives Matter" movement. During the commercial, Kendall was seen creating harmony between two opposing groups at a major protest by simply offering everyone a Pepsi. Many thought it insulting that Pepsi suggested such a sensitive topic could be remedied through something as trivial as handing out soda.

11) Life-Work Balance — Tightrope Tales

Society appears to be divided on the notion of work-life balance. In one camp we have the start-up mentality that glorifies the 80+ hour work week. Successful billionaires such as Elon Musk and Jack Ma openly support aggressive work schedules. The other camp longs for balance between the demands of work and the freedoms of life. People from all walks of life, including millennials and Generation Z, see more to life than work. They work to live, not live to work. They have set a new standard that retailers, suppliers and other stakeholders have had to adapt to.

4-Day Workweek

Companies across a number of industries are moving to a four-day work week[281]. A survey across eight countries and involving 3,000 employees showed that almost half of the respondents thought they could get their weekly work completed in four days. Companies that have piloted the four-day work week, such as Perpetual Guardian, a trust company, and Planio, a software company, have reported a reduction in employee stress and an increase in employee engagement.

In Emma Thomasson's 2018 article in Reuters, she quotes Lucie Greene, a trends consultant: "People are starting to take a step back from the 24-hour digital life we have now and realize the mental health issues from being constantly

---

[281] Thomasson, Emma. "Burnout, stress lead more companies to try a four-day work week." *Reuters*. December 26, 2018.

connected to work."

The article also addresses how we tend to take our time and have longer coffee breaks when we know we have five days to get things done. In a four-day working scenario, we tend to be more efficient with our time.

FIRE Movement

There is a new movement based on the premise of FIRE or "Financial Independence, Retire Early.[282]" In Scott Rieckens' recent book, "Playing with FIRE: How Far Would You Go for Financial Freedom?" he challenges conventional consumerism. In its place he presents a liberation of people to have the money to work less or stop working altogether and enjoy life on a modest budget.

12) Distrust of Elites — True Lies

Although the movie Elysium didn't win an academy award, it was an important forerunner for where society is headed. Like many sci-fi flicks, it shows a future where the world is polarized between elites and everyone else. In case you haven't noticed (see boiling frog analogy), we are well down the road to becoming Elysium Light. Our society has become two-tier again. The ruling class and the working class. The middle class was an anomaly.

Trust but Verify

In its 20th anniversary survey of public trust in institutions, Edleman, a public relations outfit, analyzed responses from 34,000 people across 27 countries. The responses were disturbing but not surprising. Major areas of concern include income inequality, future job prospects, corruption and more. Citizens are skeptical about institutions such as business, government, media and non-government organizations (NGOs). At the same time, people are looking for leaders to step up and resolve these concerns. Overall, 56 percent said capitalism hurts more than helps. Ninety-two percent want their CEOs to speak out about ethical issues such as climate change and technology. Eighty-three percent are afraid of not having a job in the future. Sixty percent say that governments do not understand technology well enough to regulate it and that it's moving too fast. Just under 50 percent of respondents do not trust rich people, governments or religious leaders. People do trust members of their community and scientists. Almost 75 percent said that a

---

[282] Smith, Elaine. " 'Juice worth the squeeze.' " *The Toronto Star*. October 7, 2019.

company can both enhance its community and make money[283].

WTF? WEF

One of the symbols of elitist power in business and government is the World Economic Forum (WEF) held every year in Davos, Switzerland[284]. This is the annual meeting of world leaders, captains of industry and other government officials. While this meeting is sometimes perceived to be the place where the world's problems are solved and the common citizen is taken care of, it has failed in this regard at least most recently.

Michael Hewson, chief market analyst at CMC Markets in the U.K., was quoted as saying the following on the WEF: "Judging by the state of the world right now 10 years on from the financial crisis, and the dysfunctional state of global politics I would suggest that these annual events have achieved the sum total of diddly squat."

In an article from Bloomberg, Lionel Laurent discusses how about 10 years ago one of the "big" questions for elites to solve was "What must industry do to prevent a broad social backlash?"[285] The answer, he says, "probably wasn't 'Double, triple or quadruple the wealth of the most prominent conference attendees, while letting median household income stagnate back home.'"

21st Century Fox

A lot has happened since 2008. There have been winners and losers. Winners have included anyone with assets in equities and real estate. Interest rates were held low for so long that money was cheap to borrow and share buybacks and other financial games drove corporate profits to an all-time high. The bull market has been running for 10 years and counting. With cheap money, housing prices inflated in many cities as competition pushed prices up. Losers have pretty much been everyone else. Wages have remained relatively flat while housing and other costs have soared.

---

[283] Dill, Kathryn and Wilberding, Kurt. "Capitalism draws fire, despite strong global economy." *The Wall Street Journal*. January 21, 2020.

[284] Wiseman, Paul and Keaten, Jamey. "Under assault by populists, global elites regroup in Davos." *The Associated Press*. January 21, 2019.

[285] Laurent, Lionel. "The problem with Davos? The backlash." *Bloomberg*. January 22, 2019.

Jet Lag

The hangover from globalization finally surfaced. As countless firms offshored production and services to low-cost countries, profits soared, benefiting executives and shareholders. To globalization's credit, it made the developing world a lot better off in terms of GDP growth and standard of living. But not everyone shared equally in globalization's benefits. Workers in the developed world were left behind as jobs moved across oceans.

Populism Parade

We now find ourselves in an environment where populism has flourished in countries such as the United States, the U.K., Brazil, Italy, Canada (provincially, anyway) and others. To quote Paul Sheard from Harvard University's Kennedy School: "The winners from globalization have had the megaphone. The losers have been somewhat silent, but now are starting to express themselves through the ballot box and through the political process."

This is the disenchanted populist's only power left. Eventually, the elite of society, such as big-pay CEOs, will come under fire, whether they deserve it or not, as a method to take frustration out for the poor standard of living and future prospects of the developed world.

Entitlements

Take the recent construction of New York City's new Hudson Yards mixed-use complex. It is estimated that New York taxpayers payed developers subsidies of $6 billion US[286]. Developers get a lot richer and the average citizen gets what? A few thousand low-paying service jobs or construction jobs? The privilege of spending thousands of dollars on luxury goods or watching the top one percent do the same?

13) Ultra Luxe

Products and services that cater to the super wealthy have started to emerge. With the one percent gaining so much wealth over the last decade, it makes sense to offer extreme luxury to this select group of consumers.

---

[286] Haag, Matthew. "Deal for Amazon pales against aid to Hudson Yards." *The New York Times*. March 12, 2019.

Airbnb has launched a new offering targeting rich customers[287]. The new service, called Airbnb Luxe, includes about 2,000 listings. According to an article in Bloomberg, the average weekly price is $14,000 US per week. The top end will run you $1 million US for your own island near Tahiti. The Bloomberg article goes on to list other examples, including a French villa, the place in Jamaica where Ian Fleming got inspired for the James Bond books and a hacienda in Mexico.

It looks like Under Armour is taking advantage of the publicity of Virgin Galactic's upcoming $250,000 US space trips. The clothing maker launched his-and-hers space suits and boots[288]. Limited market, but big media spin and potential brand credibility play.

14) Health and Wellness: Gym Rat

A trend that has been here for a while has been health and wellness. Getting and staying fit and healthy has never been more popular. From what we eat to staying active, consumers care about their physical and mental well-being.

Best Buy recently announced it was adding fitness equipment in 100 stores[289]. Each location will have treadmills, rowing machines and flywheel bikes. The retailer wants to reinforce its destination for healthy technology. Other technology-enabled fitness firms such as Peloton and Mirror have been aggressive in this growing space.

15) Too Much Choice: Don't @ Me

Consumers can face an overwhelming number of choices, which makes some

---

[287] Carville, Olivia and Ballentine, Claire. "New Airbnb tier aimed at super-rich." *Bloomberg*. July 19, 2019.

[288] Novy-Williams, Eben. "Under Armour seeing stars with new suits." *Bloomberg*. October 21, 2019.

[289] Thomas, Lauren. "Best Buy will sell Flywheel bikes, Hydrow rowing machines in over 100 stores by the end of the year." June 18, 2019. Retrieved from: https://www.cnbc.com/2019/06/17/best-buy-will-sell-spin-bikes-rowers-in-over-100-stores-by-years-end.html

categories too confusing to make purchase decisions.

According to a recent article by The Wall Street Journal, the average U.S. supermarket carries more than 300 different types of yogurt[290]! With all of these varieties and choice you might think sales have exploded. Just the opposite has occurred. The simple reality is that the category has become too hard to shop and more is less in this case.

Retailers need to be careful not to offer too many choices in certain categories. It is a fine line, though, as customers want more custom-made products or one-of-a-kind items. The key is to research how customers buy a given category and design assortments, plan-o-grams and online offerings around that. Some basic categories only require good, better and best or the top three flavours of a given food. Make it easy and natural for a customer to shop. More often than not, Pareto's rule comes into play: 80 percent of your sales come from 20 percent of your assortment.

16) Forever Young

I've noticed that some people are reliving or trying to relive their childhoods through familiar experiences or products. Perhaps a way to escape modern-day stress.

An example of this phenomenon is Lego. The Danish toy maker has identified stressed-out adults as a major growth segment for high ticket sets that can retail for hundreds of dollars[291]. One product that appeals to this group is the $800 US Star Wars Millennium Falcon set.

EMPLOYEES

17) Management Power: Under My Rump

In retail and other industries, the balance of power over the last few decades has been tipped in favour of management and owners over labour. From the breaking of

---

[290] Haddon, Heather. "Yogurt sales sour as options proliferate." *The Wall Street Journal.* April 10, 2019.

[291] Bhattarai, Abha. "Lego sees adult market as block to build on." *The Washington Post.* January 18, 2020.

unions to the growth of the gig economy, retailers and other firms have diminished the rights and power of workers in society.

Sharing is Caring

In an op-ed, Barrie McKenna cites a recent McKinsey report that shows the share of GDP paid in the form of salaries, wages and benefits in developed economies between management and labour[292]. In the United States, labour's share of GDP dropped from 62 percent in 1980 to 56 percent in 2017. In Canada, this metric drops from about 59 percent to just over 55 percent over the same time frame. The good news according to McKenna, is that the graphs have been stabilizing over the last few years. Have we reached a new equilibrium in offshore production and automation? I propose that we have not and the worst is yet to come.

A recent OECD survey of 22,000 people across 21 developed countries showed that an average of 68 percent indicated they wanted governments to tax the wealthiest citizens more to help provide for have-nots[293]. Other major wants included: better pensions (54 percent), health care (48 percent) and guaranteed basic income (37 percent).

Life in the Staff Lane

One dynamic that can lower morale in workforces involves companies paying top dollar for new employees while limiting wage growth for existing staff[294]. In his article published in The Globe and Mail, Guy Dixon includes the following statement from Hays Canada: "Despite 61 percent of employers going overbudget to recruit specific candidates, only 23 percent of employers gave workers a raise of more than three percent this year."

Dixon goes on to quote UBC business school professor emeritus Mark Thompson, saying: "The wage-stagnation conundrum baffles a lot of people. Employers, they please the shareholders first, the customers second and the

---

[292] McKenna, Barry. "Future of labour not as bleak as imagined." *The Globe and Mail*. May 25, 2019.

[293] Thomas, Leigh. "Majority in rich countries want higher taxes on the wealthy: poll." *Reuters*. March 20, 2019.

[294] Dixon, Guy. "A vicious circle: Attractive offers and stagnant wages." *The Globe and Mail*. December 12, 2018.

employees come a distant third."

Free Lunch

For some, employers expect unpaid hours even for low-wage service jobs such as in restaurants[295]. It is common for employees looking to work at a restaurant to put in a few hours or even a shift without pay to see how they do. In addition, some workers are expected to come in and do food-prep an hour early with no pay. Some restaurants take advantage of immigrants, who are nervous about complaining or contacting the labour authorities for fear of deportation.

If You Heave Me Now

Employees are no match for big retailers. Take the recent case of Amazon and non-compete clauses. As written in a recent article in The Associated Press, Amazon lobbyists succeeded in creating an exemption to new state legislation prohibiting non-compete clauses[296]. Under the revised plan, workers in the state making above $100,000 US would not be subject to this law and could be made to sign non-compete agreements up to 18 months with employers, albeit the employer would need to pay the employee during the blackout period. Although one can see Amazon's point, the situation demonstrates the power large companies have and their ability to sway governments.

Getting the Boot

If one looks at legendary outdoor products retailer L.L. Bean, one can get a feel for how retail and manufacturers have operated recently. In 2017, the famed retailer stopped providing employees performance bonuses for the first time in 10 years[297]. Over the years before 2017, L.L. Bean reduced its workforce, made its return policy less liberal for customers, and placed restrictions on free shipping. To the company's credit, perhaps after blowback from its 5,400 workers, it reinstated a five percent bonus in 2018.

---

[295] Sagan, Aleksandra. "Unpaid work exploitative for people in precarious positions." *The Canadian Press*. March 16, 2019.

[296] "Amazon lobbies to exempt employees from protections." *The Associated Press*. March 9, 2019.

[297] "L.L. Bean restores worker bonuses after solid 2018." *The Associated Press*. March 16, 2019.

Need-to-Know Basis

Sometimes employees are forgotten as a key stakeholder or simply ignored. Take the recent case of Tesla[298]. Tesla made a snap decision in the spring of 2019 to close all of its stores. This decision was later scaled back. But when the original decision was made, some store staff found out via social media.

I remember when Target decided to pull out of Canada in 2015. That day, 22,000 Canadians lost their jobs. It was a big deal. I also remember hearing about employees who found out their store was closing on the radio on the way to work before their manager advised them.

18) Sharing Economy Hits Puberty

Since The Great Recession, contract work has grown significantly but has generated much debate about its impact on society.

From an employer perspective, the gig worker business model is ideal. It lacks the traditional overhead and higher cost of legacy employment. No need to pay benefits, vacation pay or offer a severance for terminating an employee. It also allows employers to scale up and scale down labour in short notice to match revenue.

For the contract employee, benefits can include flexibility and supplemental income through sometimes limitless hours. Many people have used the gig economy to top up earnings from another job.

Swing Space

To understand the impact that flexible work has had on society, one needs look no further than WeWork, the global coworking company[299]. Although the firm derailed in 2019, it remains an interesting business model. The firm rents floors in buildings in urban centres through long-term leases. It then re-leases out short-term, flexible offices at a premium to customers such as IBM, Microsoft, free-lancers, contractors and start-ups. Its spaces are modern and welcoming with full amenities, food, drink and even alcohol available to clients. The open-concept facilitates

---

[298] Hull, Dana. "Tesla staff shocked by store-closing plans." *Bloomberg*. March 6, 2019.

[299] Ross Sorkin, Andrew. "Economic downturn could become a new lease on life for WeWork." *The New York Times*. November 17, 2018.

collaboration and networking (if desired) and most importantly offers companies super flexible terms so they can scale up and down quickly and cheaply. According to Coworking Resources, a website, "The company offers four levels of membership: hot desks, dedicated desks, private offices and custom build-outs[300]."

Seattle Seed Money

Amazon recently announced it is willing to front employees up to $10,000 US to quit and start delivering packages for it full time[301]. If you are accepted into the program, you quit your part-time or full-time job with Amazon and get start-up money plus three months salary to start gigging for the behemoth. Amazon needs to get more packages to customers quicker as the space race for same-day delivery heats up.

Grand Opening

In a recent op-ed in The Globe and Mail, Linda Nazareth explores the rise of the gig economy, defines it and discusses both the pros and cons of this new way of working[302]. Nazareth addresses cash pressures on business, demographic dynamics and the role of technology in her assessment regarding the growth of the industry. Her final paragraph in the article summarizes society's current position regarding the gig economy: "It's too late to prevent the explosion that has taken the labour market into a dozen different directions. Pandora's box has been opened, and there's no closing it now. The question, then, is this: How do we move forward in a way that will benefit all concerned?"

Living at the Margin

Those who rely on contract work are sometimes vulnerable from a financial standpoint[303]. Based on a study by the U.S. Federal Reserve, about 30 percent of Americans are participating in the gig economy. Gigs can range from driving Uber

---

[300] Huang, Yifu. "The WeWork Business Model." *Coworking Resources*. February 17, 2019. Retrieved from: https://www.coworkingresources.org/blog/the-wework-business-model

[301] "Amazon offers to help employees start businesses." *The Associated Press*. May 14, 2019.

[302] Nazareth, Linda. "The fragmented future of work." *The Globe and Mail.* January 24, 2019.

[303] "Gig workers living on financial edge, research finds." *Bloomberg*. May 28, 2019.

and Lyft to cleaning homes. The report addresses how about 20 percent of gig workers use this kind of work as their main source of revenue. Of the 20 percent, about half are running so tight financially they may or may not be able to handle an unexpected $400 US expense. The Fed goes on to say "A decade after the Great Recession, financial fragility and economic uncertainty remain concerns for many households."

Not everyone has been marginalized. In some industries, like information technology, many workers prefer to work on contract because it can be much more lucrative[304].

Pressure on App Firms

In Toronto, food delivery app Foodora's workers have used social media to try to organize under the Canadian Union of Postal Workers (CUPW)[305]. This could set a significant precedent for gig workers to obtain better wages and additional benefits. Gig app companies such as Uber, Lyft and others tout worker flexibility as a major advantage for independent contractors. These firms threaten that this flexibility will be diminished if they are forced to classify gig workers as employees. App providers feel that as independent contractors, workers forfeit the right to strike. It is difficult for governments to fully comprehend how many gig workers there are, but the debate on the fair treatment of these people has been hotly debated. In February 2020, the Ontario Labour Relations Board ruled that Foodora drivers had won the right to unionize[306]. In the spring of 2020, Foodora announced they were leaving Canada.

DoorDash, too, is under fire. In an article in The New York Times, DoorDash's newly-revised driver pay policy is examined[307]. Under the previous policy, customer tips were not shared with drivers. The company got them. The firm has changed its

---

[304] Dixon, Guy. "A vicious circle: Attractive offers and stagnant wages." *The Globe and Mail*. December 12, 2018.

[305] Doherty, Brennan and Saba, Rosa. "What Foodora's union effort means for the gig economy." *The Toronto Star (Calgary)*. August 10, 2019.

[306] O'Kane, Josh. "Ontario Foodora Couriers win right to unionize in labour board ruling." *The Globe and Mail*. February 25, 2020.

[307] Newman, Andy. "DoorDash promises couriers will earn more." *The New York Times*. August 26, 2019.

payment model so drivers, or "Dashers" as they are called, will receive higher minimum base pay. Drivers will make on average more but specific details of how much more are fuzzy. Unlike Uber Eats, drivers will be shown the potential earnings for a given delivery before they decide to accept or reject it. More driver promotions will be offered during certain hours to entice drivers. Some drivers prefer the old system, as pay had less variability. Second Measure, an analytics firm, claims that DoorDash has a 36 percent share of the U.S. food delivery app market.

An op-ed by Nura Jabagi, a PhD candidate at Montreal's Concordia University, discusses how Uber caused quite a stir regarding a recent driver pay proposal. The firm petitioned the U.S. Securities and Exchange Commission to allow it to offer stock to its drivers[308]. Uber (and other sharing economy platforms) has faced criticism based on how little gig contractors make. Uber drivers have organized and made demands on Uber for better compensation. Jabagi makes an argument that stock issuance, although a positive step, is not as good as higher pay and benefits.

19) Aye, Robot

One of the biggest trends in retail is the automation of work. It started in factories and distribution centres with robots in the 1990s, but has recently become popular with customer-facing jobs at the store, head office and other areas. In some cases, technology has not replaced workers but has been used to manage them. The benefits to retail is cost reduction and efficiency. The drawbacks include higher unemployment and negative customer sentiment.

<u>Cashing Out</u>

One of the best examples of employee automation in retail is self-scanning cash registers and checkouts. First used at grocery stores and later at mass merchants, this approach has become common at virtually all retailers that sell high-volume, low-ticket consumer goods. Walmart has been actively testing robots to check for out-of-stocks on shelf. Amazon is a case study in retailers using automation to minimize people in the distribution process.

<u>Mechanized Manager</u>

What if your boss was a machine? This is already happening through the use of technology to manage employees sometimes without the intervention of human

---

[308] Jabagi, Nura. "Why gig companies need to evaluate issuing stock to their workers."

managers. In his recent article in The Wall Street Journal, Greg Ip reports on how Amazon has used such a practice[309]. Ip's article quotes one law firm, saying: "Amazon's system tracks the rates of each individual associate's productivity and automatically generates any warnings or terminations regarding quality or productivity without inputs from supervisors."

At its warehouses, Amazon uses its ADAPT tracker (Associate Development and Performance Tracker) to review each employee's output versus predetermined productivity targets. One Amazon spokesperson said, "Managers make final decisions on all personnel matters." Ip's article suggests that machines can theoretically work in an employee's favour as they don't have the same bias as people do.

Time to Punch Out

Some companies are using technology to estimate when an employee is about to quit[310]. IBM is offering AI-driven technology that can help firms predict with 95 percent accuracy when employees will leave. It's called the "proactive retention" tool and IBM currently uses it internally. Brian Kropp, group vice president at Gartner, says almost all Fortune 500 firms have a "talent analytics" head in place. In 2016, about 10 to 15 percent had such a role. When you think about it, companies already use this type of approach for *customer* retention through popular firms such as Salesforce.

Give Them the Finger

Several companies have taken flack over their use of biometric data to track employees[311]. Firms operating in the restaurant and warehouse industry may have been the first to use such data. Fingerprints and retina scans are used to verify employee in's and out's. Some companies use biometrics to add a layer of security to customer access of accounts. Charles Schwabb and Fidelity use voice recognition to OK access to customer data when passwords and such are not available. A recent Gartner study of firms in Canada, Europe and the U.S. found that six percent were using biometrics to keep tabs on staff. Numerous law suits have been filed by

---

[309] Ip, Greg. "For lower-paid workers, the robots are here." *The Wall Street Journal*. May 1, 2019.

[310] McGregor, Jena. "Data can predict if you'll quit." *The Washington Post*. April 15, 2019.

[311] Chen, Te-Ping. "Workers push back as firms gather fingerprints, retina scans." *The Wall Street Journal*. March 28, 2019.

employees who claim they were not made aware of how their data was being tracked or used. Could an employer sell this data to a third party? What if the employer was hacked?

Retraining

Retailers know they don't need as many people in the future and have started to devise plans to manage this transition. Retraining and other measures are being announced to help soften the blow to their reputation and lower their legal liability.

Amazon recently announced it would spend $700 million US on retraining 100,000 employees between now and 2025.[312] Amazon is automating its process rapidly and won't need all of its 630,000-plus employees. It *will* need workers who can program and work with computers. That's what the training is focused on.

The specific program will change depending on an employee's aptitude and interest. Part of the challenge for Amazon is having enough skilled workers to meet its future needs. Creating a homegrown workforce that is educated in its systems and processes will help.

The effort will help Amazon's reputation, which has taken a hit recently. The retailer is sometimes seen as an employer of commoditized, robot-like workers who are given higher and higher productivity targets to meet. The firm is carefully positioning the training as a benefit to employees inside or outside Amazon. This may help lower the legal and moral liability the firm could face as it downsizes significantly in the future.

American manufacturers, too, are adapting to the prevalence of robots and AI and have started to retrain workers. As discussed in an article by Agam Shah in The Wall Street Journal, firms such as Marlin Steel Wire Products and Radwell International have identified workers with the aptitude for coding and other IT interfaces and have redesigned jobs to facilitate the emergence of technology in production[313].

Loblaw recently signalled it was looking to retrain workers due to AI and robotics.[314] Loblaw president Sarah Davis was quoted as saying: "Across the

---

[312] Pisani, Joseph. "Amazon to spend $700-million by 2025 to retrain workers." *The Associated Press*. July 12, 2019.

[313] Shah, Agam. "Factory workers become coders as companies automate." *The Wall Street Journal*. May 21, 2019.

[314] "Loblaws retaining workers to be future-ready." *The Canadian Press*. May 3, 2019.

economy and our industry, artificial intelligence and automation will change the nature of the work that is done in our offices, in our distribution centres and in our stores."

Loblaw has grown the use of technology in areas such as e-commerce, self-checkouts and electronic shelf labels.

20) Throw Them a Bone

As overall compensation for labour has stagnated, retailers and other firms have used other economical means to entice and retain workers.

Dress for Success

One concession that companies have made to appease employees is incorporating casual dress at work. Some more than others. If you work in the technology sector, it's almost an anything-goes proposition. Shorts, t-shirts and flip-flops for engineers. For a CEO it's a blazer, t-shirt, jeans and running shoes. Even mainstream employers such as Target and Goldman Sachs have switched to business casual[315]. This has actually created significant challenges and opportunities for retailers from a sales perspective. The U.S. men's suit market has shrunk more than eight percent to about $2 billion US since 2015, while sports apparel (which includes several sub-categories, not just men's wear) has grown 17 percent to $44 billion US over the same time.

Poodle Programmers

Amazon has gone to the dogs. That's a good thing for pet owners who work at the giant's Seattle office. Workers can bring their dogs to work. As of 2019, there are 7,000 pooches registered to have access to Amazon's complex, up from 6,000 in 2018[316]. Studies show that dogs can reduce turnover and increase morale.

---

[315] Kapner, Suzanne. "Men ditch suits and retailers struggle to adapt." *The Wall Street Journal*. March 26, 2019.

[316] Read, Richard. "Workers at Amazon bring pups to work – 7,000 of them." *Los Angeles Times*. June 29, 2019.

21) Service Mentality – People Business

Sometimes companies learn the hard way that retail can be a people business, especially when you're trying to sell $1,000 camping gear.

Take MEC (the retailer formally known as Mountain Equipment Co-op). It lost $11.5 million Cdn in its most recent year (ending February 24, 2019) on sales of over $460 million Cdn. As part of a plan to turn the co-op around, the firm announced it would be offering 950 non-permanent, casual store workers part-time or full-time employment. This means they will begin to receive a minimum number of hours per week as well as dental and health-care benefits. This group represents 70 percent of all store workers. MEC needs to reduce staff turnover, which was an astonishing 80 percent of casual workers in 2019[317].

22) Women's Movements: Never Again

Important developments for workers in all industries are the "Time's Up" and "Me Too" movements.

Women have said "enough is enough" and demand professional behaviour from men. Several large companies have exited senior executives due to breach of code of conduct incidents. Retailers and brands have not been immune to this movement. They are front and centre.

McDonald's is a case study on how poor judgment can result in significant damage.

<u>Broken Code</u>

McDonald's is one of the biggest employers in the world, with almost two million employees in 100 countries[318]. The industry was rocked in the fall of 2019 when McDonald's fired all-star CEO Steve Easterbrook for having a consensual

---

[317] Krashinsky Robertson, Susan. "MEC's next step: How the outdoor and sports retailer plans to stay in the race." *The Globe and Mail*. January 20, 2020.

[318] Ryzik, Melena. "Time's Up legal fund takes on harassment at McDonald's." *The New York Times*. May 22, 2019.

relationship with another McDonald's employee[319]. This relationship broke the firm's code of conduct. A few days later, the head of human resources, David Fairhurst, also left McDonald's.

These departures are consistent with what some feel is a broken culture at the food service giant. The American Civil Liberties Union and Fight for $15 (US) have accused McDonald's of allowing workplace harassment[320]. The groups have cited situations where McDonald's supervisors and management have engaged in groping and inappropriate comments. When workers speak up, the groups claim, they face retaliation. U.S. Democratic Party leaders Elizabeth Warren and Bernie Sanders have also criticized McDonald's for not making franchisees adhere to code of conduct policies and just "encouraging them" to do so.

In November 2019, it was announced that McDonald's was served with a class-action lawsuit for sexual harassment[321]. The suit was filed by former employee Jenna Ries against McDonald's and one of its Michigan franchisees. Ries joins at least 50 other employees or former employees who have filed suit against the burger giant since 2016. The U.S. Equal Employment Opportunity Commission has received the complaints.

SUPPLIERS

23) Brands Selling Direct – Bringing on the Mart Ache

One of the biggest trends in retail is the frequency to which branded manufacturers are selling direct to consumers.

Whether through their own websites, pop-up stores or permanent locations, brands have crossed into the traditional forbidden zone at the anger and confusion

---

[319] "Second McDonald's executive out after CEO fired." *The Associated Press*. November 5, 2019.

[320] Patton, Leslie and Eidelson, Josh. "C-suite exits show perils of stumbling in #MeToo era." *Bloomberg*. November 5, 2019.

[321] Durbin, Dee-Ann. "Class action addresses sex harassment at McDonald's." *The Associated Press*. November 13, 2019.

of select retail partners. Why are brands doing this and why will it continue to grow? It's a combination of hedging bets and not being held hostage to volatile retailers coupled with the opportunity to connect directly with end consumers and make more money by cutting out the middleman.

New Skid in Town

With the undercurrent of retailer winners and losers, it makes for a tough time to pick and stay with legacy channel partners who are often pounding vendors for lower net costs. With the advent and proliferation of e-commerce and social media, brands have the opportunity to chart their own course and obtain data about core customers. This data enables them to find new ways of building brand equity through direct relationships with customers. Selling direct to consumer, if executed in a cost-effective manner, can offer a brand greater profits. They hold retail price and pocket the gross margin their retail partner would normally make. This trend will continue as traditional retailer and supplier lines blur. The luxury industry was one of the first industries to see this trend.

I read an interesting op-ed from Jane Lee, co-founder of Launch Pop, who discusses the direct-to-consumer (DTC) movement[322]. The article addresses how big CPG companies have been negatively impacted by DTC brands by $40 billion over four years. DTC firms such as Away and Glossier are becoming household names — in part because they have garnered the trust of younger shoppers who feel these indie brands are more authentic and care about people and planet. This is really, really hard for big companies to replicate, although some have tried and failed. Many have resorted to buying DTC brands as they rise up. P & G bought DTC brand Native while RXBAR was acquired by Kellogg. Even the venture capital industry has taken notice and has started funneling start-up cash to DTC brands. However, DTC brands are not guaranteed successes. Some companies can't make money as scale economies elude them. Some have started selling large retailers to get volume and to grow their brand. Like any change in retail, it will take time to perfect the business model.

Let's look at Canada Goose as a case study in DTC excellence.

Canada Goose

Canada Goose has been magnificently successful based on a dual value proposition of technical superiority and premium luxury fashion. A rare combination.

---

[322] Lee, Jane. "Direct-to-consumer brands are becoming massive, but Canada is falling behind." *The Globe and Mail.* April 29, 2019.

Once a wholesaler to high-end sporting goods and department stores, Canada Goose's direct-to-consumer strategy has taken flight as the firm announced in April 2019 that it was opening six new stores in a variety of markets[323]. The new stores are in Milan (Via della Spiga), Paris (Rue St. Honoré), Minneapolis (Mall of America), Toronto (CF Sherway Gardens), Edmonton (West Edmonton Mall) and Banff (Alberta). This is on top of its existing 11 stores. The firm has also opened its own stores in Hong Kong and Shanghai.

The company has taken experiential retailing seriously with frigid rooms in some stores where consumers can try on a Canada Goose coat in -25 C weather[324]. This simulation lets the brand put its money where its mouth is so to speak and prove its actual warming capabilities. I toured this store and offer more comments later in the book.

A significant portion of Canada Goose's growth has come from DTC. It has also enjoyed significant margin growth and has successfully migrated from solid supplier to retail to power brand in its own right. All while growing sales and profits double-digit per annum.

24) Big Food Brands for Sale - Musical Chairs

Once-great CPG companies are dismantling brands and selling them off so they can reinvent their businesses.

As discussed previously, take the recent sale of the Keebler brand by Kellogg to Ferrero for $1.3 billion US[325]. Kellogg jettisoned its cookie and fruit snack brands to focus on core brands like cereal. Steve Cahillane, the CEO of Kellogg, was quoted as saying that the sale "will lead to reduced complexity, more targeted investment and better growth."

Kellogg is not alone.

---

[323] "Canada Goose targets European fashion centres." *The Canadian Press*. April 10, 2019.

[324] Rastello, Sandrine. "Canada Goose adding freezers to some stores." *Bloomberg*. November 20, 2018.

[325] Sutherland, Jeff and Shanker, Deena. "Kellogg sells Keebler brand, snacks to Ferrero for $1.3 billion." *Bloomberg*. April 2, 2019.

General Mills and Campbell Soup both said they are looking to sell part of their brands. Nestlé has also been busy rightsizing its portfolio as it sold its U.S. candy business to Ferrero. Campbell recently announced it was selling its Yellow and Kettle brand potato chip business in Europe for $80 million US[326].

25) Discount Dictatorship

One of the biggest grocers in Canada is Empire, which sells under several banners including Sobeys, FreshCo, Farm Boy and more. In the spring of 2019, Empire advised suppliers via a letter that some vendors would automatically be paid in 60 or 90 days — in some cases double Empire's current payment period[327]. Other suppliers were advised they would be paid earlier but that they would need to increase cash discounts[328]. The new policy was to take effect the next day!

The vendor base snapped and the media wrote about it. Mike Medline, Empire's president, deferred the implementation by two months to give suppliers time to adjust.

About one year earlier, Canada's largest grocer, Loblaw, did something similar by advising vendors that they would be charged .79 percent for supply chain costs. No discussion. No negotiation. No choice.

MANAGEMENT

26) Executive Behaviour: Braking Bad

Retail executives have earned a bad reputation. Their actions often impact front-line workers and garner a lot of media attention when employees are laid off. But

---

[326] "Campbell to sell Europe potato chips business for $80M." *Bloomberg*. September 3, 2019.

[327] Strauss, Marina. "Sobeys to delay changes to supplier payment terms by two months." *The Globe and Mail*. April 6, 2019.

[328] Strauss, Marina. "Suppliers, Sobeys at odds after grocer overhauls payment terms." *The Globe and Mail*. April 3, 2019.

there is more to it than that. Retail and brand executives continue to get caught making poor moral decisions in favour of financial gain. Society has taken notice, too.

Wall Street Weasels

In her Toronto Star article, Jennifer Wells refers to a story by Susan Faludi, a reporter at the Wall Street Journal. It was 25 years ago that Faludi wrote the story about the moral implications of business decisions by executives on everyday employees. Faludi's investigation told the story of one worker, James White, who took his own life after he was fired from Safeway in 1987. Mr. White lost his job after Safeway was bought through a leveraged buyout (LBO) by Kohlberg, Kravis and Roberts (KKR). A trucker for Safeway for 30 years, he was one of the 60 percent of 63,000 former employees who could not find full-time work a year after losing their jobs. A recipient of the Pulitzer Prize, Faludi said the following during her acceptance speech: "I think any story that sort of forces business executives to look at the moral consequences of their decisions is important."

Moral Compass Defect

Wells goes on to discuss the 2018 closing of all US Toys "R" Us stores and termination of 33,000 workers. At first there was no severance made available to these workers. Rise Up Retail, which fights for retail worker rights, stated: "We call on Congress to take bold policy action to regulate Wall Street to stop them from killing jobs and hurting our families. Predatory Wall Street firms pushed hundreds of thousands of retail workers from their jobs when they bankrupted employers like Sports Authority, Payless, Gymboree, and now Toys 'R' Us."

Only after tremendous pressure from Rise Up Retail and Senator Bernie Sanders did two of the original three private equity firms put up $10 million US each. Although this was an unprecedented gesture from these two firms, it fell far short of resembling any reasonable severance package[329].

Buyback Bullsh*t

In an article by Geoff Zochodne from The Financial Post, he talks about the

---

[329] Wells, Jennifer. "For jobless Toys 'R' Us workers, $20 million is nowhere near enough". November 20, 2018. Retrieved from:
https://www.thestar.com/business/opinion/2018/11/20/for-jobless-toys-r-us-workers-20-million-is-nowhere-near-enough.html

proliferation of corporate stock buybacks[330]. In the piece, he quotes University of Toronto's Dan Breznitz who says: "The implicit moral hazard in allowing management to do that to a degree of billions of dollars a year is something that makes me sleep less at night. If you really don't have anything to do, pay dividends."

Zochodne also quotes William Lazonick's 2014 Harvard Business Review article that proclaims that "Buybacks are 'effectively stock-price manipulation.'"

Three White Stripes

Sometimes there are disconnects between brand positioning and company culture. Take the case of Adidas. In an article written by Julie Creswell and Kevin Draper from the New York Times, they discuss the culture of Adidas from the point of view of several African Americans[331]. Adidas made billions by selling to blacks and by paying black athletes and celebrities to endorse its shoes. Yet, according to the article, the same firm marginalizes blacks who work at its Portland head office. Through interviews with 20 current or former employees, Creswell and Draper learned of how blacks were subtly told to sit together at lunch, had ideas and feedback quashed at meetings and faced racist slurs.

Dollars and Sense?

Walmart recently eliminated the popular store "greeter" role in 1,000 stores in favour of a new, more holistic "customer host" role. This new, revised position involves performing a number of expanded duties including keeping the front of the store clean, checking receipts to minimize shoplifting and, of course, welcoming customers. The only problem is that many current store greeters are disabled and are not physically capable of performing these new duties. So guess what? They were to be let go. Customers and employees started petitions and Facebook groups to try to help these vulnerable employees. Greg Foran, the boss of Walmart U.S. stores at the time, stepped in and instructed stores to use every effort to try to find these folks another job.

After Sales Disservice

An article by Jackie Crosby from the Star Tribune discusses a recent finding from researchers at the University of Minnesota. The research team concluded that some

---

[330] Zochodne, Geoff. " 'The American Disease.'" *The Financial Post*. August 24, 2019.

[331] Creswell, Julie and Draper, Kevin. "Adidas trades on Black style, but workers feel marginalized." *The New York Times*. June 22, 2019.

firms make it incredibly difficult for customers to complain on purpose. These companies create barriers so that customers give up, thus saving on refunds or replacement parts[332].

Self-Awareness

In a recent op-ed, Prana CEO Thierry Jean discusses his time spent at big food. He describes how both the industry and society have faced problems due to business putting shareholders ahead of people and planet[333]. These problems include food waste and shortage, the use of pesticides and the increase in pollution. According to Jean, food companies and in fact all companies have a responsibility to manage to a triple bottom line: people, planet and profits.

Retribution

Corruption at the top is certainly nothing new. What is new is that boards are acting on it like never before. In part due to social pressure.

Jena McGregor wrote a piece for the Washington Post that had a rather interesting headline: "More CEOs forced out for ethical lapses than poor returns." McGregor references a Strategy and PWC report that shows that in 2018, of the 89 CEOs who got fired, 39 percent were dismissed after a "scandal or improper conduct" while 35 percent were fired due to poor financial results. Finally, 13 percent were let go due to board conflicts. This is in stark contrast to 2008 when the numbers were: 52 percent fired for financial targets not being met, 35 percent fired due to board conflicts and a mere 10 percent fired due to CEOs behaving badly.

The study points out that CEO turnover reached a new high in 2018 with 18 percent of the top 2,500 biggest global firms making a change.

Radio Free Europe

The media, too, can encourage companies to grow a conscience.

In August 2019, Apple announced it was halting its practice of keeping recordings of customer conversations with Siri[334]. It also said it would allow only Apple

---

[332] Crosby, Jackie. "Your call is (not actually) important to us." *The Star Tribune (Minneapolis)*. January 7, 2020.

[333] Jean, Thierry. "How to fix a broken food system." *The Globe and Mail*. July 24, 2018.

[334] Nellis, Stephen. "Apple to halt practice of keeping Siri recordings." *Reuters*. August 29,

employees, not contractors, to listen to the recordings. This came after the Guardian newspaper ran an article exposing the process.

27) Out of Touch and Insensitive: Retail Rudeness

We have seen more and more brands making stupid, insensitive gaffs that pi*s off society.

<u>Product Equality</u>

Adidas was heavily criticized for its almost entirely white running shoe that was supposed to be part of a celebration of Black History Month. Gucci sold a black sweater with a balaclava attached that, when worn in full, showed a pair of red lips[335]. Other brands that have made similar stupid mistakes include Dolce & Gabbana, Prada, Zara and H&M. These brands have alienated millions of customers through their thoughtless product and marketing decisions.

Nike dropped the ball in 2019 when it launched and then stopped selling a controversial shoe. The giant decided to cancel the Air Max 1 Quick Strike Fourth of July shoe because it featured the 13-star Betsy Ross flag[336]. The flag has sometimes been associated with racism and alt-right groups.

<u>Sleep Country</u>

Boston-based Wayfair felt the wrath of ignoring employee ethics in June of 2019[337]. The firm was filling an order to provide beds to asylum-seekers in detainment camps near the U.S. Mexican border. Employees took exception to Wayfair profiting off this. The employee group gathered 500 signatures and sent a letter to management demanding Wayfair donate the profit to a not-for-profit agency

---

2019.

[335] Sylvers, Eric and Kapner, Suzanne. "Gucci's social-media status fell. So did North American sales." *The Wall Street Journal*. September 17, 2019.

[336] Garcia, Sandra E. and Chokshi, Niraj. "Nike drops 'Betsy Ross flag' sneaker after Kaepernick criticizes it." *The New York Times*. July 3, 2019.

[337] Criscitello, Sammy and Wu, Janet and Holman, Jordyn. "Wayfair workers protest border camps." *Bloomberg*. June 27, 2019.

offering legal services to the detainees. Management first refused but later rescinded after employees walked off the job in protest and the media carried the story for a week. The firm ended up donating the profits from the order — about $100,000 US to the American Red Cross.

28) Gangsters Pair a Dice

Beyond exhibiting poor moral judgment, executives do things that are illegal, too. This not only destroys brands but also makes retailers and suppliers subject to significant fines.

Rotten Wood

Take the case of Lumber Liquidators. In March of 2019, the company agreed to pay a $33 million US penalty for misleading investors regarding buying and selling formaldehyde-laced flooring made in China[338]. This fiasco came to light from a *60 Minutes* show that ratted them out. This fine is on top of the $36 million US it agreed to pay about 760,000 consumers who bought the contaminated flooring. This is not the first brush with the law the company has faced. In 2016, it paid $23 million US in penalties and fines for selling product made from wood from Russian endangered tigers' sanctuaries.

One Bad Apple

In a recent piece in the Washington Post, the U.S. SEC filed a lawsuit against former Apple legal eagle Gene Levoff. The SEC alleges that Mr. Levoff was guilty of insider trading in 2015 and 2016. Levoff was the senior director of corporate law and the corporate secretary at the time. He reportedly sold $10 million US worth of Apple stock before information was made public regarding an iPhone sales miss.

Stinky Cheese

Consumer packaged goods giant Kraft Heinz recently had to restate financials after an investigation by the U.S. SEC. Apparently, the procurement division did some irregular things from an accounting standpoint. People lost their jobs but the firm was quick to point out that senior management was not involved in this situation.

---

[338] Weiner, Rachel. "Lumber Liquidators fined for misleading investors." *The Washington Post*. March 13, 2019.

Jerks & Jackas*es

In Lisa Girion and Chris Kirkman's investigative report in Reuters, they expose Johnson & Johnson's efforts to deceive consumers. They found that J & J made efforts "to continue to push baby powder even as concerns mounted over the health effects of talc." The article goes on to proclaim that "Johnson & Johnson targeted minority and overweight women" with its product. J & J knew for tens of years that its baby powder contained a small amount of asbestos.

29) CEO Compensation: Fatter Stacks

CEO compensation has grown out of control and society is starting to notice.

Bay Bucks

Marina Strauss writes about how HBC faced significant criticism over its CEO Helena Foulkes' $29.4 million compensation package. The irony about the pay package is that HBC shares had dropped 35 percent under her watch as of June 2019. Nothing against Ms Foulkes. I think she had done a nice job trimming unneeded brands and selling off assets to pay down debt. I think HBC has a greater chance of success based on her work. Having said that, does it make sense for a firm's boss to make so much money while the company is suffering? HBC argues that they need to pay more to get an "all-star" executive. Governance and proxy experts aren't so convinced. York University associate professor Richard Leblanc was quoted as saying: "Shareholders can be forgiving for executive pay if they also benefit. This is not the case here… Is this good pay governance? Probably not."

Proxy advisor Glass Lewis & Co. also commented with: "A properly structured pay program should motivate executives to drive corporate performance, thus aligning executive and long-term shareholder interests. In this case the company has not implemented such a program."

Foulkes would go on to leave HBC in March, 2020.

Lion King

Another big-name CEO whose pay has come under fire is Disney's Robert Iger. And Abigail Disney, Walt's granddaughter, is the one doing the criticizing. Iger made a cool $65 million US in 2018. Research firm Equilar Inc. said that Iger's compensation represents about 1,400 times the median Disney worker. Ms Disney was quoted as saying: "I like Bob Iger. I do not speak for my family but only for myself. But by any objective measure a pay ratio over a thousand is insane."

The world listened. The company recently lowered Iger's target compensation twice in 2019, most recently by some 28 percent[339]. Iger would go on to leave Disney in early 2020.

30) A New Hope: The Empathetic Executive

In an article by Joe O'Connor from the Financial Post titled "Farewell to the alpha boss," he describes the story of Jeff Davis[340]. Davis won the prestigious Counsel of the Year award in Toronto in June of 2019 for his work as top lawyer at the Ontario Teachers' Pension Plan, a $190 billion Cdn pension fund.

The win is not the story, though. The story is that during his acceptance speech, he thanked his family and friends for helping him through depression. With 600 of his peers and colleagues listening, he showed vulnerability — the very thing traditional corporate leaders are taught never to do.

But Davis is not a traditional leader. He is perhaps the new type of modern-day boss who is human and offers compassion to employees and team members in an industry known for cold, hard numbers — all while succeeding in the highest way possible in his industry.

INVESTORS

The retail industry suffered in the past with the great dot-com bubble of 2000. Numerous online players had tremendously high valuations with little in the way of assets or profits.

Since then, the industry has been dominated by technology companies such as Amazon, Apple, Shopify and others. Amazon has had the benefit of an enormous valuation despite intermittent profitability as it invests further in infrastructure. The department store sector has been hammered by investors as this channel loses relevance and seeks shelter through privatization.

---

[339] Melin, Anders and Zhou, Jenn and Palmeri, Christopher. "Disney cuts CEO's future pay by millions." *Bloomberg*. March 5, 2019.

[340] O'Connor, Joe. "Farewell to the alpha boss." *The Financial Post*. June 22, 2019.

Retailers and other brands have felt significant pressure from activist investors while some companies adjacent to the industry have used less-than-traditional accounting practices to try to show a path to profitability. IPOs are not what they used to be, as investors are weary of lofty, would-be valuations with no earnings in sight.

31) E-commerce Profitability: Loss Leader

The reality with much of retail is that firms are hiding their online losses. We are in transition. Legacy brick and mortar retailers need to operate two businesses at the same time. Everything built and developed over that last 100 years has been designed for sales at physical retail stores. Over the last decade or two, retailers have had to migrate toward a different business model: online selling. For many retailers, the economics of online shopping don't work yet. Low volume coupled with high overhead costs result in losses. Not a pleasant sight for investors.

Sell Online. Lose Money

Take the case of Walmart. In a recent article published by Lauren Thomas at CNBC, she discusses how the giant was expected to lose $1 billion US in 2019 in its online division[341]. This has caused significant friction within Walmart. There are reports of Walmart jettisoning digitally-native brands such as ModCloth.

32) Stock Prices: Games People Play

Helium Stock

Amazon truly is the envy of every other CEO. Why? Because it can reinvest much of what it makes into infrastructure and its share price continues to soar beyond belief.

---

[341] Thomas, Lauren. "Walmart's e-commerce biz is reportedly racking up $1 billion in losses and that's only one problem it has." July 3, 2019. Retrieved from: https://www.cnbc.com/2019/07/03/walmarts-e-commerce-business-on-track-to-lose-over-1-billion.html

Most other companies have to show steady profit growth every quarter or their stock tanks as investors punish them. Those rules don't apply to Amazon. Every now and then Amazon throws investors a bone by declaring a profit. An example of this is in Q1, 2019 when it doubled net income and blew away investor expectations[342]. Then it forecasted Q2, 2019 earnings at $3.6 billion US, down from analysts' forecasts of $4.2 billion US. Either way, the share price remains high.

California Dreaming

Sometimes management plays around with numbers to look better than it really is. Switching verticals for a moment, one needs look no further than Uber and WeWork[343].

Anxious to look sweet to investors for a big fat IPO, Uber came up with "core platform contribution profit" which ignores select expenses. Based on this measure, Uber would have made about $940 million US in 2018. In reality, with generally-accepted accounting principles (GAAP), the firm lost a staggering $3 billion US! WeWork uses something called "community-adjusted EBITDA." WTF? Under this new metric, the firm would have made about $470 million US versus its loss of some $1.9 billion US in reality. Feels a little like the dot-com bubble. As Yogi Berra used to say, "It's déjà vu all over again."

Big Apple

Apple recently made headlines and stirred some controversy when it signalled it was looking to buy back about $75 billion US of its stock[344]. In 2018, Apple, along with a number of firms, repatriated earnings from offshore subsidiaries to the tune of over $200 billion US. (It was sitting on $252 billion US!) It went on to use about $100 billion US to buy back its own stock. It looks to use another $75 billion US to do more of the same.

Between the recent U.S. tax cuts and the cash grab offshore, Apple has been

---

[342] Dastin, Jeffrey and Panchadar, Arjun. "Amazon's profit soars, but earnings forecast is flat." *Reuters*. April 26, 2019.

[343] Winkler, Rolfe. "Uber, Lyft get creative with numbers, but investors aren't blind." *The Wall Street Journal*. May 15, 2019.

[344] Nicas, Jack. "Apple plan to buy $75B of its stock fuels debate." *The New York Times*. May 2, 2019.

criticized for using the windfall to benefit shareholders versus other stakeholders such as employees. The thinking behind the criticism is that some of these gains should be used to increase wages or build new factories to employ Americans.

Proponents of share buybacks say that flowing the money to investors is the right thing to do. The firm does not have a better use for it at the moment, they say, and this trickle down to investors will benefit the economy through spending and other investments.

33) Adjusted Earnings – Smoked & Mirrored

One problem in retail financial reporting is the notion of adjusted earnings. Too many retail companies, vendors and service providers have used the crutch of focusing on adjusted earnings to mislead investors.

Adjusted earnings involves a company reporting real earnings via GAAP (generally accepted accounting principles), then reporting adjusted earnings based on company-specific adjustments. When you read about a firm's performance in the media, the focus is often on adjusted earnings.

These adjustments can include the omission of one-time expenses or write-downs year over year. They may also exclude mergers and acquisitions or divestitures. They may also account for currency fluctuations. One might argue that this is preferred as it normalizes results and focuses on the true run rate of a company.

I argue that it is not preferred, as it defeats the purpose of holding all firms to the same standards. That is what GAAP is for. So investors can accurately compare one company to another and track a company over many quarters and years consistently. I think this is not appropriate and we lose credibility as an industry by focusing too much on adjusted earnings.

I know that both GAAP and adjusted earnings can be helpful, but I think they can be deceptive. For less-sophisticated investors, these results may appear misleading and optimistic, which can influence stock price and valuation.

In a recent op-ed by David Rosenberg in the Globe and Mail, he discusses how public companies are deceiving investors with earnings reports[345]. Rosenberg talks

---

[345] Rosenberg, David. "The deception of corporate earnings." *The Globe and Mail.* February 6, 2020.

about the current trend of firms to hide "bad stuff" through alternate GAAP accounting methods. He cites the current 15 percent difference between what S&P 500 companies are reporting versus GAAP. This difference represents $200 billion US, according to his estimates.

34) IPOs – What a Fool Be-Leaves

Firms of all sorts, including retailers and service providers, have come to realize that investors have become more skeptical of IPOs and shiny objects that profess to disrupt the world.

Panda-monium

Take Chinese newbie Luckin Coffee. Luckin's IPO was much anticipated, but investors soon went sour on the profitability of the firm[346]. Its stock increased 53 percent on the first day of trading only to plummet 43 percent once investors sobered up. Investors learned that the company was pulling an Amazon and was looking to reinvest profits into growth domestically. Add into the mix a U.S-China trade war and shares cooled quickly.

Sucker Punch

It appears Silicon Valley has matured. In an article by Rob Copeland from the Wall Street Journal, he discusses how Silicon Valley venture capital has gotten smarter and is less apt to sign blank checks to start-ups without proven results[347]. Copeland cites some of the recent start-up flops including messaging company Hustle, meal kit service Munchery and Ford Motor company's ride-sharing service Chariot.

To quote Josh Wolfe of Lux Capital, the industry has changed from "fear of missing out" to "fear of being suckered." Venture capital has grown tired of funding great ideas with huge start-up burn rates — often the result of lavish amenities and high-priced talent without sales to justify their existence.

---

[346] "Starbucks rival burns investors as stock sinks 43%." *Bloomberg*. May 24, 2019.

[347] Copeland, Rob. "Silicon Valley's optimism turns to 'shame of being suckered.'" *The Wall Street Journal*. January 23, 2019.

Posh Platform

In a recent article about Shopify, David Berman and David Milstead make the argument that the Ottawa-based technology darling is significantly overvalued[348]. The duo goes on to highlight how, as of November 2019, Shopify had a price-to-sales ratio of 22.3 times. The average of the same ratio on the S&P/TSX, Toronto's main stock market, was three!

What stood out was the number of unique revenue streams that Shopify currently enjoys: commission on merchant sales, monthly subscription fees to use its software, point of sale hardware fees, shipping fees, Shopify capital fees, fulfillment network fees, payment fees, referral fees and others.

Shopify has become a one-stop shop for someone starting an online business. Like many tech firms, it rarely makes money. Although I would agree that the firm is overvalued at the moment, I *do* think the firm has some great runway ahead as an alternative to Amazon.

35) Activist Investors: Game of Bones

Activist investors are the new corporate power players, wielding significant influence over boards and management teams.

Honky Tonk Linen

Take the continuing saga of Bed Bath & Beyond. Activist investors pushed the firm to put in five new independent directors and shake up the board. Two of the ousted directors included Bed Bath & Beyond co-founders Leonard Feinstein and Warren Eisenberg[349]. The activist investors were still not happy. They wanted the CEO out and thought the new board members did not have enough retail chops to turn the retailer around. The firm of course disagreed.

Hedge funds flex their muscles too. Just look at L Brands, former home of Victoria's Secret and current owner of Bath & Body Works. In March of 2019,

---

[348] Berman, David and Milstead, David. "Shopify: How high can Canada's latest tech darling fly?" *The Globe and Mail*. November 9, 2019.

[349] "Bed Bath & Beyond co-founders step down amid investor pressure." *Reuters*. April 23, 2019.

Barington Capital called for the two chains to be spun off from each other[350]. The hedge fund also told the retailer to get rid of any board member who had been around for 30 years or more.

36) Hail Mary: Department Store Privatization

As stock markets punish department store stocks, some seek the shelter of privatization. This enables struggling or undervalued retailers to repair performance without the scrutiny of public investors.

<u>Swedish Street Ball</u>

The Nordstrom family is looking to take the retailer private according to the Wall Street Journal[351]. With its shares down, the family is supposedly looking to increase its stake from about one-third to over half. A recent rift between independent directors and the family has been aired publicly.

In 2017, the family offered $50 per share to take the firm private, a 25 percent premium at the time. But the offer was rejected by the board's special committee. The Nordstrom family had a tough time raising the money needed, as lenders wanted a significant premium to cover risk.

Nordstrom, generally regarded as one of the best department stores in a challenged sector, opened its first Manhattan store in the fall of 2019. It is also launching a new format called Nordstrom Local, which will have a significantly-reduced assortment. It has also been fairly aggressive in acquisitions, buying subscription-based Trunk Club and flash sale retailer HauteLook.

<u>HBC – Private Dining Room</u>

In June of 2019, HBC's majority shareholders launched a bid to take the company private. Richard Baker and his fellow investors, who own 57 percent of the company, offered the balance of public shareholders about $1 billion Cdn or $9.45

---

[350] Lombardo, Cara. "L Brands urged to split Victoria's Secret, Bath & Body Works." *The Wall Street Journal*. March 6, 2019.

[351] Lombardo, Cara and Benoit, David. "Nordstrom family prepares proposal to increase stake in retailer." *The Wall Street Journal*. August 1, 2019.

per share[352]. This represented a 40 percent premium when the privatization bid was launched. There was much debate among pundits as to Baker's intentions with the company. Would he invest in the business and fix it or would he break it up and sell it? What would happen to North America's oldest company?

Oh Sh*t

Something came back to haunt HBC that could have derailed the bid. At a conference in September 2018, CEO Helena Foulkes, allegedly said the firm was worth about $28 per share based on its real estate.

Talk to the Hand

Independent directors on the HBC board said the original offer was "inadequate." Land & Buildings, a New York-based activist investor, said that the offer by Baker was "woefully inadequate" or "dead on arrival."

In July 2019, the HBC special committee charged with reviewing the June offer invited minority shareholders to comment on it and offer potential alternatives[353].

Sticks & Stones

In early August 2019, Land & Buildings publicly called for the resignation of HBC chairman Richard Baker if his privatization bid failed[354].

In late August 2019, Catalyst Capital bought 10 percent of HBC's public shares. It acquired almost 18,500,000 shares at a total cost of about $187 million Cdn[355].

In October 2019, HBC announced its board of directors had approved a sweetened deal from Baker's group to take the company private at $10.30 per

---

[352] Willis, Andrew. "Expect Richard Baker to raise his HBC bid." *The Globe and Mail.* August 20, 2019.

[353] Jones, Jeffrey. "HBC committee invites shareholders to discuss privatization bid, alternatives." *The Globe and Mail.* July 26, 2019.

[354] Younglai, Rachelle. "Hedge fund calls for ouster of HBC's Baker if privatization bid fails." *The Globe and Mail.* August 9, 2019.

[355] Sagan, Aleksandra. "Catalyst Capital buys nearly 18.5M HBC shares." *The Canadian Press.* August 20, 2019.

share[356]. The proposal would still need the majority of minority shareholders to accept the bid, which was $100 million US higher than the previous offer. The latest offer valued the firm at $2.6 billion US.

Pure as New York Snow

HBC hired outside companies to value its real estate. Baker's group highlighted volatility in retail real estate. He also outlined how the latest offer enabled minority investors to cash out at a premium versus the pre-takeover share price.

In November 2019, HBC released an appraisal from the CBRE Group that estimated its real estate to be worth $8.75 per share. This was in stark contrast to the 2017 valuation of $35.24 per share. HBC said this drop was a function of previous asset sales as well as a steep decline in its Saks Fifth Avenue flagship store. The report indicated that the flagship had a best-use value of $2.1 billion. This represented a $2.7 billion drop from the property's value in 2014 based on an independent analysis. CBRE highlighted the building's heritage status as well as a decrease in rent on Fifth Avenue in New York as rationale for the drop[357].

Catalyst for Change

Catalyst increased its holdings in HBC to 17.5 percent and began discussion for financing its own bid for the firm. Minority shareholders were scheduled to vote on Baker's bid during a December 17 meeting. Baker's group indicated that its current June bid was its highest and final offer for the company. Dissident investor Sandpiper Group indicated it did not support Baker's June offer. In a statement, the group said:

"Richard Baker's real estate monetization and value optimization strategy that he is now pursuing for his and his supporters' benefit should be executed upon under his and the board's leadership for the benefit of all owners of HBC.[358]"

---

[356] Willis, Andrew and Younglai, Rachelle. "HBC board accepts sweetened takeover bid from Baker." *The Globe and Mail*. October 22, 2019.

[357] Edmiston, Jake. "How much is Saks flagship worth?" *The Financial Post*. November 21, 2019.

[358] Jones, Jeffrey and Younglai, Rachelle. "HBC's sinking shares spell doom for Baker's privatization bid." *The Globe and Mail*. November 26, 2019.

In late November, Catalyst Capital announced a rival bid for HBC of $11 per share — higher than what Baker's group was offering in October. The Baker group dismissed Catalyst's offer, citing that it was not interested in selling the retailer to another investment group. The two firms traded comments in the media[359].

Hey, not Fair!

In early December, a special committee at HBC formally rejected the Catalyst bid. Catalyst filed for a hearing with the Ontario Securities Commission (OSC). Catalyst wanted to block the Baker bid and postpone the December 17 shareholder meeting[360]. The OSC agreed to hear the complaint on December 5.

Knight to Remember?

Ortelius Advisors, a New York minority investor in HBC, filed a lawsuit against the retailer. The firm owned .5 percent of HBC and looked to block the Baker deal and be reimbursed for damages. Peter DeSorcy, a managing member of Ortelius, was quoted as saying:

"[Baker's] interests were no longer aligned with minority investors in maximizing shareholder value, but in minimizing the purchase price for the continuing shareholders.[361]"

Ortelius cited the virtually-simultaneous announcement by HBC in June that it had sold off its European division for $1.5 million US and that majority shareholders were making an offer to take the firm private. Ortelius claimed that HBC's share price would have doubled with the news of the first announcement alone. The subsequent announcement limited the upside on the share price and investors suffered as a result.

Torn Between Two Rudders

In December, influential shareholder proxy advisory firm Institutional Shareholder Services (ISS) issued a report that called for minority shareholders to

---

[359] Edmiston, Jake. "Battle for The Bay heats up." *The Financial Post*. November 28, 2019.

[360] Rastello, Sandrine and Deveau, Scott. "HBC rejects Catalyst Capital's $2B bid." *The Toronto Star*. December 4, 2019.

[361] Deveau, Scott. "New York investor files suit against Hudson's Bay, chairman." *The Financial Post*. December 7, 2019.

reject the Baker bid. HBC's independent directors countered the report, indicating it was based on assumptions that were no longer valid[362]. Glass, Lewis & Co., another prominent proxy advisory firm, endorsed the latest Baker bid and encouraged minority shareholders to accept it[363].

Law & Order

In late December, the OSC hearing took place. The regulator indicated that the Baker group must update its circular on its proposed deal to minority shareholders and that the December 17 vote would need to be postponed until 2020. The new circular must include any new information uncovered since the original version, including OSC hearings on the role of the special committee in evaluating offers[364].

The Forgiven

In January 2020, it was announced that the Baker group and Catalyst had reached an agreement that Baker would increase his offer to match Catalyst's $11-per-share bid.

Take the Money and Run

At a shareholder meeting in February 2020, HBC minority shareholders approved the takeover offer of $11 per share. HBC stopped trading publicly at the end of the day Wednesday, March 4, 2020.

The Departed

In March of 2020, HBC announced CEO Helena Foulkes would be leaving the retailer after two years and Richard Baker would be taking over in the top job[365].

HBC was getting ready to celebrate its 350th anniversary in May, 2020.

---

[362] Jones, Jeffrey. "HBC directors say report against Baker-led bid is 'flawed.'" *The Globe and Mail*. December 10, 2019.

[363] "Competing HBC bids win key support." *Bloomberg*. December 12, 2019.

[364] Edmiston, Jake. "Shareholders need to know more about HBC bids, OSC says." *The Financial Post*. December 20, 2019.

[365] "HBC Chairman Baker replacing Foulkes as CEO." *The Canadian Press*. March 4, 2020.

RETAILERS

Retailers represent the moment of truth for the consumer. The place where it all happens. The magic. The rest of the industry plays a support role for the retailer — financing, manufacturing, supply chain, marketing and more. But retailing is a hard business. Margins can be low. Operational costs can be high. Sales are unpredictable. Not for the faint of heart.

On top of the brutal economics of being a retailer, you have to deal with change. Even if you become a successful retailer, you can't stand still. Everything is changing around you. There is a temptation to remain the same. Don't fix what ain't broke. But this is a recipe for failure. Retailers adapt. It's what they do. It's what they were born to do. And adapt they have, unlike any other recent time.

This section discusses the many trends that are happening from a retailer's perspective. I also highlight specific retailer formats in the market and how they address these trends.

37) The Growth of E-commerce – Back to Life

The biggest trend to impact retail over the last decade or two is the re-emergence of e-commerce. After the dot.com bubble burst in 2000, online shopping all but died. Since then, slowly but surely, it has grown to become significant again and has staying power this time.

In a recent article by Nicholas Sokic in the Financial Post, he talks about how the retail e-commerce market will hit $4.9 trillion US in 2021, up from $2.8 trillion US in 2018[366].

Reuters published an article in late January 2020 that showed U.S. shoppers spent more using e-commerce during holiday 2019 than in-store[367]. This could have been in part due to a shortened selling season that included six fewer shopping days.

For all of 2019, U.S. online sales represented 14.6 percent of total retail sales

---

[366] Sokic, Nicholas. "Instability? What instability?" *The Financial Post*. September 3, 2019.

[367] Balu, Nivedita. "Record online sales give short holiday shopping season a boost: report." *Reuters*. January 26, 2020.

and rose 18.8 percent year over year.

Some Kind Of Mag-click

E-commerce has grown in part due to lower pricing. But how can online retailers sell products for less than brick and mortar stores? The economics can be attractive if an e-tailer avoids the cost of running numerous brick and mortar stores.

Heavy Weight

To open and run a store, you need to lease or rent a space (or make payments toward principle if you buy it), pay employees, pay insurance and pay other utilities such as electricity. You also need to hold inventory, buy equipment such as cash registers and pay for fixtures and signage.

Light Weight

Online sellers can avoid these costs, except their head office and warehouse. They may operate with lower overheads, which may allow them to sell individual items for less.

Not all Rainbows and Lollipops

Challenges for e-tailers include added fulfillment costs of pick-up and delivery and the higher cost of liberal returns. E-tailers may also pay higher product costs from suppliers if volume is low. Like any business, online pureplay needs a specific volume threshold to break even. Many have not reached that point yet and may never do so.

Side Effects

Boomerang Business

As e-commerce has grown, so have returns. In a January 2020 article published in Reuters, UPS estimated that in the United States it will see a 26-percent increase in parcels returned to retailers on January 2, 2020. This day is known annually as "National Returns Day." According to the National Retail Federation (NRF) and Appriss Retail, 10 percent of products sold in retail are returned. This represented $369 billion US in 2018. Some categories have online return rates as high as 50 percent[368].

---

[368] "U.S. holiday returns surge with booming e-commerce." *Reuters*. January 2, 2020.

One survey by BodyBlock revealed that in 2018, half of online shoppers expected to return a clothing item due to poor fit[369]. The report indicated that 30 percent of fashion items such as clothes and shoes do not represent the size communicated to customers on the label. This isn't just small boutiques. Big brands such as Adidas, the Gap and Benetton share this frustration. One can see how this can impact online returns. That's why brands employ models to try on samples in advance to minimize this issue. In addition, retailers such as H&M and Zara have launched technology to try to obtain a customer's size based on data such as weight, height and what else they have purchased.

Forced Entry

Food delivery apps are all the craze these days. But the meteoric growth in the industry has led some providers to push the envelope on restaurant relations etiquette. Take San Francisco-based DoorDash, for instance. According to an article published by Ann Hui in the Globe and Mail, DoorDash has been adding restaurants to its app without its consent[370]. DoorDash claims it has had demand in the restaurants' trading areas and that it is simply trying to facilitate the transaction. Some restaurant owners are understandably upset at its actions.

Smoke Gets in my Lies

Daniela Hernandez from the Wall Street Journal wrote an article that talked about how customers can find tools online to create illegal counterfeit vaping devices[371]. Hernandez was able to find vaping devices and packaging materials on Instagram, empty vape packaging on a third-party site on Amazon and THC-laced vape products on Facebook's Marketplace. All of these big tech firms have policies and procedures designed to limit this kind of activity, but criminals can work around them.

Box Cutter

Major cities around the world were not designed to handle the degree to which society buys things online. Take the example of New York City as described by

---

[369] "Models say brands fit poorly." *Reuters*. December 22, 2018.

[370] Hui, Ann. "Delivery without permission." *The Globe and Mail*. May 22, 2019.

[371] Hernandez, Daniela. "Sales of illicit vaping products find home online." *The Wall Street Journal*. September 23, 2019.

Matthew Haag and Winnie Hu from the New York Times[372]. The duo reports that 1.5 million parcels are being delivered to the city on a daily basis and existing roads, sidewalks, bridges and tunnels have become even more congested.

38) Omnichannel Mania — I Like It Like That

With online shopping came a new concept called omnichannel retailing. Omnichannel, or all-channel, retailing became a buzzword in retail as online shopping hit its tipping point and became a table stake for traditional brick and mortar retailers.

Omnichannel retailing is when a retailer sells customers the way they want to be sold. That is, if you want to buy in-store, online or have a sales person come to your home, the retailer offers it your way. It also means that you obtain the product or service the way you want. Whether it be at store, delivered to your home or place of work or left at a pick-up locker. And all of the activities above are done so in a seamless, frictionless manner. In other words, it works smoothly. No hiccups, out of stocks, delays, price errors or discrepancies.

Sears the Seer

Selling the consumer across numerous channels is not new. Sears was doing it decades ago with its catalogue, phone-in orders, brick and mortar stores, hometown-dealer stores and catalogue pick-up partners. It was a pioneer.

I Can't Get No Satis-friction

What *is* new is the degree to which omnichannel has become commonplace. We have seen pure play online retailers build brick and mortar stores to allow customers to touch and feel product, connect with staff and offer community. Sometimes these shops are built more for brand experience versus actually ringing a sale through the cash register.

We have also seen virtually all brick and mortar retailers refine their own online offering to attempt to offer sales in a seamless, integrated fashion with their legacy storefronts. Both e-commerce and in-store working in harmony. As the growth in online shopping continues, some have felt it is the beginning of the end of traditional

---

[372] Haag, Matthew and Hu, Winnie. "Internet brings chaos to N.Y. streets." *The New York Times*. November 2, 2019.

brick and mortar stores. I vehemently disagree. Stores have a different role, which I talk about later in this section.

Pumping Iron

Omnichannel retailing requires significant re-engineering of processes, an infusion of capital, new teams and greater overhead. It requires a leap of faith. Retailers incur heavy costs before they see significant sales and profit contribution. In addition, online sales can result in losses as low volumes and high returns eat at gross margins. Investors and management must have patience — something in short supply, especially in public markets. Some retailers have been slow to adapt to omnichannel retailing and are seeing their businesses falter. Others have embraced this change and are thriving.

Click and Forget

One of Canada's foremost food experts, Dr. Sylvain Charlebois, wrote an op-ed in the Globe and Mail in late 2018 whereby he declares that "click and collect," or BOPIS (buy online pick up instore) as it is also known, is destined to fail in the food category[373]. He argues that as e-commerce for grocery becomes more developed, home delivery will, to some degree, replace grocery stores due to the convenience of the service and the fact that customers will pay for this convenience.

39) The Retail Hourglass – for Richer or for Poorer

As many pundits have cited, retail has become polarized. It has become polarized with growth at the low end and growth at the high end and a shrinking middle segment.

A product of income and wealth inequality, consumers have either become a lot richer or, more often than not, a lot poorer. With their changing lifestyle, we have seen the growth of Amazon, Costco, Walmart and the dollar channel. On the other end of the scale we have seen an increased presence of luxury brands not only in emerging markets such as China but in the developed world as well. Those who historically found themselves selling to the middle class have struggled and have either slid into bankruptcy, been acquired or attempted a major reinvention to pursue a more sustainable path.

---

[373] Charlebois, Sylvain. "'Click and collect' food shopping is set to fail." *The Globe and Mail*. December 27, 2018.

40) Malls – Unloveable

The role of the mall has changed radically. Online shopping has softened traffic year after year and malls have had to change to reflect society. Malls aren't dead. But like retail overall, they have changed significantly over the last 10 years.

Retail Closings

In 2019, 9,302 stores closed in the United Sates, up almost 60 percent from 2018[374]. This number does not include Forever 21. This is the largest number of closings since Coresight Research began tracking the data in 2012. Bankruptcies in the retail sector intensified in 2019 and many struggling chains cut stores.

In 2019, Payless ShoeSource announced it was closing all 2,100 stores it had in the United States. Gymboree announced it was closing its remaining 750 units. Gap announced it would close 200 Gap and Banana Republic stores over the next three years.

According to Coresight Research, other retailers to close stores in 2019 include: Shopko, Fred's, Charlotte Russe, Family Dollar, GNC, Charming Charlie, Avenue, Sears, Destination Maternity, Walgreens, the Kitchen Collection, Signet Jewelers, Rent-A-Center, Samuels Jewelers, Foot Locker, GameStop and more[375].

Polarization

Malls have polarized. Much like retailers themselves, successful malls take one of two forms — either super luxury for the wealthy or value for everyone else. Value-driven, stand-alone retail such as Walmart, Target and Costco, as well as dollar chains, have done well. Rural powercentres lack traffic. More folks reside in larger cities. Online shopping has hurt, as have demographic changes, with millennials preferring their own brands. Retailers are building more and more city stores, trying to make the economics work on smaller, urban footprints that cater to downtown

---

[374] Meyersohn, Nathaniel. "More than 9,300 stores closed in 2019." December 19, 2019. Retrieved from: https://www.cnn.com/2019/12/19/business/2019-store-closings-payless-gymboree/index.html

[375] Meyersohn, Nathaniel. "More than 9,300 stores closed in 2019." December 19, 2019. Retrieved from: https://www.cnn.com/2019/12/19/business/2019-store-closings-payless-gymboree/index.html

condominium owners or renters.

Luxury

Tier one luxury malls are doing very well. These are the malls with high-end brands and premium amenities. Many are located in dense urban areas where the affluent live and work. Luxury dining has become a focal point, as have luxury services including valet parking and personal shopping. Some of these malls have been built as mixed use.

Consider the newly-minted Hudson Yards project in New York City[376]. Malls aren't something that normally work well in New York. Unique to the city, this $2 billion US mall is the epitome of newly-formed, mixed-use plazas. Office towers, stores, museums, condominiums and restaurants have positioned this once-forgotten area as a tourist destination. At 28 acres, this entire city within a city is as bold a move as any in the belief that bricks and mortar retail is alive and well. The mall itself is 720,000 square feet and includes space for 100 stores. An important part of the value proposition for Hudson Yards is customer service. Filled with roaming, iPad-toting helpers, this mall personifies the concept of using people as the key differentiator to online shopping.

Neighbourhood Malls

The malls or plazas that catered to the middle class have struggled the most. Often located in once-flourishing suburbs, these malls have tier-three and tier-four tenants and just don't have the draw they once did. The once-great department store anchors have faded into irrelevancy. Legacy grocery stores may be keeping them afloat, but barely.

As the Kmarts and Sears continue to exit the retail world, what will come of traditional neighbourhood malls? We have already started to see mixed-use development that includes condominiums, apartments, offices, medical centres, fitness centres and more. Mall owners realize that the role of malls has changed for all of the reasons discussed previously. Demographics, online shopping, income and wealth disparity and more.

---

[376] Katz, Lily and Bhasin, Kim. "Hudson Yards spends $2 billion on new Manhattan mall." *Bloomberg*. March 9, 2019.

More Mall Challenges

Showroom Blitz

Tough retail times have created tensions between landlords and retailers. Gap recently filed suit against major mall landlord Westfield over allocation of expenses for select properties[377]. Gap joins Starbucks and Saks Fifth Avenue in recent formal disputes with landlords.

Weight Loss

Things are tough in the United Kingdom. A mall in Scotland sold for 310,000 pounds. That's about 25 percent less than the price of an average London condominium[378]. Like the United States, Canada and other markets, U.K. online shopping has hurt brick and mortar sales and malls have lost value. About 20 percent of retail sales in the U.K. are done online.

Electric Jell-O

When one looks at Tesla and its recent yo-yo thinking on retail stores, one can appreciate the continued volatility of malls[379]. Even prime malls. Tesla revolutionized the car-buying experience by skipping dealerships and opening stores in affluent malls near the Apple Store. Then, suddenly, the company decided to close its stores. A few days later, it partially reversed that decision and kept a portion of the outlets. Whiskey, Tango, Foxtrot?

Opportunities

Working Out

Co-working offices have made the jump from office buildings to retail malls[380].

---

[377] Cherney, Mike. "Gap sues Westfield over mall expenses as retail tensions rise." *The Wall Street Journal.* July 18, 2018.

[378] Sidders, Jack and De Paoli, Lucca. "Mall sells for less than condo in London." *Bloomberg.* February 6, 2019.

[379] Boudette, Neal E. "Tesla switches gears on its retail model." *The New York Times.* March 8, 2019.

[380] Strauss, Marina. "Co-working: Mall owners racing to attract more shoppers." *The Globe and Mail.* March 12, 2019.

Given the square footage that has been emptied with numerous store closings and bankruptcies, one can understand the appetite of retail landlords to try something new.

WeWork, despite its recent implosion, has been the most visible co-working company to see retail space as its next target. In 2017, HBC announced it would lease the top floors of its Toronto and Vancouver stores to WeWork, in addition to its New York Saks Fifth Avenue store.

Staples Canada launched its own co-working concept in 2019. The store offers 20 percent less merchandise and boasts value-added services such as printing, design and repair, guest speakers and a café. Staples realizes that more of its business is moving online and it doesn't need as much space. It already has stores, so why not play landlord itself and repurpose some of that space to become a destination for workers needing more flexible office space. Time will tell if this concept pays out though, as it represents a bold but risky move for the office products chain.

Bezos Buddy

Believe it or not, Amazon has transformed from foe to saviour for many mall landlords[381]. Often blamed for retailer bankruptcy, Amazon is an easy target. But landlords began to see Amazon for what it is: a growing retailer in need of a brick and mortar footprint. From expansion plans for Whole Foods, to its plans on ramping up Amazon Go stores, this horse is one to bet on. Don't forget Amazon's recent announcement to launch a grocery chain, not to mention its flirtatious pop-ups, book stores and Amazon 4-Star stores. Amazon is well financed and is in no danger of going away anytime soon.

Sterling Silver Lining

One person's garbage is another person's treasure. Take the Sterling Organization, a private equity firm. It looks for distressed malls and shopping centres in need of tender love and care. With some investment and upgrades, Sterling drives handsome returns in an otherwise battered industry[382]. With target returns in the mid to upper teens, the fund is taking advantage of high vacancy rates and divestiture of malls. It often leases space to non-retail entities such as medical centres or brings in

---

[381] Fung, Esther. "Amazon, long seen as a threat to malls, is now a hot tenant." *The Wall Street Journal.* March 6, 2019.

[382] Fung, Esther. "Property investors scrounge through retail ruins for bargains." *The Wall Street Journal.* July 18, 2018.

new anchors at current market rents. This is one of those times when private equity can actually help retail!

41) Channel Wars: Rise of The Store

Injured by the dark lord retail apocalypse, the store has come back with a vengeance! This once-mighty warrior has risen again. Albeit with new powers and a new purpose.

The role the store plays has changed. It has become part of a larger team that serves customers in different forms. Sometimes it's experiential and sometimes it's functional. It may be used for brand building or to fight off online evil spirits. It can even take smaller forms not unlike master Kiosk himself.

Either way, this shapeshifter is as important as ever.

Experiential Retailing

<u>Nike House of Innovation 000</u>

I spent time in New York City in December 2018 and one of the stores I visited was the new Nike flagship in Manhattan. Called the "Nike House of Innovation 000," the retail trade praised this store and for good reason. Nike offers a best-in-class example of how to create engaging experiential retail.

When I first approached the Fifth Avenue, 68,000-square-foot, six-floor store, I was immediately impressed by the corner location and overall vibe. You could tell you were in for something unique.

The store is part shrine, part museum, part retail store and part factory. The beauty of this concept is it appeals to numerous Nike target customers, from the avid, die-hard sneaker freak to the tourist to the casual Nike purchaser. Cashier-less, this flagship uses the Nike app to facilitate payment and other amenities.

One of the focal points in the store is the massive "sport beacon" that hangs through the open space between floors — a crazy-a*s chandelier that inspires creativity in a psychedelic sort of way. It looks like an inverted Stanley Cup on steroids with a side order of digital screens and lights. Very hip.

As I ascended the stairs and conquered each floor, I enjoyed the embedded

Nike specialist areas. Nike employees were busy working away on customized orders all within a magnificent fishbowl for all to see. Great way to build credibility and engage customers.

The store includes numerous other important features like QR-coded mannequins. Scan the code to see if your size is available or to order the product to a fitting room. Speaking of fitting rooms, they are accessed through a VIP customer concierge and appointment centre that looks like a 1970s massage parlour. The dedicated footwear floor offers numerous sneaker walls that mesmerize. Product fixtures go way out in space to delight drooling customers. All of the features are delivered with digital prowess and experiential value.

While the store will sell a lot of product at great margins, it does something much more important: it fans the flames of a continued Nike love affair with customers. Probably the best retail store I have ever seen, it is definitely worth checking out even if you don't own or plan on owning running shoes.

Canada Goose: The Journey

During holiday 2019, I made the trek to Canada Goose's new experiential store called "The Journey."[383] Located in an affluent west Toronto mall called CF Sherway Gardens, the store does not disappoint. Customers wait outside the location which, like a nightclub, has no windows.

Once inside, participants walk through a simulated crevasse with jagged walls and sounds of cracking ice and moving visuals at their feet. Customers are brought into a circular room with 360-degree, 4K video screens portraying an arctic landscape. The room changes with shopping seasons. With cool temperatures, customers see a display of parkas and accessories on mannequins.

Shoppers then proceed to a staging area called the "Gear Room" where associates fit them with a Canada Goose coat. They then enter a "Cold Room" where temperatures drop to -12 C and they can touch and feel real snow. The walls of the room are mirrored so they can see themselves and take selfies.

When shoppers are done, they take their parkas off and are led into an area that houses digital kiosks for ordering. There is no inventory on site. Products are delivered to their houses or other convenient locations.

---

[383] Rastello, Sandrine and Sambo, Paula. "For Canada Goose shoppers, winter's 'in store.'" *Bloomberg*. December 5, 2019.

I really liked the store. It was the first time I had tried on a CG parka and it was, indeed, very warm. The experience left me inspired and I couldn't help but feel underwhelmed by other stores I visited that day.

FAO Schwarz

On the same trip to New York, I stopped by toy retailer FAO Schwarz's flagship store at 30 Rockefeller Plaza. I was thoroughly impressed with the unit.

As you walk up to the store, several staff dressed up as Nutcracker soldiers greet you and invite you into this toy wonderland. There were many vendor demonstrations and an incredible energy flowing through the store.

The highlight for many was the opportunity to relive the scene from *Big* when Tom Hanks plays the floor piano. From a branding perspective I was impressed with the amount of private label product the retailer was selling. This not only boosted margins but also built brand loyalty.

Lululemon

Lululemon recently opened an experiential store in Chicago's Lincoln Park. Customers can take a fitness class and use the store's workout wear if they forgot their own[384]. The 20,000-square-foot gym/store allows patrons to work out at $25 US per class, chill out in the meditation area and grab a beer or a healthy salad in the café. The store is designed to appeal to men and women and offers expanded assortments. Classes range from yoga to weightlifting.

Crate & Barrel

Crate & Barrel added a restaurant at its prototypical Chicago store[385]. If you like the chairs, tables, plates and other products you use during your meal, you can buy them. Crate & Barrel joins many other retailers that have embedded services or experiences in-store. You can do your laundry at American Eagle. You can get your nails done at DSW.

---

[384] Patton, Leslie and Rastello, Sandrine. "Lululemon lets you try before you buy." *Bloomberg*. July 12, 2019.

[385] Holman, Jordyn. "Come for salad, leave with the bowl." *Bloomberg*. July 10, 2019.

William Ashley

In the summer of 2018, William Ashley made a bold move in Toronto. The firm opened a 15,000-square-foot store on Bloor Street that screams experiential retail[386]. Knowing shopping has changed, William Ashley created a cool hangout spot for millennial shoppers to learn about, connect with and engage with the storied brand. Like most new concepts these days, the store includes a café where customers can throw parties and have dinners. The store is designed to complement online shopping, not take its place. Technology is interwoven into the store with purpose. Seminars on making cocktails and arranging flowers are also offered.

Eataly

In a recent interview with Andrea Guerra, Eataly's executive vice president, Jake Edmiston from the Financial Post discussed some important components of the storied Italian retailer[387]. The part restaurant, part grocery store opened its first Canadian store in Toronto in the fall of 2019.

The Toronto location is a massive 50,000 square feet and stands three levels tall. The Canadian flagship includes coffee shops, four restaurants, a fresh food market and a grocery retail section and is sure to wow customers. Guerra was quoted as saying, "It's a bit like going to a theatre, where you're not observing a play but you're enjoying it, you're part of it." The firm is also eyeing other key Canadian markets such as Vancouver and Montreal.

Brand Connection

Glossier

During my New York trip, my daughters took me to see Glossier. This digital native served up a wonderful brand experience like no other I have seen.

Located on the second floor, customers are welcomed into a product showroom with tables to experiment with the brand's makeup and other products. Staff wore pink lab coats and offered product knowledge and real-time ordering

---

[386] Immen, Wallace. "Big stores still opening in a digital age." *The Globe and Mail.* July 17, 2018.

[387] Edmiston, Jake. "We're not a food hall." *The Financial Pos*t. August 20, 2019.

capabilities through tablets. There was a cool selfie area with giant lipsticks that personified the fun personality the brand portrays.

The best part was the on-site fulfillment process. Once a customer orders product in the showroom, a team on the first floor immediately picks and packs the order and places it on a hanger conveyor that takes it up to a pick-up desk on the second floor.

The store had that magical vibe that cool, relevant retailers have.

Levi's

Levi's New York flagship store was good but not great. It had lots of videos and lights and felt like a club, but was missing an experiential aspect.

On a positive note, the store had a tailor shop built into the sales floor and offered signage that spoke to inclusivity and environmental protection. I did like the giant 501 decal on the floor and the history lesson on the brand, but outside of that the store fell flat.

Sorry Levi's, I still love you!

Baskin -Rebrand as Scoops Ahoy

During the summer of 2019, my daughters and I went to Toronto's Woodbine Centre to check out the Baskin-Robbins shop-turned-Scoops Ahoy rebrand. As you may know, Netflix's wildly popular *Stranger Things 3* takes place at a local ice cream hangout called Scoops Ahoy, where Steve and Robin work.

The rebrand was a brilliant move on the part of Baskin-Robbins as it created an excitement that is often lost in today's retail environment. *Stranger Things* is a hot property and connects with so many generations at once. This store capitalizes on a key retail trend — mixing entertainment with bricks and mortar. Although this rebrand was only temporary (ran from July 4 to 16, 2019), it catapulted Baskin-Robbins from a sleepy legacy brand to one that is on point and topical.

The ice cream business has changed. A few shops down from the Baskin-Robbins is a Sweet Jesus location. Sweet Jesus is just one of the many new ice cream concepts that target Gen Z and millennials with exotic, premium, Instagram-worthy portions. For that moment anyway, the crowd was all around Scoops Ahoy and not its competitor.

We saw a family that had on their *Stranger Things* shirts and made this a Saturday afternoon adventure. Most of the customers spent as much time snapping photos as enjoying the ice cream. As one of only two Baskin-Robbins stores to rebrand (the other was in Burbank, California), the promotion added a flavour of exclusivity and sense of urgency that plays on FOMO (fear of missing out).

The menu was modified to include special Stranger Things flavours and desserts such as: U.S.S Butterscotch Sundae, Byers' House Lights Polar Pizza, Upside Down Pralines, Elevenade Freeze and Demogorgon Sundae[388].

Staff wore Scoops Ahoy sailor outfits, while management had co-branded t-shirts celebrating the Baskin/*Stranger Things* partnership. A must-have selfie prop completed the visit. It even had a brand ambassador outfitted in staff clothing for fun, share-worthy pictures.

Wayfair

Wayfair, the U.S.-based furniture and home products e-tailer, recently announced that it was opening up a full-service retail store in fall of 2019[389].

Like other online pure-play brands, Wayfair realizes the benefit of customers being able to touch and feel product before buying it. The full service store allows customers to buy in-store and have the product delivered. Wayfair joins a number of other brands that started online but have recently opened stores. These include Glossier, Casper and many others.

Saks Fifth Avenue

Saks Fifth Avenue has been under pressure to perform at a higher level. Owned by HBC, this luxury chain has scrambled to stay relevant in an ever-changing retail world.

Saks recently spent $250 million US on upgrades at its heralded New York flagship[390]. The upgrades include a new layout that boasts a main floor handbag emporium with price points up to $50,000 US.

---

[388] Shephard, Tamara. "Baskin-Robbins redesigns Woodbine Mall store for Stranger Things season première." www.toronto.com. July 8, 2019.

[389] Chin, Kimberly. "Wayfair is latest online seller to go bricks and mortar." *The Wall Street Journal.* March 27, 2019.

[390] Kapner, Suzanne. "Saks turns prime space into a handbag emporium." *The Wall Street Journal.* February 6, 2019.

In addition, the store opened a L'Avenue restaurant — the only one of its kind outside of Paris. In a seemingly high-risk move, the beauty category was relocated upstairs.

Saks is not alone as it invests a disproportionate amount of capital in "A" stores while rationalizing other lower-volume locations.

Tim Hortons

Tim Hortons launched a premium location in Toronto's financial district during the summer of 2019[391]. The part test store, part brand showcase offers high-end coffees and donuts, a big departure from the chain's traditional menu. The store is in the same building as its head office at King Street and University Avenue. It also sends a strong brand message, using hockey as a focal point. Some experts feel it may be too drastic a departure for the firm as it feels like a Starbucks.

Functional Retailing

Walmart

In June of 2019, I toured Walmart Canada's new prototype in west Toronto. The Supercentre was a fairly radical departure from the retailer's traditional units.

One of the biggest differences was the use of technology to enable purchase. Customers downloaded the Walmart app and scanned products as they shopped. They then proceeded to a finish line-looking checkout area where an associate quickly verified payment. The store also showcased expanded categories such as toys, party supplies, pets and more.

The location even had a Miniso (Japanese minimalist dollar store) attached that was accessible directly from Walmart. Lighting-backed signage directed customers to categories effectively and new, large KVI (key value item) signs were amazing. There were dozens of self-checkouts and an impressive grab-and-go food section.

The store felt like a Target and I liked it.

---

[391] Rubin, Josh. "Tim Hortons goes upscale with boutique location." *The Toronto Star*. July 13, 2019.

Aldi

German privately-held grocer Aldi has revolutionized discount grocery shopping[392]. The firm has 1,800 stores in 35 U.S. states and by the end of 2022 is expected to have 2,500. This would make it the third-largest U.S. grocer, only behind Walmart and Kroger.

Aldi offers little in the way of service and amenities, but offers tremendous savings. Stores are small, at 12,000 square feet, and 90 percent of the brands it sells are its own. It carries only 1,400 items, which increases buying power and simplifies inventory management. Product is merchandised in shipping boxes to save labour normally spent to stock shelves. Customers need to pack their own groceries and deposit 25 cents to use and return a cart.

Some industry experts estimate that Aldi's operating cost is about half of a traditional grocer. Its prices can be as low as 15 percent below Walmart, according to Wolfe Research. The retailer's Facebook account has over 50,000 members.

Amazon 4-Star Store, New York

Amazon has leased a 4,000-square-foot store and filled it with product based on customer ratings. Select items from its U.S. website that have a four-star and above (five-star maximum) aggregate rating are merchandised along with new, trending items and top sellers.

The store succeeds because it reinforces Amazon's (and society's) use of collective ratings and reviews to assist one in making a purchase decision. That is, many of us feel more comfortable buying something that other customers have told us is great. Great may refer to quality, functionality or performance, among other things. It also wins by adding a physical dimension that eliminates one of the remaining barriers to online shopping: not being able to touch and feel the product.

I liked the store for its simplicity and use of analytics to offer assortments based on what the masses prefer. I wouldn't say the store was exciting or offered

---

[392] Meyersohn, Nethanial. "How a brutally efficient grocery chain is upending America's supermarkets." May 17, 2019. Retrieved from: https://www.cnn.com/interactive/2019/05/business/aldi-walmart-low-food-prices/index.html

a unique experience, but that wasn't the point. Each item is electronically signed and shows aggregate customer ratings along with the Prime member price and the non-member price. Electronic signage shows daily featured items.

The store uses physical cross merchandising. It highlights products that are traditionally bought together online. In the smart home section, Alexa products are merchandised with other Alexa-compatible items. It's much easier to tell a category story in-store versus online. I also like how Amazon highlights specific New York favourites.

Amazon Grocery

Amazon has its eye on additional retail concepts. In a recent article in the New York Times, Karen Weise discusses an Amazon internal memo from 2017 that contemplated an Amazon grocery store[393].

Later that year, Amazon bought Whole Foods. That's not the end of it though, says Weise. Many see the Whole Foods purchase as just the beginning. The memo, as well as discussions with former staff at Amazon, paint a picture of a potential store that incorporates fresh food, online pickup and other features that could significantly change grocery retail. Dry goods could be ordered in-store via app, ready for collection once shoppers complete their fresh food shopping.

In February 2020, pictures surfaced of a new Amazon grocery store under construction in Los Angeles[394]. The only thing remarkable about the store was how much it looked like an everyday supermarket. Don't underestimate Amazon, though. Looks can be deceiving.

Apple

Apple recently expanded authorized repair depots to include mom and pop shops[395]. These outlets aren't allowed to do warranty work, but can repair products

---

[393] Weise, Karen. "Whole Foods just Amazon's appetizer?" *The New York Times*. July 31, 2019.

[394] Day, Matt; Stone, Brad and Buhayer, Noah. "A first peek inside Amazon's new grocery store concept in Los Angeles." February 13, 2020. Retrieved from: https://www.bloomberg.com/news/articles/2020-02-13/amazon-groceries-a-sneak-peak-inside-the-e-tailer-s-new-chain

[395] McMahon, Tamsin. "Apple to add independent shops to its iPhone repair network

out of warranty.

The expanded network will be able to obtain manuals and spare replacement parts directly from Apple. Starting in the U.S. with plans to expand to Canada, the program could have resulted from recent pressure from consumer groups about ease and ability to have technology repaired.

The "right to repair" movement accuses big tech firms of making it too expensive to repair devices, thus making buying a newer version of the same device more economical. The Federal Trade Commission (FTC) in the U.S. has been reviewing this issue. The program is designed to avoid end consumers repairing devices themselves.

Online Killer Countermeasures

19th-Century Market for a 21stCentury World

A recent op-ed by Jeff Guthrie, chief sales and marketing officer for Moneris, a Canadian payment provider, makes good points about how small retailers can survive in an Amazon world[396].

In a survey administered by Moneris, only 36 percent of small businesses had a website. A must have. More importantly, Guthrie talks about the differentiators that small retailers can implement, such as memorable customer service and patron connection. In addition, he talks about curated assortments, bespoke products and meaningful, relevant experiences and services — attributes Amazon can't provide in its current form.

Guthrie says small retailers can win "by taking a page from the 19th century – when main street was a collection of cobblers, tailors and dressmakers – and focusing on delivering one-of-a-kind products and experiences."

I subscribe to his thinking. Independent retailers need to carve out a niche to set them apart from large chains and online retailers. What better way than exemplary customer service and unique products that can't be found anywhere else.

---

amid calls for more consumer ease." *The Globe and Mail*. August 30, 2019.

[396] Guthrie, Jeff. "Canada's small retailers can survive the 'Amazon effect.'" *The Globe and Mail*. December 21, 2019.

Retail Before, During & After COVID-19

Dunham's

In a truly inspirational article by Michael Corkery from the New York Times, he talks about the one-of-a-kind department store called Dunham's in rural Pennsylvania[397]. This Wellsboro, PA gem is an anomaly. No online shopping capabilities, no Black Friday specials, no fancy modern assortments. Just furniture, clothing and housewares, and at higher prices than what you would see at the Walmart about 12 miles away.

Yet this retailer survives. Why? There are probably a few reasons, including everything from family love and commitment, local shopper loyalty and convenience. The store picked a niche and gives shoppers what they want. An anti-big box approach.

When a big retailer exits a particular product line like older women's clothing, Dunham's expands its offering. Many people who shop at Dunham's don't shop online or even own a smart phone. The store was one of the first omnichannel retailers back in the early 1900s when it outfitted a "rolling store," which was a truck filled with candy and clothing that would travel to local farms. One customer, Jim Rice, a 77-year-old former glass worker, drives 28 miles to shop at the store. Rice is quoted in the article as saying, "I always liked this store. They know how to treat you."

The store doesn't pay high wages. It can't afford to. It does, however, employ many local seniors who use the job to subsidize their social security payments. The store hardly offers the latest trends in fashion. In an ironic twist, the store recently started serving Starbucks coffee, which has helped bring in temporary workers from the local oil fracking operations.

TD Bank

In the cutthroat financial services industry, fintech (financial technology) plays the role of e-commerce to retail. TD (Toronto-Dominion Bank) has moved to make branches a competitive weapon[398]. Unlike fintech, TD offers face-to-face interaction at local branches. This is how customers want to bank for complex decisions such as mortgages, investments and other products.

---

[397] Corkery, Michael. "Quaint family retailer forgoes bells, whistles and Black Fridays." *The New York Times*. November 23, 2018.

[398] Kiladze, Tim. "Investing in branches key to TD's new strategy." *The Globe and Mail*. December 1, 2018.

But the look and operation of the branch has changed. Fully integrated with technology, branches have fewer tellers, less square footage, more room for wealth advisors and large meeting rooms. This new approach is research-driven and allows the bank to differentiate from fintech by offering customers the ability to talk to a real person.

Micro-Retailing

The concept of micro-retailing will be explored later in this chapter as a separate trend. In the interim, here are a few examples.

Stackt

Toronto recently launched a new retail format called Stackt. This metal marketplace includes about 120 shipping containers that have been converted to temporary retail shops[399]. The containers occupy about 100,000 square feet of city land in a mostly vacant space near downtown Toronto. Stackt has its inaugural showing from April 2019 to September 2020.

Glory Pops

In a recent article by Emily Baron Cadloff in the Globe and Mail, she discusses Glory Pops and its owner, Jacqui Keseluk[400]. Keseluk makes frozen treats and sells them in Halifax, Nova Scotia via a three-wheel, spruced-up Dickie Dee bike. Glory Pops is one of a number of retail concepts getting creative to cut costs and make more money. Keseluk avoids the overhead costs of having a physical storefront.

Coffee Lab

Joshua Campos is the owner of Coffee Lab in Vancouver. He uses an 18-square-foot space to sell coffee to nearby patrons[401]. With the sky high price of rents, this entrepreneur takes advantage of high traffic without the high rent to make the economics work. Smart selling!

---

[399] McPherson, David. "Old shipping containers carry a new retail vision." *The Globe and Mail*. August 13, 2019.

[400] Baron Cadloff, Emily. "Vendors give new life to ice-cream bikes." *The Globe and Mail*. August 26, 2019.

[401] Sagan, Aleksandra. "Downsizing operations to upsize profit." *The Canadian Press*. January 14, 2019.

42) Home Delivery: The Last Mile Space Race

As online retailing continues to grow, retailers, suppliers and service companies will obsess over solving the riddle known as the last mile.

The last mile is a term used in e-commerce that refers to the delivery of a parcel from the last point of mass distribution, such as a warehouse or store, to a customer's home. This step is the most costly and often kills any level of profitability that retailers try to sift out of an online sale. It is a tricky game, especially as free shipping, same-day shipping or one- to two-hour delivery become table stakes in the e-commerce value proposition.

According to SJ Consulting Group, the U.S. market for last mile delivery was $8.9 billion US in 2018, up 10 percent year over year[402]. There has been significant consolidation in this portion of the transportation industry as players are looking to gain national scale and lower cost to serve.

Bezos' Cube

Companies will continue to look for innovative ways to make last mile math work. So far, these have included: drones, driverless cars, pick-up lockers (at your local store), pick-up towers (at your local store), pick up at local partners (like drug stores), offering discounts for in-store pick up, third-party service companies such as Instacart or Uber Eats, retail employees dropping off packages on the way home and more.

It appears scale is one obvious way to solve this dilemma. That is, having so many packages delivered that it pays to have someone driving them around, like the postal service. But getting scale is really hard unless your name is Amazon. Let's take a look at some recent examples of what leading retailers are doing in this arena.

Food Delivery

Burger King recently announced that it plans to launch a food delivery service for those stuck in traffic[403]. It tested the program in Mexico City and will be rolling it out to LA, Shanghai and Sao Paulo shortly. Customers use an app that uses voice

---

[402] Black, Thomas. "As millennials 'buy everything online,' truckers reap riches." *Bloomberg*. January 12, 2019.

[403] "Stuck in traffic? Burger King sees a selling chance." *Bloomberg*. May 15, 2019.

activation software to take and confirm the order. It then uses special GPS technology to allow delivery staff to get the order to customers safely and accurately. Customers need to be within a three-kilometre radius of a local Burger King in order to guarantee the food tastes good. There are a few bugs to take out of the system, but one can't argue with the convenience factor the service offers.

Starbucks is rolling out delivery to its U.S. stores in a partnership with Uber Eats. Starbucks has already launched delivery in China, which is another key market for the retailer.[404]

Amazon recently announced it has invested in U.K. delivery company Deliveroo[405]. Amazon led a $575 million US round of funding for Deliveroo as it takes on European food delivery firms such as Delivery Hero, Just East and Takeaway.com. Deliveroo leverages some 60,000 motorcycle and cyclists who pick food up from about 80,000 restaurants across 14 countries.

Not everything Amazon touches turns to gold. The e-commerce giant announced in June 2019 that it was shutting down its U.S. restaurant delivery service called Amazon Restaurants[406]. The business was in place for four years and competed with other providers such as Uber Eats and Grubhub.

In Canada, food delivery is growing like a weed. Apps such as SkipTheDishes, DoorDash and Uber Eats have fueled significant growth in the $4.3 billion Cdn (2018) category[407]. Gen Z and their older cousin millennials make up the majority of users. The service also skews to urban regions such as Toronto. Not all is rosy, though. Based on data collected by Restaurants Canada, about 37 percent of restaurants say delivery apps have hurt on-premise dining. About 80 percent say they are making some money from third-party apps. Just over 20 percent say they are in the red.

---

[404] Jargon, Julie. "Starbucks to offer delivery across U.S. in bid to expand reach." *The Wall Street Journal*. December 17, 2018.

[405] Holton, Kate. "Amazon takes stake in Deliveroo as it challenges Uber in food delivery." *Reuters*. May 18, 2019.

[406] Herrera, Sebastian. "Amazon ends restaurant delivery in face of competition." *The Wall Street Journal*. June 12, 2019.

[407] Sokic, Nicholas. "Canadians show their appetite for ordering in." *The Financial Post*. May 29, 2019.

Retail Before, During & After COVID-19

<u>Grocery Delivery</u>

It looks like Amazon has chosen grocery for its next full frontal assault on traditional brick and mortar retail. Reuters reported in March 2019 that Amazon is planning to add dozens of grocery stores across the United States. Supposedly the Seattle retailer is scoping out regional chains and will develop a brand that does not conflict with Whole Foods[408]. Amazon is targeting Philadelphia, Los Angeles, Washington, DC, Seattle, Chicago and San Francisco for the new units. One has to assume that delivery will be a big part of these new stores' service offering.

Walmart, the largest food retailer in the U.S., is aware of the plan and is preparing for battle. Walmart has indicated that by January 2020 it will have more than 3,000 stores that are click-and-collect-capable and by the end of 2020 will have 1,600 stores that offer home delivery. The retailer is also offering $10 same-day grocery delivery.

<u>One is the New Two-Day Shipping</u>

During the summer of 2019, Amazon reported a quarterly cost hit of $800 million US as it looked to reduce prime delivery from two days to one[409]. This measure took a direct shot at competitor Walmart, which had moved to two-day shipping with no fees.

In retaliation, Walmart announced free, next-day delivery for online orders over $35 US on popular items[410]. The new service included about 220,000 items and was rolled out to 75 percent of the U.S. by the end of 2019.

It started back in 2005 when Amazon began offering Prime members two-day delivery. Walmart followed suit for millions of items for orders of at least $35 US. Target currently offers free, two-day delivery for orders at or above $35 US. Walmart and Target are using their enormous store count to offer free pick-up for online products as well.

---

[408] Panchadar, Arjun. "Amazon prepares new grocery-store business, report says." *Reuters*. March 2, 2019.

[409] Rana, Akansha and Dustin, Jeffrey. "Amazon ramps spending on faster delivery." *Reuters with files from Bloomberg*. July 26, 2019.

[410] D'Innocenzio, Anne. "Walmart ups its game with next-day delivery." *The Associated Press*. May 15, 2019.

The war continues. In October 2019, Amazon cut its forecast for holiday sales and profit below street expectations[411]. The company continues to invest in one-day delivery for Prime members. Amazon expected delivery costs for one-day delivery to increase from $800 million US in the second quarter of 2019 to $1.6 billion US in the fourth quarter of 2019. These costs include having more inventory closer to customers, increasing capacity of home delivery and forfeiting fees customers used to pay for one-day shipment.

Infrastructure Wars

Amazon learns from its mistakes or the mistakes of its partners. In an article by Sebastian Herrera and Vanessa Qian from the Wall Street Journal, the pair discusses how Amazon has quietly built its own shipping network across the U.S.[412]

It all started in 2013 when Amazon's customers were let down by a variety of carriers during the all-important holiday season. According to MWPVL International, Amazon has since increased the number of U.S. facilities from 65 to 400. According to Rakuten Intelligence, these facilities deliver, sort and fulfill about half of Amazon packages, up from less than 15 percent in 2017. Amazon now reportedly spends $61.7 billion US on shipping (2018) per annum, up from $5.5 billion US in 2010. The online behemoth even rents planes by the dozens to handle air shipments and has flirted with ocean freight management as well. This has all enabled the firm to become somewhat independent of third-party providers such as FedEx, UPS and the U.S. Postal Service.

Amazon announced in the fall of 2019 that it would be opening its first warehouse near Montreal in 2020[413]. The giant will have six fulfillment centres in Ontario and will employ 6,000 people in Canada. The new facility in Lachine will employ 300 workers.

In Canada, Amazon recently announced a partnership with Mississauga-based Cargojet Incorporated. The agreement allows Amazon to purchase almost 15 percent

---

[411] Dastin, Jeffrey and Rana, Akansha. "Amazon's sales forecast misses estimates amid plans to speed up delivery." *Reuters*. October 25, 2019.

[412] Herrera, Sebastian and Qian, Vanessa. "How Amazon's shipping empire is challenging UPS, FedEx." *The Wall Street Journal*. August 30, 2019.

[413] "Amazon Canada to build fulfillment centre in Quebec." *Reuters and The Financial Post*. November 9, 2019.

of the service provider within 7.5 years[414]. The option cost Amazon $600 million Cdn and will enable Amazon to control more of its infrastructure in Canada to facilitate one-day and same-day shipping.

In March of 2020, Costco bought Innovel Solutions for $1 billion US from Sears. Innovel, a logistics firm, focuses on last-mile delivery solutions[415]. Costco is looking to increase capabilities in home delivery of hardlines products as its e-commerce business continues to grow significantly.

43) Micro-Retailing — Small Ville

More and more people are opening up their own store fronts, whether virtual or physical, to supplement income or turn a hobby into an occupation.

Companies such as eBay, Amazon and, more recently, Shopify and Facebook provide a virtual storefront for would-be merchants to try their hands at retailing. Not unlike people driving Uber or Lyft to make extra cash, people buy and sell things or make and sell things. One just needs to look at the popularity of websites such as Etsy or Shopify. There is also an accompanying movement to buy local. Millions of people prefer locally-grown foods and locally-made products.

Hand Made Tale

Since 1975, the One of a Kind Show has been held twice a year, in the spring and fall, in Toronto. It features hundreds of vendors offering unique products often handmade by local merchants. The show was a big hit for customers looking for special, hard-to-find gifts[416]. The show runs twice a year in the spring and fall. Products range from holiday lights and ornaments to hats and sculptures.

---

[414] McLeod, James. "Capacity in Canada locked in by Amazon." *The Financial Post*. August 24, 2019.

[415] "Costco buys logistics firm Innovel for $1 billion." March 17, 2020. Retrieved from: https://business.financialpost.com/pmn/business-pmn/costco-buys-logistics-firm-innovel-for-1-billion

[416] "No two are the same: A personal touch." *The Toronto Star*. November 28, 2019.

Small Fry

The ability to earn by promoting brands on social media has cascaded down to the regular consumer (or almost) with the emergence of the nano-influencer[417]. Brands spend huge amounts of advertising dollars on influencers or those who have more than one million followers on Instagram. These folks can make millions of dollars endorsing a product or service. Then there's the micro-influencer, who makes less based on having tens of thousands to hundreds of thousands of followers. Still a pretty good gig! The nano-influencer has about 1,000 followers and is paid in small amounts of money or free product to promote a brand. As society polarizes into the haves and have-nots, customers look for authenticity. Who better to connect with the everyday consumer than another everyday consumer. A little like virtual Avon.

Discount Brokerage

A not-so-new side hustle that has gained popularity is retail arbitrage[418]. That is, looking for products on heavy discount at a local Walmart or Target (or other big box stores) and buying a huge quantity of them only to sell them at a higher price on Amazon. As described in Rachel Siegel's article in the Washington Post, one couple, the Herberts, estimates they make $150,000 US per year doing this.

Boxing Day

Small entrepreneurs have more options available to market on the cheap. One example is subscription sample boxes[419]. In a recent article by Denise Deveau in the Financial Post, she discusses this relatively new way to get a brand known through trial. Montreal-based Little Life Box helped entrepreneur Priscilla Everett get her Made By Bees product out to potential customers through its subscription box program. Accenture, a consulting firm, estimates that close to 70 percent of Gen Z consumers and over 50 percent of millennials like subscription boxes. What started with food is now common in cosmetics and fashion merchandise. Look at the popularity of Birchbox. Younger consumers have become conditioned to paying through subscription to get variety.

---

[417] Maheshwari, Sapna. "The Instagrammers next door, plugging brands for peanuts." *The New York Times*. November 17, 2018.

[418] Siegel, Rachel. "Amazon enabling a resale renaissance." *The Washington Post*. February 11, 2019.

[419] Deveau, Denise. "Subscription packages link small business to consumers." *The Financial Post*. April 17, 2019.

Enablers

Back End Beauty

Shopify has become a massive publicly-traded company. It rents its e-commerce software to entrepreneurs who want to sell online but don't want to build a website themselves. Shopify uses a monthly subscription model to eliminate upfront capital that companies require to build their own site and offers a one-stop shop to get in the online business.

The firm has set up a services division, too. This division allows customers to tap into other companies such as marketers and photographers that they can hire as needed. Shopify recently opened up a Los Angeles branch to connect with local entrepreneurs, offer seminars and host events[420]. The firm is positioned as an alternate to Amazon as it gives entrepreneurs another online channel to sell through. It's also not in the business of selling products itself. That is, unlike Amazon, it does not compete with its own customers.

Fleas R Us

Facebook created a new service called Facebook Marketplace[421]. It's free for Facebook users. The firm makes money by showing users advertisements. About 30 percent of Americans use the service. The site can be a convenient way to buy and sell products. Privacy has become a concern, though, as merchants and buyers share full profile information. This includes names, addresses, pictures and more. The site has also enabled numerous scams and crimes. Facebook appears to take a hands-off approach to managing the service.

Warp Drive

Montreal-based Lightspeed POS Inc. helps small retailers, restaurants and other ventures by providing point of sale (POS), inventory management and affiliated transaction-based services[422]. Legacy stationary POS systems in cash registers are in

---

[420] McLeod, James. "Shopify takes on the Amazon 'gorilla.'" *The Financial Post*. April 13, 2019.

[421] Safdar, Khadeeja. "Facebook Marketplace: The wild west of e-commerce." *The Wall Street Journal*. August 16, 2019.

[422] Rastello, Sandrine. "Blockbuster IPO is propelling Lightspeed." *Bloomberg*. September 27, 2019.

decline. Web-based, portable systems like Lightspeed are mobile friendly as well as fully integrate offline and online sales. The firm also offers integrated accounting and analytics upgrades. Some experts feel this company could be the next Shopify.

44) ESG – Not Just Board Bull Sh*t Anymore

About 10 or 15 years ago, companies started talking about corporate social responsibility or CSR. You started to see this buzzword pop up on annual reports and in corporate shareholder meetings. CSR can mean many things, including how a company treats its entire stakeholder group, not just investors. It can refer to the balance of profits, people and planet.

Since then, the term ESG, or environment, social and governance, has gained more prominence. We are at a point now where ESG is more than lip service to please NGOs or special interest groups. It has become real. Customers and even investors demand it.

<u>Button Down</u>

Some companies, even old companies, show they get it. Take American icon Levi's[423]. Having started in 1873, the brand has had a renaissance because of what management calls "profits through principles."

In this company's case, this means a few things. Its prospectus says: "It means never choosing easy over right" as it relates to sourcing, environmental considerations, using its global reach to push a good cause, treating people fairly, giving back to the community and operating ethically. Many brands make similar statements, but Levi's actually lives by it.

<u>Investor Pressure</u>

Large institutional investors, such as Blackrock and Vanguard, are demanding ESG responsibility from firms they invest in. From 2016 to 2018, the amount invested in ESG-friendly funds increased from $8.1 trillion US to $11.6 trillion US.

This trend is echoed in a recent article from the Wall Street Journal that talks about how big multi-nationals such as Mondelez have committed to making

---

[423] Wells, Jennifer. "Manufacturing 'profits through principles.'" *The Toronto Star*. March 23, 2019.

meaningful changes to packaging based on pressure from both consumers and investors[424].

In her piece in the Toronto Star, Jennifer Wells addresses a significant change in investors' desire for environmental stewardship[425]. Wells describes a move by investors to concentrate not just on overall governance but environmental and social issues — ESG — when evaluating a company's performance.

Public companies are now ranked according to an ESG Index that rates them across a number of criteria. These include global sanctions screening (how much a particular country relies on or deals with a country that is currently under sanctions from groups like the U.N.), ethical screening (financing as well as use of pesticides, etc.), energy and extraction screening and more.

Role of Executives

In August 2019, the Business Roundtable, a group made up of 200 of the most powerful CEOs in America, announced that it could no longer serve only the shareholder as the stakeholder that guides all decisions[426]. Its statement consisted of the following:

"Americans deserve an economy that allows each person to succeed through hard work and creativity and to lead a life of meaning and dignity."

It goes on to say that the members of the group "share a fundamental commitment to all of our stakeholders." That include employees, communities, suppliers and, of course, customers. It also said:

"We commit to deliver value to all of them, for the future success of our companies, our community and our country."

Of the 192 members of the roundtable, 181 signed the statement.

---

[424] Krouse, Sarah and Francis, Theo. "Firms make room for investors pushing climate, social issues." *The Wall Street Journal.* May 2, 2019.

[425] Wells, Jennifer. "The corporate mind shift is underway." *The Toronto Star.* May 4, 2019.

[426] McGregor, Jena. "CEOs say maximizing profit can no longer be primary corporate goal." *The Washington Post.* August 20, 2019.

Reaction to the announcement was mixed. Some applauded. Some thought it was just talk and meant nothing until action followed.

Lawyer's Light

A few weeks before the Business Roundtable announced its new doctrine, I read an article written by Andrew Ross Sorkin in the New York Times. Sorkin tells the story of former corporate lawyer Jamie Gamble[427].

Gamble retired as a partner at the law firm Simpson Thacher & Bartlett about a decade ago. Since then, he has proclaimed that corporate leaders "are legally obligated to act like sociopaths" due to the legal system. Gamble has further written that "The corporate entity is obligated to care only about itself and to define what is good and what makes it more money." He goes on to say, "Pretty close to a textbook case of anti-social personality disorder. And corporate persons are the most powerful people in our world."

Gamble offers a new set of rules and laws that make corporations and executives have a balanced duty of care to a wider spectrum of stakeholders. He discusses potential built-in guardrails that would contemplate the environment, employees, future generations and, of course, customers in addition to shareholders.

Executive Incentives

Emily Chasan, a reporter at Bloomberg, wrote an intriguing piece in the fall of 2019 that talks about the need for boards to set financial incentives for CEOs based on environmental targets[428]. She cites the example of Unilever's Seventh Generation division, which, through launching the product line in Asia, was awarded bonuses for doing right by the planet.

The team at Unilever had a financial incentive for using recycled packaging. This incentive guided decision making for a product launch date that eventually was deferred until packaging standards were met. Without this incentive, the firm would have launched without the proper packaging, which would have negatively contributed to environmental targets.

---

[427] Ross Sorkin, Andrew. "Corporate lawyer's idea: Rein in 'sociopaths.'" *The New York Times*. August 3, 2019.

[428] Chasan, Emily. "Paying CEOs incentives to protect planet one way to slow climate change." *Bloomberg*. September 20, 2019.

General Motors is another firm that has set CEO targets. The firm awards bonuses based on selling a specific number of electric vehicles. In Europe, this practice is more widespread, according to Chasan.

Profits Through Planet

Numerous companies are finding that environmental initiatives can also be big cost savers. Chris Martin and Millicent Dent from Bloomberg wrote an article that talks to this. The duo cites firms such as Nike, United Airlines, Walmart, Clarion Hotels, Patagonia, Nestlé and others that have reduced cost by reducing size, weight, specification, idle time and the like[429]. These efforts allow companies to win on two fronts: higher profits and lower environmental impact.

Here are some examples of what leading companies are doing to act more responsibly:

Environmental Footprint

Amazon made an about face when the firm launched the "Climate Pledge," a commitment to meet goals of the Paris climate agreement, a decade earlier than planned[430]. This is significant not only because of Amazon's massive scale, but because it appears the company is listening to its employees and outside activists. Jeff Bezos was quoted at the launch, saying, "We have been in the middle of the pack on this issue. We want to move to the forefront. We want to be leaders." Bezos also committed that his company will, by 2024, be 80 percent compliant to using renewable energy and that by 2030 will be fully compliant at 100 percent.

The firm also announced in 2019 that it set a target to be carbon neutral on half its shipments by 2030[431]. It cited the increased use of electric vans (see below), reconfigured supplier packaging and solar power as a means to reaching this goal. The initiative is called "Shipment Zero."

---

[429] Martin, Chris and Dent, Millicent. "Green initiatives are actually reducing company overhead." *Bloomberg*. September 23, 2019.

[430] Stone, Brad. "Amazon's Bezos vows to meet Paris pact early." *Bloomberg*. September 20, 2019.

[431] "Amazon announces plans to make half its shipments carbon neutral by 2030." *The Associated Press*. February 19, 2019.

In February 2019, Amazon committed to disclose its carbon footprint by the end of the year. The firm later announced it had emitted 44.4 million tons of CO2 in 2018.

Amazon has placed a 100,000-unit order for electric vans and vehicles to use for delivery in 2021. The firm also said it was donating $100 million US to the Nature Conservancy to help pay for reforestation.

The timing of the announcement was strategic. The next day, Amazon employees marched in protest at the climate strike led by 16-year-old Greta Thunberg, prior to her speech at the United Nations.

In February 2020, Bezos announced he was contributing $10 billion US of his own fortune to fight climate change by creating the Bezos Earth Fund.

IKEA Canada is also conscious of its environmental footprint. The retailer changed its tagline in 2010 to "the beautiful possibilities" and is walking the talk. Since then, IKEA stores have incorporated solar technology and have invested in wind farms. IKEA also offers electric vehicle (EV) charging stations and has eliminated single-use plates and cutlery at several of its food cafés.

Employee Wages and Benefits

Numerous retailers have voluntarily increased wages. Companies are doing this not because they have found a soul. They are doing this because they realize that one of the only ways they can differentiate from folks like Amazon is through in-store experience.

When employees are paid more, they leave less often and are happier. They treat customers better as well. These companies realize that millennials and Generation Z shoppers want to buy from companies that treat people and the planet with love. Some call this societal marketing. That is, marketing a company as not only serving shareholders but also mother nature and workers, too. This represents an important departure for numerous retailers and vendors.

In a recent letter to shareholders, Amazon CEO Jeff Bezos challenged the industry to match Amazon's $15 US per hour employee wage[432]. But when Amazon raised its own minimum wage to this new high, it was criticized for lowering or eliminating monthly stock awards and bonuses to offset employee gain.

---

[432] Boyle, Matthew and Roeder, Jonathan. "'Do it!':Bezos coaxes retailers to raise minimum wage." *Bloomberg.* April 12, 2019.

Amazon is not alone in its wage increases. Target, Walmart and Costco have also raised minimum wages. Walmart now offers an $11 US per hour minimum wage, while Target is at $13 US per hour. Costco recently increased its minimum wage to $15.50 US per hour.

Some say comparing wages at Amazon to wages at brick and mortar retailers is not fair. The vast majority of Amazon's employees work in warehouses where pay is naturally higher.

Lululemon announced it will be increasing employee parental leave benefits[433]. The popular chain has started offering three to six months of paid parental leave to full-time U.S. employees. This gesture is designed to keep and continue to attract great people. The firm was quoted as saying, "We just see this as something that's right to do for our people."

IKEA tries to do the right thing, too. The global furniture retailer recently announced that due to changes in its business model it would need to lay off about 7,500 workers worldwide[434]. These changes include urbanization of consumers, growth in online shopping and more. To counter these layoffs, IKEA will be employing 11,500 workers in new areas for a net gain of 4,000 jobs.

Animal Welfare

McDonald's said in 2015 that by 2025 it would sell eggs only from cage-free chickens in the U.S. and Canada. As of April 2019, it is one-third of the way there[435]. McDonald's buys approximately two billion eggs per annum in the United States alone. The firm has significantly increased supply of cage-free eggs and thus lowered the price for the entire industry. This has helped other restaurants adapt cage-free practices.

In a recent article by Michael Lewis from the Toronto Star, he talks about how prominent U.S. retailers such as Bloomingdale's and Macy's have gone fur-free[436].

---

[433] Holman, Jordyn. "Lululemon enhances parental leave benefits." *Bloomberg*. February 14, 2019.

[434] "IKEA says coming layoffs will lead to net gain of 4,000 jobs." *The Associated Press with files from The Canadian Press*. November 22, 2018.

[435] Patton, Leslie. "Cage-free scrambles egg market." *Bloomberg*. April 12, 2019.

[436] Lewis, Michael. "When will Canadian retailers ditch fur?" *The Toronto Star*. October

Other retailers and brand owners see it differently. Nordstrom, Saks Fifth Avenue and Canada Goose all continue to sell products with real fur. Other leading brands that have stopped selling fur include Tommy Hilfiger, Vivienne Westwood, Calvin Klein, Gucci and Michael Kors.

Guns and Ammunition

Retailers have made bold political moves in effort to change as society changes.

Dick's Sporting Goods CEO Ed Stack removed firearms from 125 stores and decided to stop selling guns to anyone under 21[437]. He also removed assault-style weapons from all stores. This was a direct result of the infamous Parkland, Fla. shooting. This move negatively impacted sales in the short term as some hunters stopped shopping at Dick's. The retailer is fighting online growth from rivals and must reposition itself to appeal to current and future outdoors and sporting goods customers.

Walmart announced in the fall of 2019 that it would stop selling ammunition for handguns[438]. The retailer has faced enormous pressure based on a number of shootings in the United States — some inside Walmart stores. The firm has also asked customers to refrain from bringing firearms into stores in carry states.

Other

Walmart announced in September 2019 that it would stop selling e-cigarettes and other similar devices at its U.S. stores[439]. This comes on the heels of growing concern about the safety of vaping products as hundreds of youth have become ill and some have sadly passed away. Amazon had done the same.

Oxford Properties, a real estate landlord and developer, has incorporated a vegetable garden on the rooftop of one of its largest malls, Yorkdale Shopping

---

29, 2019.

[437] Nassauer, Sarah. "Dick's Sporting Goods to remove guns from 125 stores." *The Wall Street Journal*. March 13, 2019.

[438] D'Innocenzio, Anne. "Walmart to stop selling handgun ammunition." *The Associated Press*. September 4, 2019.

[439] Bose, Nandita. "Walmart to stop U.S. sales of e-cigarettes, devices amid health controversy." *Reuters*. September 21, 2019.

Centre. The harvest from the garden is sent to a local food bank. The mall also includes a rooftop beehive.

45) The Green Giant

The world of retail will continue down its journey of environmental friendship. Not because the industry wants to (some actually do), but because they have to. Younger generations of millennials and Generation Z will demand it from brands.

Bogreenian Rhapsody

Green is the new black not only with consumers but with investors and big CPG companies are listening. In a recent survey by CPD, a non-profit group of 16 well-known consumer goods companies, results indicated that many of these firms are working hard to become more green[440]. The giants are reviewing supply chains and looking to reduce carbon emissions. Companies are looking to change products and processes to reduce the amount of water that is used in production and also during consumer use as in the case of laundry detergent. As meat and dairy have big negative impacts on carbon emissions, some firms are looking to vegan brands as a growing substitute. The fact that the survey showed European CPG firms were ahead of U.S. in terms of preparedness for climate change is not a surprise given the EU's green position.

The Scream of the Buttress Fly

On September 26, 2019, the world saw a global protest on climate change led by 16-year-old Greta Thunberg. At a time when many retailers are singing the green song and trying to act green, two Canadian chains closed their operations to protest and allow employees to protest[441]. MEC (Mountain Equipment Co-op) and Lush, both Vancouver based, walked the talk. Both brands stand for values consistent with this movement and put values above profit.

---

[440] Jordans, Frank. "Companies turn to green policies as climate change threatens profits." *The Associated Press*. February 26, 2019.

[441] Sagan, Aleksandra. "MEC, Lush to close shop in honour of climate strike." *The Canadian Press*. September 26, 2019.

Shut-Up Toy

McDonald's recently faced a firestorm over single-use plastic in its Happy Meal toys in the U.K[442]. As of July 2019, the petition had over 325,000 signatures. McDonald's is currently looking to remedy the issue by using recyclable plastic in its toys to be more environmentally responsible.

Let's review some of the common ways that retailers and brands are going green.

Food Waste

Beautiful

The U.S. Department of Agriculture says that about a third of the 430 billion pounds of food supplied to Americans goes uneaten. That's a lot. There are many firms looking to minimize the amount of wasted food tossed out at grocery stores. Various grocers have tested selling "ugly produce" or produce that is perfectly fine to eat but looks a little different in shape, size or colour[443].

But Walmart and Wholefoods recently ended their ugly food test. Although these initiatives sound good from a social responsibility perspective, grocers may have found that ugly food cannibalizes sales of regular food at full price. In addition, one could assume that it takes away from the look and feel of traditional produce sections. These sections are often the crown jewel of the retailer and set a first impression with customers. I still think there is something here and over time society will put pressure on big retailers to reinstate these sections as environmental concerns grow and food affordability for millennials and Generation Z comes into question.

Last Call

S-market, a grocer in Finland, is reducing food waste in an interesting way[444].

---

[442] Chaudhuri, Saabira. "McDonald's Happy Meal toys caught in backlash over plastic." *The Wall Street Journal*. July 9, 2019.

[443] Choi, Candace and McFetridge, Scott. "'Ugly produce' trend may have limits, as grocers end tests." *The Associated Press*. February 23, 2019.

[444] Segal, David. "The world wastes tons of food. A grocery 'happy hour' is one answer." *The New York Times*. September 11, 2019.

The 900-store chain uses a form of "happy hour" that marks down food that will soon perish. The sale starts at 9 p.m. and the subject food is marked down by 60 percent. This markdown is on top of a 30 percent reduction prior to 9 p.m. Retailers do the same for end-of-season garments. Why not food on a daily basis?

Loblaw has partnered with Toronto firm Flashfood to sell excess food to customers via an app. Shoppers can view surplus food that is set to expire by store and are offered a discount to purchase it[445]. Stores upload pictures of the food and place it in a special fridge at the front of the store for customers to pick up at their convenience. The app handles payment and order particulars. Flashfood makes a commission on sales generated.

Single-Use Plastic

Less Fizz

You know the green movement is mainstream when beverage giants Coke and Pepsi start using cans for bottled water instead of plastic[446].

The Coca-Cola Company announced that starting in September 2019 it will sell its Dasani water brand in aluminum cans in the U.S. northeast region to reduce plastic waste. The plan is to roll the change out in 2020. Coke said the change will actually increase profits. That appears to be the new trend. Firms can save the planet and boost profits at the same time. Win-win.

Meanwhile, Pepsi has signalled that it is looking to have a canned option for its Aquafina water for select stadiums and restaurants.

Dasani and Aquafina are the two largest bottled water brands in the U.S. and have been an easy target as society cracks down on the waste that single-use plastic bottles create.

Eat With Your Hands

One trend that is definitely here to stay is the reduction of plastic in food service. KFC and Walmart Canada recently joined the chorus of brands that have

---

[445] Silcoff, Sean. "Startup Flashfood teams up with Loblaw to cut waste." *The Globe and Mail.* June 12, 2019.

[446] Giammona, Craig. "Coca-Cola putting Dasani water in cans." *Bloomberg.* August 14, 2019.

made commitments in this regard[447]. These two firms, along with others including Mondelez, Nestlé, Starbucks, McDonald's, Coca-Cola and Pepsi, are on board. Each brand's programs vary, but most aim to eliminate all non-reusable, non-recyclable or non-compostable packaging in a few years.

Everybody Pitch Inn

Those small plastic bottles you keep stealing from hotels will be a thing of the past. In a recent article written by reporter Dee-Ann Durbin from the Associated Press, she talks about how numerous hotel chains are moving away from single-use, small-size toiletries[448]. Big players such as Marriott, IHG/Holiday Inn and Disney are all in. Companies are taking advantage of the recent green movement to switch from small bottles to larger ones or wall-mounted units to save on waste. The impact is big. IHG says it will eliminate about 200 million bottles per year by 2021. Marriott says it will eliminate about 500 million bottles per annum.

Frod-out Baggins

Canadian grocer Sobeys has taken the lead in environmental stewardship as it announced it would be banning single-use plastic bags by February 2020[449]. This bold move, which will save about 225 million plastic bags a year, helps the grocer differentiate from rivals. The firm also plans to stop using plastic bags in the produce aisle by introducing reusable mesh bags that are made from recycled bottles.

Package Composition and Reduction

Gilligan's Hut

KFC announced it will be testing a new bamboo packaging for poutine in 2020[450]. Why poutine? If you are from Canada, you know why. It is incredibly hot

---

[447] Reinicke, Carmen. "KFC, Walmart Canada latest to target plastic use." *Bloomberg*. January 25, 2019.

[448] Durbin, Dee-Ann. "Time running out for tiny toiletries." *The Associated Press*. August 29, 2019.

[449] Sagan, Aleksandra. "Sobeys to eliminate plastic bags by 2020." *The Canadian Press*. August 1, 2019.

[450] Rubin, Josh. "KFC picks poutine for bamboo package tests." *The Toronto Star*. November 6, 2019.

and messy. The chain figures if it can work for this Quebec favourite, it can work for anything!

Unboxing

Toy giant Hasbro announced it will eliminate all plastic from packaging for all new toy products by 2022[451]. Existing products will not fall under this plan. The company is also looking to reduce single-use plastics in actual products, where possible.

Refillable Containers

Milk Money

Big consumer packaged goods companies have banded together to test refillable containers in a radical new business model being tested in several major cities including New York, Paris, Toronto and Tokyo[452]. The program, called Loop, includes big retailers such as Kroger and Walgreens, as well as courier UPS[453]. Unilever, PepsiCo, Procter and Gamble and Nestlé top the 20 companies participating in the test, which is run by TerraCycle. Consumers will pay a deposit for the reusable package, then pay as they buy for the product inside it — like the milkman delivery model from the 1950s and earlier. The brands will pick up used containers, drop off new ones and clean and reuse the dirty ones. This approach speaks to environmentally conscious consumers and allows big brands to save on packaging over time.

In Canada, grocery giant Loblaw plans to test selling food in reusable containers in Toronto in 2020[454]. Loblaw is tapping into the Loop program driven by TerraCycle as above. The test will start with online orders. According to a study by

---

[451] Deaux, Joe. "Toy maker Hasbro to phase out plastics in packaging." *Bloomberg*. August 21, 2019.

[452] Chaudhuri, Saabira. "Big brands to test refillable containers." *The Wall Street Journal*. January 25, 2019.

[453] Telford, Taylor. "Big brands inspired by boomer-era strategy to reduce waste." *The Washington Post*. May 25, 2019.

[454] Rubin, Josh. "Loblaws to launch reusable container pilot in Toronto." *The Toronto Star*. June 7, 2019.

Dalhousie University, about 94 percent of Canadians are looking to reduce use of single-use plastic because it hurts the environment. The study also cites how only 38 percent of Canadians are willing to pay more for different packaging options, so retailers need to be careful about charging a premium.

Canadian grocery giant Metro recently announced it would allow customers to use reusable containers and bags at its Quebec stores for food from the deli, fish section, pastry section and other spots[455].

Green Trike

British consumer goods giant Unilever is an industry leader in waste reduction. The firm has partnered with Algramo, a start-up from Chile. The two use an app to summon an electric three-wheeled vehicle to act as a vending machine for household liquids[456]. The goal is to reduce plastic containers and bottles that are purchased weekly for household products. These containers often end up in landfills. Users are encouraged to use one container for each product for life and simply refill it each week or whenever they need more.

Message in a Plastic Bottle

With negative public opinion on single-use plastic bottles, two heavyweights in the industry are looking to take new approaches for consumer consumption.

Pepsi and Coke have rolled out fresh water-dispensing machines at select places of work and colleges where users supply their own bottles[457]. Customers can add flavours and bubbles to spice it up.

Pepsi has been on the acquisitions trail, as it purchased Israel-based SodaStream in 2018 for $3.2 billion US. Pepsi also launched Drinkfinity, which offers flavoured capsules that come in reusable plastic bottles.

In Europe, Coke is using 100 percent reusable plastic bottles and is testing

---

[455] "Metro grocery stores to permit reusable containers." *The Canadian Press*. April 16, 2019.

[456] Wells, Jennifer. "Unilever's cool ideas for cutting plastics." *The Toronto Star*. October 12, 2019.

[457] Maloney, Jennifer. "Coke, Pepsi want to sell water without the bottle." *The Wall Street Journal*. June 24, 2019.

aluminum cans for its water brand, Dasani.

Environmental Footprint

The Green Arches

McDonald's Canada, in what is often a test country for global initiatives, has opened a new green concept store in two markets. In 2018, Greenpeace was critical of McDonald's by naming it one of Canada's top five plastic polluters[458].

The two "green-concept restaurants," which opened on August 19, 2019 in Vancouver, B.C. and London, Ont. have marked differences from other Canadian locations. Cutlery and stir sticks are made from wood and straws are made from paper. Packaging for drinks consists of fibre lids that do not require a straw. Soft drink cups are recyclable as well.

In Canada, where being green is important, McDonald's has already rolled out changes to help the environment. Coffee is served in lighter-weight cups, Happy Meals include recycling instructions, breakfast platters and gravy bowls have been eliminated and McWraps are sold in thinner paper. The changes will save about 1,500 tons of packaging yearly. The firm has a target of having all consumer packaging sourced from recycled and renewable-certified suppliers by 2025.

Simon Says

Simons, a Canadian department store, has invested heavily into incorporating sustainability by opening its first net zero location[459]. The store generates as much energy as it consumes. It has solar panels on the roof and in the parking lot. It also uses a special geothermal heating system. But these modifications aren't cheap and would be difficult to justify for a public company focused on short-term payback. As Simons is privately held, the firm can measure return over multiple decades, not quarters. This gives it a green advantage.

Green Lantern

There has been some confusion in retail as companies use different definitions

---

[458] Deschamps, Tara. "Golden Arches are getting a green overhaul." *Corporate Knights*. August 10, 2019.

[459] Kerr, Kathy. "Retailers go green, from the roof on down." *The Globe and Mail*. November 27, 2018.

of what "climate positive" means. IKEA, H&M and Henkel all give the term a different meaning. Executives within the industry feel an independent certification body may be best to alleviate this inconsistency[460].

Green Products

In January of 2020, Barclay's released a report titled "Green is the new black," which indicates that the clothing industry has an opportunity to generate $123 billion US in value through environmental initiatives. These initiatives include better management of chemicals, waste, energy and water. The report goes on to indicate that the industry could lose $50 billion US of profit by 2030 if the status quo remains for such issues[461].

Work Horse

You can now buy a Polo shirt made out of recycled plastic bottles[462]. Ralph Lauren has jumped on the environmental bandwagon with this new garment, which is made in Taiwan from local bottles pulled from the ocean. Each shirt takes about 12 bottles to make and uses zero water to dye it.

The brand also announced it is targeting to take 170 million recycled bottles from landfills and oceans by 2025. Ralph Lauren also said it hopes to use only sustainable cotton and sustainable packaging for all its products by 2025. It is not alone as other big fashion brands such as H&M, Burberry and others have committed to the new Fashion Industry Charter for Climate Action.

Pea In Your Pants

Lululemon may be using pea protein byproducts to make garments in the future. The idea was presented by the Vancouver-based retailer at the Protein Industries Canada (PIC) summit in June of 2019[463].

---

[460] Chaudhuri, Saabira."Companies can't agree how to save planet." *The Wall Street Journal.* December 14, 2019.

[461] Cooke, Jeremy. "Greener fashion industry has billions in potential." *Bloomberg.* January 18, 2020.

[462] Italie, Leanne. "Ralph Lauren unveils shirts made out of plastic bottles." *The Associated Press.* April 18, 2019.

[463] Sagan, Aleksandra. "Don't look now, but there could be pea in your yoga pants." *The Canadian Press.* June 27, 2019.

Electric Vehicles

Posh Protectors

Porsche simultaneously launched its first electric car, the AG Taycan, in three locations in September 2019 to make a point. The locations included a solar power site in Germany, Niagara Falls, Canada and a wind farm in China[464]. The basic model will start at just under $100,000 US with the deluxe version priced at $185,000 US. The AG Taycan is designed to compete with Tesla. At launch, Porsche reportedly had pre-orders of 30,000 units.

Smashing Idea

In November 2019, Tesla launched its Cybertruck and received 200,000 pre-orders. The vehicle starts at $39,900 US and can travel between 400 and 800 kilometres per charge[465].

Marketing

Ever grab a coffee in Canada, eh? Well, if you did, there is about a 70 percent chance you got it at Tim Hortons. Tim Hortons has an evergreen promotion called Roll Up the Rim to Win, but has been getting flack for its environmental impact[466]. Tims sells millions of coffee cups during the promotion, which generates a lot of waste. The campaign that ran during 2019 fell flat even though the company gave more prizes away. The brand blamed the fail on numerous factors. One thing that caught the eye of observers was the blowback on the amount of waste created.

Tim Hortons has updated the contest for 2020 to include digital capabilities that should reduce this issue. However, it has added an enormous amount of complexity with the new program. It shortened the promotion from 10 weeks to four weeks and decreased the retail value of prizes being given away from $71.3 million Cdn to $29.9

---

[464] Rauwald, Christopher and Elliot, Hannah. "It's a true Porsche." *Bloomberg.* September 5, 2019.

[465] Knowles, Hannah. "Preorders for Tesla truck hit 200,000." *The Washington Post.* November 26, 2019.

[466] Charlebois, Sylvain. "RBI proves to be behind the ball on long-overdue Roll Up the Rim revamp." *The Globe and Mail.* May 1, 2019.

million Cdn[467]. It also created a hybrid, whereby for the first two weeks customers were supposed to use paper cups to roll up the rim, but after that were told to switch to an app.

It was planning on giving away 1.8 million reusable coffee cups just before launch, which would have helped save waste. But this was scrapped. Tims also cancelled its traditional coffee cup rim roll, planned for the first two weeks, in favour of random giveaways using cash registers. The last two weeks remained app-based. What a mess!

Other

Another issue retailers have had to wrestle with involves chemical-coated paper receipts[468]. Thirteen big retailers in Canada received a letter from a group of labour, health and environmental activists urging retailers to find an alternative for BPA-coated paper receipts used in cash registers. The group claims BPA can cause cancer, diabetes and ADHD in kids. The Canadian government labelled BPA a toxic substance in 2010. Select stores eliminated BPA from receipts but began using a similar chemical called BPS.

Greenwashing Machine?

There is a false sense of green in the recycled clothes business. A recent article in the Wall Street Journal estimated that only about one percent of recycled clothes make it back into new garments[469]. This is mostly a function of lack of appropriate recycling technology and mixed fibres in today's items. Many recycled clothes are made into wiping clothes or are dumped into landfills.

46) Amazon is the New Walmart

As Amazon has gotten bigger and bigger and enters more and more markets, it

---

[467] Charlebois, Sylvain. "Changes to Roll Up The Rim another misstep for Tim Hortons." *The Globe and Mail.* February 25, 2020.

[468] Sagan, Aleksandra. "Retail giants urged to ditch chemical-coated paper." *The Canadian Press.* August 23, 2019.

[469] Chaudhuri, Saabira. "Why your used shirts are destined for the dump." *The Wall Street Journal.* October 3, 2019.

has taken the place of Walmart as the poster child for big companies behaving badly. That's what happens when you dominate and disrupt to the degree that Amazon does. The firm has woken up to this and has started to take steps to change its reputation.

Break a Few Eggs

When an industry is disrupted, there is always carnage. Job loss, competitor bankruptcies, government push-back, monopolies or virtual monopolies, machines taking the place of workers and much more. When you become the largest you use the most energy and water, expropriate the most land, generate the most pollution, use the most fossil fuels and more.

Left-leaning politicians will want to break Amazon up, but realistically this won't happen because Amazon enables hundreds of millions of people to save money on products and save time through convenience. Add on the hundreds of thousands of people Amazon employs and you see my point. Besides governments, NGOs (non-government organizations) and special interest groups will continue to put Amazon in the crosshairs. That is, until the next 800-pound gorilla comes along.

Society has developed a love/hate relationship with Amazon. Let's review some of the recent articles written on the giant in a less-than-flattering way.

Regulatory

British Bulldog

In the U.K., the government has published a report calling for an e-commerce tax that would level the playing field with struggling brick and mortar shops[470]. Amazon and other e-tailers such as Asos and Boohoo have built up a less-than-favourable reputation of not paying their fair share.

Based on lower profits as a result of infrastructure investments, Amazon paid approximately one percent tax in the United Kingdom in 2018. Amazon shrugs off the report and counters by reminding the government that it has invested $12 billion US in the U.K. since 2010. The report called for an online sales tax, higher value-added taxes and green taxes to help make up for the thousands of stores and employees that have lost their jobs in the retail sector over the past few years. In 2018, approximately 70,000 retail jobs were lost in the U.K.

---

[470] Milligan, Ellen. "Tax web retailers to save shops, report says." *Bloomberg.* February 22, 2019.

The Associated Press announced in July 2019 that the competition bureau in the U.K. was taking a closer look at Amazon's stake in Deliveroo, the European food delivery app[471]. Britain's Competition and Markets Authority is in line with other European regulators who are watching American big tech and its impact on the trade area.

European Vacation

Amazon has found its way into some hot water in Europe. The European Commission has opened an antitrust investigation into Amazon's relationship and use of data of its third-party merchants[472].

Business Operations

In a recent article written by Patricia Callahan in the New York Times, she talks about the dark side of the increase in online shopping. Specifically, she talks about Amazon's business model as it relates to delivery accidents and deaths in the United States[473].

Callahan cites the use of third-party delivery companies and contractors that buffer Amazon from liability for any damages as a result of delivering packages. Each third-party transportation company indemnifies Amazon from any mishaps. This business model works well for Amazon as it can ramp up and ramp down delivery capacity without as much fixed overhead on its expense structure. Amazon requires that for every 1,000 parcels delivered, 999 of them be on time. If a driver is running late, will that driver speed through a neighbourhood to make up time?

Just Pull It

There was a lot of chatter when Nike announced in November 2019 that it was

---

[471] Kirka, Danica. "U.K. investigates Amazon stake in food delivery firm." *The Associated Press*. July 15, 2019.

[472] Schechner, Sam. "Amazon to overhaul terms as part of German settlement." *The Wall Street Journal*. July 18, 2019.

[473] Callahan, Patricia. "When Amazon's fast, free shipping delivers heartbreak." *The New York Times*. September 9, 2019.

halting direct sales to Amazon[474]. Always labelled as a test, new CEO and former eBay head John Donahoe made it clear that Nike was better off without the Seattle retailer. The whole idea behind Nike's test was to circumvent unauthorized third-party sellers on Amazon, but it failed to do so adequately.

Rating Game

In late 2018, Joanna Stern wrote a piece in the Wall Street Journal that discussed Amazon's star-based review system and the prevalence of fake reviews[475]. Stern boils Amazon reviews down to four categories: 1) legitimate reviews 2) Vine reviews 3) incentivized reviews 4) fake reviews.

To its credit, Amazon works hard to try to weed out fake reviews and eliminate them from the site. Stern recommends the following approach to minimize a customer's probability of getting bamboozled: 1) Forget the stars and just read the reviews. 2) Use a separate review rating site. 3) Don't believe everything you read; use it directionally (grain of salt approach).

Muzzle

In an article by Jay Greene in the Washington Post, he reports that Amazon has warned activist employees they could be terminated if they criticize the retailer publicly[476].

Pole Position

Jefferson Graham from USA Today warns that when searching for a product on Amazon, the products you see at the top could very well be sponsored[477]. Like Google, brands pay to get the coveted top view on the landing page for a particular

---

[474] Novy-Williams, Eben and Soper, Spencer. "Nike pulling its products from Amazon website." *Bloomberg*. November 14, 2019.

[475] Stern, Joanna. "Is it really five stars? How to spot fake Amazon reviews." *The Wall Street Journal*. December 26, 2018.

[476] Greene, Jay. "Amazon warns activist workers they could be fired for criticism." *The Washington Post*. January 3, 2020.

[477] Graham, Jefferson. "Sponsored ads swamp Amazon searches." *USA Today*. November 12, 2018.

searched category. One needs to be aware of this as some customers believe the best sellers are at the top of Amazon's product pages. In fact, these sponsored ads are on the rise according to researcher eMarketer. They predict Amazon will grow this business from about $1.8 billion US in 2017 to a projected $10.9 billion US by 2020.

Third-Party Merchants and Suppliers

Hired Help

Amazon has been getting flack for treating third-party merchants on its marketplace like dirt. The company has announced it is spending $15 billion US on "helping" third-party vendors increase sales[478]. The money will be used on infrastructure build such as warehousing, staff and engineers, new services and dashboards as well as training. The firm did not disclose if these costs were typical for a given year or are increasing.

Partners in Crime

In July 2019, Amazon announced it was launching a program called Accelerator to offer select third-party marketplace suppliers a unique partnership[479]. The deal, which is not compulsory, involves Amazon offering a particular brand prominent marketing support in consideration for Amazon obtaining the rights to buy the brand at a fixed price within 60 days' notice. According to the Wall Street Journal, the fixed price may be as low as $10,000 US. The third-party vendor can sell the same product through other retailers, as it retains IP ownership. However, the product cannot be sold under the same brand that Amazon nurtured.

Dura Sell

Amazon recently announced it was testing a pop-up on its app that showcased its own low-priced products on suppliers' product pages[480]. That is, if you went looking for branded batteries, you may get a huge pop-up that shows you AmazonBasics batteries. Retailers have been doing that for years by merchandising private labels beside national brands.

---

[478] "Amazon antes up U.S. $15B to help merchants." *Bloomberg.* August 24, 2019.

[479] Emont, Jon. "Amazon offers sellers a leg up, with a catch." *The Wall Street Journal.* July 19, 2019.

[480] Greene, Jay. "Amazon tests pop-up touting its lower-priced products." *The Wall Street Journal.* March 18, 2019.

47) Digitally-Native Brands: Smells Like Screen Spirit

Much has been written about digitally-native brands. These are retailers or brands that started online with no physical presence — brands such as Indochino, Warby Parker, Fabletics and more. Some have focused on direct-to-consumer exclusively, while others have explored partnering with other retailers, whether online or in-store.

BFFs

With the rise and proliferation of digitally-native brands with millennials and Generation Z consumers, the relationship between a brand and a consumer has changed. In an article by Janine Wolf from Bloomberg, she discusses the truly intimate connection that successful brands must create to resonate with younger customers[481]. Today's relevant brands have created a two-way, digital, real-time dialogue with consumers, much like the relationship between a person and their best friend. Wolf talks to young brands such as Hims, Harry's, Dollar Shave Club, Warby Parker, Away, Casper, Figs, SmileDirectClub and others, and examines how they have broken traditional consumer purchase decision moulds to engage customers in new ways.

Joker

Humour is often the currency that connects these brands with users. One of the benefits of being a DTC brand is the ability to connect with customers directly. If any one of these brands relied on a retailer for distribution, the customer relationship would be layered and the true connection would be harder to create and maintain. Not only do DTC brands capture the entire margin pie, they harvest data directly and in real-time, which beats even the most frictionless supplier-retailer relationship hands down.

Too Big To Fail

Small is the new big. Even in the high-profile world of beauty products. In a clever article written by Jaewon Kang in the Wall Street Journal, she discusses how start-up beauty brands such as Glossier, Kylie Cosmetics, Anastasia Beverley Hills, Milk Makeup and more have become more relevant to young consumers than legacy brands.

---

[481] Wolf, Janine. "Brands no longer want your loyalty, they also want your love." *Bloomberg*. February 9, 2019.

Public Figure Profits

One of the secrets for success for DTC brands is the founder's celebrity personality. Kylie Jenner, Emily Weiss, Pat McGrath and more have used their millions of followers on social media to generate awareness and drive conversion. In 2017, Indie brands grew 24 percent while the whole U.S. beauty industry grew just six percent, according to Kline, a research firm. Legacy drugstore and discount brands such as Clairol, Revlon and CoverGirl have stagnated. Estée Lauder and L'Oréal have taken to acquisition to gain relevance. Estée Lauder bought Becca and Too Faced, while L'Oréal bought Urban Decay and IT Cosmetics. If you can't beat them, join them.

Union of the Schnake

Speaking of joining them, the owner of Schick recently bought Harry's for $1.37 billion US[482]. This deal is not unique. The market leader acquires a start-up that threatens to take market share from the incumbent.

Not all of these acquisitions work, though. Supposedly Unilever still hasn't made money off its $1 billion US purchase of Dollar Shave Club. Procter and Gamble has cited challenges with making money on DTC brands as well.

Bentonville Bride

Sharon Terlep from the Wall Street Journal discusses some of the challenges digitally-native DTC brands face[483]. Terlep addresses the need for these brands to sell to large national retailers in order to build recognition and secure volume. Specifically, Terlep describes how consumers wish to buy consumables such as razors and other health and beauty products during their weekly shopping trip versus through subscription. Many DTC brands have succeeded by selling to either Walmart or Target or another large retailer. Even Kylie Jenner's makeup company decided to tie up with Ulta Beauty before selling a $600 million US equity position to Coty Inc.

Love at First Site

Many DTC brands see strong brand engagement and sales increases in markets

---

[482] Olson, Alexandra. "Schick owner buys Harry's in slick new shaving alliance." *The Associated Press*. May 10, 2019.

[483] Terlep, Sharon. "Why brand success still rests on store shelves." *The Wall Street Journal*. December 14, 2019.

where they add their own store[484]. This makes sense as customers get to touch and feel products. It enables more of an emotional connection with the brand as well. At Casper stores, customers can book an appointment to have a nap and try its mattress first-hand. Digitally-native brands are finding that the cost to acquire new customers can be reduced significantly with a store. In some cases, these retailers are able to negotiate favourable lease terms as vacancy rates have increased.

48) Madison Avenue in the Main Aisle

The battle for advertising dollars in retail has taken a new spin. Retailers have been milking vendors for ad dollars for decades to pay for flyers and circulars, TV commercials, catalogues and even endcaps in store.

What *is* new is the advent of digital media and the ability to directly connect advertising dollars to purchase. In a recent article by Matthew Boyle from Bloomberg, he talks about how Walmart sees advertising as a major potential revenue stream[485]. With its 4,600 stores and 300 million monthly brick and mortar visitors, the discounter has an enormous, captive audience.

Mad About U

Walmart isn't the only one to wake up to this opportunity. Target, Kroger, Loblaw and others have this business in their sights. They need the help to offset the impact of online shopping — specifically, narrowing margins from online sales and capital investment required to build online capabilities. According to Magna, a research company, U.S. sales of advertising spending was a staggering $208 billion US in 2018 and about half of that consisted of digital advertising. A first.

Alcatraz

According to eMarketer, a digital data tracking company, the digital side of the business is dominated by Facebook and Google, which make up about 50 percent of the market. Amazon represents about six percent of that pie. Chinese retailer Alibaba uses ad revenue to drive about 60 percent of its revenue.

---

[484] D'Innocenzio, Anne. "From clicks to bricks." *The Associated Press*. December 26, 2018.

[485] Boyle, Matthew. "Amazon has a big advertising business. Walmart wants one." *Bloomberg*. February 12, 2019.

Thirty something

Amazon has grown its advertising business to an estimated $125 billion US per year, according to Morgan Stanley[486]. Amazon sells ads to big brands that work with Amazon staff to place promotions on specific product pages based on search results.

Cafeteria Marketing

Amazon has broadened its self-serve advertising service, which allows companies and agencies to design their own campaigns based on budget and customer profile. Facebook and LinkedIn have been offering something similar for a while now.

Big Brother Seattle

The unique part of the Amazon program is the directness to product purchase. If I was a brand looking to sell children's hockey skates, I would target parents who bought children's hockey equipment within the last week or so. Unlike Google, which taps into search, and Facebook, which taps into interests, likes and groups, Amazon has a much more direct sample of target consumers to market to: customers who have already spent on Amazon in the category in question. Advertisers can use new Amazon tools to predict behaviour and establish correlation. If 80 percent of parents who bought children's shin pads also bought skates, skate brands can target that specific customer group efficiently with greater ROI. Considering Amazon's growing global reach, it's not hard to imagine a world where their service takes the number one position in marketing spend.

Pavlov's Hot Dog

Loblaw, a large Canadian grocer and drug chain, is launching a test where its most loyal customers, members of the PC Optimum program, will start seeing ads online[487]. For each ad customers see, they will be given Optimum points. How many points customers would receive for each ad is not public yet. Loblaw is treading carefully though and is quick to talk about how customers can opt out and how the internet is tracking customers anyway.

---

[486] Weise, Karen. "Amazon uses customer database to build $125 B ad business." *The New York Times*. January 26, 2019.

[487] Edmiston, Jake. "Loblaw looks to leverage loyalty." *The Financial Post*. April 3, 2019.

49) M&A — It Takes Fluke to Make a Thing Go Right

When an industry is under pressure, it is common to see significant consolidation. Some brands fall flat and are weak — prime targets for another company to buy them at a discount. Other brands are strong, well-funded and are growing. They have money to burn and see acquisitions as a sound way to grow even quicker. Some are start-ups that have valuable technology, brands, distribution or specific customers — perhaps an easy way for mature legacy brands to appeal to millennials or Generation Z. Sometimes big dinosaurs join together to realize synergies. Top line is flat, but added profit can be had by jettisoning duplicate employees, factories and so forth to reduce expense.

<u>Synergy Drink</u>

Often, merging or acquiring another company involves synergy. This can take on many forms: cost synergy (lowering total cost as a percentage of revenue), technological synergy (leveraging a technological advantage to drive revenue or lower cost), operational synergy (improving productivity and output to lower cost), financing synergy (providing capital to a growth business or lower debt cost) and more. The idea is that if you join two companies together, the sum of the parts is worth more than each individually.

Probably the most common synergy is cost synergy. This usually translates into firing redundant staff and negotiating harder with suppliers. This has significant implications for retail — everything from increased supplier or buyer power, lower consumer disposable income due to layoffs, less price competition and so forth. The strong get stronger and the weak get acquired or disappear.

<u>Love In Vein</u>

But many unions don't work. Cultural mismatches, politics, poor integration and other potential hazards can await those that come together. Usually, the larger the target company, the worse the end result. I have seen better results when large, stable companies buy small companies and leave them alone for a while. Another formula that works is when big companies buy small to medium size companies and utilize their best-in-class integration capabilities to make the transition seamless.

Let's review just a handful of the recent acquisitions within retail.

<u>Live and Let Fry</u>

One of Amazon's strengths is how it runs mergers and acquisitions. The firm is known for acting quickly, making relatively small deals often, without investment bankers, and keeping the deals under the radar[488]. According to Dealogic, a research firm, Amazon has quietly amassed $20 billion US in deals since 2017. Pundits believe it hard for Amazon to continue with this approach as regulators put Amazon, as well as its big tech peers, under more scrutiny. Some in government believe that these companies have become too big and have too much power.

Hang the Dee Jay

Doug Putman has guts, that's for sure. The Canadian millennial bought distressed U.K. music chain HMV in 2019 for $149 million Cdn. The acquisition complements the Sunrise music chain he bought in Canada a few years earlier.

Putman is relaunching HMV in Britain with a new experiential store in London and announced he would be reopening HMVs website in the fall of 2019[489]. HMV had been in Administration (U.K.'s version of U.S. Chapter 11 bankruptcy protection) in 2013 and in 2018. The retailer had been hammered as music morphed from vinyl and CDs to digital formats. It appears Putman is counting on a resurgence of vinyl. He also wants to connect with customers though experiential stores that showcase artist performances.

Value Vibe

Canadian dollar store and previous stock market darling Dollarama has made the jump to international markets by purchasing a share in Dollarcity. The Montreal-based retailer will own a 50.1 percent stake in the company. Dollarcity serves Latin American countries such as El Salvador, Columbia and Guatemala[490]. The two firms have worked together over the past several years to obtain sourcing synergies.

Back in the New York Grooming

In a tag team approach, Barneys New York has been bought by Authentic Brands Group LLC who, in turn, will license the brand to be sold in about 40 Saks Fifth Avenue stores, owned by HBC[491]. Authentic Brands is expected to close several

---

[488] Mattioli, Dana. "Amazon's deal making threatened by D.C. scrutiny." *The Wall Street Journal.* July 5, 2019.

[489] Ritchie, Greg. "Canadian to relaunch HMV's online store in Britain, open new retail sites." *Bloomberg.* October 11, 2019.

[490] "Dollarama buying stake in Dollarcity." *The Canadian Press.* July 3, 2019.

[491] "Barneys awarded to Authentic Brands as no rival bids materialize." *Bloomberg.*

stores and warehouses and keep just eight units.

Authentic Brands is no retail slouch, with ownership of brands such as Aeropostale, Juicy Couture, Nine West and Nautica. The firm, created in 2010, also has the rights to license Elvis Presley and Muhammad Ali.

Power Lunch

Lunchtime has been tough on restaurants as more employees are bringing their lunch to work. Sushi provider YO is trying to buck that trend with its announcement to purchase 700-unit SnowFox, the grocery kiosk vendor, for about $ 100 million US[492].

Sushi is healthier than many other lunch or dinner options, and the $1 billion US category has been growing 13 percent per annum. YO is known for its U.K. and European restaurants and bought Bento Sushi in 2017, adding 600 North American stores to its network.

Vision Statement

The company that makes Ray-Ban glasses is buying a rival called GrandVision for $6.1 billion US[493]. EssilorLuxottica, the company that owns Ray-Ban, will have a commanding 5,300 stores in Europe once the deal is completed. The firm already has 9,000 stores globally, with brands such as LensCrafters, Pearle Vision and the like.

Amazon Understudy

Shopify announced in September 2019 that it was purchasing Boston-based 6 River Systems for $450 million US[494]. The acquisition gives Shopify access to the firm's 20 facilities in North America and Europe and supports Shopify's expansion

---

November 1, 2019.

[492] Dummett, Ben. "Sushi chain YO reels in grocery kiosk operator." *The Wall Street Journal*. July 3, 2019.

[493] Dummett, Ben. "Ray-Ban maker strikes $6.1 B deal for European rival." *The Wall Street Journal*. August 1, 2019.

[494] Silcoff, Sean. "Shopify buys warehouse robotics company for $450-million." *The Globe and Mail*. September 10, 2019.

into logistics services for its customers. The firm also signalled it was looking to spend $1 billion Cdn on supply chain infrastructure over the next few years. Shopify proclaimed it will enable two-day shipping on hundreds of thousands of its U.S. merchant customers' products by the end of 2019[495].

Trick of the Wrist

In November 2019, in a move that will be sure to garner attention from regulators, Google announced it was buying Fitbit[496]. The purchase price was $ 2.1 billion US.

If the deal goes through, it would mean that two of the largest tech firms, Apple and Alphabet (Google's parent), would own the wearables market. According to Strategy Analytics, a research firm, at the end of Q2, 2019, Apple had a 46 percent share of the market, while the smaller Fitbit had 10 percent.

Cash Register

Lightspeed POS is on a roll. It recently announced its third purchase in a year as it bought Australia's Kounta Holdings Pty Ltd. — for $35 million US in cash and $7.7 million US in stock[497]. The competitor from down under manages the point-of-sale needs for 7,000 merchants in New Zealand and Australia. In January 2020, Lightspeed announced it was acquiring German POS provider Gastrofix for $100 million US to strengthen its position in Europe[498].

Don't Eat in the Car

Uber recently announced its purchase of a majority stake in grocery delivery app Cornershop for an undisclosed amount[499]. Cornershop offers one-hour grocery

---

[495] McLeod, James. "Shopify aims at Amazon fulfillment network." *The Financial Post.* June 20, 2019.

[496] De Vynck, Gerrit and Baker, Liana. "Fitbit deal may face scrutiny." *Bloomberg.* November 4, 2019.

[497] Silcoff, Sean. "Lightspeed to pay up to $ 61-million for its largest acquisition to date." *The Globe and Mail.* October 22, 2019.

[498] O'Kane, Josh. "Lightspeed to acquire Gastrofix for $100-million." *The Globe and Mail.* January 8, 2020.

[499] Sherwood, Dave and Laing, Aislinn. "Uber to buy online grocer Cornershop." *Reuters.*

delivery from leading stores including Walmart, Costco and others in markets including Canada, Peru, Mexico and Chile. Plans are for the brand to expand in a number of markets with the reach and guidance of Uber.

C Movie

U.K. cinema behemoth Cineworld bought Canadian Cineplex for $2.2 billion US, creating the largest movie theatre chain in North America. Cineworld needs to make up for lost revenue from the proliferation of streaming services. The U.K. firm is known for offering a monthly subscription service for would-be moviegoers for unlimited visits[500].

50) Private Label and Other Differentiators

Private label is a great way for retailers to win. It gives them more sourcing flexibility, higher margins and differentiates them from competitors.

One need look no further than Lululemon as an example of this. Lululemon, like other smart retailers, realizes the path to long-term success rests in part in owning its own brand.

In my opinion, one of the make-or-break determinations for which retailers survive rests upon the ability to leverage controlled brands. In other words, if you sell everyone else's brands you will probably fail.

Why? Because there isn't enough profit left for two companies in a transaction. Also, with Amazon's 550-million SKU assortment, eventually most national brands will be listed there and no one will be able to match Amazon on price.

Digital Killed the Radio Star

In a 2018 article by New York Times reporter Holly Shively, she discusses five

---

October 12, 2019.

[500] Krashinsky Robertson, Susan. "U.K. movie-theatre giant to buy Cineplex in $2.2-billion deal." *The Globe and Mail.* December 17, 2019.

changes to digital shopping we would see in 2019[501]. I will outline her article in more detail later under "technology." However, the third change she discussed includes the increase in retailer private labels. Look for more digital ads and pop-ups to feature store brands.

Several key retailers have already embraced this dynamic. A major initiative for Target is private label expansion. Some of Target's private brands include Cat & Jack, Pillowfort, Colsie, Stars Above, Good & Gather and Auden. Walmart has also been busy securing captive brands and businesses. As discussed earlier, FAO Schwarz uses private label in the commoditized toy category. Canadian Tire has recently acquired captive brands such as Helly Hansen, Raleigh and more.

Top of the Pops

Amazon recently began testing a new "Top Brand" label for national brands on its platform[502]. The new rating is based on popularity with customers and may help satisfy big brands' need for differentiation on the site. The label joins other Amazon product designations such as "Amazon's Choice" and "best seller." Top Brand is being tested on fashion goods.

Label Maker

According to Bain & Company, 85 percent of U.S. shoppers are open to trying a store brand[503]. Costco's Kirkland brand reportedly sells about $40 billion US a year.

51) Retail Partnering — Speed Dating

Companies are partnering at unprecedented rates and in unconventional ways to expand or stay alive.

---

[501] Shively, Holly. "Digital shopping is about to change." *The New York Times*. December 8, 2018.

[502] "Amazon tests 'Top Brand' label for fashion names." *Bloomberg*. August 17, 2019.

[503] Meyersohn, Nathanial. "How a brutally efficient grocery chain is upending America's supermarkets." May 17, 2019. Retrieved from: https://www.cnn.com/interactive/2019/05/business/aldi-walmart-low-food-prices/index.html

With technology moving faster and consumer preferences changing quicker, the need to form an alliance has never been more important. Gone are the days when retailers or retail partners had the time or resources to build breakthrough technologies and processes on their own.

Coupling with the right firm can vastly accelerate a company's technological capability. In addition, when the right partners get together, both capital and risk can be shared. Finally, complementary infrastructure can benefit all partners through increased reach. All these scenarios make for potential synergies that both partner firms would not have realized had they not met and tied the knot through an alliance.

We have already seen strange bedfellows. In some cases these partners may have previously been classified as competitors. An example of this is Walmart and Google. Although their alliance was short lived, the two united to battle Amazon using Google's voice recognition software and Walmart's massive assortment and distribution network.

David and Goliath

One needs to look no further than the Kohl's/Amazon tie up. In 2017, the pair announced that Amazon customers could return products at select Kohl's stores. In addition, many of Amazon's infamous pop-up stores have been located inside a Kohl's location. For Amazon, this represents a low-risk test. For Kohl's, it represents a short-term life raft to keep afloat with new customer traffic and scraps of revenue from Amazon to monetize unproductive retail space. Kohl's is increasing participating stores for the program[504].

New Princess

In a recent article by CNBC's retail reporter, Lauren Thomas, she discusses Target's partnership with Disney[505]. Target opened 25 Disney stores-within-a-store in October 2019 with plans for another 40 in 2020. Target will also open a small store near Disney's Florida resort in 2021. Both share a similar customer.

---

[504] Safdar, Khadeeja & Kapner, Suzanne. "Target and Kohl's gain as rivals shrink." *The Wall Street Journal.* March 6th, 2019.

[505] Thomas, Lauren. (2019, August 25th). *Disney is putting dozens of stores inside Target locations while Target set to open at Walt Disney World Resort.* Retrieved from: https://www.cnbc.com/2019/08/25/disney-and-target-are-teaming-up-to-open-stores-with-each-others-help.html

Paid Likes

PayPal and Facebook recently partnered to create Instagram Checkout[506]. Both benefit from this partnership. Facebook opens another revenue stream and PayPal fights off rivals with 40 million new customers.

TV Dinner

Celebrity chef Rachael Ray has partnered with Uber Eats to offer her recipes in 13 cities[507]. The food will be cooked at virtual restaurants bearing the Rachael Ray to Go name. The offering will run until the end of 2019 and Ray will use the trial as a test to determine if she should open permanent restaurants. The service will run in New York, Toronto, Los Angeles, Chattanooga, Portland, Houston, Baltimore, Miami, Dallas, Minneapolis, Houston, Fort Lauderdale and Seattle.

Home Theatre

Recently-purchased Canadian movie theatre operator Cineplex is trying to turn lemons into lemonade. The Toronto-based firm is positioning itself as a great spot for streaming giants like Netflix, Amazon and now Apple and Disney to launch their films first before they move to the small screen. Movie theatres have generally suffered as traffic has been challenged due to the value of streaming from home.

Legacy movie houses like Cineplex can play an important marketing role to promote new proprietary films and create a buzz before they launch to a more captive viewership. Theatres love added traffic to sell advertising and ring in add-on sales such as popcorn and cold drinks to help build margin. Cineplex and others argue that theatres offer a social experience that cannot be replicated at home.

52) Loyalty Programs — Inn dah Club

Customers aren't as loyal as before. Millennials and Generation Zs cherry pick whichever retailer is offering the best deal at a given time. Other generations are tired of one-sided programs that give users nominal benefits while making millions off purchasing data.

---

[506] Rausch, Natasha. "Shopify falls on Facebook competitor." *Bloomberg.* March 21, 2019.

[507] Krader, Kate. "Rachael Ray recipes on request." *Bloomberg.* October 11, 2019.

The loyalty industry is littered with programs that offer rewards that are lukewarm at best and boring and irrelevant at worst. Users have a few points here and a few points there in a fragmented purchasing world. There are significant opportunities to disrupt this industry.

Here are a few examples of recent loyalty programs.

Paid Loyalty – Sweating Money

One trend that I find quite interesting is the expansion of consumer paid loyalty program. This involves a consumer paying a monthly or annual fee to be part of a brand's inner customer circle. This is nothing new. Amazon has over 100 million Prime members. Costco and Sam's Club are built on membership fees.

Retailers such as Lululemon and Loblaw have tested and rolled out these types of plans[508]. At Lululemon, the customer pays $128 per year and gets a free pair of yoga pants or shorts, monthly classes and free expedited e-commerce delivery[509]. This is clever. Not only does the program build in switching costs (you feel silly shopping anywhere else now that you've paid your fee), it subsidizes the challenged economics of online shopping. The Lululemon program also creates community. Members recognize each other when wearing the program's unique garments. Finally, it enables retailers to obtain their best customers' data and purchasing habits, which is used to sell them more things. Brilliant!

Defensive Programs – Tims' Empty Net

Tim Hortons recently launched a loyalty program in Canada[510]. Tims has been in a brawl with McDonald's up here and has been scrambling to remedy soft sales. Specifically, McDonald's has been taking market share from Tim Hortons' coffee business, which still has 70 percent of the market.

The Tims program rewards customers based on visits, not specific purchases.

---

[508] Rastello, Sandrine. "Lululemon gets tighter with its most loyal customers." *Bloomberg*. December 12, 2018.

[509] "Loyalty program response strong: Lululemon says." *The Canadian Press*. December 8, 2018.

[510] Edmiston, Jake. "Tims loyalty plan to focus on visits." *The Financial Post*. March 21, 2019.

That is, you don't get stamps or tear-offs for each coffee purchase. The chain rewards customers after seven visits with a free coffee, tea or baked good. The program is not paper- or cup-based and is managed via a plastic card.

Unfortunately for Tims, the program is not working. The retailer blames the program for deflation in its fourth-quarter 2019 results. Tims is looking to modify the program to get customers using an app instead. The app would allow the firm to better track individual customer data and create targeted purchase incentives to grow the average sale.

Commitment Issues

Toronto-based Drop Technologies recently received $44 million US from investors to expand its unique millennial loyalty offering[511].

Drop links up with other loyalty cards and keeps all consumer purchase data in one spot. No swiping of loyalty cards at point of sale. The purchase is tabulated automatically. When customers use the program, they earn Drop points that allow them to cash in for gift cards at millennial-focused brands such as Uber Eats, Sephora, Amazon and Starbucks. The perceived benefit for users is that their data is all in one spot and rewards are more relevant and attainable. So far, about three million users have opted in and about 300 brands have participated.

53) New Business Models – Some Won Like U

As retail changes and existing verticals become commoditized, crowded or disrupted by new technology, retailers and partners need to keep moving. Even existing disruptors like Amazon and Apple cannot stand still. Moving to new arenas that are ripe for disruption, less competitive and that offer stronger margins can make sense for hungry investors. These moves take guts, capital and time. Let's review some examples.

Casper the Friendly Chef

Virtual or ghost kitchens are on the rise. These are restaurants without the customer interface or retail storefront. Often located off main street where rents are cheap, they make food under different restaurant brands for the growing food app

---

[511] McLeod, James. "Startup secures US$44M to expand." *The Financial Post*. August 23, 2019.

business[512].

This trend has spread throughout the U.S, Canada, China and Europe. This approach works well with food delivery apps as overheads are lower including staff, décor, furniture and rent. This enables ghost kitchens to make money while still paying Uber Eats and others their hefty commissions.

Chat Room

Best Buy was beaten up by the new retail normal and has emerged a better company as a result. As half the chains' sales were made up of smart phones and computers, it was vulnerable and had to act[513]. Best Buy has succeeded by offering in-store advice as well as services such as delivery and installation that online retailers like Amazon do not.

Porch Pirates

Amazon is ready to disrupt another big business. Residential shipping[514]. The firm announced in January 2019 that it would expand its test for Amazon Shipping from Los Angeles and London to other cities.

The service will eliminate many of the irritating fees that FedEx, UPS and other shipping companies charge. Many big couriers charge a fuel surcharge and other extra fees for residential delivery. They also charge extra for busy times like during holidays.

Amazon Shipping offers guaranteed seven-day delivery and is designed to cost customers less. This business will help Amazon obtain additional volume, allowing it to build out more of its own network.

---

[512] Isaac, Mike and Yaffe-Bellany, David. "Virtual kitchens are clear for business." *The New York Times*. August 16, 2019.

[513] Kumar, Uday Sampath. "Best Buy issues tepid holiday forecast, boosts full-year outlook." *Reuters*. November 21, 2018.

[514] Ziobro, Paul. "Amazon's pitch to woo shippers: fewer fees than FedEx, UPS." *The Wall Street* Journal. January 24, 2019.

Service Merchandise

Apple needs help. As mentioned previously, sales of its hardware products, specifically its iPhones, are flattening out with the market's domestic saturation. In addition, Apple faces formidable competition from low-priced Huawei in international markets.

In the fourth quarter of 2018, Apple's device sales fell eight percent in units. Therefore, it was no surprise that the company announced it is making a bigger push into the services business[515]. Services is not a new arena for Apple. The category makes up about 15 percent of its yearly revenue and has been growing at 20 percent per annum.

The new services include Apple News+, offering curated news articles, Apple TV+, a streaming service, and Apple Arcade, a game service. The firm wants to leverage its existing 1.4 billion customers to get a greater share of the subscription market. Most of the content will be exclusive, but in some cases it will be available on competitors' devices such as Samsung phones and Amazon Fire TV. The exact formula for revenue sharing with partners remains a mystery, but you can bet that Apple has stacked the deck nicely in its favour. In September 2019, Apple provided more details on the services, which are designed to compete with Netflix and Amazon. At the same event, Apple announced the launch of its own credit card in the United States.

Fruit Market

In an op-ed by Peter Misek, partner at Framework Venture Partners, he discusses what he calls "Fintech 2.0" and its potential future impact on the world[516].

The Apple titanium card, issued in partnership with Goldman Sachs, complements existing Apple Pay, which has been around for years and has received positive traction. One of the advantages of the Apple Card is that it updates financial purchases and loyalty points in real-time. The card offers cash back and does not charge a fee. The real benefit for consumers and a differentiator for Apple will be the seamless integration of payment and perhaps one day finance into Apple customers' lives.

---

[515] McMahon, Tamsin. "Apple makes a play for subscription services." *The Globe and Mail*. March 26, 2019.

[516] Misek, Peter. "With its new credit card, Apple gives us a glimpse into the future of finance." *The Globe and Mail*. April 2, 2019.

Misek discusses how this may one day be part of a larger service called "Apple Finance." This offering will use AI to help navigate users through their financial lives in an easy, one-stop fashion. This could be a significant development and no doubt has traditional financial institutions worried.

Misek cites how younger customers, namely millennials, are in dire need of financial coaching as estimates show only 24 percent have an understanding of basic finance, according to PWC. The data that this service would generate would be invaluable.

Alphabet City

Speaking of finance, in November 2019, Google announced it was getting into the banking business by offering chequing accounts[517]. The tech giant will partner with Citigroup and a credit union at Stanford University for the offering. Google joins Facebook, Apple and Amazon as other tech firms that have either launched or have talked to financial institutions about entering the business.

House of Lords

In late August 2019, HBC announced it was selling Lord & Taylor. Sort of. The firm sold off its brand names, inventory and operations to Le Tote, a U.S.-based clothing rental company. HBC received $132.7 million US in the deal, which also gives HBC 25 percent equity in the service[518].

The San Francisco-based Le Tote charges customers a monthly subscription fee, which allows users to rent luxury garments from the likes of Calvin Klein and Kate Spade. At the time of the deal, the inventory value in the stores was $284.2 million US. Le Tote will inherit $27 million US in loyalty liabilities and will operate 38 stores.

Couch Surfing

The co-founders of popular food delivery app SkipTheDishes are bringing their

---

[517] Rudegeair, Peter and Hoffman, Liz. " Google focused on consumer banking." *The Wall Street Journal.*" November 14, 2019.

[518] Krashinsky Robertson, Susan. "HBC selling Lord & Taylor to focus on core brand and Saks." *The Globe and Mail.* August 29, 2019.

expertise to the home furnishing market, albeit in a different manner[519].

Brothers Daniel and Joshua Simair have launched Pivot, which allows customers to rent furniture for a monthly fee. Members pay a $9.99 monthly subscription that includes delivery and returns as well as assembly and disassembly after use. Customers pay for the rental of each item (on top of the $9.99 fee) and can rent to own later if they decide to. The business is targeting transient millennials who may change jobs and apartments a few times in their 20s and 30s. There are no long-term commitments or hidden terms.

Gym Shark

ClassPass offers gym frequenters a membership-based program that allows them to gym hop and class hop as desired, but at a rate lower than typical gym drop-in prices[520].

Gym owners need to be careful, though, as they sell their services at a discounted rate. Some gyms see the app as a great marketing tool to bring in new customers or to fill open spots. Others see it as a harmful drug that feels great at first, but does more harm than good once you get hooked on it. Smells a lot like food delivery apps.

Ventura High Way

Big brands are fighting to drive innovation, too. Take the recent $100 million US investment by Starbucks with Tesla investor Valor Equity Partners to help fund start-ups in technology and foodservice[521]. Tyson Foods recently did something similar, starting "Tyson Ventures" in 2016 to develop plant-based proteins.

---

[519] Bouw, Brenda. "Co-founders of SkipTheDishes food app to launch home-furniture rental service." *The Globe and Mail*. April 15, 2019.

[520] Bouw, Brenda. "Fitness subscription service ClassPass brings new business to studios, but at what cost?" *The Globe and Mail*. March 25, 2019.

[521] "Starbucks sets up US $ 100 M fund for startups." *Reuters*. March 21, 2019.

54) Well Travelled

We are seeing more and more retailers and brands expand internationally. Facing saturated domestic markets, companies eye new markets like China and India (discussed later). Many are looking to the large U.S. market and in some cases are using Canada as a test before entering.

New Commitments

Northern Beauty

It was recently announced that U.S. makeup retailer Ulta Beauty was entering Canada[522]. It's the firm's first foray outside the United States. The chain will face significant competition from Shoppers Drug Mart, Hudson's Bay, Sephora and U.S. department stores Saks Fifth Avenue and Nordstrom.

Italian Wedding

Italy's illycaffè has announced it's looking to partner with another retailer in America. The chain wants to increase its store base in the U.S. by roughly 10 times to 200 units[523]. The family-owned firm has tapped Goldman Sachs with the task of finding a suitor.

Coffee Machine

RBI's Tim Hortons announced it was making the jump to China[524]. The chain said it will open about 1,500 shops over the next 10 years. It will be up against some formidable competition. Starbucks has 3,600 stores in 150 cities and has been in the market for 20 years. Luckin operates almost 1,400 stores in more than 25 cities. Including Burger King, Popeyes and Tims, RBI has set a target of growing from 26,000 to 40,000 restaurants globally over the next eight to 10 years[525].

---

[522] Strauss, Marina. "New Look: U.S. cosmetics chain's plan to enter Canada to intensify competition in crowded market." *The Globe and Mail*. April 15, 2019.

[523] "Illycaffe seeks partner to expand U.S. café network." *Reuters*. September 27, 2019.

[524] Wells, Jennifer. "Global growth will be a tall order for Tims." *The Toronto Star*. May 18, 2019.

[525] Sagan, Aleksandra. "Tim Hortons parent RBI aims for 40K locations worldwide." *The*

Recent Failures

Bitter Taste

Starbucks can't make it everywhere. Taste Holdings Ltd., the holder of the Starbucks licence for South Africa, recently sold its 13 stores to a local shareholder group[526]. The brand was launched to much fanfare in 2016 and made a splash for a little while. But cheaper competitors coupled with a soft economy hurt the financial results of the venture.

Amsterdam Amendment

HBC announced in September 2019 that it was closing its 15 stores in the Netherlands[527]. These stores were opened in 2017 and were branded The Bay.

Jury's Out

Red, White and Blue?

Is Lowe's pulling a Target? That is, has the U.S. home improvement chain dropped the ball with its Canadian acquisition and expansion? That topic was discussed in a recent op-ed by Konrad Yakabuski in the Globe and Mail[528]. In 2016, Lowe's bought Quebec-based Rona for $3.2 billion Cdn and, unlike its U.S. big box stores, inherited a dog's breakfast of different-sized locations and ownership arrangements.

In 2018, Lowe's wrote off $952 million US on the deal and closed 31 stores. Comparable store sales have been soft at the Canadian chain according to U.S. CEO Marvin Ellson and, most recently, Canadian head Sylvain Prud'homme left suddenly. There have been reports that Lowe's Canada will be outsourcing accounting to the U.S. and technology to India. This has caused bad blood in Quebec as jobs could be

---

Canadian Press. May 16, 2019.

[526] York, Geoffrey. "Starbucks license holder sells South African outlets for cheap." *The Globe and Mail.* November 4, 2019.

[527] "HBC to close its 15 Bay stores in the Netherlands." *The Canadian Press.* September 21, 2019.

[528] Yakabuski, Konrad. "Is Lowe's repeating Target's mistakes?" *The Globe and Mail.* November 6, 2019.

lost.

Lowe's Canada faces a much larger and more entrenched competitor in the heavy do-it-yourselfer market. Home Depot expanded into Canada long before Lowe's and has a strangle hold on that customer. The light do-it-yourselfer market is dominated by Canadian Tire and Home Hardware.

When it rains, it pours. Rona has been ordered by the Ad Standards regulator to stop using "Proudly Canadian" and "Truly Canadian" as a result of its U.S. ownership[529]. In late November 2019, Lowe's Canada announced it was shuttering 34 stores and simplifying its banners. The retailer closed 31 units in the fall of 2018 as well.

55) Cannabis – High and Dry

Being a Canadian, I might lose my citizenship if I didn't mention the legalization and development of the cannabis industry. Although weed has been legal in select jurisdictions for a couple of decades here and there, it has become a mainstream business over the last couple of years. In Canada alone, consumers purchased $1.2 billion Cdn of legal pot in 2019[530].

Don't Fear the Reefer

On October 17, 2018, Cannabis became a legal substance across all of Canada. Dry flower and oils were the first to get the nod and exactly one year later, other cannabis derivatives became legal as well. Edibles, vapes, beverages, topicals and concentrates. In the U.S., dozens of states have legalized cannabis for medical and/or recreational use, but the product has not been legalized from a federal standpoint. Weed has two main parts. THC is the part that gets you high, while CBD has therapeutic properties that can allegedly help with illness.

They Go Low We Go High

Billions have been made and billions have been lost from an investment

---

[529] "Rona ordered to stop calling stores 'Proudly Canadian.'" *The Financial Post*. November 13, 2019.

[530] Subramaniam, Vanmala. "Canadians bought $1.2B worth of legal weed in 2019." *The Financial Post*. February 22, 2020.

perspective as this new volatile category stabilizes. Retail takes on a critical role as the customer interface for this important category. Many former CPG and retail executives have been recruited to bring best practices to the weed market. Many of the retail stores I have seen are exciting and inspiring. The category has the potential to offer solid margins once the dust settles in the industry.

Woodstock Therapy

Some are focusing on the development of medicinal psilocybin (magic mushrooms) and medicinal MDMA (Molly or Ecstasy). Bruce Linton, former CEO and co-founder of Canopy Growth, the world's largest pot firm, is on the board of Toronto-based Mind Medicine. This company is currently investing in these two substances to help patients with mental illness[531].

If you're interested, I wrote a three-part article on the weed industry in Retail Insider in May 2019 titled *The New Kid In Town*.

56) Shrink Epidemic

An article by Matthew Boyle of Bloomberg discusses a growing problem affecting many retailers in the United States: Shrink.

Shrink is the retail industry term for theft and retailers including Home Depot have indicated it has gotten so bad it will begin to affect operating margins in a material way.

Some blame the opioid crisis and organized crime. According to the National Retail Federation (NRF), U.S. retailers lose about $51 billion US per annum in sales due to shrink[532].

---

[531] Ligaya, Armina. "Former Canopy co-CEO Bruce Linton sees big opportunity in psychedelics." September 17, 2019. Retrieved from: https://www.ctvnews.ca/business/former-canopy-co-ceo-bruce-linton-sees-big-opportunity-in-psychedelics-1.4597006

[532] Boyle, Matthew. "Home Depot ties theft surge to opioid crisis." *Bloomberg*. December 12, 2019.

57) China and India — The Glim' r Twins

China and India are the future of consumption. Both have populations over 1.3 billion and both have standards of living that are rising. China is currently the second-largest economy in the world (behind only the U.S.) and India is the fifth.

Many consumer packaged goods firms and retailers have China and India strategies. But both markets are not making it easy on large foreign firms looking to dominate.

<u>Young and Restless</u>

In a recent op-ed by Regina Chi from AGF Investments, she makes the case to target millennials in emerging markets such as China and India[533]. Unlike millennials in North America and Europe, emerging market millennials, or EMs as she calls them, are positive about their prospects.

With wages growing and wealth increasing, these folks are optimistic. Chi states that about 80 percent of the world's millennials are in emerging markets, with 61 percent residing in Asia, including India sub-continent. Like millennials in the developed world, these EMs have an interest in fitness and wellness, experiences, food and travel.

China

As I write this book, the U.S. and China are embroiled in a nasty trade war. According to the International Monetary Fund (IMF), China's economy is slowing, with GDP growth at 6.5 percent, the lowest since 2001[534]. Let's not forget that China's GDP grew by an average of 9.6 percent from 2000 to 2014. From 2015 to 2019, it slowed to an average of 6.8 percent. It will be significantly lower in 2020.

<u>Living it Up</u>

Luxury goods companies are particularly over-invested in China from a sales standpoint. Chinese consumers make up one-third of all luxury goods sales for

---

[533] Chi, Regina. "Millennials in emerging markets are driving growth." *The Globe and Mail*. July 19, 2019.

[534] Chidley, Joe. "'An elephant starting to run': all eyes turn to India." *The Financial Post*. December 6, 2018.

industry leaders Louis Vuitton, Burberry and Chanel[535]. Chinese spend a higher percentage of disposable income on luxury products, which has enabled outstanding growth for these brands. With China now vulnerable to a slowing economy, the industry is bracing for a slowdown.

Shopping Trip

For brands like Tiffany & Co., globalization has been a double-edged sword. The brand, like many luxury goods providers from the West, has benefited significantly from the growth of luxury shoppers in China[536]. However, when trade relations go sideways, like now, or when U.S. tourism drops, Tiffany looks less shiny. Luckily for Tiffany, LVMH bought the firm in the fall of 2019 for $16.2 billion US.

Fuel Pump

Harley-Davidson has announced it's partnering with a Chinese company to build smaller bikes in China. These models will serve markets outside the U.S.[537] In an effort to lower costs and avoid tariffs, the storied firm plans to source 50 percent of its cycles outside of the U.S. by 2027 and sees China as a huge opportunity.

Team Canada

Shopify announced in October 2019 that it had begun building a team in China — it recognizes the enormous market potential for its services[538]. The path to dominance won't be easy, though. China has entrenched national champions including Baozun, which offers similar services to Shopify. The country already has national powerhouses such as Alibaba, JD.com and WeChat. The new team's first task? Build integrative relations with payment processing firms and social media providers.

---

[535] Ryan, Carol. "Luxury-goods industry has a China problem." *The Wall Street Journal.* January 2, 2019.

[536] Winkler, Elizabeth. "Don't be lured by Tiffany's." *The Wall Street Journal.* June 5, 2019.

[537] "Harley-Davidson to build smaller bike in China." *Reuters.* June 20, 2019.

[538] Hemmadi, Murad. "Shopify begins building a team in China amid global expansion push." *The Logic.* October 4, 2019.

Retail Before, During & After COVID-19

Red Bricks

Lego is working hard to stay relevant to technology-driven children, but sees huge opportunity in emerging markets such as India and China[539].

Lego's new assortments incorporate technology such as augmented reality. In 2019, the firm planned on opening 80 stores in China where sales have risen double digit. In total, the manufacturer/retailer planned to open 170 stores around the world in 2019. This would take their global store count to a surprising 590 units.

Dragon's Lair

Chinese online behemoth Alibaba announced in November 2019 it was tapping Hong Kong stock markets to raise an expected $13.4 billion US to fund expansion[540]. This is the second time the firm has leveraged public markets through an IPO. In 2014, the company raised $25 billion US in New York. A record at the time.

The new money will be used to drive business at travel platform Fliggy, build out additional home delivery capacity and grow services site Ele.me. In addition, it will fund Youku, a video-sharing platform that is already one of the biggest in China.

Home Alone

Singles Day continues to set records in China. Alibaba reported that the 2019 shopping event produced sales of $17 billion US in the first hour, an increase of 32 percent over 2018[541]. Also known as "double eleven," the event was started in 2009 by Alibaba's founder, Jack Ma, as a sarcastic pun on Valentine's Day.

In 2019, the 24-hour extravaganza featured Jackson Yee, a local artist, and international American pop superstar Taylor Swift. Alibaba has grown Singles Day from $24 billion US in 2017 to $31.9 billion US in 2018 and $38 billion US in 2019.

---

[539] Chaudhuri, Saabira. "Lego's bid to beat the pack results in sharp drop in profit." *The Wall Street Journal*. September 4, 2019.

[540] Murdoch, Scott and Hughes, Jennifer. "Alibaba launches Hong Kong listing to fund expansion." *Reuters*. November 14, 2019.

[541] "Alibaba says Singles Day hit $ 17 billion in first hour." *Reuters*. November 11, 2019.

Taking Care of Business

Alibaba recently launched business to business (B2B) services for U.S. companies, effectively competing with Amazon and others[542]. The service will enable U.S. wholesalers, distributors and manufacturers to sell their products and services to other global and American companies. This service is operated separately from its consumer-facing sites, which include Tmall.com and Taobao.com. Amazon opened its own B2B site in 2015.

Fake it to the Limit

Alibaba is a force to be reckoned with for sure, but continues to face criticism over the amount of counterfeit goods on its Taobao.com site[543]. U.S. trade officials indicated that Alibaba was working to reduce this issue, but stopped short of removing the firm's marketplace from its list of 'notorious markets.'

J.D. Power

JD.com, a Chinese powerhouse in online shopping, opened its largest brick and mortar location in western China on November 11, 2019 — Singles Day[544]. The 50,000-square-metre store is located in Chongqing and is called JD E-SPACE. The experiential store connects consumer and products through technology.

The location features numerous brand-experience stores that showcase best sellers from Apple, Microsoft, GE and more. Key categories include electronics, beauty products, home appliances, digital accessories, office supplies, health and fitness and many others. Shoppers can use QR codes to order and have products delivered in 24 hours or pick up on site.

---

[542] Xu Klein, Jodi. "Alibaba to take on Amazon, opening business-to-business services to US companies." July 23, 2019. Retrieved from: https://www.scmp.com/business/companies/article/3019805/alibaba-take-amazon-launching-new-business-business-platform-us

[543] Mauldin, William. "Taobao.com still 'notorious' despite improvements, U.S. says." *The Toronto Star*. April 27, 2019.

[544] "JD.com opens its largest offline store to date, and in western China." Retrieved from: https://jdcorporateblog.com/jd-com-opens-its-largest-offline-store-to-date-and-in-western-china/

Dance Off

American social media giants have some serious competition in the form of TikTok. Owned by a Chinese firm called Bytedance, the app has some 1.5 billion downloads globally, of which 122 million are from the U.S. alone, according to researcher Sensor Tower[545]. In October 2019, Sensor Tower reported that new users had declined by four percent year on year[546]. This was the first time that new users had decreased since the app was launched back in 2017.

Foreigner's Greatest Hits

Costco opened its first store in China in August 2019 to wild fanfare[547]. The massive customer crowd resorted to fisticuffs and waited hours in line to buy products from the American discount store. The Shanghai store had to close down in the afternoon as a result.

Make Up Artists

Not all brands are taking a hit in China. Estée Lauder and L'Oréal are doing just fine there[548]. Millennials are making good money and shelling out for cosmetics both in retail shops and at airports where duty-free shopping is available. Estée Lauder has been pushing its brands on Tmall, Alibaba's ubiquitous e-commerce marketplace, which dominates the country.

River Runs Dry

Even Amazon has struggled in China. After trying for more than 10 years, Amazon announced in April 2019 that it was mothballing its Chinese e-commerce business. The firm will continue shipping products from one of its other

---

[545] Yuan, Li. "The firm behind TikTok's domination." *The New York Times*. November 6, 2019.

[546] Huang, Zheping and Banjo, Shelly. "Teen sensation TikTok's appeal now waning." *Bloomberg*. October 25, 2019.

[547] "Costco's China debut sparks customer fights, long queues." *Bloomberg*. August 28, 2019.

[548] "Estee Lauder sees no slump in China, beats expectations." *Reuters*. August 20, 2019.

international sites[549]. Amazon bought Joyo.com back in 2004 for $75 million US, but rebranded it in 2011 to its namesake. More recently, Amazon promoted its Amazon web services division as well as its Kindle products.

India

As China slows, the world is looking to India. The IMF estimates that India's GDP growth was 7.3 percent for 2018/2019, up from 6.7 percent the year before. India has a young, educated population with 67 percent being of working age. India's middle-class population is projected to be 500 million by 2025[550].

But India has many challenges, too. Infrastructure is in desperate need of development. The banking system needs improvement and must be built to foster entrepreneurship and economic growth. Corruption and the lack of enforcement of the rule of law are also issues, as is the fluctuation of the rupee, which can bring inflation when its currency weakens.

The re-election of Prime Minister Narendra Modi in 2019 has provided some certainty for businesses, but much work must be undertaken. Like China, income and wealth disparity is widening, which puts stress on the infant middle class. Finally, governments must walk a fine balance between driving foreign direct investment (FDI) while protecting local Indian companies.

Flip Flop

In India, the government passed regulation that prohibits non-Indian online sellers from holding their own inventory[551]. Amazon and Walmart (through its Flipkart acquisition) have invested billions in India and are obviously frustrated by this development. The retailers built a workaround where local affiliates held inventory for them, but this loophole was subsequently closed. Some say India looked to China's restriction on foreign ownership to create national champions such as Alibaba and Tencent. India's e-commerce market is expected to grow to about $72 billion US by 2022, so the stakes are high.

---

[549] Weise, Karen. "Amazon backs away from China as company struggles to gain traction." *New York Times News Service*. April 20, 2019.

[550] Chidley, Joe. "'An elephant starting to run': all eyes turn to India." *The Financial Post*. December 6, 2018.

[551] Purnell, Newley and Abrams, Corinne. "India's e-commerce rules frustrate Amazon and Walmart." *The Wall Street Journal*. January 5, 2019.

Oh Poop

Procter and Gamble has faced significant pressure from India to dispose of single-use diapers and sanitary pads[552]. The market for diapers in India is expected to grow 59 percent, so you can see why P & G has been giving India a lot of attention.

Cashmir

Lego sees massive opportunity in India. CEO Niels Christiansen was quoted as saying, "Within the next 10 years there will be more than 100 million kids in India living in middle class families." In big mature markets like the U.S., sales have been flattish recently and emerging markets are where the growth is.

Fashion Fruit

Apple has had to change its approach in order to have a chance at success in India. The American giant started making its iPhone XR in India through partner Foxconn[553]. This move benefits Apple in at least two ways. First, it allows the firm to lower its cost, thus making products more accessible versus rivals. Second, it allows Apple to demonstrate the required local content and investment to pave the way for its namesake retail stores. India has been a tough market to crack for Apple based on lower costs from competitors.

TECHNOLOGY

One of the only things that one can be sure of is the continued development of technology in retail and in our everyday lives.

As with all technological innovations, some will be successful and some will fail to gain traction. Just walk through the annual National Retail Federation (NRF) show in New York and view the plethora of technology available to the industry. Retailers know they need to utilize technology, but which ones and how?

The short answer is it depends.

It depends on what lines of business you are in, who your target customers are,

---

[552] Chaudhuri, Saabira. "P & G faces backlash over diaper, sanitary waste." *The Wall Street Journal*. April 4, 2019.

[553] "Apple starts selling locally assembled iPhone XR in India." *Reuters*. October 22, 2019.

how they buy and other inputs. It can be difficult for retailers, suppliers and service providers to wade through the number of new technologies available while managing budgets and customer engagement.

Some companies make the rookie mistake of assuming technology solves all problems. They throw the newest technology at the problem to please the board or buy some time. But if a company has a tarnished brand, broken process, too much debt, corrupt executives or whatever else eating it away, technology just makes the chaos happen quicker.

Don't fall into this trap. Get your house in order first. Then add technology to make your well-oiled machine run faster.

The Five

As mentioned previously, New York Times reporter Holly Shively discussed five changes to digital shopping we would see in 2019[554].

The first change involves more online grocery shopping. Experts expect online grocery shopping to grow from two percent now to 20 percent by 2025. Third-party delivery providers such as Shipt and Instacart have partnered with retailers to manage the heavy lifting of delivery.

The second change discussed is voice retail. Think Alexa and her competitors (Google Assistant, etc.), which now include the ability to order products through voice activation on smart phones and in vehicles. Kroger announced plans to roll out Alexa-enabled voice ordering.

As mentioned previously, the third change discussed includes the increase in retailer private labels.

The fourth change Shively discussed is the growth in artificial intelligence. AI allows retailers to know customers' purchasing habits and preferences so well they can predict what shoppers want before they realize it. This increases conversion, as offerings are almost 100 percent relevant to what the customer wants or needs.

The final point in the article is interactive aisles. Through the use of augmented reality (AR), stores like Macy's have developed technology to enable customers to visualize how furniture will look in their homes before they decide to purchase it.

---

[554] Shively, Holly. "Digital shopping is about to change." *The New York Times*. December 8, 2018.

Virtual reality (VR) will also be important as retailers look to make the store more experiential and interactive to complement online shopping.

58) Trojan Horse Race

One of the most common business models in technology is Trojan horse data monetization.

This involves a company offering its service for free so it can later sell users' data to third parties or use it itself to charge third-party firms to advertise on its platform.

The degree to which these tech platforms openly state their intentions can be suspect. Perhaps in the fine print or the legalese. The list of these tech platforms is long. Google, Facebook, LinkedIn, Amazon, Instagram, YouTube, etc. When these platforms originally launched, society didn't pay much attention to the horse as it was wheeled into the castle. Consumers felt that they were getting great value using a site for free. Free, after all, is a rare thing these days.

One-Way Contract

As time went on and these platforms got larger, consumers realized that companies were making tens of billions of dollars off their data. Also, some of these companies were using customer data in ways that surprised users. We all read about the Facebook/Cambridge Analytics scandal. One can argue that was the tipping point when society woke up to see the Trojan horse we all invited into our lives.

Law Society

This development has spawned a tidal wave of debate and potential legislation to manage tech firms. One of the first products of this was the General Data Protection Regulation (GDPR) in Europe. The GDPR has teeth. Violators can be fined up to the greater of four percent of global sales or 20 million euros.

One can argue that big tech already has what it needs. It has your data and your life is too intertwined with these platforms to stop using them. These firms have already won and are not going away.

The ZEX-Files

Harvard scholar Shoshana Zuboff sent a seismic shockwave through the tech industry with her book "The Age of Surveillance Capitalism"[555]. Her 700-page analysis was a bestseller in the U.K. and Canada and is being translated into more than 15 languages. According to an article by Frank Bajak of the Associated Press, one of the main points Zuboff makes is:

"Tech companies put out new apps designed to suck up our data trails; companies then use those insights to steer us toward our next YouTube video or Facebook interaction or Amazon purchase – and to develop their next apps. Rinse and repeat."

Current Tech Landscape

In a recent article in the New York Times, Sapna Maheshwari describes findings from walking the 2019 Shoptalk show in Las Vegas[556].

No surprise that data and automation were forefront at the event as retailers scramble to keep up with Amazon and other tech-savvy retailers and customers.

FedEx showcased its last mile delivery robot.

FaceFirst talked about its facial-recognition software that can recognize customers and send them messages while they shop in particular stores. Its software builds a customer profile that captures data such as customers' previous online purchases, how long the customer spent in that store last time and what they bought during that trip.

Orbital Insight demonstrated how it can use geolocation data from customers' cell phones to gauge and monitor mall traffic flows.

Let's review the major technology available and being used in retail along with some examples, where available.

---

[555] Bajak, Frank. "How she shook the tech industry." *The Associated Press*. December 26, 2019.

[556] Maheshwari, Sapna. "Future of retail stores to know exactly what you want." *The New York Times*. March 12, 2019.

59) AI (Artificial Intelligence)

AI has become sexy. Everyone is talking about it. Are you using AI? What are you using it for? How has it helped?

In a recent article by James McLeod in the Financial Post, he addresses some of the nuances of this powerful technology[557]. AI has the potential to significantly increase efficiency across almost all businesses. In short, AI acts like humans from a thinking and smarts standpoint.

One component of AI that is very popular is machine learning. Basically, machine learning is a system where the program learns like we do. Machine learning has a subset called deep learning, which is also receiving a lot of attention. This tech uses something called neural networks, which simulates our brains. Neural networks have garnered a lot of attention, according to McLeod, because they can process an incredible amount of data including pictures, posts, likes, comments, videos and more, incredibly quickly. They then identify patterns that enable future outcomes to be predicted.

All big tech brands use AI. Some examples are Microsoft, Amazon, Uber, Google, Facebook and many more. Managers of this technology need to be careful as the system cannot identify biases that may go against company goals — biases such as racism, sexism and others.

Sunny Ways

In a move to bolster its automation, McDonald's announced in March 2019 that it was purchasing Dynamic Yield, an AI firm, for $300 million US[558]. The firm's software will enable McDonald's to customize recommended drive-thru and restaurant kiosk orders based on a number of variables including time of day, weather and even how busy a particular location is.

Millie Van-illy

In a race to assist brick and mortar retailers from differentiating from e-

---

[557] McLeod, James. "Absorption targeted, not just kicking something off." *The Financial Post*. November 29, 2018.

[558] Elejalde-Ruiz, Alexia. "McDonald's buying AI firm Dynamic Yield for $ 300 million." *Chicago Tribune*. March 27, 2019.

commerce, some companies are using AI-driven robots. Take Twenty Billion Neuron's life-sized avatar, 'Millie'[559]. This AI acts as a salesperson, prompting customers to try products and even complements them.

Sp-eye Games

RBC, a large Canadian bank, has started to use AI alternate data to help look beyond traditional company financial statements[560]. The bank has employed AI to use tools such as web-scrapping, social media posts and satellite-image intelligence. This allows it to look for trends and consumer sentiment as inputs into its banking practice.

If a brand experiences increasing negative posts on social media, that could be a leading indicator to sales or net promotor score. If a company has too much inventory and it is stored outside, satellites can pick that up before the balance sheet shows it.

Convoy

NFI Industries, a logistics firm, started using AI to predict when its trucks need servicing before they break down[561]. This $2 billion US company uses AI to anticipate when parts on its almost 9,700 trailers and 2,200 trucks need to be recalibrated or replaced. This new approach is anticipated to save the company between $1.5 million and $2 million US per annum.

Gouge

Canadian grocer Loblaw recently announced that it used AI algorithms to try to increase margins. The effort backfired, as higher prices negatively affected sales and lowered profits[562].

---

[559] Kahn, Jeremy. "This 'Millie' really is thoroughly modern." *Bloomberg.* December 28, 2018.

[560] Shufelt, Tim. "Banks turn to Big Data for research tools." *The Globe and Mail.* August 10, 2019.

[561] Murawski, John. "A logistics provider looks to AI to keep its trucks on the road." *The Wall Street Journal.* March 13, 2019.

[562] Sagan, Aleksandra. "Loblaw's focus on margins hits sour note." *The Canadian Press.* July 25, 2019.

60) Social Media

In a July 2019 op-ed by technology entrepreneur Qasim Mohammad, he discusses the growing role of social media in the purchase decisions of shoppers within the millennial and Gen Z segments[563]. He talks about how, through mediums such as YouTube and Instagram, shopping has become a collective venture and not an individual task.

Mohammad cites a study from eMarketer that claims that between 2016 and 2018, social media was growing seven times faster than paid search in driving shoppers to e-commerce websites. In another study, the percentage of shoppers who claim social media sites drove purchase decisions increased from 27 to 36 percent in the U.S. from 2015 to 2018.

Crowd Control

Mohammad references China's Pinduoduo as an example of crowdbuying. The firm's platform of 500 million users works in groups to provide feedback and confirmation on vendor designs and get a discount by recommending the product to friends. This movement involves live interactions and curated assortments that are reinforced through social media groups tapping into celebrities and influencers.

Mohammad also discusses Mogu. The brand claims that 24 percent of its sales are made during live events, where its 48,000 influencers market to its 62 million users.

Finally, Drake-backed, Los Angeles firm NTWRK has been called the "QVC for Gen Z" based on the use of the practices above.

Buzz Cut

BuzzFeed is not known for product development. But the massive millennial platform has upped its game thanks to a new service to help brands co-develop products[564]. In an article by Gerry Smith of Bloomberg, he outlines the success that Scotts Miracle-Gro experienced by partnering with BuzzFeed to develop Lunarly, a

---

[563] Mohammad, Qasim. "Community-driven commerce represents a new era of consumerism." *The Globe and Mail.* July 5, 2019.

[564] Smith, Gerry. "BuzzFeed will tell you what millennials want…for a fee." *Bloomberg.* November 19, 2018.

subscription business. Based on the lunar calendar, customers are mailed gardening products from the firm. BuzzFeed executive Ben Kaufman came up with the idea and brought in experts to brainstorm ideas for his client. Kaufman was quoted as saying:

"Companies make a thing, then tell media companies 'Please tell the world about this.' It should work in a more collaborative fashion. We should say, 'Here's what we think the world needs. Can you make this?'"

Dislike

In Canada, Instagram removed the public visibility of the number of likes a user receives for a particular post. This has been a good move for society overall, but perhaps not for small business owners who rely on likes to demonstrate customer popularity of products and posts[565].

Many small businesses don't have the big marketing bucks to formally spend on social media, and Instagram is a cheap and cheerful way to create awareness. Will this test be rolled out to the balance of Instagram markets? What can companies do to work around this?

61) Voice Activation and Smart Home

Voice activation technology has increased in popularity due in large part to Amazon's Echo system. The technology is convenient, relatively inexpensive and has numerous applications. Many pundits feel this technology will be used for retail extensively.

McLabour Savings

McDonald's announced in September 2019 that it had bought start-up Apprente Inc. for an undisclosed sum[566]. Apprente offers voice-activation software that can replace employees when customers order at McDonald's drive-thrus. McDonald's does about 70 percent of its business through drive-thru ordering and

---

[565] Devlin, Megan. "Instagram changes prompt business owners to rethink marketing strategies." *The Globe and Mail*. August 5, 2019.

[566] Patton, Leslie. "McDonald's bets on automated drive-thru ordering." *Bloomberg*. September 11, 2019.

this development can save labour. McDonald's is also using this acquisition to start its own Silicon Valley technology lab for further innovation. The Apprente system is already in place at a Chicago McDonald's and, depending on the results, is targeted to roll out across all markets eventually.

Echo Beach

Amazon is upping its game and giving Alexa a makeover. Launching in 2020, the new Echo is wider, with more space for sound and other capabilities. The firm has to defend its position. With a commanding 60-plus percentage share of the home assistant market, it leads second-place Google with just over 30 percent. Other smaller players include Apple's HomePod and Sonos. Amazon is also working on a rolling robot that follows Alexa's instructions. The item, known internally as "Vesta," is still in the works.

Stockholm Smarts

IKEA recently announced it is making a major push into the smart home segment[567]. The Swedish giant hopes to offer customers affordability and simplicity in its offering in comparison to other large tech companies.

Talking Fruit

Apple is playing catch-up in the smart-home market. The giant signalled that it wants to gain ground on well-established rivals Amazon and Google[568]. Apple entered the market in 2014 with its HomeKit service.

The Word of Zuck

Facebook recently confirmed that it's working on its own voice assistant to go up against Amazon's Alexa, Google's Assistant and Apple's Siri[569].

---

[567] "Ikea jumps into smart-home technology." *The Logic.* October 3, 2019.

[568] Gurman, Mark. "Apple revamps smart home efforts to catch competitors." *Bloomberg.* November 12, 2019.

[569] "Facebook working on voice assistant to rival Alexa." *Reuters.* April 18, 2019.

62) Facial Recognition

One technology that is gaining popularity across many industries, including retail, is facial recognition.

Also known as biometrics, this technology has gone mainstream. The software is already being used at airports for security clearances. Perhaps the defining moment for this technology was its inclusion on the Apple iPhone in 2018. But with this exciting technology comes significant privacy concerns.

Say My Name

In an article by Katherine Bindley in the Wall Street Journal, she explores facial recognition technology and its applications for retail[570].

One of the potential applications in retail is quick payment. Step forward and let the scanner read your face and that new shirt is yours. Another potential application that Bindley discusses is in-store marketing and customization. Imagine walking into a store and facial recognition software instantly recognizes you from past purchases or even scans your social media history or search history. Magically, video screens show you products that algorithms predict you will be interested in. You get an alert and see that the retailer has texted you a special offer. The software could alert a store associate and he or she may address you by name and let you know about a particular promotion the system has designed specifically for you. Sounds great, right? Not necessarily.

First-Mover Disadvantage

According to Bindley, there are numerous retailers that are wary of this technology. Who wants to violate shoppers' privacy at a time when it is so controversial? When the technology *does* appear in retail, brands will claim to gather generic information only. Retailers will say they capture only high-level, anonymous data such as gender, ethnicity, height, weight and age. But this will change quickly. Specific user data will soon be captured, as that is where the money lies.

Minority Rapport

The fear with facial recognition is that our biometric data will be captured and

---

[570] Bindley, Katherine. "Facial recognition goes mainstream." *The Wall Street Journal*. September 22, 2018.

sold to third parties or bad actors. These firms could use the data to effectively market to customers every waking moment. Even worse, they could use the data to steal identities. We are already bombarded with ads on smartphones, but at least you can turn your smartphone off. You can't wear a mask in society to stop facial-recognition software from tracking you down.

Or can you?

Professor Arun Ross from Michigan State University's department of engineering and computer science is quoted as saying, "It is likely that some of the data that we have provided in the past will come back to haunt us."

63) Apps

Apps are commonplace in retail and have become a table stake to compete in many verticals. Any brand targeting millennials or Generation Z pretty much has to have one. Even boomers and Gen Xers are comfortable with them.

The real question for retailers, then, is *why* have an app? What value does it add for your customers? Does it make their life easier? Does it solve a problem? Or is just for show so you can say you have one? Can you use an app to differentiate from your competitors? If so, how?

Search Mart

Google continues to focus on retail and will soon launch its own standalone shopping app[571]. At a conference in 2019, the firm committed to update its shopping experience by offering personalized products and a digital shopping cart.

Two-Faced

For many retailers and suppliers, Google acts as both advertising partner and competitor. With $116 billion US in digital advertising revenue in 2018, it leads the market. But the company faces competition from Amazon and Instagram as marketers try new mediums and diversify their spend.

---

[571] Bergen, Mark. "Google unveils slew of new digital ad formats." *Bloomberg*. May 15, 2019.

American Snipe-R

As a result, Google has added more options for retailers and suppliers to target consumers with their ads. It will add targeted ads for Gmail, its voice-activated personal assistant and its YouTube mobile app, Google Images. It will also make its personalized news feed, Discover, available to advertisers and even allow YouTube watchers to buy products right from the video they are watching.

Let's Buy a Gram

Facebook recently announced it was launching Instagram Checkout[572]. This new service allows customers to shop and buy online without switching platforms.

Meal Jockeys

We are seeing consolidation in the high-growth, crowded food app arena. During the summer of 2019, U.K.'s Just Eat and Amsterdam's Takeaway.com announced they were merging[573]. The two firms want to become global brands and more effectively compete against Amazon-affiliate Deliveroo, Uber Eats and others.

Deep-Dish Downer

One segment of the restaurant and food service market that isn't thrilled with the plethora of food delivery apps is the pizza business[574]. Both Domino's Pizza and Pizza Hut have felt pressure on same store sales as a direct result of this dynamic.

64) Mobile

Mobile is the king and queen of retail technology. As Anne D'Innocenzo writes about in the Associated Press, the mobile phone, once a threat to retailers, is now their BFF[575]. Retailers used to see mobile phones as an enabler to showrooming —

---

[572] Rausch, Natasha. "Shopify falls on Facebook competitor." *Bloomberg*. March 21, 2019.

[573] Sandle, Paul and Meijer, Bart H. "Takeaway.com and Just Eat agree on terms of merger." *Reuters*. August 6, 2019.

[574] Devlin, Megan. "Losing a slice of the pie." *The Globe and Mail*. July 17, 2019.

[575] D'Innocenzio, Anne. "Retailers embrace smartphones." *The Associated Press*. December 13, 2018.

comparing prices online from competitors and then leaving the store to buy the product online.

Retailers now understand the importance of this technology. Retailer apps allow customers to use phones to enhance in-store experience through product knowledge, digital maps and scan-and-pay capabilities. According to Adobe Analytics, 33 percent of U.S. Black Friday sales were made via mobile phone in 2018. This is up from 29 percent in 2017.

D'Innocenzo highlights areas for improvement. These include spotty Wi-Fi, unreliable 'click-and-collect' and more.

Hard Body

Customers at Nike's flagship in New York City can use their phones to scan products on mannequins, have them sent to a change room and ultimately purchase them.

Crooked Queue

Walmart Canada resorted to something called "line rushing" to speed up customer payments during Black Friday 2018[576]. The process consisted of store associates using mobile technology to scan products that customers wanted to buy while they were standing in line. The associate would then print out a slip that the customer would present to the cashier for payment. Simple but effective.

Posh Parade

Other retailers, such as Saks Off 5th, have used mobile payment technology to scan and process credit card and debit transactions throughout the store, allowing customers to avoid lines altogether.

Missing Link

Moneris, a Canadian payment processing company, has found a way to track digital advertising with in-store purchases[577]. Tracking the effectiveness of digital

---

[576] Stancu, Henry. "Retailers using new tricks to keep the lines moving." *The Toronto Star.* December 27, 2018.

[577] Krashinsky Robertson, Susan. "Moneris links digital ads to offline sales as data collection faces greater scrutiny." *The Globe and Mail.* November 5, 2018.

advertising for online shopping has been in place for some time. But as most retail purchases are still in-store, this new tool has value.

Moneris asks advertisers to embed a tracker in each digital ad it shows. The firm can then triangulate mobile and stationary devices that have viewed the ad with credit card numbers that have made in-store purchases.

Flash Drive

Starbucks recently announced an equity deal with Brightloom to enable improvement in speed of mobile ordering and payment[578].

65) Robots

Robots have become popular in retail. From warehouse fulfillment to home delivery and shelf management, they reduce labour costs and increase efficiency. They usually require a sizable upfront investment, but pay for themselves over time.

Let's look at a few applications.

In-Store

Discount Droid

Like other retailers, Walmart is using automation to reduce store labour costs so it can reallocate staff to fill online orders. In a recent article in the Wall Street Journal, Walmart was highlighted for its use of robots to unload trucks, clean floors and monitor store inventory[579].

About 1,500 Walmart stores will get automated cleaning technology, 1,200 will get backroom conveyor belts, 300 will get electronic shelf scanners to look for out-of-stocks, and 900 will use automated pick-up towers. This allows click-and-collect

---

[578] Haddon, Heather. "Starbucks takes stake in tech company Brightloom." *The Wall Street Journal*. July 27, 2019.

[579] Nassauer, Sarah and Cutter, Chip. "Walmart is rolling out the robots." *The Wall Street Journal*. April 10, 2019.

customers to get in and out quickly, without human interaction.

Walmart recently hired about 40,000 workers to pick and pack e-commerce orders as it competes with Amazon.

Fulfillment

Kung Fu Grip

Using robots in warehousing is nothing new. Using robots that can grip products like a human *is* new. Kindred Systems Inc. has managed to do just that[580]. With its proprietary Sort system, a robot uses sensors to identify products and learns how to grip objects with the right pressure and at the right angle.

The robot learns from humans and is programmed to call a worker over when it doesn't know how to handle a particular product. Like other AI systems, the robot learns from each human correction and gets smarter the more orders it manages. The system is being tested with several retailers including The Gap. Although the speed of the system needs to improve, pundits see potential in this technology as fulfillment infrastructure becomes more automated.

Micro Machine

Loblaw is testing an in-store click-and-collect solution from Takeoff Technologies that enables a "micro fulfillment centre" at one of its Toronto stores[581]. In 2020, the grocer will use 12,000 square feet of less-productive space at one of its Real Canadian Superstores and pilot the concept. The space will be used as a hub for other nearby stores to fulfill click-and-collect and home-delivery orders. Currently, Loblaw tasks employees to walk the aisles and shop on behalf of customers. This takes time and congests the space for other in-store shoppers.

Schnitzel Maker

Germany is a tough market for grocers. Germans are incredibly price sensitive and competition is fierce. Any edge is critical. Selling fresh food online, even for Amazon, involves manual labour to ensure product is fresh and visually appealing.

---

[580] Nowak, Peter. "This smart robot packs potential for large retailers." *The Globe and Mail*. November 22, 2018.

[581] Krashinsky Robertson, Susan. "Loblaw food sales flat as rivals keep prices in check." *The Globe and Mail*. November 14, 2019.

German Grocer Rewe Group has developed a warehouse that automates fresh food like no other[582]. Rewe's 20,000-SKU fresh warehouse cost about $120,000 US to build and is compliant with Germany's strict fresh food temperature control standards. The closest thing would be U.K.'s Ocado, which has licensed its technology to Kroger in the U.S. and Empire in Canada.

Double Rink

Speaking of Ocado and Empire, Sobeys recently announced it now has two Ocado warehouses in Canada to deliver groceries[583]. With a capital budget at $190 million Cdn, these warehouses aren't cheap.

In the U.K., where Ocado currently operates, the online grocery market is eight percent of grocery retail sales. In the U.S., that number is four percent. Currently at about one percent in Canada, many feel this number will grow significantly.

Sobeys' approach differs from Loblaw, which, like Walmart, has used Instacart for delivery and heavily markets click-and-collect as a preferred channel.

Last-Mile Delivery

Captive Courier

Bloomberg recently reviewed "Beep boop," FedEx's new delivery robot[584]. The device is designed to deliver packages from local stores to customers' homes. With a range of 13 kilometres and a speed of about 16 km/h, this little workhorse has no problem dodging people, tackling curbs and even going up steps.

FedEx confirmed that Walmart, Lowe's and Target will test the unit. FedEx is the biggest, but not the only, company to invest in this technology, as Starship Technologies and Kiwi offer a version as well.

---

[582] Weiss, Richard. "Playing Tetris in Germany to keep Amazon Fresh at bay." *Bloomberg.* November 17, 2018.

[583] Strauss, Marina. "Sobeys doubles down on e-commerce technology." *The Globe and Mail.* May 9, 2019.

[584] Black, Thomas. "'Beep boop' is robot for your package has arrived." *Bloomberg.* February 28, 2019.

Delivery Boy

Amazon has decided to expand tests of its autonomous delivery robot, Scout[585]. Amazon has been busy mapping select suburban regions of America to test Scout in a special design centre. Originally tested in Seattle, the bots have begun delivery in Irvine, California.

66) Cashierless Stores

One of the most discussed topics in retail at this time is cashierless store technology. Amazon made this concept a reality when it launched its Amazon Go stores. One can see how this innovation makes shopping easier for the time-starved customer. It also lowers payroll costs in the low-margin grocery industry, where the technology has so far been applied.

A recent article by Matt Day and Spencer Soper from Bloomberg highlights the rush by technology companies, investors and retailers to emulate Amazon Go capabilities[586].

Launched in early 2018, Amazon Go made noise with all retailers as a better option than scan-and-go technology recently tested at stores like Walmart. According to PitchBook, U.S. venture capital firms invested $111 million US to fund companies that are in the store automation arena. Some of the tech firms that are jockeying for position include Mighty AI, AiFi, Caper and many more.

Walkin' on Funshine

As mentioned, in February 2020, Amazon opened its first full-sized, cashierless grocery store in Seattle called Go Grocery[587]. In March 2020, it announced it would be selling this technology — called "Just Walk Out technology by Amazon" — to

---

[585] Holley, Peter. "Amazon to expand delivery by robots." *The Washington Post*. August 13, 2019.

[586] Day, Matt and Soper, Spencer. "Amazon Go, one year old, has attracted a lot of imitators." *Bloomberg*. January 23, 2019.

[587] Pisani, Joseph. "Amazon expands no-cashier stores." *The Associated Press*. February 26, 2020.

other retailers [588].

Golden Gate

San Francisco is also becoming a test ground for cashierless shopping technology[589]. The biggest and most famous is, of course, Amazon with its Amazon Go store. The Seattle firm has four such locations in the city. According to Sebastian Herrera at the Wall Street Journal, there is a stretch of about a square mile where numerous start-ups, including Standard Cognition and Zippin (Vcognition Technologies Inc.), have joined Amazon to demonstrate their technology in a live test environment. The technology for all three players is similar. Numerous cameras feed images into computers that use machine learning to capture each transaction.

Go Limey, Go!

Amazon has opened 16 Amazon Go stores in four different cities as of October 2019, with another 3,000 potentially on the books by 2021. Sizes of Amazon Go stores currently range from 450 square feet to 2,300 square feet. Amazon has been scouting out London, England for its Go concept and already operates seven Whole Foods Markets in that market.

Porto Programmers

A Portuguese start-up called Sensei is giving Amazon's cashierless technology a run for its money[590]. At least in Europe. The company confirmed three large U.K. grocers are onboard to use or test its technology. Sensei uses cameras and AI to enable transactions and, like Go technology, requires customers to use a payment card or mobile phone code to begin.

Buggy Builder

New York-based Caper Inc. and Seattle-based Veeve Inc. have developed smart

---

[588] Porter, Jon. "Amazon will start selling cashierless Go system to other retailers." March 9, 2020. Retrieved from: https://www.theverge.com/2020/3/9/21171230/amazon-just-walk-out-technology-cashierless-go-stores-third-party-retailers

[589] Herrera, Sebastian. "Silicon Valley takes on Amazon's cashierless Go stores." *The Wall Street Journal*. October 19, 2019.

[590] Milligan, Ellen and Kahn, Jeremy. "Amazon facing a supermarket battle." *Bloomberg*. April 8, 2019.

Retail Before, During & After COVID-19

shopping carts.

Canadian grocer Empire announced in October of 2019 that it would be testing Caper's smart carts at its stores. The carts would allow customers to shop, place items in the cart, see a running total of what they have bought, pay and leave. The first store is in Canada's affluent Oakville, outside of Toronto.

The grocer says the carts will one day be able to plan meals with customers and help them find the most efficient path in the grocery aisles to procure what's on a shopping list. The goal of the test is to reduce time spent shopping for time-starved, technology-friendly customers.

Shopping Spree

As mentioned, Walmart Canada launched a prototypical store of the future in west Toronto in late spring, 2019. One of the key features of this store is the ability for customers to use their "scan-and-go" app[591].

Shoppers can walk around the store and scan products with their phone, bag them as they go, then line up in a designated "fast lane" to confirm payment to their credit card. If customers don't want to use the app, they can use one of six human cashier lanes. The store has 18 self-checkouts as well. Walmart Canada says the new approach can save customers between 10 percent and 25 percent in time spent shopping.

Not for Everyone

In the U.S., Walmart tested a version of scan and go, and results were mixed. It kept it at Sam's Club but discontinued it at its namesake stores.

Cashier Crusade

Recent changes to the payment process at stores, including self-checkout using portable scanners, has some customers annoyed. In a recent article by Tara Deschamps from the Canadian Press, she cited how some customers said the technology was "cumbersome" and that it actually took a longer time to complete grocery shopping[592]. One customer felt the technology was OK if you buy a few

---

[591] Strauss, Marina. "Walmart tests fast-shopping app in Canada in digital push." *The Globe and Mail*. May 29, 2019.

[592] Deschamps, Tara. "Self-checkouts, portable tech leave patrons less free than

items, but if you have a cart full of food, it was quicker and easier to have the cashier scan the items old-school.

Retailers need to be very careful, as any time they try to push labour onto the customer without a meaningful benefit in return, they balk.

Beaver Damn

Canadian grocery giant Metro has accelerated its use of automation for applications such as self-serve checkouts and electronic shelf labels to offer customers convenience, but also to lower labour costs[593].

Self-checkout lanes have become common place in Canada. I have seen them in virtually all large grocers, drug stores and general merchandisers. They save time for those customers comfortable using them. They also save retailers labour dollars. Shrink can be an issue, though, so retailers need to put processes in place to mitigate this risk while not pis*ing off loyal customers.

Weight Loss Program

In a recent article in the Wall Street Journal, the trials and tribulations of self-checkouts are examined. American retailers are experimenting with cameras to lower theft. They are finding that original equipment weight sensors are causing too much friction with customers and slowing down the checkout process. Too many "wait for assistance" alerts are popping up[594].

Box Drop

Experts have indicated that costs for store automation are coming down. It was reported that 7-Eleven was quoted about $1 million US to run a cashierless system in one of its stores a few years ago. Some say it might cost $100,000 US to $300,000 US today, depending on the number of cameras required.

---

expected." *The Canadian Press*. December 24, 2018.

[593] Sagan, Aleksandra. "Metro fast-tracks self-serve checkouts to help boost bottom line." *The Canadian Press*. August 15, 2019.

[594] Nassauer, Sarah. "Stores and shoppers agree: Self-checkout is hard." *The Wall Street Journal*. February 15, 2020.

67) Blockchain

Blockchain technology became topical in 2017 and 2018, but lacks widespread application.

Spin Cycle

In an article by Terence Corcoran in the Financial Post, he references research firm Gartner's "cycle of hype" for technology[595]. The theory revolves around technology moving through several stages. The first stage involves the "technology trigger." The second consists of the "peak of inflated expectations." The third and final stage is the "trough of disillusionment." Technology is discovered, it becomes larger than life as the be all and end all, only to have reality set in that it will never live up to its reputation.

Blue Blocks

Corcoran argues that Blockchain technology has fallen victim to this cycle. In 2016, reputable firms such as IBM promoted the technology and ran TV ads promoting it (branded IBM Blockchain). The industry was riding high on the wave of cryptocurrency popularity such as Bitcoin. Fast forward to 2019 and Blockchain has become a niche technology that provides tracking for food at retailers such as Walmart.

Here are some examples of its use:

Wake-Up Call

A company called Farmer Connect has used Blockchain technology to create a fair-trade coffee platform that provides transparency to its supply chain[596]. The coffee industry has a reputation of having an opaque, sometimes suspect sourcing process. The system includes a consumer-facing component called Thank My Farmer that gives end customers visibility into where the coffee was roasted, exported, imported, milled and farmed. It will eventually show pricing at each stage of the value chain. The system is backed by large Swiss coffee trader Sucafina and includes participation from brands such as Jacobs Douwe Egberts and J.M. Smucker. The

---

[595] Corcoran, Terence. "Blockchain stuck in the spin cycle." *The Financial Post*. January 9, 2019.

[596] Almeida, Isis. "Top coffee companies turn to tech in bid to lure customers." *Bloomberg*. September 21, 2019.

system also helps farmers build credit history for financing purposes.

Lock and Key

SecureKey Technologies has created a system using blockchain to enable banks with customer identification[597].

K-Pop

Samsung announced it was launching a smartphone in South Korea that was made for blockchain technology[598]. The phone, called the KlaytnPhone, will have specific apps designed for cryptocurrencies and is a derivative of the Samsung Galaxy Note10. The phone is named after the country's popular blockchain platform, Klaytn.

68) Drones

Sometimes technology takes longer to perfect than one anticipates. Take the case of drones. According to an article published by the Associated Press, Jeff Bezos famously claimed in 2013 that drones would be actively delivering Amazon packages by now[599].

Not the case, I'm afraid. One of the major reasons involves constraints on battery life. Another involves regulation and government approval. In the United States, the government body in charge of regulating drones is the Federal Aviation Administration, or FAA.

Under the Radar

It is estimated that in 2018, 110,000 commercial drones were in operation in the United States. This number is expected to balloon to about 450,000 by 2022. Some

---

[597] Alexander, Doug. "Banks adopt blockchain for client identity verification." *Bloomberg.* May 2, 2019.

[598] Jeong, Eun-Young. "Samsung launches smartphone meant to make blockchain friendlier." *The Wall Street Journal.* September 6, 2019.

[599] Koenig, David and Pisani, Joseph. "Amazon's customers are still waiting for the drones." *The Associated Press.* December 4, 2018.

experts feel we are about 10 years away from active drone flights, whereby a drone can fly outside of the operator's site.

Moon Shot

In the U.S., NASA is in year four of four in its efforts to set national traffic standards for drones[600]. It has used cities like Reno to test drone flights outside of users' line of sight.

Winging it

Google's sister company, Wing, has been actively testing drones for e-commerce deliveries in Australia. Local state officials cited complaints by residents as it relates to wildlife interference, privacy and noise[601]. The concerns have pointed to the need for increased regulations. Wing has used Australia as a testing ground before potentially expanding to the United States.

69) Autonomous Vehicles

This technology, once perfected, has significant opportunity in retail. Self-driving vehicles could pick up and drop off tractor-trailer loads of product, deliver products and food to homes, provide ride-sharing services and offer local bus tours.

In a recent article by Neal E. Boudette from the New York Times, he examines the journey car companies and other firms are travelling in an attempt to make autonomous vehicles commonplace[602].

---

[600] Sonner, Scott. "NASA's first-of-kind tests look to manage drones in cities." *The Associated Press.* May 25, 2019.

[601] Cherney, Mike. "Some want drones to buzz off. Would stricter rules sway them?" *The Wall Street Journal.* August 6, 2019.

[602] Boudette, Neal E. "Roadblocks aside, self-driving cars seen as a way of the future." *The New York Times.* July 20, 2019.

Pareto Parking

According to Boudette, companies are about 80 percent complete developing technology that is safe to use. The remaining 20 percent hangs in the balance and the timeline to completion is unknown.

Numerous companies are working to perfect the technology. These include Ford and Volkswagen through Argo AI, Alphabet's Waymo, Aurora (backed by Amazon) and Cruise (a product of GM but with help from Honda and SoftBank).

There have been several deaths attributed to self-driving vehicles. This demonstrates that the technology, while promising, still has a way to go.

70) Virtual Reality

Virtual reality currently has limited applications within retail. I think this will change over time, though. Look for this technology to play an important role in the future. In the short run, however, the honeymoon might be over from an investor's perspective.

A Follow for a Follow

When Facebook bought Oculus in 2014 for $2 billion US, the investor community followed[603]. At its peak in 2016, U.S. investors funded $253 million US across 24 start-ups to gain exposure to this technology.

Since then, investment has tailed off as consumers have not adopted the technology en masse. In 2018, seven million virtual reality sets were shipped worldwide. This compares to 100 million smart speakers, according to IDC, a research firm.

71) Augmented Reality

Unlike its cousin, virtual reality, augmented reality is being used in retail with greater frequency. The biggest application so far is in the furniture category. Other

---

[603] Lee, Wendy. "VR gets reality check with significant decline in investment." *The Los Angeles Times*. January 19, 2019.

uses include fashion, where customers can virtually try on different garments using special AI-driven mirrors.

Appetite for Construction

IKEA is launching a new app that allows customers to use augmented reality to visualize products in their own home, then purchase them[604]. The app integrates in-store, online and mobile channels. IKEA realizes not everyone has the time to shop at its large traditional stores.

The app will launch in France and the Netherlands. Additional cities will be added over time. As mentioned previously, IKEA has started to offer small downtown stores that carry less assortment. The app helps fill in the blanks and allows urban shoppers to shop in a simulated reality. Customers can also point their phone at a product and see different versions (colour, pattern, material) to determine what looks best.

IKEA has competition from Made.com, a digital native that added bricks and mortar showrooms. Made.com recently launched a paid interior design service that uses AI to make product recommendations with 3-D visuals.

72) 3-D Printing

So far, 3-D printing has been used scarcely within retail. Cost and application are current barriers to widespread use.

Hologram

In an op-ed by Joe Atikian in the Globe and Mail, he dispels 3-D printing as revolutionary from an application perspective. Author of *Industrial Shift: The Structure of the New World Economy*, Atikian makes the argument that the technology has limited widespread economical application. Outside of the hearing-aid industry and a few others, he sees the technology as expensive and relegated to non-critical parts such as housings and casings. He refers to a 2015 Harvard Business Review article that forecasted that 3-D printers would be widespread by now. He argues this is not the

---

[604] Thomasson, Emma. "IKEA to revamp app as strategy shifts toward online shopping." *Reuters.* May 28, 2019.

case[605].

73) Customer Lifetime Value (CLV) Software

Customer lifetime value, or CLV, software is very popular in retail.

Sometimes referred to as customer management systems, or customer relationship management systems, they allow brands to manage their customers as they would a portfolio of products.

The process involves harvesting data from customers and then classifying them and proactively managing them to drive sales, profits, retention and customer satisfaction. One of the key metrics used in this approach is forecasting what a given customer's lifetime value is to a company — their estimated profit potential in the future based on projected purchases.

VIP (Very Ignorant Purchaser) Customer

In an article by Khadeeja Safdar in the Wall Street Journal, the concept of customer lifetime value is discussed in detail[606]. Through technology from companies such as Salesforce, Zeta Global and others, customers are scored for a particular company based on potentially thousands of data points across numerous societal interactions to sort the best customers from the worst.

Carrots and Sticks

Depending on whether you are married or single, male or female, educated or uneducated, a complainer or a grin-and-bear-it type, we all have a score. Software uses this score to decide what we get from a service and offer standpoint. If you are a highly-valued customer, you get the quickest service and the best perks. If you are a royal pain in the a*s, you wait in the queue and get nothing. None of us knows what our score is and what specific criteria companies use to determine how they calculate our ranking. The algorithms are more complex than just how much we spend per year.

---

[605] Atikian, Joe. "Claims that 3-D printing will disrupt industry more hype than reality." *The Globe and Mail*. December 1, 2019.

[606] Safdar, Khadeeja. "On hold for 45 minutes? It might be your customer score." *The Wall Street Journal*. November 3, 2018.

Profiler

Your customer lifetime score is usually composed of data that is bought from a variety of companies that you interact with daily. All this is happening behind the scenes without your knowledge and probably without your expressed consent. The most telling sign in Safdar's article was the number of companies, such as Verizon and Sprint, that declined to comment on the article or provide details on how they are using your data to score you.

74) Wearables

Wearables are popular in retail as a consumer product, not as a sales-generating device. For now.

Mood Ring

According to a recent Bloomberg article, Amazon is collaborating with Lab126 to develop a wearable, voice-activated device that can read and recognize human emotions[607]. The device, categorized under health and wellness, would work with smartphones to determine how you feel based on the sound you make while talking. This, of course, could lead to customized offers based on your particular mood at that moment.

75) 5G Networks

There has been much talk about the rollout of 5G technology. This technology allows users to upload and download large data exponentially faster than today's 4G network.

The reality is that although 5G can be hundreds of times faster than existing 4G networks, it is expected to take a decade before this new technology becomes commonplace[608]. Apple is getting ready to launch its new 5G iPhones and devices in

---

[607] Day, Matt. "A device that can read human emotions." *Bloomberg*. May 29, 2019.

[608] Lewis, Michael. "Companies prepared to pay billions to roll out 5G technology." *The Toronto Star*. January 4, 2019.

2020[609]. Once the technology becomes mainstream, one can see the applications for retail, such as video streaming, real-time AI interaction and so forth.

76) Neural Implants

This technology is far from being used in retail at this time, but has the potential to revolutionize the industry several decades from now.

Six-Billion-Dollar Scan

Elon Musk's two-year-old Neuralink start-up looks to connect the human mind with computers[610]. Musk and team have targeted medical applications and have had successful tests using monkeys.

It isn't a stretch to see this technology having multiple applications beyond therapy and health care. Neuralink is making a detailed proposal to the U.S. Food and Drug Administration to obtain permission to start human trials. Other companies have been working in this space as well, including Paradromics, Facebook, CTRL-labs and Kernel.

77) Pick-Up Towers

Automated, in-store pick-up towers are gaining popularity. Walmart has rolled out the towers in about 700 stores in the United States. Canadian retailer Canadian Tire has piloted the towers in five stores and is rolling them out further[611].

Tinder Block

The 16-foot towers can hold between 250 and 300 packages and can dispense

---

[609] Gurman, Mark. "Apple announces three iPhone 11 models, new watch, iPad." *Bloomberg*. September 11, 2019.

[610] Hernandez, Daniela and Mack, Heather. "Elon Musk's Neuralink advances brain-computer interface." *The Wall Street Journal*. July 20, 2019.

[611] Stancu, Henry. "Retailers hope that self-serve towers will reduce wait times." *The Toronto Star*. November 6, 2018.

products in less than a minute. Customers buy online and then receive an email once the product is ready and loaded.

78) Window Dressing

FrontRunner Technologies has made vacant retail storefronts sexy and exciting. It found a way to take vacant stores and use them to project big-screen images that captivate passersby while collecting valuable data[612].

The firm's Firefly system uses translucent film that is placed on property windows, which acts as a screen for laser projectors inside the property. The result: a dynamic, attention-getting ad or message that gets folks to stop and check out what's happening.

The company uses an application called WindowFront, which gathers data from smartphones of people within 100 feet of the shop. This, along with special cameras, allows FrontRunner to provide its landlord clients with demographics and analytics to help determine interest and opportunities. The system generates data such as how many unique people passed by, how long they stayed, if they were male or female, what their approximate age was, their ethnicity and how they felt about the vacancy based on facial expressions.

This program is in play in several cities across North America. The company hoped to have 200 of these by the end of 2019 and 5,000 up and being used by 2021.

79) Supply Chain Transparency: Forrest Grump

Canadian not-for-profit environmental organization Canopy (not the weed firm) has developed a tool that enables a more transparent supply chain for viscose, the raw material made into rayon[613]. Previously, there was little knowledge of which forest a particular batch of viscose originated from. This concerned the fashion industry, as preserved forests could be used to harvest the material nefariously.

---

[612] Immen, Wallace. "Virtual window dressing is revitalizing vacant retail space." *The Globe and Mail*. August 27, 2019.

[613] Roston, Eric. "Fashion turns to technology to save trees." *Bloomberg*. November 12, 2018.

H&M, as well as NGOs, provided research into which forests were protected, while Canopy brought satellite imagery.

80) Other Tech Applications

Fit Bit

Canadian start-up Passen Technologies has developed software that measures clothing fit for specific customers[614]. The advantages to the industry, the consumer and the environment are great.

After using the software and uploading a specific size, consumers can buy online with confidence, knowing what they ordered will fit. Retailer returns and waste will be reduced significantly. The firm cites 2018 data that indicates $30 billion US of clothing bought online was returned.

Cookie Cutter

True Fit is another firm offering a solution to sizing. The firm gathers measurement specifications from a variety of labels and, through customer-provided measurements, finds a better fit[615]. Human Solutions, another firm, scanned 18,000 people in Canada and the U.S. to try to understand the magnitude of the issue. Of those, 70 percent said finding the right size was tough. My Size Inc. is another firm working on this issue through customer scans.

Kiss and Make Up

Sometimes it's the little details that can be the biggest pain points. Toronto- and Waterloo-based Convictional offers software that easily integrates online retailers' systems with suppliers' systems. Its platform makes order management and delivery

---

[614] Toneguzzi, Mario. "Canadian startup launches digital measurement technology to revolutionize retail industry." May 28, 2019. *Retrieved from:* https://www.retail-insider.com/retail-insider/5/canadian-startup-launches-digital-measurement-technology-to-revolutionize-retail-industry

[615] Kapner, Suzanne. "It's not you. Clothing sizes are broken." *The Wall Street Journal.* December 21, 2019.

seamless and eliminates manual ordering and follow-up[616].

My Feet Don't Lie

Verily, a company related to Google, has designed a new smart shoe. At the prototype stage, this shoe can track users' weight, movements and activity[617].

---

[616] Serebrin, Jacob. "Ex-Shopify staffers' Convictional platform links retailers and suppliers." *The Globe and Mail.* December 2, 2019.

[617] Brown, Dalvin. "Google sister firm working on smart shoe." *USA Today.* February 25, 2019.

Bruce Winder

DURING COVID-19

Bruce Winder

RETAIL DURING COVID-19

"Lost in a Roman wilderness of pain
And all the children are insane
All the children are insane
Waiting for the summer rain[618]"

(The End, The Doors)

My Reaction

I heard rumblings about the virus in late December and into early January, but thought it would probably be contained in China. At the worst, it would make its way to some parts of the rest of the world, but like other viruses, would be managed accordingly. I live in Toronto, ON, which was one of the hotspots for SARS and we got through it. I was sure we would be OK.

Through the balance of February and into early March, the world realized this virus was in control and we went from playing offense to playing defense in a matter of weeks, if not days. This was real. This was different than SARS. I was stunned at how quickly the world was held hostage by COVID-19. By the end of March, the world was effectively shut down.

Most stores were closed. Grocers and other stores that carry food and essentials remained open. That was it.

At some point, the weight of the situation sunk in. How the f*ck were these retailers, suppliers, service providers and others going to stay in business with no cash coming in? What about the employees? I felt a deep sense of grief for these people — small- to medium-sized entrepreneurs, staff and all the people who make retail happen.

<u>Shock and Awe</u>

Before the pandemic, sometimes I would drive to a small plaza called Six Points

---

[618] The Doors. "The End." *The Doors*. 1967. *Spotify.*
https://open.spotify.com/album/1jWmEhn3ggaL6isoyLfwBn?highlight=spotify:track:5Ug T7w6zVZjP3oyawMzbiK

in west Toronto to shop for some fresh produce at a small mom-and-pop grocer called Valley Farm Produce. The store wasn't much to look at, but the vegetables looked fresh and were cheap. I also enjoyed giving my business to a local firm. I drove by in early April as the virus plagued Toronto and noticed that the grocer looked very different. As I got closer to the storefront, I noticed it had created large yellow and orange fluorescent signage that offered customers fresh produce boxes for delivery or pick-up. Customers could order at the front door through a small window or online. The storefront looked like something out of an apocalypse movie. This little grocer was trying to innovate like hell to survive.

Striking Out

As the tsunami of cases hit North America in March, I could feel the anxiety building at the potential societal and economic impact that was anticipated. On March 22, I wrote the following on social media:

During this time, some brands will put people above profits. Some brands will put profits above people. Some brands will help society by retooling factories and paying employees who have been laid off. Some brands won't be able to because they just don't have the resources. Some brands will need our help just to stay in business. Some brands will fall. Some brands will thrive. Some brands will claim to be here for you but are just taking advantage of the moment to build goodwill. Which brand are you?

Marketing Madness

In early April, after being bombarded by advertisement after advertisement, I felt annoyed at the commercialization of the pandemic and the sleezy snuggling up of brands to consumers for financial gain. Soon after, I wrote the following on social media:

Tired of every ad:

"We at (insert brand) know we are in uncertain times. We are doing (insert trivial self-serving COVID-19 change) for you because we have your back."

Marketers of the world, unite and show mercy!

Self-Expression

In early April, as I realized what was happening, I felt a sense of shock in terms of the magnitude of the pandemic and its sudden impact on society. After a few days of thinking and taking in hours of cable news, I had to express myself through a post I made on the retail industry. It would later be published in Retail Insider:

Retail Before, During & After COVID-19

Retail's Journey Through the Abyss: COVID-19

The retail industry is on a perilous journey. To a place it has not been before. A retailer's worst nightmare. No sales. No cash flow. Bills piling up. The retail sector faces bankruptcies in the thousands, store closings in the tens of thousands and employee layoffs in the millions. All because of something we can't even see. Something we can't kill. Something no one talked about in 2019.

Most large retailers will weather the storm. With strong balance sheets and access to loans based on large asset bases, big brands will make it through to the other side. Some large brands that were teetering on insolvency before this crisis will enter bankruptcy protection and will be sold off in parts. My first thought is department stores and middle retail with weak value propositions. They were destined to fall anyway. This just accelerated the process.

Many small- and medium-sized retailers and suppliers will run out of cash over the next several weeks or months and will close. Some will go into a retail hibernation of sorts to lower as much cost as possible and emerge lean and mean on the other side. Some will call it quits for good. Not worth the stress of potentially using personal assets as collateral to secure financing.

If too many small or medium retailers cease to exist, it will create an unhealthy industry where we are left with only large retailers, suppliers and service providers. Too much power will be given to the select few. This will reduce choice, reduce service and create an oligopoly where prices increase. This will also impact jobs as big retail continues to turn to automation and e-commerce to save cost. The strong will buy the weak for a song and will grow even more dominant.

When this is over, many consumers will have a newfound sense of thrift. Savings will be depleted, credit cards and lines of credit will be stretched and stock portfolios and pensions will be decimated. You will see an extreme flight to value. Dollar chains, value grocers and used-clothing stores will thrive. Many consumers will think twice before spending. They will make existing products last longer. More items will be repaired versus replaced. Those with cash will invest in the dip, buy assets on the cheap and make a fortune when stock markets and society returns to some form of normal. All these factors will create a new retail landscape that further polarizes our industry and society between the wealthy and the wealth-less.

On the bright side, retail will survive but will take a different form. We will see a reincarnation of business as retailers and suppliers sprout up and start again from the ashes. More retailers will be built on variable cost and capital light models. More businesses will be digitally native, at least to start. We will also see a renewed sense of collectivism in our society as people help each other more and try to shop locally. E-commerce, having proven itself a valuable asset, will grow as a percentage of sales.

The air will be fresh and the waters will be clear. The environment will catch its breath and begin to heal, if only for a little while.

The Economic Damage

Beyond the immeasurable societal toll the pandemic has brought, the economic carnage the world is facing is beyond compare. We have not seen anything like this since The Great Depression of the 1930s. This crisis makes The Great Recession of 2008/2009 look like a speed bump in comparison to what global economies are dealing with. The International Monetary Fund (IMF) added some clarity.

<u>IMF Perspective</u>

The IMF announced its forecast for the global economy in mid-April. The agency forecasted that the world economy would shrink by three percent in 2020 — a six percent drop for developed economies. The IMF detailed how, if the pandemic lingers beyond what's expected and if a second outbreak were to occur in 2021, the world could see an eight percent economic decline below its base-case projections[619].

Individual, country-specific 2020 GDP forecasts vary significantly. The U.S. is estimated to be down almost six percent while China is forecasted to be up just over one percent. The U.K. is forecasted to be down six-and-a-half percent. South Korea is estimated to be down just over one percent. Germany is estimated to be down seven percent. Italy is forecasted to be down just over nine percent. Canada is expected to be down just over six percent[620].

<u>Stock Slide</u>

The S&P 500 lost about one-third of its value from February 20 to March 23, 2020, the low point so far. The index has since rebounded, but remains off fifteen percent from its high as of mid-May.

The Dow Jones Industrial Average lost about 37 percent from February 12 to March 23, its low point as well. Like the S&P 500, it rebounded but is still off about 20 percent as of mid-May.

---

[619] Parkinson, David. "Canada's economy to shrink 6.2% this year amid dire global outlook, IMF warns." *The Globe and Mail*. April 15, 2020.

[620] Lewis, Michael. "Canadian economy ripe for historic fall." *The Toronto Star*. April 15, 2020.

The Nasdaq Composite Index fell 30 percent on March 23 from highs on February 19. The index has since levelled off to be down about eight percent as of mid-May.

In Canada, the S&P TSX Composite Index, like its U.S. counterparts, fell 37 percent on March 23 from its high on February 20. The index has since recovered to be down about 18.5 percent as of mid-May.

Unemployment

In the United States, 40 million Americans have filed for unemployment benefits since mid-March. This represents over 20 percent of the people who are looking for work[621].

Almost 21,000 Americans lost their jobs in April 2020, bringing the unemployment rate to about 15 percent.

In Canada, workers lost one million jobs in March. In April, job losses totalled two million as the unemployment rose to about 13 percent. In Toronto, almost a quarter of all jobs have vanished since the crisis began[622].

New Home Builds

According to CNBC, U.S. home construction decreased by just over 22 percent in March from February. This was the biggest monthly decrease since 1984[623]. That was just March.

U.K.

In the U.K., one agency has forecasted second quarter gross domestic product will decline by 35 percent if government restrictions continue until the end of June. The Office for Budget Responsibility, an influential government watchdog, predicts

---

[621] Mutikani, Lucia. "U.S. braces for possible second wave of layoffs." *Reuters*. May 15, 2020.

[622] Subramaniam, Vanmala. " Jobs picture has yet to fully bare its teeth." *The Financial Post*. April 24, 2020.

[623] "US home construction collapsed 22.3% in March." April 16, 2020. Retrieved from: https://www.cnbc.com/2020/04/16/us-housing-starts-march-2020.html

unemployment for the U.K. will increase from four percent to 10 percent during the same time frame[624].

China

China's gross domestic product dropped by 6.8 percent in the first quarter of 2020. This was the first decline in its economy since 1992, when quarterly GDP records began being published[625].

In mid-March, China reported both industrial output and retail sales fell double digits. China's National Bureau of Statistics reported that January and February industrial output fell over 13 percent while retail sales dropped over 20 percent[626].

McKinsey 1.0

In an April study by McKinsey, a consulting firm, it surveyed consumers around the globe from March 15 to April 19, 2020 as it relates to sentiment during the COVID-19 crisis[627]. The report offers several important insights as described below.

From a consumer-sentiment perspective, Europe has been hit particularly hard, with the exception of Germany, while China has shown a rebound. The U.S. saw a decrease of about 10 percent during early-to-mid April.

Mood

When polling for optimism after the pandemic subsides, the U.S. scored in the middle of participating countries, where respondents where neither overly optimistic nor overly pessimistic. China was significantly more optimistic, scoring in the top one-third of the scale — as was India and several other middle-eastern countries.

---

[624] Waldie, Paul. "U.K. watchdog paints grim economic picture." *The Globe and Mail.* April 15, 2020.

[625] Crossley, Gabriel and Yao, Kevin. "Hobbled by coronavirus, China's Q1 GDP shrinks 6.8%." *Reuters.* April 18, 2020.

[626] Zochodne, Geoff. "China's production slowdown bad omen for Canada, world." *The Financial Post.* March 17, 2020.

[627] "A global view of how consumer behavior is changing amid COVID-19." April, 2020. Retrieved from: https://www.mckinsey.com/business-functions/marketing-and-sales/our-insights/a-global-view-of-how-consumer-behavior-is-changing-amid-covid-19

Most other countries, including Canada, scored in the bottom half of the ranking, with considerably more pessimistic scores.

Foodie

From a category perspective, the story was consistent around the world — consumers are spending more on grocery and less on discretionary products and services. Household essentials and home entertainment fared well, while travel and transportation, services, entertainment and apparel were the biggest decliners.

Back to the Future

As China begins to exit the pandemic, spending has returned but with some significant differences. Consumers have begun to shop again on fitness, beauty, pet and child basics. In grocery, traffic has been down by about 30 percent, while average ring has increased considerably. However, Chinese consumers continue to spend less at fashion retailers and department stores — between 40 to 50 percent below pre-pandemic levels.

Wait Time

When asked about the duration of the impact of COVID-19 on personal routines and finances, about three-quarters of global respondents thought it would impact them for more than two months, while about half of respondents expected it to last more than four months.

Computer Class

In terms of new digital activities that consumers have picked up during the pandemic, online streaming, grocery delivery and restaurant delivery scored well. In the U.S., more than half of the growth in restaurant curbside pickup and store curbside pickup came from new users.

Retail Therapy

Perhaps one of the most important findings that McKinsey published estimated future shopping behaviour as it relates to pre- and post-pandemic.

The findings highlighted that in most countries, more consumers planned on shopping more in physical grocery stores after the crisis, except the U.K. and India — where more consumers would shop less. In the U.S., a net six percent of consumers said they would shop more in grocery stores after the crisis than before.

Regarding shopping again in non-grocery brick and mortar stores, many countries showed a decrease in the percentage of net consumers who would shop more at these locations. In other words, more consumers in most countries would shop less at non-grocery physical brick and mortar stores. The exceptions are Japan and Germany. In the U.S., the survey showed that about as many consumers would shop more often in these stores as would shop less often.

Several countries showed a net decrease in the number of consumers who would go to malls after COVID-19 than before the crisis started. For several European countries, the net percentage score was well into the teens. In the U.S., a net nine percent more shoppers indicated they would go to malls less often post-pandemic. In India, this number was almost 20 percent.

GOVERNMENTS

I added governments as a key influence on retail in this section because their profile and role has changed. Over the last few years, governments have been relegated to the role of pain in the a*s from a business perspective — a stakeholder that just gets in the way of getting things done with their pesky regulations and profit-sucking taxes. Big government is bad. Well, similarly to how government saved the day during The Great Recession, government is wearing the cape and rescuing businesses and consumers left, right and centre in some countries.

Governments have responded differently around the world. Australia has stopped commercial landlords from evicting tenants for six months, France has temporarily stopped all mortgage payments, rent and utilities, South Korea has reduced rent costs and Denmark has helped to pay small businesses' fixed costs for select firms[628].

United States

On April 9, the U.S. Federal Reserve announced a $2.3 trillion US relief package designed to assist local governments and small- and medium-sized businesses. Businesses work through banks to administer four-year loans to firms that have up to 10,000 employees[629]. The first wave of support was exhausted on April 16. The program included $349 billion US and was used for approximately 1.7 million loans. Unfortunately, according to Morgan Stanley, $243.4 million of the fund was allocated

---

[628] Shell, Jon. "Loans won't save local small businesses." *The Globe and Mail.* April 1, 2020.

[629] Schneider, Howard. " Fed unveils $2.3-trillion backstop plan." *Reuters.* April 10, 2020.

to publicly-traded companies[630].

In late April, president Trump signed a coronavirus relief bill that allowed for an additional $370 billion in relief for small business[631]. The Bank of America has indicated that it feels the U.S. government will need to spend up to $1 trillion US on small business loans to assist in the recovery.

The United States government reported an April budget deficit of $738 billion US, a new record. This was based on the $3 trillion US spent as of mid-May on aiding businesses and individuals as well as reduced government revenue such as taxes[632].

<u>Canada</u>

In Canada, the federal government has implemented numerous programs to assist business. One program is the $25 billion Cdn Canada Emergency Business Account (CEBA). This program is a loan to companies that spent between $20,000 and $1.5 million Cdn on payroll in 2019. It includes interest-free borrowing of up to $40,000 with a potential $10,000 of the loan converting to grant if paid back within 24 months.

Additional business support includes the Canada Emergency Commercial Rent Assistance program to help business with rent during April, May and June 2020[633].

In Canada, almost seven million people applied for the federal government's

---

[630] Franck, Thomas. "Here are the largest public companies taking payroll loans meant for small businesses." April 21, 2020. Retrieved from: https://www.cnbc.com/2020/04/21/large-public-companies-are-taking-small-businesses-payroll-loans.html

[631] Pramuk, Jacob. "Trump signs $484 billion coronavirus relief bill to boost small business, hospitals and testing." April 24, 2020. Retrieved from: https://www.cnbc.com/2020/04/24/coronavirus-updates-trump-signs-relief-bill-for-small-business-hospitals.html

[632] Dunsmuir, Lindsay. "U.S. reports record budget deficit." *Reuters*. May 13, 2020.

[633] O'Kane, Josh and Curry, Bill and Leblanc, Daniel. "Ottawa widens small business relief, looks to help with rent." *The Globe and Mail*. April 17, 2020.

Canada Emergency Response Benefit (CERB) from March 15 to April 21[634].

The Canadian government announced in mid-April that it was modifying collusion regulations during the pandemic. The Competition Bureau indicated that companies that would normally be competitors could work together if they were producing a product or service that would help in the fight against COVID-19[635].

The federal government began using quantitative easing to help drive liquidity in the country. The government will buy billions of dollars of government bonds. The government has also cut interest rates to .25 percent in an effort to ease loan payments. The Canadian government refrained from using quantitative easing during the 2008 financial crisis[636].

India

The Indian government recently announced a $260 billion stimulus package designed to enable India's self-reliance. The package is worth about 10 percent of the country's annual GDP[637].

Basic Income

Universal basic income (UBI) has gained support recently as several countries have implemented government support programs to allow non-working citizens to pay rent and buy groceries.

CUSTOMERS

I was almost afraid to read about how customers were reacting to the pandemic from a spending perspective. High unemployment, stock market roller coasters,

---

[634] Subramaniam, Vanmala. "Jobs picture has yet to fully bare its teeth." *The Financial Post*. April 24, 2020.

[635] Dobby, Christine. "Competition Bureau relaxes collusion rules during pandemic." *The Globe and Mail*. April 13, 2020.

[636] Parkinson, David. "Bank of Canada unleashes next weapon in arsenal: quantitative easing." *The Globe and Mail*. April 2, 2020.

[637] "India aims at self-reliance with $260B stimulus." *The Associated Press*. May 13, 2020.

uncertainty and fear everywhere. This is retail. Retail doesn't work unless you have customers willing to buy things. Sure enough, my fears were warranted.

<u>March Madness</u>

In the U.S., March retail sales dropped 8.7 percent. This was the most since 1992, when the Commerce Department starting tracking it. This represented $46.2 billion and was almost as large as the 16-month cumulative drop during the Great Recession — which totalled $49.1 billion.

Some of the categories that saw the biggest declines included clothing, down just over 50 percent; furniture, which dropped almost 27 percent; appliances and electronics, which dropped just over 15 percent; and vehicles and sales at restaurants and bars, which dropped over 25 percent. Not all was bad, though — grocery stores saw an almost 27 percent jump[638].

In the U.S., March consumer prices dropped by the most in five years, triggering worries about deflation. The U.S. CPI dropped .4 percent for March, led by decreases in hotels, airlines, gasoline and fashion[639].

<u>April Showers</u>

In April, U.S. retail sales plummeted 16.4 percent. A new record. Apparel was down almost 90 percent. Electronics dropped 65 percent and furniture was down almost 70 percent. Grocery was up 12 percent and online sales grew 22 percent.

Customer Segments

Depending on individual situations, the pandemic has affected people differently. For some, it has been an inconvenience. For some, a chance to spend more time with family and reconnect. For some, it has been catastrophic from an economic and personal health standpoint. Let's examine three different customer segments and how they probably felt during the shutdown.

---

[638] Mutikani, Lucia. "U.S. retail sales, factory output sink as economy reels from the pandemic." *Reuters*. April 16, 2020.

[639] Mutikani, Lucia. "U.S. consumer prices record largest drop in five years." *Reuters*. April 11, 2020.

Top of the Mountain

For folks who have a lot of money, COVID-19 didn't look the other way. The virus doesn't discriminate. Wealthy folks suffered like everyone else from a health standpoint. Economically, they were perhaps impacted less than other socio-economic classes, which had to worry about food and shelter. Some of those with cash invested when the markets crashed and have already made a good return.

Cashing In

One can see how the COVID-19 pandemic is creating further income disparity. In late April, the Institute for Policy Studies (IPS) published a report that indicted that the combined wealth of the United States' billionaires increased by almost 10 percent since the crisis started[640].

Jeff Bezos, founder and CEO of Amazon and the world's richest person, increased his net worth by tens of billions of dollars during the crisis as Amazon soared in valuation. As of mid-April, Mr. Bezos presided over a fortune of $140 billion US. Elon Musk, CEO of Tesla, made a cool $10.4 billion US in 2020 during the same time. The Walton family, part owner of Walmart, saw its net worth increase by five percent in 2020 to $169 billion US.

Separation Anxiety

According to Matt Maley, chief market strategist at Miller Tabak: "The wealth gap, it's only going to get wider with what's going on now." He adds, "The really wealthy people haven't had to worry about putting food on the table or keeping a roof over your head." Executives and directors within companies have also bought up shares on the cheap to lower the average cost of their holdings[641].

Shiny Objects

Some wealthy consumers are buying high-end jewelry during the pandemic. Sotheby's New York has enjoyed an uplift in sales of high-quality items sold online. Catharine Becket, a specialist at the firm, was quoted in a recent Bloomberg article as saying, "Clients are sequestering at home and, generally speaking, leading relatively dreary lives. They're wearing their big diamonds inside their homes because it brings

---

[640] "Net worth of billionaires up 10% in pandemic." *Reuters*. April 24, 2020.

[641] Alexander, Sophie and Maloney, Tom and Metcalf, Tom. "'Wealth gap...only going to get wider.'" *Bloomberg*. April 16, 2020.

joy"[642].

Posh Drop

According to Bain, a consultancy, the luxury-goods market could fall as much as 15 to percent in 2020. Forecasted 2020 revenue declines of 50 percent at Burberry and 15 percent at Kering (owner of Gucci) support Bain's analysis[643].

Panic Palace

Grocery stores aren't the only stores that have seen demand surge due to the virus. Providers of survival goods are busy, too. Personal shelters and underground bunkers are gaining traction for more affluent customers. Prices can start at $25,000 US and go up quickly to well over a quarter of a million dollars[644].

Home Care

Being rich can have its benefits in a health crisis. The super-wealthy have been buying up ventilators and isolating themselves and family in luxury hideaways to avoid the virus. In Russia, wealthy citizens have been setting up their own health-care facilities in their homes — some paying tens of thousands of dollars per annum for on-call doctors to treat them[645].

Airport Fees

Travel restrictions have left the super-rich in a bit of a pickle. Many are stuck for longer than thought in high tax jurisdictions, which means they may have to pay tax there[646]. Pity.

---

[642] Tarmy, James. "Bored, wealthy and buying $250K jewels online." *Bloomberg*. April 23, 2020.

[643] "Luxury sales could fall as much as 35% in 2020, report says." *Bloomberg*. March 28, 2020.

[644] Parvani, Sarah. "Sales soaring for survival suppliers." *The Los Angeles Times*. March 21, 2020.

[645] Roland, Denise and Kantchev, Georgi. "Wealthy tap ventilators and on-demand doctors to battle coronavirus." *The Wall Street Journal*. April 11, 2020.

[646] Stupples, Ben and Pendleton, Devon. "Stranded super-rich face higher bills."

Middle of the Road

Remember the middle class? Well, there are still some people out there who are part of this dying breed. With solid, white-collar jobs, many of these people spent most of the pandemic working from home — maintaining their salary through the chaos. Not all, though. Some got laid off just like hourly workers as companies tried to save cost.

Gilded Cage

For many middle-class workers, their only trip outside was to get groceries once per week. And even that wasn't certain as online grocery orders soared. Their life consisted of sleep, food, work, food, news, Netflix, more food and repeat — no need to buy or consume much else. Maybe puzzles and board games. Annoyed at the drop in their 401K or their RRSPs, they were OK for a while and could weather the storm.

Leave it to Beaver

Numerator, a research firm, reported that 30 percent of Canadians are buying products online that would have normally been bought at a store.

Chill

In April, Netflix announced it had garnered an unprecedented 15.8 million new subscribers in the first quarter of 2020 — double analysts' expectations[647].

Inn-Convenient

In Toronto and Vancouver, Airbnb's revenue decreased by 70 percent from mid-January to mid-April 2020[648].

Motown Slowdown

Vehicle sales have, not surprisingly, tanked during the pandemic. For the first

---

Bloomberg. May 13, 2020.

[647] Shaw, Lucas. "Netflix posts explosive growth, but boom may not last long." *Bloomberg*. April 22, 2020.

[648] Younglai, Rachelle. "Short-term rental bookings plummet in big cities." *The Globe and Mail*. April 18, 2020.

quarter of 2020, GM reported a sales decrease of just over seven percent, while Fiat Chrysler reported a 10-percent decline. Other vehicle manufacturers such as Mazda, Hyundai, Honda and Volkswagen all saw March sales drop by 40 percent or more[649]. In May, Toyota reported its fiscal fourth-quarter profit was down 86 percent[650].

<u>Zoom-Wear</u>

As more people work from home, comfortable clothing has seen a sales spike. Old Nay, Gap, Lululemon, Uniqlo, Everlane and others have seen significant growth in online demand for leggings, yoga pants, jogging pants, stretchy sweatpants and sweatshirts. Numerous marketers have updated advertising to focus on these categories[651].

<u>Self-Salon-ing</u>

In early April, Walmart U.S. reported it had seen a significant uptick in sales of personal grooming products, hair dyes and sewing machines[652].

Economically Challenged

Sadly, many less-fortunate consumers either lost their jobs or became our newest super hero — the frontline worker. Either way, it was tough. You either lost your low-paying job (or saw your hours significantly reduced) or you took your life into your hands each day as you worked at hospitals, grocery stores, drug stores, drove transportation or supported the aging at care homes.

<u>Survival</u>

For those who lost their income, spending on anything outside of groceries or

---

[649] Coppola, Gabrielle and Welch, David and Naughton, Keith and Dawson, Chester. "Demand for vehicles evaporates." *Bloomberg*. April 2, 2020.

[650] Kageyama, Yuri. "Pandemic drives Toyota's profit down as sales, production halt." *The Associated Press*. May 13, 2020.

[651] Krashinsky Robertson, Susan. "Leisure wear sales surge with increase in work from home." *The Globe and Mail*. April 15, 2020.

[652] Reagan, Courtney. April 9, 2020. Retrieved from: https://twitter.com/CourtReagan/status/1248323937437650949

paying the rent was out of scope and out of mind. Food and shelter was all that mattered and, sadly, many of these people struggled to keep their fridge stocked and a roof over their head. Many went further into debt (assuming they could get it) to survive. Like retailers, these people had no cash flow while bills continued to pile up.

New Behaviours

We saw some new consumer behaviour show up during the crisis — some innovative and some down-right nasty and selfish.

Hoard-Game

We have all heard the stories or seen first-hand how consumers were hoarding food and home essentials. It started with toilet paper and hand sanitizer in March. Then all hell broke loose and there was a run on grocery stores and consumers bought whatever they could get their hands on. Grocers and discounters sat back and enjoyed the business while they scrambled to keep shelves full. No limits on anything not on promotion. Cleaners, canned goods, dairy, meat all sold out. Finally grocers, perhaps realizing that they were now an essential service, began limiting quantities.

Some consumers even hoarded medications. In late March, some pharmacies indicated that customers were attempting to fill several months' worth of medication at once. As this practice can cause shortages and put citizens' lives in danger, many pharmacists discouraged this behaviour[653].

Gouging – Price Pointed

Some jack*sses who hoarded basics started selling them online on eBay, Walmart.com and Amazon at significant premiums. To their credit, these retailers swiftly kicked them off their platforms. I remember one guy, whom I saw on social media, who had a garage full of hand sanitizer that he could no longer sell online. Sorry buddy, karma's a b*tch, isn't it?

Traders

Bartering has become popular again. Since the crisis hit in March, many consumers and small business owners are trading products for food or other essential items. With cash in such short supply, social networks Nextdoor and Facebook have

---

[653] Saba, Rosa. "Pharmacies warn against stockpiling drugs." *The Toronto Star – Calgary Bureau*. March 20, 2020.

lit up with offers to trade[654].

Playing Chicken

Eggs have suddenly become a star and costs are going up as a result. A recent article in the Wall Street Journal discusses how egg prices from wholesalers have increased more than 300 percent. Demand at grocery stores has soared, as eggs are an economical source of protein. Supply is fairly fixed, at least in the short term, as farmers have recently reduced flocks based on low profitability over the last few years[655].

Farm Box

Meal kits have soared in popularity as consumers look to try to eat healthy while enjoying the safety of home.

Greenback Burner

One needs only to review Maslow's hierarchy of needs to relate to the fact that for many consumers, being green took a back seat during the crisis. When we are under threat, we focus on food, shelter and safety first. Other more noble concerns are pushed to the back burner.

Even for those who saw through to help the planet, the virus sometimes took that from us as well. Grocery stores stopped accepting reusable bags and food service brands such as Starbucks prohibited reusable cups. Tim Hortons was poised to give away 1.8 million reusable cups this spring as part of its Roll Up the Rim contest, but cancelled the gesture due to concerns regarding employee safety[656].

Fitting Faux Pas

CNBC reported that according to a study by First Insight, 65 percent of women

---

[654] Kharif, Olga. "Swapping eggs for toilet paper: Bartering makes a comeback." *Bloomberg*. April 6, 2020.

[655] Kang, Jaewon and Bunge, Jacob. "For grocers, eggs are getting more expensive amid coronavirus." *The Wall Street Journal*. April 7, 2020.

[656] Krashinsky Robertson, Susan. "Tim Hortons suspends cup giveaway, won't use refillable containers." *The Globe and Mail*. March 7, 2020.

don't feel comfortable using a fitting room during COVID-19. The number changes to 54 percent when asking men. Similar numbers to the data above were reported when asked how comfortable both would be dealing with a store associate during the pandemic[657].

Bake Off

According to an AMC global survey, 60 percent of respondents have been cooking from scratch more — one-third plan to continue to do so when the pandemic passes. One-third are baking more and 20 percent plan on continuing to do so post-crisis. Twenty-eight percent are eating more prepared meals[658].

Canuck Consumers

Canadian consumers' purchasing habits changed during the worst of the shutdown. Sales of the following items increased: wine and beer, coffee filters, hair dye, canned goods, toilet paper, condoms, hand sanitizer, baking supplies, snacks, office supplies, arts and crafts, fitness equipment, electronics, butter, margarine, milk, eggs, video games, games and puzzles, hair clippers, bread makers and espresso machines[659]. Cosmetics saw a decrease during the shutdown[660].

EMPLOYEES

One of the biggest changes during the COVID-19 pandemic has been how society views essential frontline workers. Society has been turned upside down. Low-

---

[657] Thomas, Lauren. "Here's how you'll be safely shopping for clothes as stores begin to reopen." May 11, 2020. Retrieved from: https://www.cnbc.com/2020/05/11/coronavirus-how-to-safely-shop-for-clothes-as-stores-reopen.html

[658] Brehaut, Laura. "Some lockdown food habits may stick around." *The National Post*. May 15, 2020.

[659] Krashinsky Robertson, Susan. "Retailers fight to survive amid pandemic." *The Globe and Mail*. May 9, 2020.

[660] Lewis, Michael. "Canadians' quarantine shopping lists." *The Toronto Star*. May 12, 2020.

wage earners such as bus drivers, delivery people, PSWs, nurses, grocery-store workers and warehouse staff are the new pandemic soldiers. Our new heroes.

Self-Worth

Essential

As a result, we have seen numerous retail workers temporarily receive wage increases — as much to minimize legal liability as to keep them showing up each day. Retail workers have finally received something close to what they deserve. Respect and the ability to make a living wage.

Non-essential

Retail workers outside of essential businesses have been devastated through sudden job loss. Millions of frontline and head office employees have been furloughed at best with uncertain prospects in terms of what the future will bring — and not just retail workers, but all workers supporting non-essential categories. Product or service designers, factory workers, marketing staff, sales staff, administrative staff and the list goes on. Non-essential retailers, suppliers and service providers are in survival mode. They need to save cash and save it quick — and one of the fastest ways to do so is through staff reduction.

Homework

Many employers have asked staff to work from home. Forbes estimates that almost 60 percent of U.S. "knowledge workers" are now working from home. In North America, as of late March, about double the average number of people are working remotely[661].

Empty Office

In a recent survey of 1,335 Canadians conducted by Forum Research, it was found that just over 30 percent of survey respondents are working from home due to the pandemic. Another seven percent above and beyond these people were working from home before the virus struck.

---

[661] Koetsier, John. "58% of American knowledge workers are now working remotely." March 20, 2020. Retrieved from:
https://www.forbes.com/sites/johnkoetsier/2020/03/20/58-of-american-knowledge-workers-are-now-working-remotely/#71286a443303

Weekday Get Away

Of the 30 percent who are new to working from home, about 30 percent liked working from home more than working at the office and almost 20 percent indicated they plan on continuing to do so after the crisis. Just over 60 percent said they planned to work at the office again and about 20 percent have not decided yet[662].

Fruit Pickers

Apple is using its store employees to handle technical questions from home. The program started after the brand closed all stores and promised to pay employees anyway. Employees are being encouraged to temporarily join the AppleCare team and work from home to handle customer calls[663].

Laid Off

According to the Washington Post, U.S. retailers laid off one million workers the week of March 30 alone. During the Great Recession, retailers eliminated 2.8 million workers in total. As of early April, Coresight Research reported that 16,000 retail stores closed over the weeks since the pandemic hit the U.S.[664]

The hotel industry has been devasted by COVID-19. The American Hotel and Lodging Association has estimated that about four million hotel workers have been or will be laid off as a result of the crisis. The industry has asked for $150 billion in loans to weather the storm. Many of the hotels in the U.S., including national branded properties, are franchised and individual owners face steep mortgage payments that could force them into bankruptcy[665]. In May, hotel giant Marriott

---

[662] Subramaniam, Vanmala. "Working from home the place to be for some." *The Financial Post*. April 23, 2020.

[663] "Apple store staff asked to take on tech support roles." *Bloomberg*. April 1, 2020.

[664] Bhattarai, Abha. "Retailers furloughed nearly 1 million workers this week. But the industry's troubles are just beginning." April 3, 2020. Retrieved from: https://www.washingtonpost.com/business/2020/04/03/retailers-furloughed-nearly-1-million-workers-this-week-industrys-troubles-are-just-beginning/?arc404=true

[665] Creswell, Julie. "Big-name hotels are going empty and smaller owners face closing." *The New York Times*. March 28, 2020.

posted first quarter 2020 profit down almost 92 percent[666].

The food sector outside of grocery has been affected as well. Restaurants don't need as many people when they turn to drive-thru and delivery exclusively.

In Canada, the food-service sector laid off two-thirds of workers in March. Restaurants Canada reported that about 800,000 employees were laid off and estimated that about 30 percent of restaurants would close for good if the crisis persisted until May[667].

In Canada, Boston Pizza announced in late March that it laid off 50 percent of head office staff. The layoffs are across three offices and affect approximately 95 workers[668].

Freshii, a fast-casual chain, announced in March that it was laying off a number of head-office staff but would not specify how many. The restaurant chain also announced it was delaying filing its latest financials as it manages through the crisis[669].

Hiring

The irony about this situation is that while many sectors of retail close and lay off workers, others are booming. Grocery stores and essential-product retailers that sell online are seeing double digit jumps in demand. With this demand comes the need to grow capacity. The quickest way to grow capacity is often through adding people. Especially where business models can scale up quickly, like delivery apps. Job websites are flooded with temporary positions to work in grocers. Some retailers are offering bonuses to those who join the front line.

Amazon is one of the firms benefiting the most from the COVID-19 crisis. The

---

[666] Sebastian, Dave. "Marriott posts lower profit as occupancy drops." *The Wall Street Journal.* May 12, 2020.

[667] Edmiston, Jake. "Restaurants laid off 800,000 in March." *The Financial Post.* April 3, 2020.

[668] "Boston Pizza laying off half of 192 corporate staff across Canada." *The Canadian Press.* March 28, 2020.

[669] "Freshii cuts office staff, delays financial results." *The Canadian Press.* March 31, 2020.

firm announced it was hiring an additional 150,000 workers to help meet demand[670].

In late March, Walmart U.S. announced it was hiring an additional 150,000 workers. The workers will be used for the retailer's 150 warehouses and 4,750 U.S. stores[671].

Canadian book retailer Indigo has rehired 545 workers with government help. The Canadian federal government launched a program that would pay employers up to 75 percent of employee wages under certain conditions to assist with employment. The retailer originally laid off 5,200 workers in March when they closed their stores[672].

Shield

One of the key challenges for retailers is keeping their staff safe. Some retailers and service providers have done a better job than others. Workers are not taking poor working conditions lying down, either.

In mid-April, the Washington Post published an article that addressed the state of grocery-store workers in the United States. It was estimated that as of April 12, 41 grocery workers had died of COVID-19 — with thousands more testing positive for the virus. The article describes the fear and anxiety that many of the three million American grocery store workers feel — all for low wages. Some grocery clerks have quit, leading to a boom in job postings for grocers around the country — an increase of 60 percent according to ZipRecruiter[673].

Some employees are striking and signing petitions to fight for better protections. Most grocers have added plexiglass panels at the cash register and offer employees masks and gloves to assist in their protection. They have also begun controlling how

---

[670] Herrera, Sebastian. "Amazon hired 80,000 of 100,000 planned workers." *The Wall Street Journal*. April 3, 2020.

[671] Boyle, Matthew. "Walmart beefs up with 150,000 new U.S. hires." *Bloomberg*. March 21, 2020.

[672] "Subsidy helps Indigo rehire 545 workers." *The Canadian Press*. April 14, 2020.

[673] Bhattarai, Abha. "'It feels like a war zone': As more of them die, grocery workers increasingly fear showing up at work." April 12, 2020. Retrieved from: https://www.washingtonpost.com/business/2020/04/12/grocery-worker-fear-death-coronavirus/

many customers can shop in a store at the same time[674].

In May, Noam Scheiber wrote an article in the New York Times that discussed the fear workers have about companies pulling back on employee safety protocols. The article addressed worker outcries at retailers such as Starbucks, Whole Foods and Costco, as social distancing measures were put to the test. Workers protested during "May Day" events that increased the profile of their concerns[675].

On April 17, Walmart sent a message to all associates across all U.S. banners, warehouses and offices advising them that they must wear a face covering at work[676].

Amazon announced it was implementing worker protection policies that include temperature checks in the U.S. and Europe and providing workers with masks. These changes came as numerous employees complained that the Seattle-based behemoth wasn't doing enough to protect them[677].

U.S. restaurants expedited the delivery of masks as government guidelines changed. As the pandemic hit full force, regulators recommended that citizens wear face masks in public. Since the announcement, brands such as Subway, McDonald's, Domino's Pizza and Starbucks have rushed to secure inventory. Starbucks went so far as to ask its baristas to make their own masks in the interim[678].

In late April, Walmart Canada began testing employees' health before allowing them to work at one of the brand's warehouses in Mississauga. The retailer calls these

---

[674] Bhattarai, Abha. "'It feels like a war zone': As more of them die, grocery workers increasingly fear showing up at work." April 12, 2020. Retrieved from: https://www.washingtonpost.com/business/2020/04/12/grocery-worker-fear-death-coronavirus/

[675] Scheiber, Noam. "Reopening prompts agitation over worker safety." *The New York Times.* May 16, 2020.

[676] "Our next step to protect you, our customers and our members." April 17, 2020. Retrieved from: https://corporate.walmart.com/newsroom/2020/04/17/our-next-step-to-protect-you-our-customers-and-our-members

[677] Herrera, Sebastian. "Amazon hired 80,000 of 100,000 planned workers." *The Wall Street Journal.* April 3, 2020.

[678] "U.S. restaurants scramble for masks as guidelines change." *Bloomberg.* April 9, 2020.

"wellness checks" and includes asking employees a number of health-related questions as well as taking each employee's temperature. If an employee has a temperature of thirty-eight degrees or more, they are sent home but paid. The program was expected to roll out to other facilities and all stores[679].

In this new abnormal, app delivery drivers are concerned about being asked to deliver medicine to sick customers. The Toronto Star recently published an article that described how, in Toronto, delivery app Foodora had pivoted to delivering throat sprays, inhalers, lozenges and other products from pharmacies. The article notes that couriers were being asked to deliver such products without providing contractors with personal protective equipment such as masks or gloves. Ironically, Foodora announced the last week of April they were pulling out of Canada in May[680].

Danger Pay

Many U.S. retailers have temporarily increased the wages of hourly workers by as much as $2 to $3 during the COVID-19 crisis. Some of the retailers that have given wage increases include: Amazon, Walmart, Target, BJ's Wholesale Club, Sheetz, Albertsons, Starbucks, Trader Joe's and Costco, to name a few[681].

Walmart also announced it was providing U.S. hourly employees with a bonus of $300 for full-time workers and $150 for part-time workers. It also advanced its next quarterly bonus from May to the end of April. For Walmart, the bonuses will tally up to about a year's worth of net income from U.S. operations — or $550 million US[682].

In Canada, Amazon has increased overtime pay for warehouse workers by one hundred percent. This is on top of a recent $2 Cdn per hour raise. The firm has also

---

[679] Krashinsky Robertson, Susan. "Walmart begins staff 'wellness checks.'" *The Financial Post*. April 21, 2020.

[680] Mojtehedzadeh, Sara. "Food couriers fearful of delivering medications." *The Toronto Star*. April 2, 2020.

[681] Cain, Aine. "9 retailers that have hiked wages during the coronavirus pandemic." March 25, 2020. Retrieved from: https://www.businessinsider.com/retailers-pay-increase-bonus-temporary-coronavirus-pandemic-2020-3

[682] Boyle, Matthew. "Walmart beefs up with 150,000 new U.S. hires." *Bloomberg*. March 21, 2020.

taken additional measures to protect warehouse employees after facing criticism[683]. The retailer announced in mid-May that it was ending its wage premium and bonuses for Canadian staff at the end of the month[684].

In Canada, food giant Nestlé has given a temporary $3 Cdn per hour raise to all warehouse and production employees retroactive to March 16. Salaried workers in the facilities will receive a bonus if they cannot work remotely[685].

Mental Health

One of the dark sides of the pandemic, outside of the obvious sickness, is the impact COVID-19 is having on the mental health of many — from frontline workers who face the trauma of going in to work day after day to people fighting substance abuse on their own with limited support. We are social creatures and are not meant to be in isolation. The pandemic has brought increased anxiety, depression and other serious mental-health issues. Sadly, we will soon face a significant increase in post-traumatic stress disorder (PTSD) after the worst is over and government and business need to ensure they have the right support in place as COVID-19 turns into a mental-health crisis.

Employee Abuse

Some retail employees have faced abuse by customers as they grow angry at new store-level procedures. A worker was shot at an Oklahoma McDonald's in early May when a customer entered the dining room and got into an argument over the fact that the area was closed[686].

---

[683] Mojtehedzadeh, Sara. "Amazon doubling OT pay in Canadian warehouses." *The Toronto Star*. March 26, 2020.

[684] "Amazon will end pay bump after May." *The Canadian Press*. May 17, 2020.

[685] "Nestle giving raises to factory and distribution workers." *The Canadian Press*. March 27, 2020.

[686] Razek, Raja and Maxouris, Christina and Alonso, Melissa. "Customer shot a McDonald's employee after being told to leave due to coronavirus restrictions, police say." May 7, 2020. Retrieved from: https://www.cnn.com/2020/05/06/us/mcdonalds-employees-shot-coronavirus/index.html

Gratitude

In a recent op ed in the Globe and Mail, Linda Nazareth examines the probable phase-out of many of the workers we so desperately rely on during these difficult times. She specifically cites grocer workers and delivery drivers and how, over time, these jobs will be replaced by technology. Nazareth discusses how we are not only facing a cyclical downturn in the economy, but also structural changes too. These structural changes involve technological advancements that are changing the way we work and live. She uses the example of how voicemail was used during previous recessions to reduce headcount for administrative personnel[687].

SUPPLIERS

Much like retailers, suppliers to retail have faced enormous challenges during this crisis. Outside of essential product or service suppliers, much of the industry has shut down. In the U.S., April industrial production decreased by 11.2 percent. Factories led the charge with a drop of 13.7 percent. Factory utilization skidded by 8.3 percent to 64.9 percent. These drops represent the worst monthly performance in 101 years[688].

According to an article in the Globe and Mail, a March survey showed 54 percent of manufacturers in the U.S. were thinking about moving a portion of offshore production back to North America. In April, Thomas, a research and analysis firm, claimed that the same metric rose to about 64 percent in April[689].

As retail sales dive, inventory builds up at stores and supplier orders get cancelled. With supply chains moving at a snail's pace, numerous component parts used to make products are stuck in ports. Factories stop assembly lines. Most people go home. But not everyone has followed this path. Some suppliers have started to produce personal protective equipment (PPE), hand sanitizer and other products to help governments fill backlogs.

---

[687] Nazareth, Linda. "Pandemic heroes could see pink slips postcrisis." *The Globe and Mail*. April 20, 2020.

[688] Mutikani, Lucia. "U.S. downturn 'sobering if not downright scary.'" *Reuters*. May 16, 2020.

[689] Younglai, Rachelle. "Supply chains get redundant." *The Globe and Mail*. May 16, 2020.

Role Reversal

Legacy processed food brands are back in favour. Carol Ryan from the Wall Street Journal wrote an article that discusses how comfort food is back in vogue as a result of the pandemic[690].

Traditional brands like Hershey's have regained momentum in the confectionary market versus healthy up-and-coming brands such as Challenger. Ryan references a Bain & Company study that shows insurgent brands, those growing 10 times faster than a given category overall, have dropped from representing 35 percent of the growth in their categories in January and February of 2020 to five percent in March and April. The article also discusses how, as retailers streamline assortments, some of the smaller brands may be getting pushed out of the assortment and off the shelf.

Ryan also discusses how the enormous production scale big brands have can play in their favour as volume suddenly surges and they can react. In addition, Ryan highlights how supply chain capabilities factor into the situation, as smaller brands may use third-party providers that have increased costs 20 percent during the crisis in some markets. As big brands have more clout with transportation companies, they can get their product to store shelves cheaper and quicker than smaller rivals[691].

Rat Race

If you find yourself a supplier of essential products or services, you are probably running your operations 24/7 to try to keep up. Grocery suppliers, PPE suppliers, hand sanitizer suppliers, toilet paper suppliers, delivery app providers, trucking companies and many more fall into this category.

Un-Lean Manufacturing

For many suppliers who rely heavily on workers, costs are soaring and productivity is plunging as firms attempt to respect social distancing protocols and enhance cleaning. Since it takes a lot longer to produce a product, volumes drop and therefore a factory's fixed costs are distributed over fewer units. This increases product costs and forces suppliers to increase wholesale prices or eat the margin. In addition, as lead times for parts and finished products increase, producers need to

---

[690] Ryan, Carol. "Disruptive food brands get taste of their own medicine." *The Wall Street Journal.* May 16, 2020.

[691] Ryan, Carol. "Disruptive food brands get taste of their own medicine." *The Wall Street Journal.* May 16, 2020.

carry more inventory, which ties up working capital.

Winners

Some suppliers will benefit from the virus. Producers of essential products like food, PPE as well as cleaning products and other household items will have record years. Other service providers, such as cleaners and warehouse companies, will benefit as well.

Soup Surprise

Campbell Soup is having a moment. The manufacturer is operating plants 24 hours a day, seven days a week. During one week in March, orders rose over 350 percent. The firm is hiring more workers as consumers buy canned goods for safekeeping in case food supplies run short. It wasn't long ago that Campbell found itself on the wrong end of recent food trends as mentioned earlier in the book[692].

Tide Times

P&G has benefited greatly from changing consumer purchase patterns as a result of the virus. In mid-April, the consumer products company reported that fiscal third quarter sales jumped 10 percent in the United States. Some categories have grown 20 percent — mostly everyday essentials. One category that has slowed is personal care. Sales of products in the grooming and beauty lines have declined[693]. Unilever reported similar results, noting that personal care categories such as deodorants, hairstyling, skin care and shampoos have seen considerable declines since the virus spread[694].

Overtime

In Canada, 80 percent of food manufacturers increased production to try to meet the increase in demand from consumers during the last two weeks of March. Some producers saw demand as much as 500 percent higher than the same period in

---

[692] Sagan, Aleksandra. "Plants run 24/7 to meet consumer demand for food." *The Canadian Press*. April 21, 2020.

[693] "P&G wipes up as consumers stockpile toilet paper and cleaning products." *Reuters*. April 18, 2020.

[694] Evans, Judith. "Lockdown shifts personal hygiene, grooming standards." *The Financial Times*. April 24, 2020.

2019. Specific products that were in demand the most included: household cleaners, pasta, rice, baby foods, eggs, water, canned goods, baking supplies, milk, medicine and, of course, paper products[695].

CSIs "R" Us

Sarah Nassauer penned an article in the Wall Street Journal that reviewed the sudden success of Aftermath Services — a deep cleaner that often focuses on cleaning locations where people die. With COVID-19 wreaking havoc on brick and mortar stores, retailers need to clean more often and more thoroughly. Since late February, Aftermath has handled about 500 retail cleaning requests[696].

Skid King

Prologis Inc. could be one of the many firms that benefit from the pandemic. The warehouse provider operates in 19 countries and has 964 million square feet of supply chain space. With Amazon as one of its 5,000 customers and with online shopping growing significantly, the firm may benefit long term as a result of the pandemic[697].

Neat-Freak

Neo, a floor-cleaning robot from Avidbots, has seen demand double since COVID-19 came to town. The autonomous robot, made in Kitchener, about an hour outside of Toronto, has been busy disinfecting floors at malls, airports, universities, colleges, warehouses and more[698].

---

[695] Jackson, Emily. "Stocking up leads to surge in demand." *The Financial Post*. April 2, 2020.

[696] Nassauer, Sarah. "Crime-scene cleaners in demand…from retailers." *The Wall Street Journal*. May 16, 2020.

[697] Won, Shirley. "Real estate picks for yield-hungry investors." *The Globe and Mail*. April 1, 2020.

[698] O'Kane, Josh. "Orders spike for floor-scrubbing robots to boldly go where humans fear to tread." *The Globe and Mail*. April 27, 2020.

Retooling

Numerous manufacturers have switched what they produce in order to make in-demand crisis products. One of those manufacturers is Stanfield's. This 138-year-old company, known for its quality shorts, underwear and long johns, has started making gowns for medical use[699].

Assortment

As consumers flock to grocery stores, suppliers are focusing on manufacturing top sellers. With restaurants closed and with many consumers feeling anxious about income, more people are cooking from home. With some grocery products having shown increases as high as 400 percent, food processing plants have streamlined operations to increase output. This means producing only top sellers — avoiding costly changeovers for lower-volume products that take time and leave factories idle. Therefore, store shelves look a little different — gone are many of the fringe items that used to round out assortments[700].

Direct-to-consumer

Food suppliers have learned how to retail as restaurants close. Before COVID-19, many food suppliers relied entirely on the restaurant channel and did not develop their own direct-to-consumer business. With fresh food about to go to waste, many of these suppliers have opened the door to retail to move product and generate cash. The problem with this change is that product portions, quality and packaging for the wholesale business is significantly different than retail. The two worlds are just too different.

Boxing Match

In May, PepsiCo launched two new direct-to-consumer websites. The first, called Pantryshop.com, includes brands such as Tropicana, SunChips, Quaker and Gatorade. Customers can buy one of several pre-kitted boxes such as Family Favorites, Everyday Pantry, Snacking, Hydration, Protein, Workout & Recovery and Rise & Shine. Each kit is available in regular size at $29.95 US and in family size at $49.95 US. Delivery is free. The second site is called Snacks.com and includes brands

---

[699] Mercer, Greg. "Stanfield's pivots from underwear to medical gowns." *The Globe and Mail*. April 17, 2020.

[700] Blaze Baum, Kathryn and Krashinsky Robertson, Susan. "Food makers scale back to basics with surge in home cooking." *The Globe and Mail*. April 6, 2020.

such as Tostitos, Lay's, Ruffles, Cheetos and more. Delivery is free on orders of $15 US or more[701].

Meat Market

Toronto's The Butcher Shoppe, a meat wholesaler, previously sold to about 2,000 hotels, schools, restaurants and casinos. The firm is now trying to sell online or through its store[702].

The Incredible Bulk

Houston-based Sysco, a large food supplier to restaurants and other institutions, has launched its own direct-to-consumer food e-commerce site in Canada called Sysco at Home. Customers order bulk packaged foods online and pick them up at one of 15 warehouses around the country. The wholesaler is offering delivery in the Greater Toronto Area and plans to add other major cities such as Montreal, Vancouver, Calgary and Edmonton[703].

Cardboard Ketchup

In an interesting move, Heinz has started a direct-to-consumer initiative for its products in the United Kingdom. Originally designed for frontline workers who may not have time to shop, the program has created some controversy with retailers.

Department Store Blues

In early June, Canada Goose announced it would limit selling any additional product to department stores for the balance of 2020. The brand has indicated that it would focus on its own stores and website to generate sales where it enjoys triple the margins[704].

---

[701] Anderson, George. "PepsiCo launches direct-to-consumer sites for its brands." May 12, 2020. Retrieved from: https://retailwire.com/discussion/pepsico-launches-direct-to-consumer-sites-for-its-brands/

[702] Liu, Karon. "Meat suppliers on hunt for new distribution networks." *The Toronto Star*. April 9, 2020.

[703] Krashinsky Robertson, Susan. "Sysco Canada jumps into online groceries." *The Globe and Mail*. April 21, 2020.

[704] Sampath, Uday. "Canada Goose strategy switch". *Reuters*. June 4, 2020.

Helping Hand

Some service providers have excelled during the crisis by offering timely solutions for retailers in need of help.

Room for Advancement

Shopify has been busy lending capital to its merchant customers. The cash advances range from as high as $500,000 Cdn to as low as $200 Cdn. The firm calls the service a cash advance rather than a loan. Merchants can pay the amount back once they start making sales on the site. There is no credit check done in advance and no payment deadline. Each advance is underwritten by Export Development Canada and is also available in the United States and the United Kingdom. During the last two weeks of March, new merchants to the platform have grown by 20 percent as more people look to start their own online stores[705].

Amazon Understudy

Shopify crossed the line into consumer marketing when it announced it was launching an app called Shop. The app allows consumers to reach its more than one million merchants in one spot and saves each merchant from creating its own version. Shopify will be able to capture more merchant advertising revenue inside its own ecosystem[706].

Golden Maple

In early May, Shopify's market valuation temporarily grew to a stunning $120 billion, making it the biggest company in Canada. The stock is up almost 100 percent in 2020 thus far.

Tap Dance

In Canada, Mastercard and Visa increased the tap limit on credit cards. In a move to facilitate increased contactless transactions, the two increased the limit customers can use tap for from $100 to $250. The use of cash has seen a dramatic decline this spring as customers and retailers minimize the spread of the virus[707].

---

[705] McLeod, James. "Shopify expands capital lending." *The Financial Post*. April 21, 2020.

[706] Silcoff, Sean and Milstead, David. "Shopify steps into Amazon's territory with consumer app." *The Globe and Mail*. April 29, 2020.

[707] O'Hara, Clare. "Mastercard, Visa raise tap limits in effort to help consumers avoid

Supply Chained

Global supply chains are in disarray. Passenger airplanes, once used to move product as well as people, are grounded. Essential items, regulated at the national, provincial or state level, have rightly so jumped to the front of the line. In March, trucks were lined up at grocery stores and warehouses trying to meet unprecedented demand as customers avoided eating out. Country-specific lockdowns and stay-at-home orders have brought many labour-dependent components of global supply chains to a crawl — ports, railyards, warehouses and more. Factory productivity has dropped as workers become sick or practise social distancing. Manufacturing plants around the world were designed for maximum output, which often requires employees to work in close quarters. Even if automated, numerous manufacturers have been mandated to shut down as they are not deemed an essential service[708].

Dry Hands

As you would expect, hand sanitizer sales have soared, but so have supply chain issues. Nielson, a research company, indicated that U.S. sales for hand sanitizer increased by 239 percent in March 2020 from a year ago. As a result, at least two issues with ongoing supply have emerged. First, plastic bottles are backlogged. Second, the ingredients to make the gel that goes into the hand sanitizer is on back-order[709].

Springtime Santa

Canada Post, the country's government-owned, federal mail and package delivery service, is seeing holiday-type volumes as Canadians order considerably more online during the crisis. On April 20, the company delivered 1.8 million packages in one day[710]. That's a lot for Canada!

Production Function

As food production runs hard to keep up with demand, many facilities, known

---

touching machines." *The Globe and Mail*. April 3, 2020.

[708] Powell, Naomi. "Supply chain pain." *The Financial Post*. March 28, 2020.

[709] Porter Jr., Gerald and Ludlow, Ed. "Hand sanitizer will be hard to find for some time to come." *Bloomberg*. April 15, 2020.

[710] "Canada Post reporting 'Christmas level' volumes." *The Canadian Press*. April 24, 2020.

for workers working in close proximity, have closed temporarily to clean as workers become infected with the virus.

Shutdown

In the U.S., food processing companies such as Sanderson Farms and Smithfield Foods have had employees test positive for COVID-19 — demonstrating the risk to global food supply. As factories shut down for cleaning, farmers run the risk of seeing crops spoil. Several food companies such as Kraft Heinz, Mondelez, Cargill, Maple Leaf Foods and Campbell Soup have resorted to paying workers premium hourly rates or bonuses to compensate them for the risk of working in this new normal. Some unions in South America have threatened to strike due to dangerous working conditions[711].

Seafood

High Liner temporarily suspended operations at its Portsmouth, N.H. processing plant after confirming employees tested positive for COVID-19 in late April[712].

Chicken

Maple Leaf Foods halted production at its Brampton poultry processing operation because three workers tested positive for COVID-19. The firm deep-cleaned the plant before it reopened[713].

Meat

As numerous meat-processing plants such as Cargill battle rapid employee sickness, the entire supply chain is impacted. Cattle farmers don't know what to do with animals and are seeing lower prices as supply increases. Grocery stores and restaurants are seeing out-of-stocks and potential price increases, which will be passed on to consumers. In early May, Wendy's reported some locations ran out of beef.

---

[711] Mulvany, Lydia and Shanker, Deena and Almeida, Isis. "Workers critical to world's food supply start to fall ill." *Bloomberg.* March 28, 2020.

[712] "High Liner closes U.S. plant over virus." *The Canadian Press.* April 22, 2020.

[713] "Maple Leaf suspends operations at plant on three COVID cases." *The Canadian Press.* April 9, 2020.

Rationing

In the United States, Costco and Kroger temporarily placed limits on poultry, pork and fresh beef following meat-processing plant supply issues as a result of workers catching COVID-19.

Order Cancellations

The COVID-19 pandemic has had a ripple effect as western apparel chains cancelled billions of dollars worth of orders from Bangladesh. The Bangladeshi apparel industry is large, with more than 4,500 factories selling to more than 200 brands worldwide.

Estimates are that approximately $3 billion US worth of orders have been cancelled, some already made and sitting at the factory. Some of the brands that have cancelled orders or refused to pay for finished goods include American Eagle, J.C. Penney, Tesco, Walmart, Kohl's and others. Brands that have committed to pay for orders include Target, Marks & Spencer, Zara and H&M[714].

Walmart-owned ASDA has ruffled feathers with suppliers as the firm announced in April that it was cancelling apparel shipments and paying for only part of product that is already made. The U.K. discounter wrote to suppliers, advising them that for finished goods that have not shipped, the retailer would pay half of the value of the product. For product not completed, the retailer offered 30 percent as a "goodwill gesture." Many suppliers were reportedly angry at ASDA's position[715].

Out on Bail

In Europe, Adidas received a $3.3 billion US-equivalent aid package from the German government. The sporting goods giant will receive a revolving credit facility but must cease share buy backs and dividends during the period of the loan[716]. In mid-March, Adidas and Puma signalled they had lost $1.1 billion US worth of

---

[714] Lewis, Michael. "Pandemic threatens Bangladesh garment industry." *The Toronto Star.* April 24, 2020.

[715] Chambers, Sam. "Coronavirus: now Asda turns screw on suppliers." April 19, 2020. Retrieved from: https://www.thetimes.co.uk/article/coronavirus-now-asda-turns-screw-on-suppliers-zsbzt7l85

[716] "Adidas gets 3 billion-euro package." *Bloomberg.* April 15, 2020.

revenue in China due to COVID-19 — where over 30 percent of the firm's revenue is normally generated[717].

MANAGEMENT

Management has been on the hot seat during the COVID-19 crisis for a number of reasons.

<u>Crisis 101</u>

From CEOs down to middle management, the pandemic has been nothing but an operational nightmare — stores closing almost overnight, building online capacity on-the-fly, furloughing staff, cancelling orders, cutting costs, securing emergency financing, shipping products, communicating through videoconferencing and more. All that work just so you can have the worst year of your career, while also trying to protect your health and that of your teams. Not easy. For those who never managed through or led teams through a crisis, this was their baptism by fire.

<u>Fat Cat Diet</u>

Executive compensation is under a new level of scrutiny during this time. Kevin Thomas, CEO of the Shareholder Association for Research and Education, penned an interesting article in the Globe and Mail that addresses this issue. Thomas calls on shareholders to review previous measures that are no longer relevant in this new normal. Some executives have reduced or eliminated their pay during the crisis and society has noticed[718]. Lululemon executives have reduced their salary by 20 percent and have used the money to create a fund for furloughed workers.

INVESTORS

Retail was already in the doghouse with investors before the pandemic. Outside of highflying tech companies and big blue chip retailers like Walmart and Target,

---

[717] Thomasson, Emma. "Adidas sees US$1.1B coronavirus hit in China." *Reuters.* March 12, 2020.

[718] Thomas, Kevin. "Now is the right time to rethink executive compensation." *The Globe and Mail.* April 9, 2020.

retail was yesterday's bet.

Some of those with exposure to retail during the crisis suffered — not just from a stock standpoint. Lenders, private equity firms and others have taken a collective bath as a result of the virus's impact on retail. Those that invested in retail landlords or real estate investment trusts (REITs) before the crisis have been challenged also, as April and May rent payments were spotty at best. The value of retail real estate has taken a beating as well, as the future of brick and mortar retail and, specifically, malls, comes into question. With 2020 financial guidance retracted for many retailers, investors are flying blind.

Chip and Dip

As of April 15, 2020, the S&P Retail Select Industry Index was down about 20 percent from its year-to-date high on February 20[719] — although that's better than the 40 percent drop on March 23.

Flying V

An op ed by David Rosenberg, a researcher, discusses the probable recovery time for consumer discretionary stocks. Rosenberg cites previous financial meltdowns and how long it took for the hardest-hit sector to recover. He discusses how the tech bubble of 2000 took about 17 years, while it was seven years before U.S. financials recovered from their peak in 2007. It was 10 years before commodities rebounded after their 1980 trough. Rosenberg makes the case that consumer discretionary will take some time to make a comeback as well[720].

Fallen Angel

Sycamore Partners recently retracted its offer to buy a majority interest in L Brand's Victoria's Secret due to a change in business operations as a result of COVID-19. In May, L Brands announced it was closing 250 Victoria's Secret stores and 51 Bath & Body Works stores in the US and Canada. The firm saw a 37% decrease in revenue for the 1st quarter 2020[721].

---

[719] "S&P Retail Select Industry Index." April 15, 2020. Retrieved from: https://us.spindices.com/indices/equity/sp-retail-select-industry-index

[720] Rosenberg, David. "We won't be spending our way out of this." *The Globe and Mail*. May 7, 2020.

[721] Tyko, Kelly. "Victoria's Secret closing 250 Canadian, U.S. stores". *USA Today*. May 22,

Breakfast Coupon

There have been reports that luxury giant LVMH is looking to renegotiate it's deal with Tiffany & Co. based on the impact of COVID-19 on the luxury market. LVMH agreed to buy Tiffany for a cool $ 16.2 billion U.S. in November of 2019[722].

Greener Pastures

According to the Wall Street Journal, Pitchbook reported that venture capital (VC) money invested in consumer brands dropped 26 percent in the first quarter of 2020 from 2019. Speaking of 2019, Goldman Sachs reported that VC firms decreased their investment in consumer companies by 54 percent from 2018[723].

Corporate Bail Outs

Greed Leash

In the United States, companies are being pressured to manage dividends and share buy-backs differently. Institutional investors, regulators and unions are signalling that companies should not be laying off workers and cutting salaries while maintaining dividends or continuing to participate in share buy-backs. In Canada, there have been calls for governments to refuse aid to companies that use offshore financial centres to income shift and avoid taxes.

Happy Meal

McDonald's has maintained dividends while cutting salaries and laying off staff during the crisis. In 2019, the firm's dividend was $3.6 billion US[724]. The firm, to its credit, has at least stopped buying back its own shares.

2020.

[722] Roumeliotis, Greg and Barbaglia, Pamela. "LVMH eyes renegotiining Tiffany & Co. takeover". *Reuters*. June 4, 2020.

[723] Ryan, Carol. "Disruptive food brands get taste of their own medicine." *The Wall Street Journal*. May 16, 2020.

[724] Kerber, Ross and Scott, Alwyn and Dinapoli, Jessica and Spalding, Rebecca. "U.S. companies panned for protecting payouts." *Reuters*. April 9, 2020.

Lenders

Baby Shark

Private lenders are seeing a significant increase in enquiries as small retailers need help with cash flow. The worldwide private lending market is $812 billion US and is poised to grow significantly due to the crisis[725].

Kick in the Asset

Asset-backed lenders are feeling the pain of the pandemic. These are the firms that lend money to small businesses like restaurants and retailers and use the assets in the business as collateral. With so many small businesses defaulting, these assets are worth less as the market for recovery tightens. This has caused significant losses for these lenders as retailers close down.

2020 Guidance Withdrawals

McTurtle

Like many retailers, McDonald's withdrew its 2020 financial forecast amid uncertainty. The fast-food giant posted negative 3.4 percent comparable restaurant sales in the first quarter of 2020. March crushed the Chicago-based firm as sales for January and February were trending at a positive 7.2 percent. New CEO Chris Kempczinski announced he was reducing his base salary by half from April 15 to September 30 to save money. The firm is also reducing capital spending by $1 billion in 2020 by reducing the number of restaurants it opens[726].

Don't Sweat It

In late March, Lululemon announced it would not offer a 2020 forecast due to the uncertainty in the market. The Vancouver-based retailer was on a roll as comparable store sales grew 20 percent in the quarter ending February 2, 2020. The brand had seen direct-to-consumer sales grow 41 percent recently as it closed

---

[725] Sambo, Paula. "Private lenders face flood of calls." *Bloomberg*. March 21, 2020.

[726] Patton, Leslie. "McDonald's withdraws forecast as sales crash." *Bloomberg*. April 9, 2020.

numerous stores around the globe[727].

Loonie Lax

Canadian dollar chain Dollarama held off on financial forecasts for the balance of 2020. The retailer has seen sales of essentials such as hand sanitizer increase, but sales of discretionary categories such as Easter fall. The chain was deemed an essential service by the Canadian government, but has seen traffic fall by about half in mall-based locations. Stores outside of malls have seen traffic declines but not to the same degree. Some of Dollarama's suppliers were shut down in February (presumably in China), but are now open. The firm has also focused on restocking brick and mortar stores at the expense of online sales. Stores have added an additional associate to focus solely on cleaning, sanitization and safety. The chain has also encouraged customers to use alternate payment methods outside of cash. In its warehouse, Dollarama has put in place new policies to protect workers after various complaints[728].

RETAILERS

Retail, as you well know, has been one of the worst affected industries as a result of the pandemic. Along with travel, hospitality, sports and tourism, our industry has been challenged like never before.

In a study by JPMorgan, 50 percent of small businesses have less than one month worth of cash on hand and a further 25 percent have less than two weeks of cash available.

Sandrine Devillard, a senior partner at McKinsey & Company, discussed how, during COVID-19, high-volume, low-ticket retailers will have a harder time making money as traffic levels remain low. She said, "In a fixed-cost business, it could be hard to make that money work." She discussed how, in China, apparel chains are getting hit with transactions down 46 percent while average ring has decreased 23 percent. Devillard goes on to report that about 40 percent of Chinese apparel

---

[727] "Lululemon offers no 2020 forecast, e-commerce thrives." *Bloomberg.* March 28, 2020.

[728] Krashinsky Robertson, Susan. "Dollarama suspends earnings guidance in face of unpredictable sales." *The Globe and Mail.* April 2, 2020.

retailers will run out of cash during the third quarter[729].

As discussed previously, there is, however, a significant difference between essential retailers and non-essential retailers.

<u>Essentials</u>

Those in the fortunate position of offering essential products or services are seeing a boom. Costs have increased due to higher wages and additional cleaning procedures, but have been more than offset by increases in revenue, often at full price. These retailers are the lucky few.

<u>Non-essentials</u>

For those retailers that find themselves selling non-essentials, the pandemic has been nothing short of a nightmare. Sales and cash flow has virtually dried up. Sure, if you can offer curbside pickup or home delivery you can sell online. But for most retailers, online sales, while potentially growing, cannot make up for the loss of brick and mortar revenue. Not even close. These retailers still need to pay rent, insurance, suppliers, interest on loans and third-party providers for any equipment they may have leased. The expense side of the income statement is still there while the revenue side is significantly eroded.

Retail Hibernation

In March, as the pandemic hit the U.S., about 250,000 non-essential stores closed within the span of a few weeks. According to Neil Saunders of GlobalData Retail, this represents about 60 percent of overall U.S. retail square footage. Saunders says, "This is the most catastrophic crisis that retail has faced — worse than the financial crisis in 2008, worse than 9/11. Almost overnight, the retail economy shifted from being about things people want to things that they need"[730].

Essential Retailers — Uplift

As mentioned, some retailers, especially those that sell food, have seen strong gains during the crisis.

---

[729] Ferreira, Victor. "Ma'am, that dress is in quarantine." *The Financial Post.* May 14, 2020.

[730] D'Innocenzio, Anne. "U.S. bricks-and-mortar retailers try and stay relevant." *The Associated Press.* April 13, 2020.

In late May, Walmart announced 1st quarter comparable-store-sales increased 10% - the most in almost 20 years. E-commerce sales jumped 74% in the US during the same time as shoppers stocked up on essentials. Margins were challenged as customers bought more lower margin products and bought more online, which has higher fulfillment costs[731].

Target reported same-store sales increased 10.8% for the 1st quarter 2020 - with digital comparable sales up 141%. Product mix shifts to lower margin essentials as well as increased wages hurt margins and profitability, which fell 64% for quarter[732].

The Home Depot saw sales increase 7.1% in the 1st quarter of 2020 as customers bought essential items. Costs increased as well as the retailer spent $ 850 million U.S. on higher worker's wages and benefits[733].

Lowe's announced 1st quarter 2020 same-store-sales growth of 11.2% - with online sales growing 80%[734].

Costco posted a 9.6 percent increase in global comparable store sales in March of 2020. The club began placing limits on dry grocery goods, bottled water and cleaners due to customer hoarding[735].

Canadian grocer Empire announced a stunning 37 percent same-store sales increase for four weeks in March. Nielson, a research company, reported that consumer packaged goods sales increased $2.7 billion year-to-date as of March 28. This increase represents more than the total industry growth in all of 2019[736].

---

[731] Boyle, Matthew. "Walmart sales soar as consumers pile up goods". *Bloomberg*. May 20, 2020.

[732] Boyle, Matthew. "Target sees plenty of uncertainty ahead". *Bloomberg with files from Reuters*. May 21, 2020.

[733] "Pandemic hammers early profit for Home Depot". *The Associated Press*. May 20, 2020.

[734] Feuer, William. "Lowe's same-store sales surge 11.2% as coronavirus restrictions spark home improvement spending". May 20, 2020. Retrieved from: https://www.cnbc.com/2020/05/20/lowes-low-earnings-q1-2020.html

[735] "Virus crisis triggers surge in Costco's comparable sales." *Reuters*. April 9, 2020.

[736] Krashinsky Robertson, Susan. "Sobeys parent company sees jump in sales." *The Globe*

Metro, Canada's third-largest grocer, enjoyed a 25 percent gain in same-store food sales from March 15 to April 11. CEO Eric La Flèche indicated that customers were shopping less often but the average purchase was up significantly. Since mid-April sales have increased, but at a lower rate as customers were replenishing weekly. Metro said that promotions are down as a result of suppliers' ability to supply products, which help margins. Operating costs are up, though, as additional staff cleans stores and employees enjoy elevated wages during the pandemic[737].

In Canada, Amazon has signed a deal with the federal government to deliver personal protective equipment (PPE) to provinces and territories. Like many countries, Canada has contracted with domestic suppliers to manufacture PPE in short supply[738].

Non-Essential Retailers — Devastation

Those that found themselves in the wrong categories at the wrong time have suffered immensely. Department stores and fashion and footwear retailers have been hit the hardest. Often with weak balance sheets, some have entered bankruptcy protection.

<u>Bankruptcy</u>

J. Crew filed for bankruptcy on Monday, May 4, representing the first big U.S. retail brand to seek protection since the pandemic broke out. Chinos Holding, the parent company of J. Crew, will convert $1.65 billion US of debt into equity for hedge fund Anchorage Capital and other creditors. Chinos will keep control of the Madewell banner, which has seen positive momentum of late.

In early May, U.S. premium department store Neiman Marcus filed for bankruptcy protection. The firm hopes to reduce its debt levels by about $4 billion US when it exits Chapter 11 protection in the fall[739]. Creditors have provided interim

---

and Mail. April 16, 2020.

[737] Sagan, Aleksandra. "Metro's sales level off, but revenue up." *The Canadian Press.* April 23, 2020.

[738] Johnson, Kelsey. "Amazon tapped to distribute medical equipment." *Reuters with files from The Canadian Press.* April 4, 2020.

[739] Doherty, Katherine. "Struggling Neiman Marcus files for bankruptcy." *Bloomberg.* May 8, 2020.

financing of $675 million US so the chain can continue operations while it restructures. The retailer closed its 43 namesake stores, two Bergdorf Goodman stores in New York and about 24 Last Call outlets as a result of the virus. The brand also furloughed most of its 14,000 employees to reduce cost. Ares Management and the Canada Pension Plan Investment Board bought the firm in 2013 for $6 billion US in a leveraged buyout. The company currently has $4.8 billion in debt.

On Friday, May 15, J.C. Penney finally filed for Chapter 11 bankruptcy protection. The firm negotiated $900 million US in financing to allow it to proceed through the restructuring process. The 118-year-old department store has about 850 stores and $4 billion US in debt. The once-great retailer had 1,600 stores and employed more than 200,000 workers[740]. The retailer's trouble came to light when it announced in mid-April that it was not making an interest payment of $12 million US on a senior note due in 2036. The company also hired AlixPartners, a restructuring firm, to assist it with strategic alternatives[741]. In May, J.C. Penney announced it would close approximately 30% of its locations as it attempts to successfully restructure[742].

Privately-held footwear retailer Aldo entered creditor protection in May. The Montreal-based global retailer was in trouble before COVID-19 ravaged the industry. The firm is desperately accelerating its two-year transformation plan to be completed in six to 12 months. The plan calls for the closure of about 40 percent of the retailer's corporate-owned locations. With stores closed during the crisis, online sales have helped to generate about 25 to 30 percent of historic revenue. NPD, a research firm, indicated that the three hardest-hit categories during the closedown have been apparel, footwear and high-end beauty[743].

Montreal-based fashion retailer Reitmans announced in May that it received approval for protection from creditors under Canada's Companies' Creditors Arrangement Act (CCAA)[744]. The firm signaled weeks earlier that unless it could

---

[740] Spector, Mike. "J.C. Penney files for bankruptcy protection." *Reuters with files from newswires*. May 16, 2020.

[741] "J.C. Penney skips interest payment, eyes its options." *Bloomberg*. April 16, 2020.

[742] Kapner, Suzanne. "J.C. Penney to close nearly 30% of stores". *The Wall Street Journal*. May 19, 2020.

[743] Krashinsky Robertson, Susan. "Creditor protection forces Aldo to quicken its transition plan." *The Globe and Mail*. May 12, 2020.

[744] Krashinsky Robertson, Susan. "Reitmans gets creditor protection as pandemic takes toll on business". *The Financial Post*. May 20, 2020.

obtain suitable financing, it would cease to be a going concern. Like other non-essential stores, the chain closed its 582 stores in the middle of March and has been trying to generate as much cash as possible from online sales[745]. In early June, the retailer announced that it was shutting down all Addition Elle and Thyme Maternity stores and exiting the two brands[746].

In early June, Canadian retailer Sail Outdoors Inc. announced it filed for bankruptcy protection from creditors. The firm has 14 stores and employs about 1,800 workers. The retailer plans to restructure and continue as a going concern[747].

Lapsed Payment

The firm that owns Lord & Taylor is exploring options including filing for bankruptcy protection from creditors. Le Tote, which bought the chain (save real estate) from HBC for $100 million US, is contemplating a number of options including negotiating with creditors and seeking additional financial support. Le Tote owes HBC $33.2 million in a promissory note from the transaction[748]. Some believe that the retailer is close to re-opening all locations and liquidating its inventory.

In early May, it was reported that HBC failed to make payments due in April for two mortgage-backed securities. The April payments totalled $3.2 million US.

In late April, Gap warned it needed a cash inflow to keep operating. The retailer has drawn down its line of credit and did not make April's rent. It closed its North American locations and laid off most of its workers. By the end of the quarter on May 2, the firm said it would have only $750 million US to $850 million US of cash and equivalents on hand and that it would need to arrange additional financing[749].

Henry's, one of Canada's oldest camera stores, issued a "Notice of Intent" to

---

[745] Krashinsky Robertson, Susan. "Reitmans Canada warns business could fail if it can't secure financing." *The Globe and Mail*. May 4, 2020.

[746] Deschamps, Tara. "Thyme Maternity, Addition Elle to close". *The Canadian Press*. June 2, 2020.

[747] "Sail Outdoors files for bankruptcy". *The Canadian Press*. June 3, 2020.

[748] "Lord & Taylor mulls bankruptcy, sources say." *Reuters*. April 22, 2020.

[749] Kapner, Suzanne and Dabaie, Michael. "Gap warns it needs to raise additional funds." *The Wall Street Journal*. April 24, 2020.

creditors in early May. The notice was to advise its creditors that it cannot pay the $24 million Cdn in payables it owes them. The firm has been in operation since 1909.

Freefall

Macy's announced in May that it was using it's real estate and inventory as collateral to secure up to $ 4.1 billion U.S. to help it with liquidity during the crisis[750].

San Francisco-based The RealReal announced in early April that it would lose about $40 million US and lay off about 10 percent of staff. The luxury consignment company indicated that once San Francisco shelter-in-place orders came into effect March 17, volume dropped 40 to 45 percent year over year[751].

Under Armour has signalled that its second quarter revenue would be off 50 to 60 percent[752].

Nordstrom reported in early May that it was permanently closing 16 department stores as a direct result of the pandemic. This represents about 14 percent of its full-line store count[753].

In the U.S., Best Buy has seen sales drop by about 30 percent since closing stores and switching to a curbside pick-up model March 22[754].

---

[750] Seligson, Paula and Doherty, Katherine and Smith, Molly. "Macy's will hock key assets to borrow up to US$4.1 billion". *Bloomberg*. May 28, 2020.

[751] Van Voorhis, Scott. "The RealReal to post first-quarter loss and makes cuts including 10% of staff." April 14, 2020. Retrieved from: https://www.thestreet.com/investing/the-real-real-to-post-q1-loss-and-makes-cost-cuts?puc=yahoo&cm_ven=YAHOO&yptr=yahoo&soc_src=hl-viewer&soc_trk=tw

[752] Balu, Nivedita. "Under Armour revenue takes hit." *Reuters*. May 12, 2020.

[753] Thomas, Lauren. "Coronavirus fallout: Here are the 16 department stores Nordstrom is closing permanently." May 8, 2020. Retrieved from: https://www.cnbc.com/2020/05/08/nordstrom-store-closures-here-are-the-16-stores-expected-to-shut.html?__source=sharebar|twitter&par=sharebar

[754] "Best Buy provides business update related to COVID-19." April 15, 2020. Retrieved from: http://investors.bestbuy.com/investor-relations/news-and-events/financial-releases/news-details/2020/Best-Buy-Provides-Business-Update-Related-to-COVID-19/default.aspx

U.S. fitness provider 24 Hour Fitness is reportedly considering numerous options, including bankruptcy protection. The firm has 450 locations with estimated revenue of $1.5 billion US and four million members. Gold's Gym recently announced it was closing 30 locations and YogaWorks announced it was shuttering all New York units[755].

In mid-March, British book retailer WH Smith reported sales had dropped by 35 percent at airports. In April, sales fell 85 percent at the same locations. Airport duty-free shops and other retailers and restaurants that count on travellers have been hurt badly as travel has slowed considerably[756].

Live goods (plants, flowers, etc.) is a tough business at the best of times. With the pandemic continuing into May, this category faces steep losses. Not just for retailers, either — growers, too, who have been preparing for the season for months. In Canada, for eight weeks from late April onward, growers sit on about $450 million Cdn in plants that may have to be thrown out if large retailers close garden centre operations to the public. Mark Cullen, an industry expert, says Canada could see 30 percent of growers shut down if the industry remains closed — noting that about 80 percent of growers' sales occur in just 12 short weeks[758].

Tim Hortons reported a 45 percent decrease in comparable-restaurant-sales the last two weeks of March. The coffee shop has been using home delivery and drive-thru capabilities to try to preserve as much business as possible.

Canadian department store Simons is facing an uncertain future. In an op-ed by Konrad Yakabuski, he discusses how the 180-year-old company is facing its demise during COVID-19. With 15 stores in Canada and fresh off a major multi-year expansion plan, the firm had to push out the opening of its new $215 million Cdn automated distribution centre. Online sales have helped a little, but not enough. The private company may need to tap outside investors to help it get through the crisis

---

[755] Hanbury, Mary. "24 Hour Fitness reportedly considers bankruptcy options as the coronavirus pandemic continues to squeeze gyms across the US." April 20, 2020. Retrieved from: https://www.businessinsider.com/24-hour-fitness-considers-bankruptcy-cnbc-report-2020-4

[756] "Coronavirus hits sales at WH Smith's airport shops." *Reuters*. March 17, 2020.

[758] Kalinowski, Tess. "Garden centres facing a shady spring." *The Toronto Star*. April 22, 2020.

and the aftermath that follows[759].

Online Lifeline

One of the only saving graces during the pandemic has been e-commerce. With brick and mortar stores closed and customers fearful of shopping in person, online shopping has helped keep cash coming in.

Costco reported online sales increased 48.3 percent during March of 2020[760].

In the U.S., Target has seen its online business grow by 270 percent in April as curbside pickup helped to partially offset comparable store sales decreases in the mid-teens, according to Fortune reporter Phil Wahba[761].

In the U.K., Aldi has entered the online food business for the first time. The discount food retailer has begun selling boxes filled with a combination of toilet paper, rice, pasta, hand wash and soup. The box is selling for £24.99 GBP[762].

Best Buy U.S. announced that online sales were up 250 percent since the chain closed its stores in March and that about half of its online sales have been curbside pickup[763].

Online home products retailer Wayfair appears to be doing well during the crisis. In early April, management signalled to investors that gross revenue was up

---

[759] Yakabuski, Konrad. "After 180 years, Simons faces its biggest test yet." *The Globe and Mail*. May 13, 2020.

[760] "Virus crisis triggers surge in Costco's comparable sales." *Reuters*. April 9, 2020.

[761] Wahba, Phil. "Target's April e-commerce has nearly quadrupled as crowd controls slam in-store sales." April 23, 2020. Retrieved from: https://fortune.com/2020/04/23/target-online-pickup-driveup-sales/

[762] Armstrong, Ashley. April 16, 2020. Retrieved from: https://twitter.com/AArmstrong_says/status/1250747356724842496

[763] "Best Buy provides business update related to COVID-19." April 15, 2020. Retrieved from: http://investors.bestbuy.com/investor-relations/news-and-events/financial-releases/news-details/2020/Best-Buy-Provides-Business-Update-Related-to-COVID-19/default.aspx

over 100 percent toward the end of March across most categories in all markets[764].

Peloton is one of the firms benefiting from changing lifestyles as a result of the pandemic. As gyms were ordered closed, more people signed up with the company. The brand's stock has risen more than 40 percent year-to-date as of early May.

A report from Bloomberg claims that Amazon has recently picked up a number of brands that have decided to sell through the retailer, albeit reluctantly, as brick and mortar stores close during the pandemic[765]. The retailer also announced it was moving it's Prime Day event from July to September of 2020[766].

Challenges

Financing

Depending on the size of the retailer, its balance sheet, its cash position, its asset base and other characteristics, it may be able to borrow money to get it through the pandemic — whenever that is. Some retailers may be fortunate enough to qualify for government loans and grants. Some will fall through the cracks and will not make it through the storm. Some have already given up.

Rent

Many troubled retailers have attempted to negotiate rent deferrals with commercial landlords. Canadian restaurant A&W has sent a formal request to landlords for a two-month rent deferral[767]. Some have had success while others have not. Landlords have businesses to run, too, and have mortgages, insurance, maintenance, payroll and other costs to bear. Is it fair for retailers to stop paying rent?

---

[764] Freund, Janet. "Wayfair surges amid online furniture spree." *Bloomberg*. April 7, 2020.

[765] Soper, Spencer. "Amazon wins business from reluctant brands after virus closes stores." May 5, 2020. Retrieved from: https://www.bloomberg.com/news/articles/2020-05-05/amazon-wins-business-from-reluctant-brands-after-virus-closes-stores

[766] "Amazon pushes prime day to September". *Reuters*. May 22, 2020.

[767] Younglai, Rachelle and Krashinsky Robertson, Susan. "A&W requests two-month rent deferral from franchisee's landlords." *The Globe and Mail*. March 27, 2020.

Cash Preservation

Some retailers who face a cash crunch have slashed capital budgets. They have put off store renovations, expansion plans or capability upgrades where possible to preserve whatever cash they have on hand. Others are looking to sell non-core assets or issue new debt to generate cash.

Stop Gap

In the U.S., Gap has several initiatives underway to try to survive the crisis. These include eliminating $300 million US in capital expenditures, leaving spring merchandise on racks as long as possible, packing up spring merchandise for 2021 and delaying ordering for holiday 2020 to build in financial and inventory flexibility[768].

Added Costs

Amazon expects all would-be operating profit in quarter two 2020 to be spent on COVID-19. The retailer anticipates it will spend $4 billion US in the second quarter on employee protective equipment, testing and paying staff more.

Online Capacity Issues

Some retailers have been caught without adequate infrastructure and capacity to handle online sales during this crisis. According to Forrester Research, some retailers that are located in malls have not utilized curbside pickup to help stem offset sales decreases. Other smaller retailers may not have the budget or bandwidth to pivot to e-commerce easily. With little hope of recovery, many have closed down permanently after being open for decades.

Security

Some small retailers worry about break-ins as they leave their stores left unattended. Diane Brisbois, president of the Retail Council of Canada, was quoted in the Toronto Star, saying, "People are worried about how they're going to pay rent and how they're going to pay for inventory they ordered. And now, they have to worry about, 'Is my business going to be safe?'" Brisbois discusses how it's mostly the smaller retailers that are worried about security because they are often not in malls that have their own security.

---

[768] Wahba, Phil. April 9, 2020. Retrieved from: https://twitter.com/philwahba/status/1248361295319126023

Inventory Issues

Many retailers have been caught with spring goods that aren't selling due to the crisis, tying up cash that could be used to pay other bills.

Heavy Discounts

Brands such as Gap, Ralph Lauren, Saks Fifth Avenue, Nordstrom and J.Crew have discounted spring fashion at up to 70 percent off to try to generate cash and dispose of the goods. Some have also paused fall shipments[769]. T.J. Maxx, normally a major buyer of slow-moving fashion, is closed — making it harder to unload distressed product. The problem with inventory is that it loses value the longer it hangs around. Styles change, weather changes and packing away the product, which some call "hoteling," is expensive and consumes space. It also does little to generate cash flow.

Asset Management

In normal times, once discount outlets like T.J. Maxx or Burlington are exhausted, retailers use "jobbers" to try to move fashion at regional chains — sometimes recouping 30 to 50 percent of cost. If that doesn't work, they move on to liquidators, who may offer 10 percent on the dollar. Retailers could also donate product and produce a tax write-off — not much help to generate cash today, though. Finally, some luxury goods producers have historically destroyed product to keep it off the market at discount prices, to maintain premium brand positioning. This practice has been subject to scrutiny from environmental groups and some brands have stopped doing it.

These approaches can work in normal times, but become ineffective during a pandemic when discretionary shopping has all but dried up. Retailers will probably use a mix of whatever or whomever they can to generate cash to keep operations running for as long as they can — or enter Chapter 11 protection to try to reduce debt[770]. Some will partially liquidate inventory just to generate cash.

---

[769] D'Innocenzio, Anne. "U.S. bricks-and-mortar retailers try and stay relevant." *The Associated Press*. April 13, 2020.

[770] Kapner, Suzanne. "Closed stores get desperate to unload spring clothes." *The Wall Street Journal*. April 21, 2020.

Write-downs

In the U.K., retailer Primark is reportedly losing £100 million GBP per month with stores closed. The firm has also taken a write-down of £284 million GBP based on it carrying £1.5 billion GBP worth of inventory[771]. Clothing retailers could face inventory write-offs of as much as £15 billion GBP in the U.K., as product isn't selling. Clothing stores, classified as non-essential, closed March 16 after spring and summer merchandise arrived from factories[772].

Landlord Issues

Mall landlords will suffer significantly as COVID-19 impacts retail in the United States. In an article by Lauren Thomas from CNBC, she references UBS's recent analysis that says 100,000 retail stores will close in the U.S. over the next five years. The article also addresses the co-tenancy clause that many mall tenants have within their leases. This clause stipulates that current occupancy is based on the mall having key anchors to draw traffic. As many of the anchors potentially pull out of malls, this creates a legal issue for real estate landlords. UBS also claims that U.S. online sales will grow from 15 percent now to 25 percent by 2025 — which will further pressure landlords as malls become less popular[773].

Rent Collection

CNBC reported that according to real estate services firm Marcus and Millichap, U.S. malls with a majority of non-essential stores collected between 10 and 25 percent of April rent.

According to a study by Jones Lang LaSalle in Chicago, major Canadian mall landlords collected only 15 percent of rent from tenants for the month of May. This

---

[771] Armstrong, Ashley. April 21, 2020. Retrieved from: https://twitter.com/AArmstrong_says/status/1252543672324960257

[772] Armstrong, Ashley. "Clothes retailers face £15bn of write-offs as stock lies unsold." April 14, 2020. Retrieved from: https://www.thetimes.co.uk/article/clothes-retailers-face-15bn-of-write-offs-as-stock-lies-unsold-qv8j35cr5

[773] Thomas, Lauren. "With 100,000 stores set to close by 2025, mall owners face this legal hurdle next." April 23, 2020. Retrieved from: https://www.cnbc.com/2020/04/23/coronavirus-will-speed-up-store-closures-what-landlords-need-to-watch-next.html

is in comparison to the 25 percent for April[774].

Some large real estate investment trusts (REITs) are having a hard time getting rent from retailers. Malls, especially, have been hard hit and it's not just the small- to medium-sized merchants that have skipped paying rent.

H&R REIT received only 56 percent of its retail rent in April. Oxford Properties collected 20 percent of April rent from most malls. RioCan REIT collected a mere 66 percent of retail rent for April and publicly named Staples as one of the retailers that did not pay. SmartCentres collected 70 percent of rent at its Canadian retail sites but was "disappointed" that some big-name retailers balked at April's payments.

Many retail landlords have negotiated deferrals with retailers and expect April rent to be paid sometime in the weeks or months ahead[775]. Gap has not made April rent payments for its North American retail stores.

When North American malls closed in March, landlords and retail tenants were headed for a confrontation. Some retailers claimed they should not have to pay rent as malls were forced to close and no longer kept their end of the contract. Some landlords held the line and told retailers they expected rent in full no matter the circumstance.

Some retailers have asked for a deferral or a temporary rent reduction. Retailers explored force majeure clauses, which were designed to accommodate acts of God, insurrections and other black swan events.

Landlords, too, have commitments and mortgages to pay and voiced their concerns regarding being left high and dry. Many large landlords are using a case-by-case approach to determine if and when deferrals are in their long-term best interest.

Retailers have warned landlords that if they evict them they will have a hard time finding new tenants under these conditions[776].

---

[774] Younglai, Rachelle. "Canadian malls collect just 15 per cent of May rent from tenants." *The Globe and Mail*. May 13, 2020.

[775] Subramaniam, Vanmala. "Poor rent collection hits retail REITs, especially mall owners." *The Financial Post*. April 24, 2020.

[776] Krashinsky Robertson, Susan and Younglai, Rachelle. "Retailers seek rent relief as shopping centres close." *The Globe and Mail*. March 26, 2020.

Numerous U.S. retailers including Gap, Bed Bath & Beyond, Dick's Sporting Goods and UNTUCKit have been active renegotiating leases with landlords as a result of COVID-19[777].

CNBC reported that Green Street Advisors, a real estate services firm, indicated that by the end of 2021 half the malls that currently have department stores as anchors will close[778].

Different Course

In a CNBC article, Lauren Thomas discusses how New Jersey mall American Dream has switched its focus from retail to entertainment as a result of COVID-19. The mall, which spans a space of three million square feet in East Rutherford, NJ, has reallocated retail space from 45 percent to 30 percent since the crisis developed. Entertainment will make up the remaining 70 percent of the space[779].

RioCan, one of Canada's largest retail landlords, announced it is holding off on early-stage and new projects for 2020. This represents about $100 million to $150 million in deferred capital and cost savings[780].

Skin in the Game

One of North America's largest retail landlords announced a program to invest $5 billion US in retailers. Brookfield Asset Management Inc. has called the program

---

[777] Thomas, Lauren. "Men's shirt retailer Untuckit taps real estate restructuring firm to renegotiate deals during coronavirus." May 5, 2020. Retrieved from: https://www.cnbc.com/2020/05/05/untuckit-taps-real-estate-restructuring-firm-to-renegotiate-deals-during-coronavirus.html?__source=sharebar|twitter&par=sharebar

[778] Thomas, Lauren. "Over 50% of department stores in malls predicted to close by 2021, real estate services firm says." April 29, 2020. Retrieved from: https://www.cnbc.com/2020/04/29/50percent-of-all-these-malls-forecast-to-close-by-2021-green-street-advisors-says.html

[779] Thomas, Lauren. "Stalled by coronavirus pandemic, American Dream rethinks its future and retail becomes an afterthought." April 6, 2020. Retrieved from: https://www.cnbc.com/2020/04/06/stalled-by-coronavirus-american-dream-rethinks-its-future.html

[780] Thorpe, Jacqueline. "RioCan hits brakes on new projects." *Bloomberg*. May 6, 2020.

"retail revitalization" and will involve the landlord taking an ownership stake in select retailers that need a capital infusion during these tough times[781]. The program will focus on retailers with sales over $250 million US and that have been in business for a minimum of two years.

Mall Miss

In May, the Mall of America announced it had failed to make April and May payments toward a $ 1.4 billion U.S. mortgage-backed security held by Wells Fargo[782].

Out of the Big Box Thinking

We have seen many retailers innovate during these unprecedented times. Most have had to in order to survive. From building out online capacity to selling new lines of essential products, retailers are finding ways to generate whatever cash they can.

Restaurant to Retail

Some restaurants have pivoted to groceries during the crisis. In an article by Jim Salter from the Associated Press, he describes the activities of several eateries such as Panera, Subway and smaller brands such as Union Loafers and Gandy Dancer, which are now selling groceries. This makes sense on at least three fronts — restaurants are closed and need the business, they have residual food to draw down and they can offer an alternative to crowded grocery stores[783].

Store Stock

Austin, TX-based retailer Kendra Scott used its 108 stores as mini-fulfillment centres during the crisis. With social distancing mandated, the chain had to innovate in order to meet customers' orders via e-commerce. As warehousing became more difficult to operate when workers needed to be six feet apart, the brand innovated

---

[781] "Brookfield commits US$5B to revitalize ailing retail sector." *Bloomberg*. May 8, 2020.

[782] "Biggest U.S. mall two months behind on US$1.4B loan". *Bloomberg*. May 22, 2020.

[783] Salter, Jim. "U.S. restaurants turn to grocery sales to help offset revenue loss." *The Associated Press*. April 13, 2020.

and used its existing assets to help with delivery[784].

Hot Box

In Canada, Pizzaville, as well as many other fast-food providers, has launched contactless delivery. This process, which can be specified during ordering, allows the delivery person to drop the order on a customer's doorstep, ring the doorbell and walk away. Other companies are reengineering kitchen processes to minimize the degree of contact between staff and the food they are preparing. Numerous food service brands have launched marketing campaigns to advise customers about these changes.

Loose Thread

Walmart announced in May that it was partnering with used clothing reseller ThredUp to sell over 750,000 garments on it's website. Customers can use Walmart's vast store network for returns[785].

Cheapskate

Perhaps as a forerunner to consumers' flight to value, Apple announced it was launching an economically-priced iPhone. The model SE will sell for $399 US and be ready for delivery in the spring of 2020. This new price point represents a 40 percent decrease from the previous most economical model[786].

Package and a Show?

There are reports that Amazon is in talks to purchase AMC Entertainment.[787]

---

[784] "Kendra Scott turn all 108 stores into fulfillment centers." April 24, 2020. Retrieved from: https://www.rli.uk.com/kendra-scott-turn-all-108-stores-into-fulfillment-centers/

[785] "Walmart, ThredUp teaming up to sell used clothing". *Bloomberg*. May 28, 2020.

[786] Jesdanun, Anick. "Apple rolls out cheaper iPhone." *The Associated Press*. April 16, 2020.

[787] Edwards III, John J. "AMC Entertainment surges on report of talks with Amazon." *Bloomberg*. May 12, 2020.

Black Ops

As the pandemic has gripped the world, retailers have had to modify operations on-the-fly to make money. From increasing capacity for e-commerce to pivoting to curbside pickup to protecting staff and customers, retailers have had to re-write standard operating procedures in a hurry. Retailers know that productivity will fall considerably, but they have no choice. Either operate under these conditions or choose to close down completely.

Close Quarters

Fast-food brands have changed restaurant processes to protect employees as they close dining rooms and focus on drive-thrus and delivery. Chains such as McDonald's, Tim Hortons, Harvey's and many others have added physical distancing cues, including floor tape in kitchens. They have also changed the way they deal with cash and have tried to use workers for only one task. Not surprisingly, productivity has dropped significantly[788].

Outer Limits

Many grocers have placed purchase limits on products to avoid hoarding, which effectively translates to food rationing. When the pandemic first hit, many stores did not have such constraints on buying, unless it was a promotional item. It looks like grocery shopping has started to settle down a little, as Neilson reported that U.S. packaged good food sales grew 24 percent year over year for the week ending April 4 — down from growth of 32 percent the week before[789]. Many customers' pantries are full, so hoarding has died down considerably.

Full Line

In mid-April, Amazon announced it was slowly moving back to warehousing non-essential items in its facilities. When the pandemic hit North America, the retailer streamlined its assortment to focus on essentials such as groceries, pet supplies and medical equipment. The behemoth was also forced to relax its delivery

---

[788] Krashinsky Robertson, Susan. "Fast-food chains add safety measures to kitchens, drive thoughs." *The Globe and Mail*. March 31, 2020.

[789] Skerritt, Jen and Shanker, Deena. "Food rationing a new reality in Canada, U.S." *Bloomberg*. April 23, 2020.

promise due to the surge in demand[790].

Prioritize

Retailers that remain open due to their essential status have focused on key staples. Retailers such as Costco and Walmart have reallocated resources to fast-moving consumer goods versus fashion and other discretionary categories[791].

Thermal

T&T, a Loblaw-owned grocer, has implemented voluntary temperature checks for customers — which are mandatory for staff. Workers who have a fever are required to go home with pay, while customers showing a high temperature are refused entry to the grocer.

Form Fitting

Retailers are adjusting to how customers are trying on clothes differently. Walmart Canada closed down its change rooms and has not accepted returned clothes since March 20. Some chains are accepting returns but quarantine them for 72 hours before handling. Some retailers have asked customers to book appointments to use fitting rooms[792].

Pillow Talk

Canadian mattress retailer Sleep Country announced it would have disposable pillow and mattress protectors available for customers who want to lie down and try out its beds[793].

---

[790] "Amazon makes move to stock more non-essentials." *Bloomberg*. April 14, 2020.

[791] D'Innocenzio, Anne. "U.S. bricks-and-mortar retailers try and stay relevant." *The Associated Press*. April 13, 2020.

[792] Ferreira, Victor. "Ma'am, that dress is in quarantine." *The Financial Post*. May 14, 2020.

[793] Krashinsky Robertson, Susan. "Safety top of mind for retailers, customers as reopenings loom." *The Globe and Mail*. May 13, 2020.

BYOM

Starbucks Canada will be asking customers to wear masks when they reopen in May[794].

Raw Couture

At Holt Renfrew, a Canadian luxury chain, in-store services such as facials and makeovers will not be offered when re-opening[795].

Clean is the new Black

Aritzia CEO Brian Hill was quoted as saying that "the health and safety of customers and staff" was the fourth dimension of his store's strategy after product, environment and customer service. Aritzia will steam clean all garments that are tried on by customers in fitting rooms and each fitting room with be sanitized after each use. Alternate fitting rooms will be used to allow customers to socially distance when trying products on[796].

Tool Box

Major retailers such as The Home Depot have changed operations as a result of the pandemic. The following is from the retailer's business update April 1, 2020 under the heading "safety measures"[797]:

- Closing stores early at 6:00 p.m. to allow more time for sanitization and restocking
- Limiting the number of customers allowed into stores at one time

---

[794] Krashinsky Robertson, Susan. "Safety top of mind for retailers, customers as reopenings loom." *The Globe and Mail.* May 13, 2020.

[795] Krashinsky Robertson, Susan. "Safety top of mind for retailers, customers as reopenings loom." *The Globe and Mail.* May 13, 2020.

[796] Sagan, Aleksandra. "Retail experience to get a makeover." *The Canadian Press.* May 15, 2020.

[797] "The Home Depot announces business updates in response to COVID-19." April 1, 2020. Retrieved from: https://ir.homedepot.com/news-releases/2020/04-01-2020-110039177

- Promoting social and physical distancing practices in stores by marking floors and adding signage to help customers and associates maintain safe distances
- Eliminating major spring promotions to avoid driving high levels of traffic to stores
- Limiting services and installations to those that are essential for maintenance and repair needs in impacted markets
- Distributing thermometers to associates in stores and distribution centers and asking them to perform health checks before reporting to work

Bullseye Boundary

Target is focusing on the following measures to ensure staff and customers are safe: increased cleanliness, monitoring and metering guest access, quantity limits on in-demand items, plexiglass shields at cash registers, masks and gloves for all team members, reminders for social distancing, dedicated shopping hours for vulnerable guests and team, all stores closed by 9pm[798].

Sam Safety

Like many essential retailers that remain open, Walmart Canada has significantly modified its store processes to protect employees and customers. In an article by Jake Edmiston in the Financial Post, he interviews Walmart's Michael Gill, the person responsible for converting stores to the discounter's new measures. Some of the changes that Gill has implemented beyond plexiglass shields and social distancing floor queues include: having cashiers put receipts directly in bags, staff washing hands every 30 minutes, staff cleaning cart handles and baskets in between use and cashiers using a stylus to touch screens instead of using fingers[799]. Other retailers have used one-way aisles to minimize contact and have added staff to clean stores. Some grocers are offering customers hand-cleaning stations at the entrance and are managing lineups to allow only a certain number of customers in stores at once.

---

[798] "Target's coronavirus response." Retrieved from: https://corporate.target.com/about/purpose-history/our-commitments/target-coronavirus-hub

[799] Edmiston, Jake. "He's the man in charge of coronavirus-proofing Walmart's Canadian stores." *The Financial Post.* April 1, 2020.

The Good

In times of crisis, we often see the good in companies come out (along with the bad as discussed next section). Many retailers have chosen people over profits and have acted selflessly by putting the greater good ahead of their own short-term needs.

Testing Lot

In March, President Trump announced that several U.S. retailers would assist in testing for the COVID-19 virus. Participating retailers included Walmart, Target, CVS Health and Walgreens. Sadly, widespread testing at the retailers' stores has been spotty as each attempts to secure testing supplies and personal protective equipment for staff doing the testing[800].

Health Care Halo

Two big-name retailers are making personal protective equipment instead of their namesake products in an effort to help health-care workers. Both Canada Goose and The Gap have switched production at select factories to start making scrubs, gowns and, in some cases, masks[801].

Prime Protector

Amazon announced in May that it was making face shields available at cost on its website. The retailer has already donated 10,000 units to health-care professionals and plans to donate an additional 20,000 units once available. The firm has reallocated teams from its drone division to handle this project[802].

Shoe Angel

In the U.K., Neil Clifford, CEO of shoe retailer Kurt Geiger, has announced that the chain is paying all staff even though stores are closed. The retailer is also

---

[800] Repko, Melissa. "As demand for coronavirus testing grows, Walmart and Walgreens will soon open drive-through sites for first responders." March 20, 2020. Retrieved from: https://www.cnbc.com/2020/03/20/coronavirus-testing-cvs-walmart-opening-drive-up-sites-for-first-responders.html

[801] "Canada Goose, Gap to make scrubs, patient gowns." *Reuters.* March 26, 2020.

[802] Day, Matt. "Amazon redeploys to make face shields." *Bloomberg.* May 15, 2020.

providing all National Health Service (NHS) staff with a discount of half off when stores reopen. Clifford is also suspending his salary for one year[803].

Social Contract-or

In early April, The Home Depot stopped selling N95 masks at its North American stores. The firm made the move to enable manufacturers to redirect supply to hospitals and other frontline workers. The retailer witnessed hoarding and price-gouging before the change. Competitor Lowe's also redirected personal protective equipment to hospitals that would normally be used for contractors. The firm also announced it was donating $10 million US-worth of product to medical professionals[804].

Redemption

Tim Hortons has used the crisis to display that despite its bruised reputation, it can do good things. The restaurant was quick to close its stores to the public (March 17), while offering drive-thru and curbside pickup to coffee-craving customers. Tims has also offered free home delivery, free coffee truck service to health-care workers, provided sick-leave to workers, made food bank donations and loaned 35 trucks to deliver medical equipment[805].

The Bad

Some retailers, or at least individuals, have taken the selfish route during the crisis. They may think they are pulling a fast one on society, but customers have long memories, especially when times are tough.

Web Wankers

In late March, large online retailers faced pressure to limit third-party price gouging on essential items. Attorneys general from New York, California and other states urged retailers such as eBay, Walmart and Amazon to eliminate third-party merchants from selling products far above market prices. In some cases, hand

---

[803] Armstrong, Ashley. March 22, 2020. Retrieved from: https://twitter.com/AArmstrong_says/status/1241685448281423872

[804] Vigdor, Neil. "Home Depot halts sales of N95 masks amid shortage." *The New York Times*. April 3, 2020.

[805] Hall, Joseph. "Corporate kindness good for business." *The Toronto Star*. April 11, 2020.

sanitizer was being sold for $80 US[806].

Mercenary Merchants

Shopify announced in early April that it had banned thousands of merchants from its platform due to price gouging and making false claims about COVID-19[807].

Shameless Supermarket

In early April, U.K. grocer Tesco looked awkward as it proceeded with a £900 million GBP dividend even though it took £585 million in government support through the COVID-19 business rates relief holiday[808].

Golden Lifejacket

In a move that couldn't be timed worse from an optics perspective, J.C. Penney announced in May that it was paying out about $10 million US in executive bonuses, days before the firm entered bankruptcy protection[809].

Gaming Gaffe

EB Games faced significant criticism during the early stages of the crisis when it proceeded to allow customers to pick up two popular video games at its brick and mortar stores. In late March, Toronto EB Games allowed customers to pick up pre-ordered "Animal Crossing" and "Doom" games in store while Toronto's chief medical officer advised all non-essential stores to close[810].

---

[806] Dolmetsch, Chris and Nayak, Malathi. "Price gouging complaints widespread." *Bloomberg*. March 21, 2020.

[807] McLeod, James. "Shopify bans users for false virus claims." *The Financial Post*. April 2, 2020.

[808] Armstrong, Ashley. "Tesco defends £900m dividend payout." April 8, 2020. Retrieved from: https://www.thetimes.co.uk/article/402c6ea2-796d-11ea-a9b3-a42d54022bdc

[809] Unglesbee, Ben. "J.C. Penney pays out nearly $10M to execs as finances falter." May 14, 2020. Retrieved from: https://www.retaildive.com/news/jc-penney-pays-out-nearly-10m-to-execs-as-finances-falter/577947/

[810] Kwong, Evelyn. " Employees scoff as EB Games launch expected to draw hundreds." *The Toronto Star*. March 20, 2020.

Pâté Pirates

In late March, Toronto premium grocer Pusateri's was discovered to be selling Lysol wipes for $29.99 Cdn. Premier of Ontario Doug Ford was quoted on television, saying, "I have zero, zero tolerance for price gouging. I'm calling him out. Pusateri's. I hear that they're selling hand wipes for $30 a tin? That's disgusting. Absolutely disgusting a company like that would be selling hand wipes for that cost.[811]"

Loan Lizards

Payday lenders have come under increased scrutiny as cash-strapped consumers flock to loans outside the banking system. In Canada, some of these firms charge an annual interest rate of 390 percent[812].

TECHNOLOGY

Never before in the history of retail has technology played as important a role as during this crisis. For many, online shopping has played a critical role in transacting during the pandemic — and generating cash. Even for essential retailers that remained open, many customers chose to stay home and use online shopping instead of venturing to brick and mortar locations. For non-essential retailers, e-commerce was their only lifeline to revenue. For many grocers and restaurants, food delivery apps played a vital role in facilitating home delivery. Let's not forget Zoom, Team, Skype, Facetime and other videoconferencing technology that enabled loved ones to stay in touch and people to continue working from home.

But virtually all retailers and service providers were not prepared for the surge in volume the pandemic generated. After all, for many retailers, technology was used before COVID-19 but played second fiddle to legacy brick and mortar methods of transacting.

---

[811] "Doug Ford calls out Toronto grocer Pusateri's for 'disgusting' price gouging on hand wipes." March 26, 2020. Retrieved from: https://www.cbc.ca/news/canada/toronto/pusateris-ford-price-gouging-1.5511240

[812] Mojtehedzadeh, Sara. "Payday lenders profiteering during crisis, critics warn." *The Toronto Star*. April 11, 2020.

E-commerce

United States

According to the U.S. Commerce Department, online sales jumped to about 21.5 percent of total retail sales in January and February 2020 versus about 10 percent in 2019. From March 12 to 31, 2020, e-commerce sales increased 38 percent versus the two weeks prior, before the World Health Organization (WHO) labelled COVID-19 a pandemic[814].

Canada

A poll by Forum Research showed that 38 percent of Canadians are using e-commerce for more than 20 percent of their shopping needs — up from 21 percent before the crisis. Also, almost 20 percent of Canadians are using online shopping for more than 40 percent of their requirements versus half of that number pre-pandemic. One interesting finding was that only 61 percent of Canadians ordered takeout food delivery versus 71 percent before COVID-19[815].

Habit Forming

As more consumers try online grocery shopping for the first time, will they keep the habit after the peak of COVID-19 passes? Susan Krashinsky Robertson, retail reporter for the Globe and Mail, recently wrote an article that brought this question to the forefront. In the article, Walmart Canada's executive vice-president of e-commerce, Alexis Lanternier, was quoted as saying, "We don't have a crystal ball, but what we have seen is that online grocery is really a habit to be built — when customers try it, they usually stick to it."[816]

---

[814] D'Innocenzio, Anne. "U.S. bricks-and-mortar retailers try and stay relevant." *The Associated Press*. April 13, 2020.

[815] Ferreira, Victor. "Canadians embrace e-commerce amid pandemic, poll finds." *The Financial Post*. April 22, 2020.

[816] Krashinsky Robertson, Susan. "How COVID-19 has changed grocery shopping." *The Globe and Mail*. April 6, 2020.

Draft Pick

One of the barriers to online grocery shopping has always been the loss of the ability to pick one's own produce. Delivery firm Fresh City Farms has attempted to overcome this issue with satisfaction guarantees.

TV Dinner

The article also cites a recent survey administered by Dalhousie University that shows almost 50 percent of respondents stopped going to grocery stores as of March 23.

Big Spender

Online shopping can be more expensive than shopping in person for at least two reasons: there are often handling fees and online customers do not get as many weekly price promotions[817].

Discount Disaster

Walmart Canada has had some growing pains with grocery delivery during the pandemic. As volume has skyrocketed, Walmart customers have complained about being charged for missing items and wrestling with the retailer for refunds that can take weeks to reconcile. Other customers have complained about being shipped wrong items or being charged for their order and it never showing up[818].

A Little Late

Canadian grocer Empire was caught flat-footed in online shopping during the initial stages of the pandemic. Choosing the automated warehouse route, the firm has accelerated testing of its Voila grocery delivery service in the Greater Toronto Area. The brand has seen its existing online grocery business soar in Quebec and British Columbia, where it offers a different service[819].

---

[817] Krashinsky Robertson, Susan. "How COVID-19 has changed grocery shopping." *The Globe and Mail*. April 6, 2020.

[818] Krashinsky Robertson, Susan. "Walmart charging for missing items, skipped deliveries, shoppers say." *The Globe and Mail*. May 7, 2020.

[819] "Empire speeds launch of online grocery service in Toronto area." *The Canadian Press*. April 16, 2020.

'80s Sears Style

Canadian Tire, which lost its essential service designation in Ontario for a few weeks, resorted to asking customers to phone in curbside pickup orders. The service has had numerous glitches as customers have taken to social media to complain. Tire's website at one point directed customers to avoid using its e-commerce site between 9am and 5pm due to heavy traffic. The site read, "Due to these unprecedented times, we are experiencing a higher than normal volume of traffic to our website. We want you to know we are here for you, and to assure you that we're working hard to bring you the essentials you need."[820]

Food Delivery Apps

In late March, food delivery platform Instacart reported a 150 percent jump in order volumes in North America over the previous few weeks. The firm also announced it was hiring an additional 30,000 shoppers in Canada[821].

Pimp Your Ride

In an article by James McLeod in the Financial Post, he describes the love/hate relationship some restaurants have with food delivery apps in these unusual times. Some restaurants have voiced concerns that they are breaking even on food delivery apps as commissions can be as high as 25 to 30 percent. In better times, when restaurants had dining-room business, they could cover their overhead costs with sit-down customers and chase incremental business with food apps. But with all dining rooms closed, the math doesn't work anymore. Some say that in this environment, ghost kitchens — restaurants without a dining area, are the only companies making money though food delivery platforms[822].

Queuing

As lineups to get into grocery stores can be long, technology is being used to

---

[820] McLeod, James. "Retailers scramble to respond to e-commerce surge during crisis." *The Financial Post*. April 11, 2020.

[821] Krashinsky Robertson, Susan. "As online orders surge, grocers struggle to deliver." *The Globe and Mail*. March 27, 2020.

[822] Mcleod, James. "Delivery apps' fees hurting restaurants." *The Financial Post*. April 22, 2020.

help consumers manage through this new challenge. It can take an hour or more to get into the local big box grocery store — waiting in line with masks on, six feet apart. Developer Miki Lombardi has developed an app that uses Google Maps and relays estimated wait times to users for local stores.

Traffic Cop

Walmart Canada has developed its own app that examines traffic in and out of its own locations.

Hero Pass

Some retailers have allowed health-care workers to skip the line and shop first.

Scheduled Shopping

Mike von Massow, chair in food service leadership at the University of Guelph's agriculture department, offered additional solutions for grocers. These include allowing customers to book an appointment time — like restaurants do, or follow the "fast pass" approach theme parks use that allows customers to register and then come back when their time to enter comes up[823].

Exposure Tracing

In a rare mashup, Google and Apple have joined forces to offer help to governments to trace COVID-19 exposure. Under the partnership, government health departments would use a new app that would allow users to be notified if they were in contact with another person who was infected. Between the two tech powerhouses, about one-third of the world's population could use the system. The technology is not without controversy, though, as potential privacy issues could surface. Users would need to opt in, of course[824].

Videoconferencing

Zoom has become the new normal from a meeting perspective, growing users from ten million to 300 million during the pandemic. The firm has been criticized for weak security, though, as hackers "zoombomb" meetings. The California company

---

[823] Lewis, Michael. "Tech eases shopping stress." *The Toronto Star.* April 23, 2020.

[824] Gurman, Mark. "Apple, Google team up on COVID-19." *Bloomberg.* April 11, 2020.

has since announced it is taking additional precautions to enhance security[825]. Other providers such as Microsoft Teams, CISCO Webex, Google Meet and GoToMeeting are poised to capitalize on the crisis as well.

Other

Some retailers have taken to apps to bridge consumer engagement during the crisis. Lululemon is offering virtual classes in Europe and North America. Nike did something similar in China during its outbreak[826].

---

[825] "Zoom says platform is as safe as peers, boosts privacy tools." *Bloomberg.* April 9, 2020.

[826] D'Innocenzio, Anne. "U.S. bricks-and-mortar retailers try and stay relevant." *The Associated Press.* April 13, 2020.

Bruce Winder

AFTER COVID-19

Bruce Winder

RETAIL AFTER COVID-19

"You don't know what you're missing, now
Any little song that you know
Everything that's small has to grow
And it's gonna grow, push push, yeah[827]"

(The Song Remains the Same, Led Zeppelin)

The Aftermath

How do you predict what will happen to retail after it emerges from the worst modern-day crisis on the planet? Not an easy task.

In order to attempt this task, I put myself into the shoes of different retail stakeholders. I also thought about my experience on the retailer and supplier side. Most importantly, I put on my consumer hat. I also read everything I could on how these stakeholders were being impacted and tried to separate short-term, mid-term and long-term effects.

I thought about the different stages of retail recovery that we were going to go through. From the re-opening of stores to the new cautious normal until a vaccine is discovered and administered — until the next pandemic comes along.

What would change and what would stay the same? Why?

The CNN Moment

On April 14, I was sitting back watching CNN when I saw a headline that startled me. Chris Cuomo was interviewing Marc Lipsitch, an epidemiologist at Harvard School of Public Health and the headline read "Study: Social distancing may last into 2022 without vaccine." The gravity of the headline sunk in — we could be in this for a while. What would be the social and economic impact if the world has to socially distance for potentially two to three years? Would retailers make it?

---

[827] Led Zeppelin. "The Song Remains the Same." *Houses Of The Holly*. 1973. Spotify. https://open.spotify.com/track/59hhEeGGOgoPBVBNp3wxCd?si=Eyf6M6rzQKqj-ohESZXQqA

A Reminder

In early May, South Korea reported that it needed to close 2,000 nightclubs in Seoul. A recent re-opening of the facilities created a quick resurgence of the virus after being managed so well by the Asian country. This was a stark reminder to the world not to let our guard down.

Economic Models to Recovery

As economists ponder what the economy will look like as we exit the COVID-19 pandemic, a few different philosophies have emerged.

The first is the V-shaped forecast. This assumes a steep recovery where we get back to pre-virus levels by mid-2020.

The second is the U-shaped forecast, where the return to normal is more gradual and we see pre-virus GDP levels by early 2021.

The third scenario involves the W-shaped recovery, whereby we see a second smaller dip in economic activity after a brief and shallow gain. This model assumes that the economy recovers slowly after that and we don't get back to pre-pandemic levels until 2022.

The final approach involves the L-shaped recovery model, where the recovery is slow and lasts well beyond 2022.

These models make assumptions as it relates to virus containment, government support and consumer behaviour changes post-crisis[828].

Big Ben

Former U.S. Federal Reserve Chairman Ben Bernanke does not see a quick V-shaped recovery as some experts have predicted. He sees a gradual opening of the economy and sees a one- to two-year timeframe for when the economy will be in good shape again if "all goes well." He also felt that the 1930s Great Depression scenario that saw 12 years of hardship was not going to play out this time[829].

---

[828] Shufelt, Tim and Lundy, Matt. "The shape of recovery." *The Globe and Mail*. April 18, 2020.

[829] Miller, Rich. "Bernanke doesn't see V-shaped U.S. recovery after steep fall." *Bloomberg*. April 8, 2020.

The Don of Business

In an op-ed by Don Tapscott, a renowned thinker and educator, he describes numerous changes post-COVID-19. These include: the growth of online shopping, the decline of cash, the resurgence of global institutions, how e-commerce will deliver entertainment and services, how education will move to online, how cleanliness will take mainstage, how big governments will show their worth, the rise of universal basic income, the growth of mobile work and work from home and the need to think and understand global linkages. Probably the best article I have read in some time, Tapscott encapsulates, in my opinion, some of the most important changes this crisis will drive[830].

McKinsey 2.0

McKinsey conducted a survey with U.S. retail executives from April 6 to April 8, 2020 regarding their sentiment on their operations post-COVID-19. The survey includes a cross-section of retailers from different categories and formats including apparel, department store/off-price, beauty, specialty (big box) and specialty (small box). See below for a summary of some of the major findings[831].

Closing Time

In terms of closings, 44 percent have shut down operations as a result of the pandemic. Twenty-five percent have indicated they have closed but are using click-and-collect and home delivery to generate sales from stores. Formats with the greatest percent of closures include department store/off-price, beauty, apparel and small specialty stores.

Grand Reopening

In terms of time to recover business to pre-pandemic levels, about half of respondents feel it will take two to six months to fully recover. About 22 percent feel

---

[830] Tapscott, Don. "When all this ends – it'll be different." *The Globe and Mail*. April 4, 2020.

[831] "How retailers are preparing for the post-coronavirus recovery." April, 2020. Retrieved from: https://www.mckinsey.com/industries/retail/our-insights/how-retailers-are-preparing-for-the-post-coronavirus-recovery?cid=other-eml-alt-mip-mck&hlkid=0a9d481b045b46a7b8c53163e33c8ccc&hctky=9451477&hdpid=a7e6acd5-ca14-4f0b-b13f-05d3ff9ea4d6

it will take about six to 12 months to recover. About half of department stores/off-price retailers feel it will take six to 12 months to recover.

Eruption

Overall, retailers predicted that online shopping will grow post-COVID-19 from 17 percent of sales to 26 percent of sales. Apparel retailers forecasted the biggest increase, with online sales rising from 26 to 39 percent pre- and post-crisis.

Ready, Set

Beyond infection rates and government regulation, the top four considerations for retailers before reopening stores include: staff availability, store performance before the crisis, what competitors are doing and what the break-even level would be for each location.

Operation Recovery

The top four post-opening operational changes retailers are considering to protect customers and staff include: enhanced cleaning, social distancing measures, managing and limiting customer count at a given time and requiring staff to wear personal protective equipment.

Understaffed

Fifty-nine percent of respondents plan on reopening stores with reduced hours, while 55 percent plan on reducing staff at each reopened store. Respondents estimated they would reopen with about 22 percent less staff than pre-crisis levels.

Door Lock

As retailers reopen stores again, about 32 percent say they are considering permanently closing stores and about 34 percent say they are considering pausing new store builds.

Couple hood

About half of respondents say they are not looking to modify formats due to the pandemic. However, about 45 percent signal they are looking to better integrate online shopping in stores. This is most prominent in apparel and specialty (small box) segments.

The New Abnormal

Retail has been changed forever because of the COVID-19 pandemic. This crisis will go down in history as a major catalyst for changes in how retail works.

The fundamentals of retail are evergreen. That is, retailers find out what their target consumers want or desire and give it to them. That sounds too simple, doesn't it? But it's true. That will never change. What will change is how retail is executed. What channels retail will sell through. What, specifically, customers want. The table stakes of selling a product or a service to a customer. The economics and how to make money. The expectations from a cleanliness and safety perspective. The intimate relationship between customer and brand.

When you think about retail post-COVID-19, it has many different parts that will work differently depending on the specific stage of recovery. I have outlined how I see each stage playing out below.

Phase 1

In the spring and summer of 2020, depending on what country, state, province or other region you live in, retail will start to open up again. Depending on how the virus spreads during this initial phase and how widespread testing and data sharing is, we will see an expansion or contraction of the initial opening. This phase could start and stop and go on for potentially several months until governments, business and citizens learn to get it right. There is a real chance that once economies open up, it will be impossible to close them down again due to social unrest and depletion of government support.

Phase 2

The second phase covers the time from when we learn to operate under this new way of doing business up until we find a vaccine to cure COVID-19 or treat it aggressively. This phase could last one year or more. We could conceivably find ourselves in this phase from the fall of 2020 through to the fall of 2021 or later.

Phase 3

The third phase is when business and citizenry get as close to "back to normal" as we are going to get. With a vaccine or effective COVID-19 treatments being rolled out to the world, much of retail will resume in a different form. This phase will last for several years, up until the next pandemic occurs.

Stakeholder Paralysis

Each of the retail stakeholders and influencers discussed below will be examined to describe how they will govern, live, consume, work, supply, sell and use technology under this transformational period in retail's journey.

GOVERNMENTS

One of the unlikely heroes of the pandemic, many governments have held strong in the face of COVID-19. Far from perfect, many have been there to offer aid in a time of need. But the role of government will change as we enter the recovery stage.

Phase 1

In phase one, governments will continue to play a critical role in the reopening of retail. They will be the referees between science and capitalism. This is perhaps the toughest phase for governments, as society wants to move quickly while health-care officials err on the side of case containment. Governments will control which parts of retail and society in general open up, when they open up and how they open up.

Pressure Valve

Governments will face enormous pressure from both business and citizens to reopen the economy as quickly as possible. We will see a variety of philosophies and plans emerge based on right-wing, left-wing and centre-of-the-aisle politics. Governments will also hold the critical role of regulating when and where parts of the economy shut back down to gain control of the virus again.

Band-Aid

Governments will also continue to play the role of financial aid administrator — sending funding to consumers and business to keep both afloat. They will also use appropriate monetary and fiscal policy to keep economies alive until phase two or three of the recovery take hold.

Social distancing, face coverings and other precautions will continue to be mandated across society.

Phase 2

In phase two, governments will continue regulating the economy as it slowly starts to grow. Stepping back a little, governments will provide updates on how commerce is transitioning while ensuring that second- and third-wave outbreaks are managed accordingly. Aid packages will begin to be drawn down as personal and commercial income slowly begins to grow for some people.

Social Net

Many small- to medium-sized companies will declare bankruptcy — unable to weather the steady state drop in revenue. With the large number of retail, food service, entertainment and tourism companies permanently closing down, unemployment rates will be considerably higher than pre-pandemic levels. Governments will need to offer social assistance to these workers in the form of unemployment insurance, housing subsidies, food stamps or universal basic income.

Economic Pilots

Governments will levy fines on select businesses and citizens as they ignore rules on how they can operate. Monetary and fiscal policy will continue to support a fragile economy that continues to operate at well-below capacity. Governments will continue driving for a vaccine while incorporating global treatment options that slow the virus or lower its mortality rate.

Social distancing, face coverings and other precautions will continue to be mandated across society.

Phase 3

In phase three, governments will return to more of a passive participant in business, but with higher unemployment and large budget deficits. While most of the short-term tactics used to manage the pandemic will no longer be needed, some will stay.

Report Cards

Governments will execute post-mortem reviews of what went well and what didn't during the pandemic. Health-care processes will be reviewed and long-term health-care capacity will be adjusted for the next crisis.

Payback

Governments will sell back equity stakes in large national champions that they supported during the crisis and will reform tax systems to begin to lower debt. Business loans will be collected as due.

Cutback

Many governments will implement austerity measures to lower spending through cuts to education or other areas. Election campaigns will focus on accelerating the economy while enhancing health-care systems for fear of the next pandemic. Governments will privatize additional services and explore more public/private partnerships to pay down deficits.

Select social distancing, face coverings and other precautions will continue to exist on a voluntary basis depending on the situation.

Future Trends Now Current

I have highlighted several trends that I originally thought would become relevant several decades from now that, in my opinion, will become important in the near future as a result of the pandemic.

Regime Reduction

In the developed world, basic government services will be cut back to offset tax revenue declines from higher unemployment. Technology companies will pay additional user taxes but the percentage will be nominal.

Government-provided services such as health care, education, sanitation, snow removal (where appropriate), social services, parks and recreation, emergency services and more will be cut back significantly.

Haves will pay for these services through private companies. Have-nots will go without, use poorly-run government-service providers or use off-the-books local providers such as market dentists and doctors.

Meet Me Halfway

In the developed world, governments will be forced to provide basic income to many have-nots. Government services will be administered by those on basic income who are well enough to work.

Bumper to Bumper

As online delivery grows, we will see unmanageable traffic congestion in large cities. Delivery vehicles will bring urban roads to a standstill. Eventually, municipalities will pass laws that regulate and manage online deliveries in these zones.

Retailers and brands will change their business models to offer mostly click-and-collect, with pickup at designated locations as discussed later in the book.

CUSTOMERS

From a retail perspective, the importance of how customers feel about spending post-pandemic cannot be overstated. The entire industry is centred around the customer. Without them, there is no retail. So, how will they feel? Will they have the money to buy things? If so, what things and through which formats?

Beyond the work that McKinsey published, I examined a few other points of view before coming up with my own take on how the consumer will change from a retail perspective and look to transition out of this crisis.

China

In order to predict consumer behaviour post COVID-19, I thought it prudent to see what can be learned from China as it is further along its recovery journey than most, if not all, other countries.

In an article by Jane Li in Quartz and Yahoo Finance, she discusses how the Chinese consumer has behaved as the virus wanes in the country. Some of the key observations that Li makes include customers focusing on only what is needed versus what is nice to have, looking to buy used products through marketplaces and aspiring to save more and spend less.

Li references a survey completed by Chinese consulting firm Cefuture, which showed that just over 40 percent of respondents said they would spend less in order to get ready for future crises. Just over half indicated they would work harder to make more income and only eight percent indicated that they planned to shop more after the pandemic. This is a big problem, as Li reports that in 2019 almost 60 percent of Chinese GDP consisted of consumer spending[832].

South Korea

In South Korea, shoppers have taken to stores for "revenge shopping." As one

---

[832] Li, Jane. "'Cutting off trivial things': Chinese consumers are thinking twice about their post-coronavirus spending." April 6, 2020. Retrieved from: https://finance.yahoo.com/news/cutting-off-trivial-things-chinese-093444985.html

of the first nations outside China to see a major surge in cases, governments shut down the country quickly and effectively made use of contact tracing and testing. Now the nation is ready to spend.

Retail Surveys

I also researched North America to see what studies have been published on consumer behaviour as it relates to purchasing.

In early April, U.S. retail research firm GlobalData released the results of a survey of 2,450 consumers polled the first week of April. Over 35 percent of respondents indicated they would spend below average going forward. Roughly 23 percent indicated they would spend above average. The balance indicated they planned to spend at-average levels going forward. Of the respondents who indicated they would spend less, the biggest category declines included apparel, electronics, home furnishings, leisure and sports. Of the customers who responded they would spend above average, the biggest category increases included home furnishings, beauty, home improvement and leisure and sports[833].

Opinions

I also reviewed a number of opinions on how people thought spending would change post-virus. I describe one below.

In an article by Kevin Carmichael in the Financial Post, he discusses the potential increase in frugality post-COVID-19. Carmichael references the Great Depression and the impact it had on how consumers restricted spending — well after they had the money to resume spending. He cites some of the recent consumer pandemic trends including baking more, minimizing waste and avoiding buying discretionary goods such as fashion. He talks about how after the Great Depression being frugal became fashionable. In the 1930s, society embraced a "new modesty" as the purchase of bicycles soared in place of cars, along with denim in place of dress clothes. Could we drag ourselves into an economic depression because of this new psychological dynamic[834]?

---

[833] Saunders, Neil. "Anticipated changes in consumer spending post-crisis compared to normal levels of spending." April 8, 2020. Retrieved from: https://twitter.com/NeilRetail/status/1247929663118143488

[834] Carmichael, Kevin. "Our frugality could become a way of life." *The Financial Post*. April 23, 2020.

My Take

The pandemic will accelerate income and wealth disparity. The world post-pandemic will feel very different depending on which socio-economic class a particular customer occupied before the crisis, as well as which industry they worked in.

Top of the Mountain

As discussed previously, wealthy consumers will feel little long-term economic impact from the crisis. In fact, many will invest and buy assets such as distressed companies, brands, equities and real estate at reduced prices and build additional wealth.

Middle of the Road

A second consumer segment, those who could be called middle class before the pandemic, will fare well unless they happen to work in high-impact industries such as retail, food service, entertainment and tourism. Many of these customers worked from home during the pandemic but saw their retirement investment fall sharply as a result of temporary stock-market losses.

Economically Challenged

A third consumer segment, which lives at the margin, will have a difficult time economically, especially if they work in the high-impact industries mentioned above. These customers tend to work in blue-collar, administrative or service-oriented jobs.

They had little in the way of savings or assets before the pandemic and have limited abilities to obtain credit. Workers outside of the high-impact industries will suffer financially, but at least have the prospect of future income to rely on, once the economy opens up again. Workers in high-impact industries will suffer the greatest as numerous companies in these industries close down permanently, leaving these consumers without work.

Shopping Impact Analysis

In chart one below, I outline my thinking on consumption before, during and after COVID-19.

		Chart 1 - COVID-19 Shopping Impact Analysis by Macro Customer Segment		
		Top of the Mountain	Middle of the Road	Economically Challenged
Before COVID-19		Essentials, Discretionary & Luxury	Essentials & Discretionary	Essentials & Select Discretionary
During COVID-19		Essentials, Select Discretionary & Luxury	Essentials	Select Essentials
After COVID-19	Phase 1	Essentials, Select Discretionary & Luxury	Essentials & Select Discretionary	Select Essentials
	Phase 2	Essentials, Discretionary & Luxury	Essentials & Select Discretionary	Select Essentials
	Phase 3	Essentials, Discretionary & Luxury	Essentials & Select Discretionary	Select Essentials

Phase 1

During phase one, wealthy consumers will limit most, if not all, of their shopping to online purchases but will add virtual appointments with store owners who were previously closed. They will continue to purchase essentials, select discretionary and select luxury products and services this way.

Middle-class consumers will continue shopping online but will begin to visit select brick and mortar stores for some discretionary items under strict shopping conditions.

Low-income consumers will continue to shop online but will begin to visit select discounters and dollar stores for essential items. Discretionary purchases will be almost zero.

Phase 2

During phase two, wealthy consumers will continue shopping online. Some shoppers within this segment will complement this activity with select in-store or virtual appointments with specific specialty food stores or luxury retailers. They will continue to consume luxury, discretionary and non-discretionary products and services in controlled environments.

Middle-class customers will continue shopping online but will also visit select stores for discretionary items such as clothing and home products.

Low-income customers will continue to shop online but will return to shopping mostly at discounters and dollar stores for essential items. Discretionary purchases will be reduced significantly from pre-pandemic levels. Used clothing stores will see increased traffic, as well.

Phase 3

During phase three, wealthy consumers will continue shopping online — more than pre-pandemic levels but less than phase two levels. Shoppers within this segment will buy in-store or through virtual appointments with a variety of specialty food stores or luxury retailers. They will continue to consume both discretionary and non-discretionary products and services. Some will go to restaurants, travel and enjoy live entertainment and sporting events in controlled environments. Spending across all categories will be similar to pre-pandemic levels.

Middle-class customers will continue shopping online — more than pre-pandemic levels but less than phase two levels. They will visit select stores for discretionary items but will limit these purchases as budgets are tighter. Some will go to restaurants, travel and enjoy live entertainment and sporting events but will cut back versus pre-pandemic levels.

Low-income customers will continue to shop online — more than pre-pandemic levels but less than phase two levels. They will shop at discounters, dollar stores and used clothing stores or through apps for essential items. Very few will go to restaurants, travel and enjoy live entertainment and sporting events due to high unemployment. Discretionary purchases will be significantly lower than pre-pandemic levels.

Baseline Trend Impact

The COVID-19 pandemic has impacted several consumer trends that were discussed earlier in the book. Some have accelerated, some have decelerated and some have been paused, changed or have stayed the same. Therefore, I have classified each based on the virus's impact with comments below.

<u>Accelerated trends</u>

Customization – As consumers become used to living in more of a digital reality, through online shopping, streaming, communication and other technology, they will demand similar customization in retail.

Community – As society longs for physical connections as a result of the virus, online and digital communities will become more important.

Customer Convenience – This trend will accelerate as online shopping, home delivery, curbside pickup and other capabilities become commonplace and are built out sooner than expected.

Meat and Protein Alternatives – As numerous meat producers are impacted negatively due to worker's sicknesses, this industry will accelerate even more but will need to offer lower price point options as more consumers need to stretch their dollars.

Subscriptions – As many consumers deplete their savings and face lower wages in the future, subscriptions will increase as the ability to buy some products or services outright upfront will be diminished.

Used Products – As unemployment grows, many customers will buy more used products to save money.

Authenticity, Inclusivity, Equality and Transparency – Society will demand governments and business leaders communicate authentically. Governments will be scrutinized to ensure they allocate aid and enforce laws in a fair and equal manner.

Distrust of Elites – The pandemic has brought out numerous conspiracy theories and distrust of foreign nations, agencies and even domestic governments.

Ultra-Luxe – As the wealthy become even more wealthy during the crisis, the demand for exclusive, super-premium products and services will grow to compensate for entertainment and travel.

Forever Young – The pandemic will lead some consumers to yearn for easier times, perhaps during youth. Nostalgia will become popular as many people escape their current reality.

Decelerated trends

Healthy Eating – Although society wants to eat healthier, broken supply chains, increased cost of fresh fruit and vegetables and pressure on wages will damper this trend in the short run. Many people will eat more comfort food to relieve stress.

Health and Wellness – Similar to healthy eating, society will continue to want to take care of themselves, but gyms, spas and other wellness services will be challenged as it relates to social distancing. Many consumers will buy their own exercise products and work out outdoors more.

Paused, Changed or Stay the Same

Too Much Choice – As consumers spend more time online, on apps and on social media, marketers will bombard them with infinite email, advertisements, assortments and other prompts to overwhelm them. At the same time, some assortments will tighten to lower productions costs.

City Living – Some will avoid large, dense populations for fear of vulnerability to the current pandemic and future outbreaks. At the same time, more will flock to cities for employment and communal housing.

Future Trends Now Current

I have highlighted several trends that I originally thought would become relevant several decades from now that, in my opinion, will become important in the near future as a result of the pandemic.

The Grand Canyon

Income and wealth disparity will continue to grow as a result of the wealthy increasing their net worth during the crisis while the middle class and poor face higher unemployment. Governments will be forced to keep interest rates artificially low to try to stimulate the economy. This will allow companies to borrow money to administer share buy backs once government loans are paid back. Low interest rates will also fuel asset price growth including real estate and equities, which will disproportionately benefit the wealthy while driving inflation for other classes.

Merchant Vessel

Growing income and wealth disparity will have a significant impact on retail. Retail will continue to polarize between value and luxury — value being defined as dollar stores, low-cost online sellers, warehouse clubs, discounters and local merchants. Luxury being defined as boutiques, specialty stores and service-oriented premium merchants. Services and experiences will become a much greater mix of retail as society lives in the moment.

Glam-R-Us Life

As those who possess assets become wealthier at an accelerated rate, growth in celebrity-type lifestyles will emerge for the non-celebrity consumer. Million-dollar cars, gold-plated food and unique one-off experiences like trips to space will become more mainstream for the elite. Led by and influenced by social media stars, the extreme wealthy will begin to live a surreal life in leisure and play that is the epitome of materialistic obsession.

High-Hanging Fruit

In the developed world, fresh fruit and vegetables will become a luxury. Haves will continue to enjoy these premium-priced foods, while have-nots buy private-label vitamins and supplements to provide nutrients. Many have-nots will buy food that is close to expiry through local apps.

Greenback

As the pandemic fades and concern for the planet resurfaces, both haves and have-nots will aspire to live lifestyles that are planet-friendly, but will do so in different ways. Haves will use full-sized electric vehicles, solar-powered homes and naturally grown, organic food. Have-nots will limit consumption, buy used products, use shared transportation or low-end electric vehicles and buy local products including food that has been discarded by haves.

All In the Family

In developed countries, it will be more common for three or four generations to live under one roof in perpetuity. Grandparents, parents, children and grandchildren will live together to save money and provide daycare and senior-care service for each other as needed.

Room Service

Some have-nots will rent rooms on a monthly or weekly basis. We will see several families living together that will share a kitchen, bathrooms and other amenities. Some have-nots will rent rooms from night to night depending on where work takes them. Apps will fuel this trend.

EMPLOYEES

We will see the great sacrifice as the brunt of the economic recovery will be borne by low-income, immigrant workers and people of colour who will get sick and die for the sake of opening up the economy again. The fortunate, with office jobs, will watch from the safety and comfort of their home with a deep sense of relief and guilt. This is the society we have created. This is the horror that late-stage capitalism has facilitated.

New Heroes

One important question society must answer after the pandemic has subsided is: will frontline workers be valued more? Valued more in terms of wages and benefits as well as respect. As discussed previously, when the virus took hold, society recognized that frontline workers such as nurses and personal service workers (PSWs), grocery workers, food-service workers, warehouse workers, truck drivers, transit drivers, delivery drivers and more risked their lives while keeping everyone else alive.

Retail Before, During & After COVID-19

<u>Short Memories</u>

As mentioned, in the moment, some of these groups have received wage increases or bonuses to keep working. A noble gesture. But will it continue? Most will face wage freezes once the pandemic is over, as governments and businesses look to rebuild finances. Some will have their wages rolled back to pre-pandemic levels.

<u>Power Play</u>

In an article by Peter Shawn Taylor in the Toronto Star, he discusses past pandemics and the impact to the balance of power between labour and capital afterward. Taylor makes the argument that labour often benefits due to the devastating population loss as a result of each virus[835].

In today's world, where more jobs are automated every day and the sheer magnitude of loss is lower, I think we will see labour enjoy a short-term gain but for different reasons. I think society will shame companies and governments into providing more for these groups for a year or two — more in the way of wages and benefits, while automation continues to reduce society's dependence on them for future pandemics. After a few years, capital will gain even more power and these workers will be commoditized again.

<u>Industrial Revolution 2.0</u>

One of the issues that has already started to surface is the battle between management and labour regarding safe working conditions during the pandemic and as we open the economy up again. How will both groups strike a balance that protects workers and customers while recovering economically?

<u>Corporate Ladder</u>

The employment landscape is often closely associated with socio-economic status. That is, wealthy segments often have ownership or senior executive positions within medium-to-large businesses. Middle-class segments are often employed in white-collar jobs as senior managers or are owners of small businesses. Low-income segments are often employed in hourly positions in administration, retail, hospitality, tourism or services. There are always exceptions and certainly the classifications above do not cover everyone. But it allows for some general discussion in terms of

---

[835] Taylor, Peter Shawn. "What history says about economics of pandemics." *The Toronto Star*. April 18, 2020.

how the labour market could evolve as we move through the reopening of the economy.

Employment Impact Analysis

Chart two below captures my thoughts on how different employment segments will evolve over the life of the pandemic and into recovery.

Chart 2- COVID-19 Employment Impact Analysis by Macro Customer Segment				
		Top of the Mountain	Middle of the Road	Economically Challenged
Before COVID-19		Work from Office	Work from Office/Site	Work from Store/Site
During COVID-19		Work from Office	Work from Home/Site. Some Small/Medium Entrepreneurs Close	Work from Store/Site or Laid Off
After COVID-19	Phase 1	Work from Office	Work from Home/Site. Some Small/Medium Entrepreneurs Close	Work from Store/Site or Laid Off
	Phase 2	Work from Office	Work from Home/Site. Some Small/Medium Entrepreneurs Close	Work from Store/Site or Laid Off
	Phase 3	Work from Office	Work from Office/Site. Some Small Entrepreneurs launch New Business	Work from Store/Site or Unemployed

Phase 1

During phase one, wealthy workers will feel little difference as they continue to work from offices under new pandemic-driven protocols.

Many middle-class workers will feel little difference also, having worked from home or from sites during the pandemic. Some small-to-medium-sized business owners or managers will face some job loss as firms close down permanently as they run out of cash and fail to secure financing. Middle-class store managers, restaurant managers and distribution managers would have worked on-site during the crisis to keep operations going, albeit with a smaller staff to supervise take-out or curbside pickup.

Like frontline workers, those who return to offices to work will find a very different environment. Retail and supplier head-office employees will work with plexiglass panels around them and use one-way hallways. Office layouts will be reconfigured to limit the number of employees on each floor. Some offices will revert back to cubicles and away from open-office concepts to minimize sickness. Open spaces will need to be booked in advance, elevators will be metered with limited rider capacity. Staff will be required to wear masks and gloves in some circumstances and have their temperature checked as they enter buildings. White-collar workers will rotate work between home and office to manage capacity.

From a low-income perspective, select hourly staff will begin to generate income as retailers and other businesses open again. For those who do work, they'll face reduced hours as retail and other consumer-facing businesses limit capacity and struggle to increase revenue. Some will continue to enjoy higher wages as a result of employers increasing hourly rates and bonuses during the pandemic.

Phase 2

During phase two, wealthy and many middle-class workers will feel little difference in employment from phase one. Additional small-to-medium business owners or managers who are classified as middle class will face job loss as more of these firms close down permanently.

Low-income workers will begin to work more as retail and other select businesses open up more. For this group, income will continue to rise slowly but will remain significantly lower than pre-pandemic levels. Some will continue to enjoy higher wages as a result of employers increasing hourly rates and bonuses during the pandemic. Many small- to medium-sized businesses will close permanently during this stage, which will leave many in this segment out of work.

Phase 3

During phase three, both wealthy and many middle-class workers will see their teams grow to accommodate full staffing levels in this new abnormal. That is, employers will right-size staff counts to match new lower sales volumes and social-distancing constraints. Many white-collar teams will continue to work from home.

Small-to-medium-sized businesses that were destined to fail will have closed down permanently by now and entrepreneurs will begin to open up new businesses that operate within this new environment.

Low-income workers will work more as consumer-facing businesses open. For this group, income will continue to rise slowly but will remain significantly lower than pre-pandemic levels. Some will continue to enjoy higher wages as a result of employers increasing hourly rates, but will face wage freezes. Bonuses will be phased out. Unemployment for this segment will be high as many retail and service jobs will be eliminated.

Baseline Trend Impact

The COVID-19 pandemic has impacted several employee trends that were discussed earlier in the book. Some have accelerated, some have decelerated and some have been paused, changed or have stayed the same. Therefore, I have classified each based on the virus's impact with comments below.

Accelerated trends

Management Power – As automation and unemployment increases in many parts of the retail sector, management will gain even more power from workers. In the short term, frontline staff will have increased social power as society continues to value them and pressure employers to treat them well. This will fade as the world progresses through phase three.

Sharing Economy Hits Puberty – As more of the retail industry is driven by e-commerce, the number of sharing economy workers will soar. As restaurants rely more on food delivery apps and retailers increase the mix of home delivery, newly unemployed retail workers will turn to sharing economy jobs of all sorts to generate income. Ride-sharing drivers will suffer in phases one and two but bounce back in phase three.

Aye, Robot – This pandemic has shown the volatility of relying on people for numerous tasks. Companies will move to more automation not only to mitigate this risk of sickness and lost productivity, but to lower costs to survive margin decreases from online shopping growth.

Decelerated trends

Throw Them a Bone – As the balance of power shifts further to companies and away from workers post-pandemic, firms will need to offer less sweeteners to attract employees. Short-term wage gains and bonuses for frontline workers will fade by phase three.

Paused, Changed or Stay the Same

Service Mentality – As physical stores close and change, in-person servicing will decrease but digital servicing will increase significantly through virtual appointments and the like.

Women's Movements – Although society recognizes that much change is required in this area, it will be focused on other things for at least a few years such as economic recovery and health care.

Future Trends Now Current

I have highlighted several trends that I originally thought would become relevant several decades from now that, in my opinion, will become important in the near future as a result of the pandemic.

Free Agency

Retail workers will, for the most part, become independent contractors, not employees, as the gig economy expands. Automation coupled with pressure on margins will commoditize retail workers further.

Sharing Economy Becomes Main Economy

The majority of people will work through apps as part of the sharing economy. Executive and elected government positions will be some of the only exceptions.

The sharing economy will grow exponentially. It will offer flexible, low-wage income to billions of have-not workers. Most have-nots will work for several app firms that offer services such as ride sharing, room rentals, cleaning, personal assistance, massage and grooming, delivery and prostitution.

Lopsided

Contractors who participate in the sharing economy will feel bitter at the mega companies that reap the majority of the benefits. Technology companies will continue to make billions of dollars on the backs of contractors who earn minimum wage.

Mob Rules

We will see contractor alliances form to negotiate with large sharing economy platforms. Although large in numbers, their power will be moderate and weaker than current day unions.

Pay as you Grow

Governments will pass regulations that provide basic contractor rights and will levy a nominal tax on sharing-economy platforms.

As the gig economy grows, governments will be forced to legislate this form of precarious work. Companies that use gig-economy workers will offer nominal benefits and other basic perquisites.

The tax on sharing-economy platforms, while modest, will help make up for loss of traditional income tax from legacy employer/employee business models.

Our House

Local, micro-sharing economy platforms will emerge. These platforms will be cooperatives that are owned by contractors. They will offer basic benefits and higher wages versus traditional large technology companies. Local restaurants and retailers will band together to offer cooperative apps for delivery to cut out big app platforms that take large commissions.

Walkabout

Almost all non-executive positions in the developed and developing world will be app-based. Transient workers will country-hop so they can work while seeing the world. The legacy lifestyle of work, travel, repeat will no longer make economic sense. Air travel will become too expensive for this group. Many will travel on container ships at a fraction of the cost.

Failing Grade

As the cost of education continues to rise exponentially and real wages remain stagnant, fewer of those in the developed world will attend college or university. Haves' children will attend ivy-league schools. Most of the children of have-nots will use e-learning or opt out of college altogether.

SUPPLIERS

Much like retail, the outlook for suppliers will be polarized and complicated. Suppliers of groceries and other essential products will do well but will start to produce at more normal volumes as consumers' pantries reach capacity. Suppliers of non-essential items will struggle, at least through phases one and potentially in phase two.

Many small- to medium-sized suppliers of non-essential products and services will close permanently as they run out of cash and fail to secure financing. Select service providers will enjoy a boom while others wither away. Some suppliers will develop direct-to-consumer programs to try to sell online as brick and mortar retail begins to slowly open up. Many suppliers will work hard to reduce their cost structure by temporarily or permanently closing production facilities and reducing staff. Those who do operate will incur additional expense as employees require PPE. For many, productivity in plants will drop as employees socially distance. Some suppliers will close small satellite offices as employees have demonstrated they can work from home efficiently.

Reverse Globalization?

Could some products be made domestically again? Food, mission-critical healthcare items? Has China been given too much of the world's production? Will we see some reverse globalization occur? Will consumers pay more?

These are just some of the questions we must contemplate as we proceed through the recovery phase of the pandemic. Will supply chains remain slow and costly post COVID-19? Perhaps for a little while. Will suppliers choose short leadtimes over lower acquisition cost? When one examines the total cost of ownership (TCO) for a given product, it may make sense to manufacture it domestically. Governments may offer financial incentives to producers who employ local workers so as to maximize employment and minimize social programs. Trade relations between China and the rest of the world may change after the pandemic as countries look to become more independent and avoid having all of their sourcing eggs in one large basket. Other, south Asian countries may benefit from this as an alternative to China with attractive wage rates and government tax incentives.

Certainly, the appetite for suppliers, retailers and consumers to pay more for locally-sourcing products is low. Corporations have enjoyed the enhanced profitability that globalization has brought them over the last four decades and will not go backwards. I think we will see select categories of products made locally, but the vast majority of consumer and industrial goods will be made in China long after the pandemic subsides.

Supplier Impact Analysis

In chart three below, I outline my thinking on how suppliers will fare, depending on the type of product or service they offer and the role of direct-to-consumer (DTC) before, during and after COVID-19.

Chart 3 - COVID-19 Supplier Impact Analysis (year over year growth)						
		Essential Products & Services	DTC Offering?	Non-Essential Products & Services	DTC Offering?
Before COVID-19		Nominal Growth	Limited	Nominal Growth	Some
During COVID-19		Enormous Growth	Limited	Enormous Declines	Most
After COVID-19	Phase 1	Some Growth	Some	Enormous Declines	Most
	Phase 2	Nominal Growth	More	Some Declines	Almost All
	Phase 3	Nominal Growth	Most	Nominal Declines	Almost All

Phase 1

During phase one, suppliers of essential products and services will see some growth but will see sales grow at lower rates compared to the main weeks of the crisis. Non-essential product and service suppliers will continue to see enormous declines as retailers slowly open up. If not contemplated already, many non-essential suppliers will open up their own direct-to-consumer websites. Some small-to-medium suppliers will close permanently during this phase.

Phase 2

During phase two, suppliers of essential products and services will see sales levels that will rival pre-pandemic levels. Many non-essential product and service suppliers will begin to see some volume recovery as remaining retailers open up. Direct-to-consumer online business will grow as many consumers continue to stay away from malls and other non-essential retailers. Many small- to medium-sized suppliers will close permanently during this phase as they have run out of cash and failed to secure financing. New suppliers will emerge that cater to post-COVID-19 consumer and business requirements.

Phase 3

During phase three, suppliers of essential products and services will see traditional pre-pandemic-like sales levels. Most surviving non-essential product and service suppliers will see much of their volume return, but at less than pre-pandemic levels. Direct-to-consumer businesses will mature as shoppers buy online more. New suppliers will emerge that cater to post-COVID-19 consumer and business requirements.

Baseline Trend Impact

The COVID-19 pandemic has impacted several supplier trends that were discussed earlier in the book. Some have accelerated, some have decelerated and some have been paused, changed or have stayed the same. Therefore, I have classified each based on the virus's impact with comments below.

Accelerated trends

Brands Selling Direct – As retailers permanently close down or close stores and with more consumers buying online, this trend will accelerate as more brands form direct relationships with valued customers.

Discount Dictatorship – As big retailers get bigger, with small-to-medium competitors weakening or closing down, they will enjoy increased channel power over suppliers. As more consumers live on a tight budget, suppliers will be hammered by big retailers for additional discounts.

Decelerated trends

Big Food Brands for Sale – Suddenly, with processed food back in demand, legacy brands will become profitable, at least for a little while and will be kept by big food to harvest during the near future.

Future Trends Now Current

I have highlighted several trends that I originally thought would become relevant several decades from now that, in my opinion, will become important in the near future as a result of the pandemic.

Ambidextrous

Suppliers will become retailers and retailers will become suppliers. Outside of a few mega retailers, suppliers will have fewer firms to sell to and will develop significant DTC divisions.

Elephants and Mice

Like retailers, suppliers will polarize into two extremes: Mega conglomerates that own remaining legacy national brands, post consolidation and small local suppliers that sell in cities or neighbourhoods.

Mega suppliers will be highly concentrated with just one or two in each major category. Micro suppliers will sell locally to micro retailers and to mega websites.

Mega suppliers will mostly sell globally to the haves while small suppliers will mostly sell locally to the have-nots.

Many have-nots will become suppliers as person-to-person retail increases significantly.

MANAGEMENT

There will be changes to management as we exit the crisis and slowly open up the economy again. Managers will need to change their operating approach and management philosophy in many cases. Before the pandemic, management was mostly focused on financial results and productivity. Many thrived at being and were taught to be command and control managers — treating workers like a commodity. This will no longer be tolerated in this new abnormal. There will also be fewer low-level managers and supervisors in the retail industry as a vast number of stores close and retailers, suppliers and service providers cease to exist.

The New Manager

People Person

New requirements for managers will include the ability to display empathy and patience with employees as they collectively work through the emotional and situational turmoil of the pandemic. In addition, managers will be required to motivate and manage teams remotely as staff work from home. Managers will also need to learn how to manage through a crisis and rebuild on the other side — often after catastrophic business performance.

These managers will need to be able to re-imagine their business and operating models to be able to compete in a world turned upside down. They will need to accept that business will be brutal, in many cases for many months, if not years, yet continue to work through these challenges on a day-to-day basis.

Play Nice

Senior managers will need to be able to work with stakeholders in a new way. Executives, union leaders, governments, suppliers, investors, special interest groups and other members of a firm's ecosystem will need to work in a cooperative manner. Combative behaviour will lead to the destruction of their collective existence.

Humble Pie

There will also be zero tolerance for extreme greed and personal gain. CEOs and other senior executives or board members who enjoyed exponential growth in compensation since the Great Recession will need to be compensated in a more reasonable way. Society will be watching. As other stakeholders feel the financial pain of trying to survive and kick start business again, exorbitant pay for senior leaders will meet swift condemnation from all groups. We have already seen the rules being rewritten as large public firms are being told by government, even right leaning governments, that if they accept tax-payer aid, they must not execute share buybacks, be mindful of dividends and limit CEO compensation. A very different vibe from the financial crisis of 2008.

Some managers will earn excessive compensation during the crisis as they are terminated and are legally entitled to extremely generous compensation packages, negotiated before the pandemic began. Others will find themselves in the right industry at the right time and will enjoy significant share gains on stock options as financial markets reward companies that thrive.

Equal parts pain?

Some senior executives have announced they are taking salary cuts during the crisis. A noble gesture. But one thing to keep in mind is that a large portion of most executives' compensation consists of stock options, share grants, bonuses and other perquisites that fall outside of base salary. Salary can be a mere 20 to 30 percent of a senior executive's total compensation.

Management Impact Analysis

In chart four below, I outline my thinking on how different levels of management will fare from a total compensation perspective, depending on the level of seniority each has within a retailer, supplier or service provider.

Chart 4 - COVID-19 Management Impact Analysis				
		CEO*	Senior Managers	Managers/Supervisors
Before COVID-19		Exponetial Compensation Growth	Some Compensation Growth	Low Compensation Growth
During COVID-19		Some Base Salary Reductions	Some Base Salary Reductions	Some Base Salary Reductions
After COVID-19	Phase 1	Some Base Salary Reductions	Some Base Salary Reductions	Some Base Salary Reductions
	Phase 2	Some Base Salary Reductions	Some Base Salary Reductions	Some Base Salary Reductions
	Phase 3	Significant Compensation Growth	Some Compensation Growth	Low Compensation Growth
* Note: Large amount of CEO total compensation includes share grants and bonuses outside of base salary				

The main takeaway is that all three levels of management will take a salary reduction during the pandemic but that lower-level managers will sacrifice more as a percentage of total compensation. In addition, once we arrive at stage three, we will see a similar income trajectory as before the pandemic began — with one exception; CEO compensation will grow but not at the same rate as before the crisis.

Top Heavy

Unfortunately, a significant number of retail, supplier and service providers will permanently close and with these closings will come considerable loss of lower-level managers and supervisors. Tens of thousands of stores will close and with them store managers, department managers and supervisors will face unemployment. In addition, suppliers will close factories as they suddenly find themselves with excess capacity. Finally, thousands of retailers and suppliers will enter bankruptcy and be liquidated as they run out of cash and adequate financing to allow them to weather the storm of post-pandemic consumer markets. Some retailers, suppliers and service providers will expand and will hire some of these managers, but the net effect will be negative.

Baseline Trend Impact

The COVID-19 pandemic has impacted several management trends that were discussed earlier in the book. Some have accelerated, some have decelerated and some have been paused, changed or have stayed the same. Therefore, I have classified each based on the virus's impact with comments below.

Accelerated Trends

Gangsters Pair a Dice – With financial results cratering, some executives will resort to illegal activities to try to maintain compensation. Whether through accounting fraud, products that don't meet government standards, worker abuse or environmental abuse to save cost, get ready for some bad behaviour.

A New Hope – While some resort to unethical and illegal behaviour, the new ethical executive will rise from the ashes of the Great Recession and take power again. Society will reward firms that are led by leaders who care for people, the planet as well as deliver financial returns.

Decelerated Trends

Bad Executive Behaviour – Most executives will migrate toward acting in the best interest of society or fear swift public backlash and termination. There will be zero tolerance for unethical actions by company leadership in this new abnormal.

Out of Touch and Insensitive – As above, leaders will need to quickly develop a keen sense of what society is going through and be sensitive to what is happening outside the boardroom or face backlash and a quick exit. Society will become even more sensitive to those who do not think through the impact to marginal stakeholders before marketing products and services.

CEO Compensation – CEO compensation will grow but at a lower rate than pre-pandemic levels for at least two reasons. One, many companies will perform worse than before the pandemic and many will rely on government support. Two, society, financially devasted, will shame and boycott companies with unrealistic compensation for at least a few years.

Future Trends Now Current

I have highlighted several trends that I originally thought would become relevant several decades from now that, in my opinion, will become important in the near future as a result of the pandemic.

Loop De Loop

Left-leaning governments will implement new and more aggressive tax schemes for society's haves. In turn, more haves will move to tax havens or find new tax loopholes to avoid the full impact of this change.

Working Prototype

A new type of CEO and executive will emerge. This person will be able to work well with all stakeholders, not just investors. The everyday CEO will make more modest income and will truly manage to a triple bottom line (profits, people, planet). Customers will offer patronage to these retailers and vendors at the expense of companies with bloated executive compensation.

INVESTORS

Investors will ride the roller coaster along with other stakeholders within retail as the industry changes to survive.

In early April, Lauren Thomas from CNBC published an article that showed there was a 42 percent probability that department stores would default on their debt within 12 months. Apparel retailers fared a little better at almost 29 percent[836].

Suppliers of pandemic- and post-pandemic-centric products and services will also enjoy extraordinary valuations. Some investors will do well if they invest in the right retailers and suppliers that thrive or at least survive during the next few years. Overall, investors will follow the consumer.

---

[836] Thomas, Lauren. "Department stores top list of consumer companies most likely to default on debt." April 9, 2020. Retrieved from:
https://www.cnbc.com/2020/04/09/coronavirus-us-department-stores-most-likely-to-default-sp-says.html?__source=sharebar|twitter&par=sharebar

Bad Returns

Many investors, large and small, will face significant losses as retailers, suppliers and service providers permanently close.

Investors will receive a fraction of their investment back as retailers liquidate assets in a crowded market.

Many small- to medium-sized entrepreneurs will close and open up again under a different legal entity to re-enter the retail market, albeit in a different manner. They will seek financing from banks, private lenders and others that will charge higher interest rates to compensate them for the risk of this wounded industry.

Numerous start-ups will flame out as whatever sales they enjoyed were extinguished by the pandemic. Investors such as venture capitalists will pull their money out and cut their losses.

Large FAANGS

Valuations of online retailers will grow, as will technology companies who enable new retail to grow in a contactless world.

Facebook, Amazon, Apple, Netflix, Google (Alphabet) — known as the FAANG — and other large technology firms will thrive as they have significant cash reserves and were made to thrive in the new abnormal.

Face the Facts

Facebook is in an enviable position. With its billions of active users on both its namesake platform and Instagram, its ability to connect people will take on a new importance during these times and in the years to come. In addition, its Marketplace will enable used products growth by thrifty consumers.

River Made of Gold

Amazon, as if a seer, has spent the last 25 years building infrastructure for these times. No one else can compete with it from a mass market, cost leadership perspective. Its cloud computing business lends itself well for the droves of companies who continue to have employees work from home. In China, you will see a similar halo over the valuations of national champions such as Alibaba and JD.com. In India, Flipkart will do the same.

No Worms Here

There are a number of reasons why Apple will be successful post-pandemic. From its deep cash pockets to its billion-plus ecosystem to its connected devices and new streaming products, look for Apple to fare very well.

Invest and Chill

Netflix has already won significantly. Even with some potential flattening of new user counts for the balance of 2020 (after its huge pick-up in spring), Netflix, like these other firms, was made for the new abnormal. With brick and mortar theatres, sporting events, concerts, festivals and other entertainment forecasted to decrease significantly, Netflix is best positioned to supplement its already dominant content to expand its business significantly.

How do you spell Profit?

Google (Alphabet) will win as well, with its ubiquitous search engine and Google Meet, its version of Zoom. As more of the world lives and transacts online, Google is positioned well to capture incremental revenue through advertisements and other service fees.

Baseline Trend Impact

The COVID-19 pandemic has impacted several investor trends that were discussed earlier in the book. Some have accelerated, some have decelerated and some have been paused, changed or have stayed the same. Therefore, I have classified each based on the virus's impact with comments below.

Accelerated trends

E-commerce Profitability Gap – As online shopping grows at an even quicker rate, retailers will be forced to address the lack of profitability this channel provides. Companies will be forced to clamp down on returns and reconfigure supply chains to make money.

Stock Price Manipulation – We will see more f*ckery as it relates to share price manipulation as numerous companies face devastating earnings and valuations.

Adjusted Earnings – As above, companies will further distort accounting to make their performances somehow look good while GAAP-based financials stall.

Activist Investors – They will become significantly more powerful as economically-challenged individual investors take money out of the market to live.

Decelerated trends

IPOs – Except for a select few pandemic-inspired start-ups, many firms will remain private for at least a few years until the economy picks up, valuations increase and liquidity improves.

Department Store Privatization – Most department stores will declare bankruptcy and be sold off in parts or liquidated over the next few years. Only ultra-premium, best-in-class brands will survive.

Future Trends Now Current

I have highlighted several trends that I originally thought would become relevant several decades from now that, in my opinion, will become important in the near future as a result of the pandemic.

Broken Piggy Bank

Only the wealthy will invest in stock markets. This will be due to strains on disposable income coupled with high costs of shelter, food and products. A new form of tech-enabled micro-finance will emerge for have-nots that will help them maintain cash flow and credit for basic, everyday needs.

Wall Street Wankers

Large institutional investors will dominate financial markets. Hedge funds, private equity firms and the like will wield the tremendous asset power of the haves. Retail investors will diminish. This will change board composition and further increase the influence and control of activists in how these companies are managed. Pension funds will eventually disappear as workers stop receiving employer benefits.

RETAILERS

As retail begins to open up around the world, governments hold the unenviable position of trading off the health of their citizens with the recovery of the economy. A difficult balance. Governments cannot support businesses and citizens forever but know that if they open up too quickly, they will overwhelm an already fragile health-care system. Most governments are starting slowly, with the cooperation of retail, to try to open. The problem is that even when retail opens, many customers will continue to stay away. Why? At least two reasons. The first relates to fear of catching the virus. The second relates to reduced incomes or at least increased uncertainty with existing income.

The Opening

On Monday, April 20, Germany joined select other nations that allowed some retail to open again. The result was that crowds were light as Germans were cautious about catching the virus, according to a CNBC article. Some experts feel that consumers are reacting emotionally versus factually about the pandemic and that they are using a wait-and-see approach to shopping again. Stefan Genth, CEO of the German retail federation, believes that it will take some time before the country sees anything resembling shopping before the virus took hold[837]. Shortly after Germany reopened, the country experienced a marked increase in infection rates.

IKEA opened its new Macau store on April 23 with a two-week waiting period to enter. Not two hours — two weeks[838]. The store is using appointments to limit the number of customers in the store as it adheres to China's social distancing guidelines.

In mid-May, as I complete this book, the U.S. and Canada have started to reopen retail fairly aggressively. Time will tell what the impact to the economy and the health of each country's citizens will be.

Hold On

As parts of the world began to open up again toward the end of April, not every brand was jumping at the chance. Fitness club Equinox has opted to wait as states like Georgia begin to open up fitness centres and gyms. Executive chairman Harvey Spevak was quoted as saying, "We have chosen not to because, while we are eager to open, we also have a responsibility to continue to embrace our high standards and

---

[837] McKeever, Vicky. "Germans aren't shopping despite stores being open — experts explain why." April 24, 2020. Retrieved from: https://www.cnbc.com/2020/04/24/coronavirus-why-germans-arent-shopping-despite-stores-being-open.html

[838] Stockdill, Robert. "Ikea Macau opens – with a two-week wait to get inside." April 24, 2020. Retrieved from: https://insideretail.asia/2020/04/24/ikea-macau-opens-with-a-two-week-wait-to-get-inside/

not rush.[839]"

Retail Changes

As the world opens up, retailers will face significant changes. Some retailers will benefit from these changes, while others face a dark future. The industry at large will face significant macro-level changes as mass bankruptcies and consolidation occur. Store processes and operations will change considerably and with much greater expense. Retailers will have a difficult time raising prices to offset these cost increases as the world enters a brutal recession and perhaps a depression. Most of the changes discussed below will apply to phases one and two of retail recovery. However, some will continue well into phase three.

Macro Changes – Industry

Online Growth – Online will grow at an accelerated pace. Some say we have jumped 10 years ahead in online shopping penetration.

Lower Volume – As many non-essential retailers open, they will find their in-store volume will run at a fraction of what they enjoyed pre-crisis. Some will make up a portion of this volume loss through online orders, but there will still be a volume loss as compared to pre-pandemic levels. Some customers will avoid stores for fear of infection. Others will cut back on spending. This will drag many locations below their break-even point as costs will have risen while revenue falls. These stores will close permanently.

Store Closures – Hundreds of thousands of stores will close around the world. There will be several causes for such closures including bankruptcies and liquidation, post-pandemic rightsizing by large chains based on revised break-even points and other potential rationale.

Bankruptcy – Many small- to medium-sized retailers will go bankrupt. Select large retailers with weak value propositions and debt-ridden balance sheets will also fall. Some brands or other assets will be bought by stronger players.

---

[839] Thomas, Lauren. "Equinox chief: We are taking a 'wait and see approach' on reopening studios in Georgia." April 24, 2020. Retrieved from: https://www.cnbc.com/2020/04/24/coronavirus-were-taking-wait-and-see-approach-on-reopening-georgia-gyms-says-equinox-ceo.html?__source=sharebar|twitter&par=sharebar

Malls – Malls will struggle, especially tier two and tier three locations.

Landlords - Some small-to-medium landlords will go bankrupt as rents are not paid. Some large landlords will become owners of select bankrupt retail stores.

Consolidation – The industry will consolidate with fewer retailers left standing. This will increase channel power further and create an oligopoly in some markets. Service will fall and prices will rise.

Flight to Value - Some industry pundits believe that off-price retailers will gain market share post-pandemic. T.J. Maxx, Ross Stores and others may come out of this crisis favourably as analysts from Goldman Sachs and Credit Suisse have upgraded these firms[840]. With excess inventory at full-line stores and a recession (at the minimum) on the horizon, these retailers tend to do better in tough times.

Supply Chain Cracks – Retail supply chains will be messy for some time as workers start them again. As many of you know, there are several components to a typical retail supply chain: raw material procurement, manufacturing, transportation from the factory to a retailer's distributor (small-to-medium retailers) or distribution centre (large retailers), storage, and pick, pack and ship to stores or to customers directly for online orders. Then there is reverse logistics for returns, recalls and stock lifts. Retailer supply chains become even more complex when adding in global sourcing efforts where containers are driven to ports, loaded onto ships, unloaded at destination ports, offloaded and put on trucks or trains. Now imagine virtually all of these touch points running at less-than-capacity due to worker illness or government stay-at-home orders. Also layer on the backlog of non-essential goods that were deprioritized over the last few months as essential goods moved to the front of the line. Also, imagine that online orders have soared, putting strain on pick, pack and delivery infrastructure that wasn't built for it. See my point? Over time these issues will be remedied, but in-stock levels will be spotty until then. This will further exacerbate revenue challenges as customers can't buy from an empty bin.

Higher Costs – Overall, most retailers will see an increase in cost. These costs include higher cleaning costs, higher labour costs, higher in-store signage and fixture costs, higher inbound supply chain costs, higher outbound supply chain costs, higher insurance costs and potentially higher taxes, to name a few. As retailers hire more staff to clean and meter customers at entrances and exits, labour as well as cleaning

---

[840] Ryan, Tom. "Will off-pricers be major share gainers post-coronavirus?" April 3, 2020. Retrieved from: https://retailwire.com/discussion/will-off-pricers-be-major-share-gainers-post-coronavirus/

material costs will be incremental to pre-crisis levels. If retailers, especially essential product or service retailers, keep wages at the same level as during the crisis, they will see a higher store wage bill. Some stores will reduce staff to try to keep labour costs under control. As stores add social distancing queues and plexiglass shields at cashiers and customer-service desks, like essential retailers have done, fixture and signage costs will rise. With global supply chains in turmoil and productivity significantly down, the cost of inbound freight per product on average will increase. Helping to counter this increase in cost will be the lower cost of oil. Warehouse throughput will drop sharply as distribution centres practise social distancing and cleaning. With the mix of online shopping increasing, last-mile delivery costs will soar as retailers and service providers try to increase efficiency. Insurance costs will also increase as retailers take on the liability of workers and customers getting sick from the virus. And taxes will increase as governments attempt to lower the enormous deficits that were created during the pandemic.

Prices – Select items will be subject to inflationary pressure, such as fresh fruit, vegetables, meat and other items as supply chains slow down and become less efficient. Some promotions will decrease on essential items as demand remains above historic levels and retailers try to offset growing costs. Various country currencies will be up and down and with that volatility will come inflation for imported products or components. As mentioned, new low-price products will be engineered to cater to thrift-conscious customers. On the other end of the spectrum, super-luxury products and services will be designed for wealthy customers who take advantage of their increase in net worth.

Marketing – Many marketers will pivot from institutional, feel-good messages to new value queues that target thrifty consumers. Some will remind customers of how they were there for them during the crisis and how they gave back to society in a selfless manner. Overall, for many firms, advertising expense will be cut back to save costs. Digital marketing will grow as more customers transact online.

Business Model Adaptation – Numerous retailers will need to drastically change their business models to make money post-pandemic. Some of these changes could include new product or service offerings, change in target customers, change in price points, change in sourcing strategy and how much of their business is done online versus in-store. Many retailers will become online-only propositions and close stores. Some will use more contract staff to operate in a variable-cost model that avoids many of the fixed costs that hurt them during the pandemic. Some will exit categories that no longer make sense from a volume perspective. Several new retailers will emerge that cater to this new abnormal.

Essentials – Essential product and service retailers, all things equal, will survive and even thrive as consumers spend a greater percentage of remaining disposable income eating at and working from home.

Non-essentials – Non-essential retailers will be the most at-risk, as this is where some economically-challenged consumers will need to cut back.

Luxury – Luxury retailers will see two opposing forces at play. A negative force will consist of luxury wannabes who cut back spending to meet basic needs. A positive force will be increased demand from wealthy customers who have become even more wealthy as a result of the crisis. For luxury retailers, they will thrive or suffer depending on their customer mix. Super-premium brands will do well. Low-end luxury brands will face revenue declines.

Micro Changes – Store

Cleanliness – Stores will face heightened cleaning protocols as they reopen. This will add cost and decrease productivity considerably. Everything from shopping carts, baskets, floors, doors, windows, cash registers, counters, staff areas, washrooms and more will be cleaned frequently. Stores will close early and open late to ensure staff has enough time to follow enhanced cleaning protocols. As COVID-19 cases pop up, stores will be temporarily shut for deep cleaning.

No Touch – In many cases, retail will become a "no touch, no contact" proposition. Doors will open automatically, cash will be significantly reduced as tap becomes the norm for electronic payment. Consumers will be encouraged to touch only what they buy. Virtual fitting rooms will become popular as traditional fitting rooms are closed and merchandise must be bought before trial at home.

PPE for Staff and Customers – Most, if not all, stores will require all staff and in some cases customers to wear face coverings. Gloves and personal protective equipment will be mandated for all staff and wipes will be everywhere for all to use.

Additional Signage – Stores will continue to require incremental point-of-purchase material and in-store signage to assist customers in respecting social distancing protocols and other COVID-19 driven shopping changes.

Hand-Washing Stations – Many retailers have created customer and staff hand-washing stations throughout the store. These will remain even into phase three.

Temperature Checks – Many retailers are using temperature checks to screen staff and, in some cases, customers before they can enter the store. In some cases taking a customer's temperature is voluntary, while in other cases, it is mandatory.

Customer Limits Per Store – Retailers will place limits on the number of customers in each store based on square footage. Associates will meter customers in and out of each store to regulate this new process.

Store Services – Many in-store services will be paused or changed to accommodate social distancing, cleanliness and cash-strapped consumers. These may include home installation, in-store learning seminars, tutorials and face-to-face trouble-shooting.

In-Store Appointments – Many retailers who sell large ticket, complex products or services will offer individual appointments to customers. These appointments, designed with social distancing and cleanliness in mind, will help retailers stagger sales activities to limit customer count in physical brick and mortar locations while protecting staff and customers.

Virtual Appointments – As retailers offer in-store appointments, they will do the same with online versions of the same. For customers who don't feel comfortable going to a store, salespeople will be reallocated to hold videoconferencing appointments linked to purchase platforms.

Assortment – For a while, some assortments will be tighter to accommodate long production runs by factories to keep retailers stocked, specifically in high-demand essential items such as food. Manufacturers and retailers will re-focus assortments to the 20 percent of products that make up 80 percent of sales. As various suppliers close down for good, assortments will also contract. We will see a mix change toward value and opening price point products for many as consumers look to save money. New products will be engineered at lower specification to hit new lower price points while meeting margin targets. Some retailers and manufacturers will maintain tight assortments well into phase three to lower cost and preserve margins.

Store Layout Changes, Gondola Reduction – Some retailers will change the layout of stores to free up space and take out gondolas that were used for tier-three merchandise. One-way, racetrack-like layouts will be used to help flow customers while focusing on key high-demand categories.

Fewer Promotions – For a while we will see fewer promotions, especially for essential items as retailers enjoy higher regular demand and try to offset increases in operational costs. As consolidation occurs across the industry, we will see less competitive pressure and fewer price promotions as markets become more oligopolistic in nature.

Category Winners – There will be several categories that increase in volume: food, gardening supplies, board games and puzzles, alcohol, cannabis, sweat pants and sweat shirts, books, bicycles and more.

Category Losers – Categories that will decline include: business attire and dress clothing, nightclub wear, footwear, personal care items such as shampoo and razors, vehicles, team sports products such as hockey and football equipment, luggage, backpacks, coolers and more.

Reduced Hours – Retailers will operate at reduced hours to give employees more time to clean and re-stock shelves. Lower sales volumes for many non-essential retailers will make it uneconomical to revert back to previous hours of operations.

Less Staff – Retailers will lower staffing levels where possible and accelerate automation at retail stores to lower cost.

Less Paper Flyers/Circulars – Paper flyers will be reduced to contain the spread of COVID-19 and save cost for retailers. Electronic digital flyers will take their place for most retailers.

Local Suppliers – As supply chains become longer and more expensive, retailers will turn more to local suppliers. This change will increase goodwill as local suppliers employ local workers in the store's community.

Consignment Programs – As assortments shrink and volumes drop off for some retailers, they will offer unneeded space to local suppliers to sell their merchandise on consignment.

No Cash – Cash will all but be eliminated in favour of electronic payment. This will cause significant problems for seniors, low-income consumers and the homeless who rely on cash for everyday needs.

One-Way Aisles – Many retailers will change the flow of customer traffic to avoid contact and will implement one-way aisle traffic. This will increase the time for customers to shop, prompting additional growth in online consumption.

Outside Spaces – As retailers, restaurants and other customer facing businesses open up, they will try to spread out. Parking lots will be used where weather permits to sell product in the open. Restaurants will increase patio space to maximize business while keeping customers and staff safe. Some roads will be closed to allow shoppers more space to socially distance.

Used Clothing Stores/Used Product Stores – As more consumers look to purchase used clothing and other products, we will see retailers accelerating their entrance into this space.

Phase 3

As mentioned, many of the changes outlined above in phases one and two will carry over into phase three, when a vaccine has been discovered or effective treatments are discovered. Consumers will grow accustomed to cleanliness, the convenience of online shopping, buying through appointments and home delivery and will find a new sense of freedom from spending less. There will be fewer retailers to buy from and those remaining will have more power. New retailers will emerge that cater to a niche or offer a value-added service, many selling online initially. Vacant malls will begin to be converted into affordable housing and mixed-use developments. Online delivery will create traffic challenges in urban areas.

Fictional Individual Store Profit and Loss Statement

To illustrate what a given retailer is up against, I have used a fictional profit and loss (P&L) statement to show the potential impact of the pandemic. See chart five below.

	Chart 5 - Fictional Yearly Retail Store P & L Statement						
	Baseline	%	COVID-19 Impact	%	Break-Even with COVID-19	%
Net Sales	$1,000,000	100%	$ 750,000	100%	$ 958,285	100%
Cost of Goods Sold	$650,000	65%	$ 488,000	65%	$ 622,885	65%
Gross Margin	**$350,000**	**35%**	**$ 262,000**	**35%**	**$ 335,400**	**35%**
Rent	$60,000	6%	$ 60,000	8%	$ 60,000	6%
Payroll	$164,000	16%	$ 218,400	29%	$ 218,400	23%
Insurance	$24,000	2%	$ 24,000	3%	$ 24,000	3%
Marketing & Signage	$12,000	1%	$ 13,000	2%	$ 13,000	1%
Cleaning & Maintenance	$12,000	1%	$ 14,000	2%	$ 14,000	1%
Total Expenses	$272,000	27%	$ 329,400	44%	$ 329,400	34%
EBITDA	**$78,000**	**8%**	**-$ 67,400**	**-9%**	**$ 6,000**	**1%**
Interest	$6,000	1%	$ 6,000	1%	$ 6,000	1%
Taxes	$14,400	1%	$ -	0%	-$ 0	0%
Net Income	**$57,600**	**6%**	**-$ 73,400**	**-10%**	**-$ 0**	**0%**

<u>Baseline</u> – In the baseline case, the retailer sells $1 million a year at o location. The store is profitable with an eight percent EBITDA (earnings before interest, taxes, depreciation and amortization) margin. After interest and taxes the store enjoys six percent net income.

<u>COVID-19</u> – In the pandemic scenario, a few things have changed. Sales have dropped by 25 percent (including online sales – through curbside pickup or home

delivery). Also, payroll has increased as additional staff are required to meter customers and perform almost-constant cleaning. Marketing and signage has also increased as visual aids are required to direct customers and follow social distancing. Finally, cleaning and maintenance has increased as the store spends more on cleaners and PPE for staff and customers. In this scenario, EBITDA becomes negative at minus nine percent. Net income is -10 percent. Unless something changes, this store will close.

Break Even With COVID-19 – The purpose of this scenario is to demonstrate the volume in sales that the store would need just to break even with the additional costs that the crisis has brought on. You can see that with required sales of over $950,000, the store will face difficulty staying in business unless it gets close to pre-pandemic sales levels.

Although the numbers used are made up, you can see how challenging it can be for stores to continue to operate during the crisis and how many will choose to close because they can't make money post-pandemic.

Retailer Type Impact Analysis

The pandemic has affected retailers differently depending on their channel classification. I have created chart six below, which shows, according to my opinion, how different retailer types will perform from a comparable-store-sales perspective during the three phases of recovery.

Chart 6 - COVID-19 Retailer Impact Analysis (Comp Store Sales Growth)					
			\multicolumn{3}{c}{After COVID-19}		
	Before COVID-19	During COVID-19	Phase 1	Phase 2	Phase 3
Grocery & Drug	L	H+	M	L+	L+
Discount, Clubs & Dollar	L+	H	M	M	M
Department Stores	N	N++	N++	N+	N+
Home Improvement	M	H	M	L+	L+
Apparel & Footwear	L	N++	N++	N+	L
Specialty	L	N++	N+	N+	L
Amazon & Other Online	H	H++	H++	H+	H
H = High, M = Medium, L = Low, N=Negative					

You can see that retailers of essential products, like food, performed very well during the crisis while retailers of discretionary goods such as apparel suffered as their brick and mortar locations were closed. Amazon and online retailers have also picked up share during the crisis.

Phase 1

As the recovery moves into phase one, some essential retailers begin to see slower growth as consumers' pantries fill and they begin to trust food supply chains again. Discounters, clubs and dollar chains continue to do well as many of these retailers offer food and other essentials. Department stores and apparel retailers continue to face significant decreases as consumers remain cautious. Online retailers continue to enjoy strong growth.

Phase 2

In phase two, grocery and drug start to flatten out while department stores, footwear, apparel and specialty retailers improve slightly. Online retailers continue to enjoy growth but at lower rates. Discount, club and dollar stores continue to fare well.

Phase 3

During phase three, the industry begins to resemble sales trends before the pandemic occurred — but with some marked differences. Discount, club and dollar stores perform better as more consumers channel down to save money. Apparel, footwear, department store and specialty retailers perform below pre-COVID-19 levels as more customers shop at discount and club. Home improvement stores settle in at sales growth below pre-crisis levels as housing markets soften. Online retailers continue on similar growth trajectories as before the crisis but at much larger bases, having gained share during the pandemic.

Retailer Format Importance Analysis

Another important change retail faces as a result of the COVID-19 pandemic is the acceleration of the decline of malls. See chart seven below that I created that summarizes, from my perspective, how various shopping formats will fare after the crisis.

Chart 7 - COVID-19 Retailer Format Importance Analysis

	Before COVID-19	During COVID-19	After COVID-19 Phase 1	After COVID-19 Phase 2	After COVID-19 Phase 3
Mall - Tier 1	H	N/A	L	M	M+
Mall - Tier 2	M	N/A	L -	L	L+
Mall - Tier 3	L	N/A	L - - -	L - -	L - -
Power Centre	M	H	H	H	M
Freestanding	M	H	H	H	H
Online	L	H	H	H	M

H = High, M = Medium, L = Low

Before the pandemic began, tier-three malls and, to a lesser extent, tier-two malls were in decline. Tier-one malls were strong. Power centres and freestanding retail was holding its own while online, growing fast, was still a smaller percentage of how many consumers shopped.

As we endured the pandemic, malls shut down while online shopping peaked. Most essential product freestanding retailers remained open.

Phase 1

During phase one of the recovery, some malls will begin to slowly open but will lack traffic as customers stay away and socially distance. We will start to see small- to medium-sized retailers and department stores close permanently, further weakening malls. Online shopping will continue to be strong as will select essential category freestanding retail.

Phase 2

As retail progresses into phase two, we will begin to see malls recover a little but remain below pre-pandemic relative importance. Tier-two and three malls will suffer more as small-to-medium retailers fail. Freestanding retail will be preferred over malls in general as even tier-one malls struggle to drive traffic. These malls will at least have larger tenants who have a greater chance of paying rent and remain as going concerns. Online retailers will remain important as customers learn to shop in brick and mortar stores again.

Phase 3

During phase three, we will see a different landscape from before the crisis erupted. Tier one malls will recover while some tier-two and tier-three malls repurpose or redevelop into residential mixed-use facilities. Freestanding retail will recover as online retail grows to that of power centres from an importance perspective.

Baseline Trend Impact

The COVID-19 pandemic has impacted several retailer trends that were discussed earlier in the book. Some have accelerated, some have decelerated and some have been paused, changed or have stayed the same. Therefore, I have classified each based on the virus's impact with comments below.

Accelerated Trends

The Growth of E-commerce – Almost everyone involved in retail believes online shopping will grow as a result of the pandemic as consumers shop at brick and mortar stores less and have grown accustomed to the convenience of e-commerce during the pandemic.

Omnichannel Mania – We have already seen significant growth in home delivery and curbside pickup and it makes sense that these trends will continue post-crisis.

The Retail Hourglass – There is little doubt that society and therefore retail will polarize more between the rich and the poor. Middle retail will continue to wane as the wealthy shop at super premium stores and economically-challenged consumers gravitate to discounters, clubs and dollar stores.

Malls: Unloveable – Even tier-one malls will suffer for some time as consumers learn to shop in public again. Some tier-two malls and most tier-three malls will close and resurface as mixed use sites.

Home Delivery – As e-commerce accelerates, so does home delivery. Retailers will need to significantly build capacity and quickly to keep up. Profitability will be an issue until they learn how to modify their value proposition, which I will talk about later.

Micro-Retailing – With unemployment rising significantly and many brick and mortar merchants closing permanently, more people will open up their own businesses online.

ESG – As hourly workers, seniors and other vulnerable groups are hit the hardest during and after the crisis, companies will be forced into balancing profits with people and, later, with planet as well.

Amazon is the New Walmart – The Seattle giant is one of the greatest beneficiaries of the new abnormal based on its business model. With size and power comes increased scrutiny from media and governments.

Digitally-Native Brands – As brands close down stores and lower overhead costs, more will sell exclusively online. In addition, as new brands emerge, they will start online as it will be difficult to receive funding for new brick and mortar business models post-crisis.

Private Label and Other Differentiators – As more consumers need to lower their spending, and as remaining retailers need to offset the increased cost of pivoting to e-commerce, private label will significantly increase as a percent of sales.

New Business Models – Whether from existing retailers that need to reinvent themselves or from new firms, several new business models will emerge.

Cannabis – As society faces significantly-higher stress levels and governments are desperate for new streams of tax revenue, you will see most countries, states and provinces legalize cannabis.

Shrink Epidemic – We will see an increase in theft and scams as people become more desperate to make ends meet.

Decelerated Trends

Channel Wars: The Rise of the Store – Many retailer renovation and expansion plans will be put on hold. Experiential stores will exist at the ultra-premium spectrum of retail, but will be deferred for other customer segments as retailers focus on getting e-commerce right. Many will also reduce capital budgets in favour of operational expenses to drive frictionless omnichannel capabilities.

Loyalty Programs – Loyalty programs will flourish in premium segments but will be de-emphasized in other lower-priced retailers as customers look for the lowest price and retailers build out omnichannel capacity.

Well-Travelled – Many retailers will put foreign expansion plans on hold for similar reasons as those that influence store programs. Most retailers will need to focus on domestic operations first and re-visit international expansion in several years. Retailers that fared well during the pandemic will continue on with select international expansion.

Paused, Changed or Stayed the Same

The Green Giant – Society will be more focused on economic recovery for a few years. Similar to the Great Recession, most citizens will be consumed with making a living first.

Madison Avenue in the Main Aisle – As in-store traffic falls for a few years, we will see this initiative paused until other capabilities are built and traffic returns. Retailers will focus first on advertising to customers on websites that will see traffic increase.

M&A – Mergers and acquisitions will change. Well-capitalized retailers and select private-equity firms will buy parts of distressed retailers that close as part of the new abnormal. Some industries will take a pause on M&A as they rebuild their balance sheets. New growth industries may consolidate.

Retail Partnering – Most retail partnering will be focused on e-commerce delivery and supply-chain management as this capability gets built out. Technology companies will also see partnering opportunities as retailers look to tie up specific technologies that allow them to outperform or differentiate from competitors. Other partnership opportunities will take a pause until the economy picks up in a few years.

China and India – Both countries will have suffered greatly due to the pandemic both from an economic and social perspective. With much of its GDP based on consumer purchases, China will spend a few years getting back to full strength. Select retailers and suppliers will pull production out of China and back to their home countries or at least a different country. In India, population density and its heavy reliance on the service industry will increase pandemic challenges. Like China, the country will take a few years to get back on track. Both remain the future of consumption.

Future Trends Now Current

I have highlighted several trends that I originally thought would become relevant several decades from now that, in my opinion, will become important in the near future as a result of the pandemic.

Whales and Minnows

Like suppliers, retailers will polarize into two extremes — mega conglomerates that own remaining legacy retail banners, post consolidation and small local independent retailers that sell in cities or neighbourhoods.

Mega retailers will offer two levels of price points across different banners. Value for the have-nots and Ultra Luxury for the haves. Micro-retailers will sell locally and to mega websites.

Everyone's a Merchant

As people in the developed world get squeezed from stagnating wage growth, rising inflation, layoffs, consumer debt, cost of housing and other economic issues, significantly more people will sell products and services themselves to supplement falling income.

People will find a niche. Many of these products will be handmade and sold locally at marketplaces and online. Everything from crafts to food will be available as an alternative to mass-merchant brands.

Macy's Museum

Almost all department stores will close down. Remaining brands will have just a handful of stores left. These remaining units will cater to the haves from a nostalgic and experience/services perspective.

The End

Almost all movie theatres will close or be repurposed as mixed use. They may become rooming houses, marketplaces, grocery stores or narcotics dens. Select movie theatres will remain open and cater to haves as a premium nostalgic experience.

One-Trick Pony

As large-value retailers expand, we will see growth in niche retailers and suppliers. Most retailers and suppliers will become the best at one product or service within their specific market. This will apply to both have and have-not targeted offers. They will offer superior quality, assortment and service or unique one-off items or services in one category.

The Omnichannel Equilibrium – Balance Sheet

Online sales will continue to become a greater percentage of total retail sales. We are headed to an equilibrium point where virtually all retailers, pure play and traditional bricks will consist of some mix of online and store infrastructure sales.

There will continue to be a net reduction in brick and mortar stores as demographics change and online sales grow even more.

We will see more pick-up locations through greenfield construction or through partnering.

Home Delivery/Click-and-Collect Hybrid

As cities become more and more congested, governments will pass legislation regarding e-commerce delivery. This legislation will regulate how products flow and how many delivery vehicles are allowed in a certain zone at a particular time.

Also, as retailers and suppliers grow tired of losing money as a result of last-mile delivery costs, they will come up with new approaches. As a result, a new type of home delivery/click-and-collect hybrid will become common.

Virtually every product will be delivered to regional pick-up spots that are no more than a five-minute walk to 90 percent of the population. These pick-up spots will include gas stations, stores, restaurants, government buildings, medical centres, churches, schools, mailboxes and other existing locations. For larger, heavier items or when customers cannot or do not want to walk to a pick-up spot, home delivery will continue but at a much greater cost to consumers.

Someone will develop an app that facilitates this process — connecting merchants with pick-up partners en masse. This process will minimize last-mile delivery cost and minimize theft from porch pirates.

Go Go Club

Virtually all stores will become cashierless. From premium stores down to gas stations, almost all transactions will be executed using this technology.

Streaming Store

Online streaming services will start selling advertising to brands and will imbed technology that enables real-time purchase during use. See an action hero wearing a certain watch? No problem, just click and buy it in real time.

Automatic Replenishment – No Brainer

Some will opt into programs that send basic household items automatically to their home or local pick-up spot. Items such as groceries, sundries and consumable household items will just show up automatically unless consumers modify the weekly or daily order.

Ice Cream Man

Virtually all products, services and even experiences will be available for delivery to home or nearest pick-up location.

Immediate Shipping — Wait a Minute

As society gravitates to instant gratification and more e-commerce infrastructure is built, online orders will be filled immediately — if desired. This will cost more, though. Consumers will pay a premium for immediate delivery. Those who can wait a few hours or days will pay less.

One-Way Street

For have-nots, return privileges for online purchases will be tightened up significantly. New technology that better matches up size of product with size of person or space will enable this. Also, retailers and suppliers will no longer afford liberal return processes. They will charge a premium for the option to return items.

Living Large

Service providers will capitalize on societal changes to offer once-in-a-lifetime experiences (OIALE). These will include space travel, crime simulations, unique sexual encounters, celebrity role playing, rare food encounters, rare animal encounters and fishing trips, hiking expeditions and other exotic and premium-priced packages.

Too Posh for Private Label

National consumer brands will be targeted to haves. Have-nots will buy generic or no-name brands at a much lower price.

Worn Out

Based on lower incomes and higher costs to live, have-not consumers will buy used products almost exclusively. New product purchases will mostly be for haves. Growing consumer sentiment around environmental protection and recycling will also fuel this trend.

Hired Help

A new type of service will become popular. The personal service assistant (PSA). Haves will hire numerous personal service assistants to take care of menial tasks such as shopping, cleaning, laundry, gardening, taking children to school, etc.

Service providers will offer permanent or semi-permanent placement for qualified assistants while some will offer app-based, on-demand assistants on an as-needed basis.

Zombie Apocalypse

As society looks for immediate, economical indulgences, governments will begin to legalize virtually all drugs to increase tax revenue to offset debt and social programs. The birth of a controversial but popular legal industry worth billions of dollars will take place and will be highly regulated. Pharmaceutical-grade LSD, psilocybin, MDMA, cocaine and even heroine will be sold alongside cannabis in various forms.

Proponents of this new legal industry will cite lower crime and increased funds available to assist with addiction management. Narcotic taxes will assist with government-revenue shortfalls as fewer people work.

Licensed narcotic producers (LNPs) and licensed retailers will be omni-present much like liquor stores are today.

Love Shack

Much like narcotics, prostitution will become fully legalized with governments seeking tax revenue while consumers seek indulgence and instant gratification.

With pressure on unemployment from fading manufacturing and service jobs, prostitution will become a career option for men and women. Much like personal service assistants, hiring will be done on a permanent, semi-permanent or on-demand fashion via service providers and apps.

Reverse Annuity

Retailers, service providers and suppliers targeting have-nots will offer more and more products, services and experiences via month to month subscriptions.

Beg, Borrow, Steal

Most retailers, service providers and suppliers targeting have-nots will offer rental by the month, week, day, hour or minute depending on the category.

End of Day Eats

Some have-nots will buy their food through depots, mega chains or restaurants that sell food damaged in transit or close to expiry. Apps will enable these transactions.

Never-Ending Story

For have-nots, retail will be everywhere, all the time. Advertising will be everywhere, all the time. Consumers will be able to buy a product or service in real-time automatically through technology.

For haves, it will be more selective. They will pay to have the option of not seeing constant ads and constant retail. They will be able to turn the ability to purchase on or off at any time or delegate this activity to personal assistants.

Price Club

Local groups of have-nots will be invited to join app buying groups to procure food and other consumer products in volume to save money.

The Electric Company

There will be at least two types of electric vehicles. The first type will be for haves and offer premium features and pricing. These will include full-sized SUVs, sedans, trucks, sports cars and luxury motorcycles. The second type will be targeted at have-nots and will be basic in nature. These will include two-seater sedans as well as scooters. Electric vehicles will have numerous commercial applications such as powering trains, transport trucks, planes, ships and more.

TECHNOLOGY

As retail rebuilds life in a post-COVID-19 world, technology will play a far greater role than even today. In my opinion, many technologies will be advanced by a decade or more as they enable a new way of living. As society buys more online, becomes touchless, works from home more and proactively manages secondary and tertiary outbreaks, technology will be there to support.

Retailer Online Sales Importance Analysis

One of the most pronounced technological changes in retail that we will see post-pandemic is the growth in e-commerce or online shopping. See chart eight below that I created that shows the relative importance of e-commerce by major retailer type and how it changes post-pandemic. While the importance of online shopping peaks during the pandemic, all channels will see e-commerce grow as a percent of sales once we get to phase three.

Chart 8 - COVID-19 Retailer Online Sales Importance Analysis			After COVID-19		
	Before COVID-19	During COVID-19	Phase 1	Phase 2	Phase 3
Grocery & Drug	L	H	H	M	M
Discount, Clubs & Dollar	L	H	H	M	M
Department Stores	L	H	H	M	M
Home Improvement	L	H	H	M	M
Apparel & Footwear	M	H	H	H	H
Specialty	M	H	H	H	H
H = High, M = Medium, L = Low					

Baseline Trend Impact

I have highlighted several trends that I originally thought would become relevant several decades from now that, in my opinion, will become important in the near future as a result of the pandemic.

Accelerated Trends

Trojan Horse Race – As society relies more on technology post-pandemic, tech firms will capture even more customer data, which will be used for commercial purposes to make billions of dollars.

E-commerce – As mentioned previously, transacting through web platforms will increase from pre-COVID-19 levels. From online shopping to electronic banking, more and more commerce will take to the internet.

Videoconferencing – Not on my original list of emerging technologies pre-pandemic, this technology has become essential for society to work and for the retail industry to converse with customers. From virtual appointments to virtual fashion shows and supplier meetings, this technology has been catapulted from useful to mandatory.

Artificial Intelligence (AI) – Many of the technologies that will become even more prominent post-COVID-19 will be powered by AI, such as facial recognition, voice activation and robotics.

Social Media – As society spends more time at home, time spent on social media will accelerate as a means to communicate. Retail industry marketers will increase their spend on this medium significantly.

Voice Activation and Smart Home – As society spends more time at home, consumers will use voice activation and smart-home devices to order products and services.

Facial Recognition – One of the biggest winners that will emerge from the crisis is facial recognition. This technology supports a contactless society and can be used for numerous purposes within retail. From employee identification to consumer-purchase confirmation to customer-relationship management, this technology has room to grow. Developers are working on updates to work with face coverings.

Apps – Apps will accelerate in retail. From business to business (B2B) to business to consumer (B2C) to consumer to consumer (C2C), apps will be used as more online marketplaces and virus-tracking mechanisms roll out.

Robots – Robots will be used more in retail as a result of the pandemic. From cleaning stores and offices to delivering packages and automating distribution facilities, robots don't get sick and don't require personal protective equipment. They will perform even more tasks that virus-conscious workers or consumers wish to avoid.

Cashierless Stores – As retail returns with less contact and grocery stores enjoy post-virus growth, this technology will accelerate. No need for plexiglass panels, cashiers washing hands every 15 minutes and putting themselves and customers in harm's way.

Blockchain – As cash is used less often, society will turn to cryptocurrencies as a substitute. In addition, as food supply chains are put under the microscope from a safety perspective, blockchain will fuel this requirement as well.

Mobile – Mobile will continue to grow as online shopping grows and internet capabilities grow around the world.

Drones – As online shopping increases and home delivery grows, drone use will be accelerated for short, lightweight purchases. Governments will be lobbied to advance approval of this economical last-mile delivery method.

Autonomous Vehicles – As online shopping and home delivery grow, so will autonomous vehicle technology. With fear of contagion, ride sharing will eventually move to humanless drivers.

Virtual Reality – This technology will grow in importance as consumers escape from reality and take virtual vacations in lieu of air travel.

Augmented Reality – This will become more important as consumers shop more online and virtually try on garments or simulate how furniture will look in homes.

Pick-Up Towers – With contactless retail growing in importance, this method of click-and-collect will be used more to protect workers and shoppers and lower payroll costs.

Wearables – These will grow in importance as consumers track their health in real-time. Employers will use wearables to monitor employees for signs of COVID-19 or another virus.

Window Dressing – As more stores permanently close, this technology will be used more as landlords look to incorporate data into potential tenant marketing.

Digital Fitting – This will grow significantly as customers balk at physically trying fashion products on before purchase. Consumers will use these technologies to lower the risk of purchasing something that does not fit.

5G Networks – This technology will become more important as it enables the acceleration of technological speed and capability.

Customer Lifetime Value (CLV) Software – This technology will become even more popular as more business is done online and customer data is easier to track and manipulate.

Paused, Changed or Stayed the Same

3D Printing – This will remain a niche technology.

Neural Implants – Still a few decades out, this technology will not see a major change as a result of the pandemic.

Supply Chain Transparency – This technology will be used more for food safety tracking and less for fair-trade purposes for a few years.

Future Trends Now Current

I have highlighted several trends that I originally thought would become relevant several decades from now that, in my opinion, will become important in the near future as a result of the pandemic.

Temples of Seer-Inx

The fourth industrial revolution, as discussed below, will accelerate as society, technology and biology interact to create new ways of selling and consuming products and services.

In an op-ed by Linda Nazareth, an author and senior fellow at the Macdonald-Laurier Institute, she discusses the fourth industrial revolution, or "Industry 4.0," and the impact to society[841].

The first industrial revolution was the birth of steam power and machinery in the late 1700s. The second industrial revolution was the advent of electricity, division of labour and mass production that occurred in the late 1800s. The third industrial revolution includes digital capabilities and the internet of things over the last 50 years. Finally, the fourth industrial revolution involves the intersection of several technologies to offer artificial intelligence, blockchain and other future developments involving the combination of humans and machines.

Nazareth quotes the World Economic Forum (WEF), defining it as

---

[841] Nazareth, Linda. "Are we ready for a Fourth Industrial Revolution? This time will be different." *The Globe and Mail.* June 12, 2019.

"characterized by a future of technologies that is blurring the lines between the physical, digital and biological spheres." Nazareth points to the pace at which this fourth revolution is engulfing the planet and the winners and losers that may result.

U are Everything and Everything is U

With the proliferation of data capture and AI technology around us and imbedded in our lives, technology will anticipate a large portion of our lives for us in real-time and make recommendations.

Almost all decisions or actions in our lives will be just a "yes" away from being managed by technology for us. Whether it be smart-home technology or mobile devices, society will have a symbiotic relationship with tech.

Looker

Facial recognition coupled with biometric data will be used to provide governments and companies real-time access to virtually all data concerning a person's whereabouts, mood, health, interests and intentions.

Like other Trojan horses we have seen, this data will be gathered through free consumer apps. These apps will initially help us solve problems in our lives. They will help find lost elders or children, help avoid local sickness or enable games such as playing electronic tag with friends. Soon after, though, the data will be used for commercial purposes.

View Master

While haves live real experiences, have-nots will turn to a super-charged version of virtual reality as a means of escape. This technology will include not only sight and sound but also touch, smell, temperature control and neural stimulation to operate at an emotional level. Legal narcotics will be used to enhance the experience.

When the Levy Breaks

As governments feel the strain of higher unemployment as a result of automation, they will levy taxes on tech firms and AI service providers to help offset tax revenue losses. Although these taxes will be nominal, they will help politicians convince society that big tech is paying their fair share.

Bruce Winder

APOCALYPSE NEVER

Today, retail is in the fight of its life. The industry faces an existential threat that will punish many and reward the few. Millions of retail workers will lose their jobs, tens of thousands of stores will close, thousands of brands will enter bankruptcy and liquidate. Online shopping will grow and society will further polarize between the haves and have-nots. Consumers will become more thrifty and buy fewer discretionary items.

But retail will not die. Not even close.

Retail has been around since we've been around, which is quite a long time. Retail's basic components are the same and will remain the same. A customer wants or needs something. That customer thinks about where they can get it or how they can get it and what they have to give up to get it. Money, time, convenience, etc. They go through an evaluation process that helps them decide on the purchase, then they make the purchase or don't. Finally, they think about the purchase after the fact and evaluate how it went. This, of course, is the basic consumer purchase decision process created by John Dewey in 1910[842]. It varies considerably by product or service, country, decade, customer, geography and more, but it is the same. How the industry guides the consumer through this path is in flux. Or should I say how the consumer guides retail through this process is in flux. The method changes but the core will remain the same.

COVID-19, as horrible as it is, is not killing retail. Just the opposite. It is forcing retail to innovate — faster than anticipated. Weak formats such as department stores were destined to fail either way. Tier two and three fashion chains were headed the same way. In a cruel sort of way, the pandemic has purged retail of its brands, stores, suppliers, service providers and more that weren't going to make it anyway. I know this is callus and I don't say it with any malice or joy. Only sadness.

Maybe retail wasn't meant to be owned by private equity firms that artificially use huge sums of debt to keep chains alive — like giant Frankensteins jump-starting with debt banners that really should have died long ago. Chains that are unable to survive the stress of a downturn. Limping until they are finally taken out of their misery.

---

[842] Mehrguth, Garrett. "5 stages of the consumer decision-making process and how it's changed." June 7, 2018. Retrieved from: https://directiveconsulting.com/blog/5-stages-of-the-consumer-decision-making-process-and-how-its-different/

Maybe customers were spending too much and taking on too much debt to sustain their unrealistic lifestyles. Maybe we were buying too many things we really didn't need. Maybe we had too many stores.

Maybe some CEOs and executives were making more money than they were worth.

Maybe start-ups were operating when they didn't deserve to. With weak value propositions and zero in the way of profit, they were artificially propped up by venture capitalists.

Maybe we needed this crisis to find innovative and convenient ways to deliver products the last mile to a customer's home.

Maybe we needed to think about the pollution we generated by driving as much as we did or by consuming as much as we did.

Maybe we needed this crisis to reengage government as protector of the people, not just of big business. Maybe this crisis has shone a light on the vulnerable in society who were crying for help.

I guess this is just my way of making some sense out of this.

New retailers, suppliers and service providers will emerge and launch successful businesses that cater to consumer needs while operating in a manner conducive to the new abnormal. They will rebuild the industry for better times ahead. Retail will become more convenient, more efficient, more dynamic and will use technology like never before to delight customers and satisfy their every wants and desires.

One thing is for sure — retail will go on. It will be very different and challenging for a little while, but retail will find a way. There will always be customers and there will always be merchants. That is guaranteed!

Thanks for reading!

Bruce

Retail Before, During & After COVID-19

Bruce Winder

ABOUT THE AUTHOR

Bruce Winder is a Toronto-based retail analyst, speaker, consultant, business instructor and author. His 30 years of retail and supplier experience make him one of Canada's most sought-after pundits. Bruce has appeared on numerous TV programs including Business News Network (BNN)/Bloomberg, CBC The National, CTV National News, CTV News Channel, CP24, Global News and CityNews, offering insight on retail matters. Bruce has been quoted hundreds of times in leading business publications including Bloomberg, The Washington Post, BBC News, The UK Guardian, Reuters, Adweek, The Globe and Mail, The Financial Post, The Toronto Star, The Calgary Herald, The Canadian Press, Maclean's and many more. He is the president at Bruce Winder Retail and holds an MBA from the Smith School of Business at Queen's University. He is married and a father to two wonderful daughters.

Manufactured by Amazon.ca
Bolton, ON

44040746R00226